## About this Book

This benchmark study by two leading authorities on international development cooperation:

- Provides a comprehensive and up-to-date analysis of aid as it has evolved over the last fifty years.
- Pays special attention to the new challenges facing donors and recipients since the end of the Cold War.
- Reviews bilateral and multilateral agencies' motives, development goals and aid strategies and deals extensively with the actual delivery of aid and how donors interact with actors in developing countries.
- Deals comprehensively with the role of NGOs from both the North and the South in development.
- Examines the complex and problematic links between emergency relief, humanitarian assistance and long-term development co-operation.
- Analyses the international debates on aid impact and how aid has worked under different conditions in developing countries.
- Shows that aid has proved valuable for recipient countries in general but more so in countries with coherent development policies and strong political institutions.

The authors argue that no better alternative exists to replace taxpayer-financed aid as the main mechanism for promoting greater equality between North and South and within the countries of the South. It should therefore be continued while at the same time being made more effective and efficient, and the authors present ideas to achieve this. They conclude by examining new modes of financing development and new modes of international cooperation aimed at bringing about growth and human development.

This major study – replete with detailed statistical and factual information, comprehensive in scope, and penetrating in its analysis – is likely to stand as the authoritative account of international aid for many years.

The Publishers and the coauthor of this book, Poul Engberg-Pedersen, wish to express their deepest regret at the entirely unexpected and untimely death of Professor John Degnbol-Martinussen. He passed away while working on the final proofs of this book, and at a time when he was at the height of his powers and still vigorously carrrying on his many-faceted contribution to both the practical processes of development and our intellectual understanding thereof.

# AID

## Understanding International Development Cooperation

JOHN DEGNBOL-MARTINUSSEN
AND POUL ENGBERG-PEDERSEN

Translated by Marie Bille

Zed Books Ltd
LONDON • NEW YORK

Mellemfolkeligt Samvirke
Danish Association for International Cooperation
COPENHAGEN

*Aid: Understanding International Development Cooperation* was first published by Zed Books Ltd, 7 Cynthia Street, London N1 9JF, UK and Room 400, 175 Fifth Avenue, New York, NY 10010, USA in 2003.

www.zedbooks.demon.co.uk

Published in Denmark by Mellemfolkeligt Samvirke – Danish Association for International Cooperation, Borgergade 14, DK 1300 København K, Denmark

Originally published in Danish under the title *Bistand: Udvikling eller afvikling* by Mellemfolkeligt Samvirke, Borgergade 14, DK 1300 København K, Denmark in 1999

Translation by the generous support of the Royal Danish Ministry of Foreign Affairs, Danida, www.um.dk/english/



Cover designed by Andrew Corbett
Set in Monotype Garamond by Ewan Smith, London
Printed and bound in Malaysia

Distributed in the USA exclusively by Palgrave, a division of St Martin's Press, LLC, 175 Fifth Avenue, New York, NY 10010



A catalogue record for this book is available from the British Library.

US CIP data is available from the Library of Congress.

ISBN 1 84277 038 1 cased
ISBN 1 84277 039 X limp

In Denmark
ISBN 87 7907 159 7 limp

# Contents

# Figures, Tables and Boxes

## Figures

## Tables



## Boxes

# Abbreviations

| | |
|---|---|
| ACP countries | African, Caribbean and Pacific countries, signers of the Lomé Convention |
| ACT | Action of Churches Together |
| AfDB | African Development Bank |
| AIDS | acquired immune deficiency syndrome |
| AsDB | Asian Development Bank |
| ASEAN | Association of Southeast Asian Nations |
| ATTAC | L'Association pour la taxation des transactions financières pour l'aide aux citoyens (Association for the Taxation of Financial Transactions for the Aid of Citizens) |
| BIS | Bank for International Settlements |
| BRAC | Bangladesh Rural Advancement Committee |
| CARE | Co-operative for American Relief Everywhere |
| CDF | Comprehensive Development Framework |
| CFA | Communauté financière africaine (African Financial Community) |
| CPIA | Country Policy and Institutional Assessment |
| DAC | Development Assistance Committee |
| Danida | Danish International Development Assistance |
| DFID | Department for International Development (UK) |
| EADI | European Association of Development Research and Training Institutes |
| EBRD | European Bank for Reconstruction and Development |
| ECDPM | European Centre for Development Policy Management |
| ECHO | European Community Humanitarian Office |
| ECLA | Economic Commission for Latin America |
| ECOSOC | Economic and Social Council |
| EU | European Union |
| Eurostep | European Solidarity Towards Equal Participation of People |
| FAO | Food and Agriculture Organization |
| GAD | Gender and Development |
| GATT | General Agreement on Tariffs and Trade |
| GDP | gross domestic product |
| GNI | gross national income |
| GNP | gross national product |
| HIC | high-income countries |

| | |
|---|---|
| IAEA | International Atomic Energy Association |
| IBRD | International Bank for Reconstruction and Development, World Bank |
| ICVA | International Council of Voluntary Agencies |
| IDA | International Development Association, World Bank |
| IDB | Inter-American Development Bank |
| IDS | Institute of Development Studies, University of Sussex, UK |
| IFAD | International Fund for Agriculture and Development |
| IFC | International Finance Corporation, World Bank |
| ILO | International Labour Organization |
| IMF | International Monetary Fund |
| IMO | International Maritime Organization |
| INTRAC | International NGO Training and Research Centre, Oxford, UK |
| ITC | International Trade Centre |
| JICA | Japan International Cooperation Agency |
| LIC | low-income country |
| LLDC | least developed country |
| LMIC | lower middle-income country |
| MIC | middle-income country |
| MS | Mellemfolkeligt Samvirke (Danish Association for International Cooperation) |
| NGO | non-governmental organization |
| NIEO | New International Economic Order |
| NORAD | Norwegian Agency for Development Co-operation |
| NOVIB | Nederlandse Organisatie voor Internationale Samenwerking (The Netherlands Organization for International Cooperation) |
| ODA | official development assistance |
| ODF | official development finance |
| ODI | Overseas Development Institute |
| OECD | Organization for Economic Co-operation and Development |
| OECF | Overseas Economic Cooperation Fund (Japan) |
| OED | Operations Evaluation Department, World Bank |
| OEEC | Organization for European Economic Co-operation |
| PRSP | Poverty Reduction Strategy Paper |
| SAP | structural adjustment programme |
| SEWA | Self-Employed Women's Association |
| SIDA | Swedish International Development Cooperation Agency |
| SIP | Sector Investment Programme |
| SPA | Special Programme of Assistance for Africa |
| SUNFED | Special UN Fund for Economic Development |
| SWAps | Sector-wide Approaches |
| UMIC | upper middle-income countries |
| UN | United Nations |

| | |
|---|---|
| UNCDF | United Nations Capital Development Fund |
| UNCED | United Nations Conference on Environment and Development |
| UNCTAD | United Nations Conference on Trade and Development |
| UNDAF | UN Development Assistance Framework |
| UNDG | UN Development Group |
| UNDP | United Nations Development Programme |
| UNEP | United Nations Environment Programme |
| UNESCO | United Nations Educational, Scientific and Cultural Organization |
| UNFPA | United Nations Fund for Population Activities |
| UNHCR | United Nations High Commissioner for Refugees |
| UNICEF | United Nations Children's Fund |
| UNIDO | United Nations Industrial Development Organization |
| USAID | United States Agency for International Development |
| VSO | Voluntary Service Overseas |
| WFP | World Food Programme |
| WHO | World Health Organization |
| WID | Women in Development |
| World Bank Group | Comprises IBRD, IDA and IFC |
| WTO | World Trade Organization |

# Preface

This is a time of crisis for international development cooperation. The conditions for many areas of cooperation have changed, especially since the end of the Cold War. Cooperation between rich and poor countries has acquired a new meaning for both parties. The forms of cooperation have changed character. This applies to both bilateral and multilateral cooperation, and it also applies to the role of NGOs in both North and South.

With this book, we hope to create a comprehensive understanding of these changes and present a coherent picture of how development cooperation is carried out today. We will discuss the motives behind foreign aid initiatives and the arguments for and against various forms of aid. We will question and criticize where we find it necessary, but will also indicate positive points and make proposals for improvements, in order to stimulate a constructive debate.

It is important to think through how foreign aid can be improved at a time when this form of international cooperation is under economic and political pressure. Since 1992, foreign aid from North to South has decreased in real value, even though the problems and poverty in most developing countries have increased. In recent years, foreign aid has fallen to the lowest level since the start of the 1960s, measured as a percentage – or rather per capita – of the rich countries' national product.

Some of the central questions we will consider are the following:

- Why do we give aid and why are so many countries interested in receiving it?
- How is development cooperation carried out?
- What is the aid given to? What are the objectives – and does it fulfil its intentions?
- Should development cooperation continue as it has been, or is there need for decisive changes?
- Is there a future for aid cooperation?

This book attempts to create a comprehensive view of the various answers that have been given to such questions and to present the reasoning behind these different answers. But we also wish to create debate. We have made no attempts to hide our own views and attitudes about how aid functions and ought to function. We try to understand the viewpoints of both the different donors and recipients, but we acknowledge that our perspective is mainly that of the donor actors. This is not because we wish to give the donor side of the cooperation any kind of preferential position. However, power relations are such that donor actors in practice have the greatest influence in planning foreign aid – even though in recent years there has been much talk about partnership.

In organizing our material, we start with the donors, their motives, goals and strategies, but in the subsequent analysis of achievements, we also try to consider the interests and conditions of the recipients. Throughout the book, we attempt to analyse development cooperation within its national and international context.

The book is about the common tendencies and problems in bilateral and multilateral aid. It examines both official aid and the role of NGOs and other organizations, including international trade unions. We go back in time in order to uncover basic tendencies and patterns, but concentrate mostly on foreign aid since 1990, including the challenges now facing both donors and recipients.

Previously, there was a relatively clear division between foreign aid and emergency relief, but the tendency now is towards more integration and overlapping. Humanitarian assistance includes both areas, and new mixed forms have emerged where emergency relief is linked to more long-term efforts. We discuss the border areas but do not go deeper into the question of emergency relief itself.

The presentation is based on the very comprehensive literature on foreign aid published throughout the world, both research literature and the many publications from official aid organizations and non-governmental organizations (NGOs). We include many references to this literature in the text as a guide to the reader who wishes to investigate further. We also try to reflect on our own experience in development cooperation, where we have been involved as researchers, consultants, advisers and decision-makers.

The book is addressed to everyone who has an interest in acquiring a comprehensive view of the tendencies of change and the debates regarding international development cooperation. The primary target group comprises everyone engaged in such cooperation in one way or another, or those with an interest in following this subject relatively closely. In addition, the book is addressed especially to students at institutions of higher education who are working with foreign aid questions. The book is organized so that it can be used as a reference book.

This edition is based on a book published in Danish in 1999 (*Bistand. Udvikling eller Afvikling*, Copenhagen: Danish Association for International Cooperation). The English version, however, has been updated and revised for international readers. Some new sections have been added, including discussions of the most recent analyses and international debates. Danish foreign aid is not discussed as deeply as in the Danish edition, but it is of common interest. Relatively, Denmark gives the most aid and is also representative of what we consider to be the progressive donors that primarily attempt to relieve poverty.

We owe thanks to many people who have inspired discussions about the themes of this book. We are especially grateful to all those in the Scandinavian countries who have participated in discussions about the Danish edition.

When two such old hands in the professional debate about foreign aid decide to write a book together, it is obvious that in the process disagreements will arise about priorities, conclusions and recommendations. Instead of choosing the lowest common denominator, we have chosen to present some of our disagreements in the form of different arguments in some sections of the book, without, we hope, undermining our aim to create a cohesive whole.

Foreign aid is about development among the poorest people in the world, among the most marginalized and oppressed peoples and societies. Since 1990, traditional, project-based and taxpayer-financed development cooperation has been under threat of being dismantled as a result of the changed political world order, problems of efficiency, decreasing support, and new attitudes towards the position of foreign aid in relation to cooperation between partners in North and South. At the same time, the need for foreign aid in many countries has unfortunately become greater than ever before. This book concludes that no other, better way exists that can replace foreign aid as part of a solidary effort to achieve greater equality between countries, the people in developed and developing countries, and between people within developing countries. We therefore reject proposals to phase out foreign aid, but acknowledge the need for further development and improvement of this cooperative effort.

*John Degnbol-Martinussen*
*Poul Engberg-Pedersen*

CHAPTER I

# Introduction

§ THE structure of the presentation in the following chapters is based on the concept of international development cooperation as a process with many actors, each with their own motives, interests, goals and strategies. Within this framework, we attempt to connect the presentations and discussions in the individual chapters by focusing, throughout the book, on a few central themes. Here, we first describe the structure and then the central themes.

## The Logic of the Presentation

Figure 1.1 presents an overview of development cooperation understood as a process that begins with the background for involvement by the donor actors. The process develops further to the donors' formulation of development goals and strategies. In some cases, the donor and recipient actors formulate these goals and strategies together. The logical next step is implementation of development strategies and the achievement – or lack of achievement – of the desired results. In this connection, actors in recipient countries play a decisive role.

Today, there is a widespread tendency to obscure the actual power relationship by using words and formulations that make it appear that foreign aid comprises collaboration between equal partners. This may be the case between the NGOs in North and South and between small donor countries and large recipient countries, but in general donors set most of the agenda and the conditions for cooperation. This is the assumption on which we base our use of such terms as donor and recipient. We emphasize strongly, however, the need to discuss under what conditions and how cooperation can be more equal, a real cooperation and partnership. Appendix 1 contains a brief explanation of our use of terms, such as donor countries and recipient countries, and also reproduces DAC's latest list of countries that have the right to receive official foreign aid.

The donor actors consist of states, international organizations and NGOs. We differentiate between official donor organizations and other donor actors. The first category consists of the bilateral state aid organizations and international organizations with larger or smaller groups of states as members.

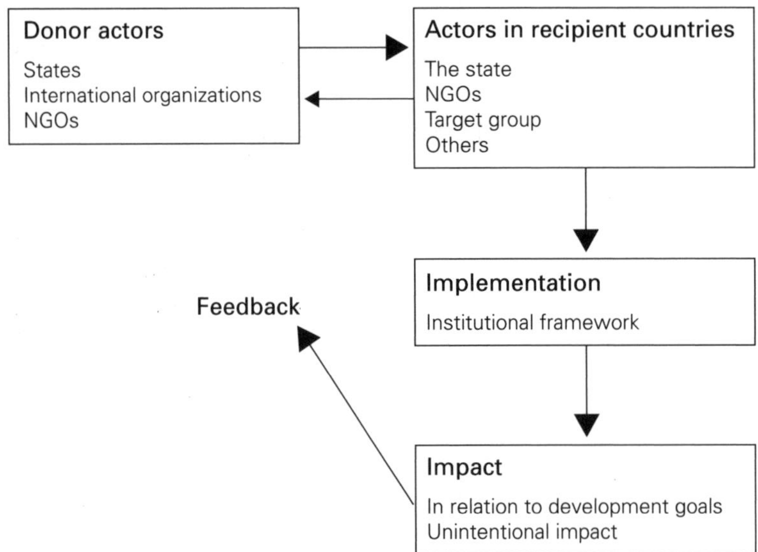


**Figure 1.1** Foreign aid as process

Other donor actors are primarily the many NGOs that participate in development cooperation. The analysis emphasizes what motives and interests are decisive for the donor actors' involvement. We also examine what development goals they set up for their involvement in aid, and the different strategies they have designed to realize these goals.

The next step in the analysis is to involve the actors in the recipient countries in order to understand their motives, interests, development goals and strategies. We must acknowledge, however, that the main emphasis throughout the book is on the donor actors and their perspective.

There are significant differences in all the named respects between the donors themselves and between the actors in recipient countries. There are also significant changes over time. We have chosen to account for these differences and changes by first, in Chapter 2, presenting the motives and interests in development cooperation in a historical perspective, and then presenting a more detailed description of the different types of motives and interests. A special section discusses the theoretical reasons for and against providing and receiving aid. In principle, this chapter covers both actors in donor and recipient countries. Chapter 3 discusses the development goals that have been formulated by the different types of actors. Chapter 4 examines the strategies of development cooperation, discussing the most important forms of aid and the changing priorities and procedures since the 1960s. The important differences in the various aid strategies used by different types of donors are also discussed.

In order to give an impression of the scope of foreign aid, its composition and distribution, Chapter 5 presents an overview based on available statistics. This chapter also contains a section on foreign aid's scope in comparison with other forms of resource transfer between the industrial countries and developing countries.

Chapter 6 is especially concerned with official bilateral aid and presents a more detailed introduction to the actual foreign aid policies of five selected countries during a period of several years. These countries, the USA, Japan, France, United Kingdom and Denmark, are representative of the great variations that exist in donor priorities and strategies.

Chapter 7 treats multilateral aid in a similar way, with emphasis on both the great variations and changes over time. The chapter describes the strengths and weaknesses of the most important multilateral aid organizations: the UN, the World Bank and the European Union.

Chapter 8 directs attention towards NGOs and their involvement and strategies in development cooperation. The chapter discusses NGOs from both the North and the South.

Following these three chapters with their focus on the different types of donor actors, Chapter 9 discusses their interaction, both with each other and with actors in recipient countries. The analysis is developed further in the total process, with an investigation that emphasizes the institutional framework for implementation of development cooperation.

Chapter 10 discusses emergency relief and humanitarian assistance. The emphasis is on the efforts to link these two forms of initiative for the purpose of organizing emergency aid so that it can be followed up by more long-term assistance.

Chapter 11 looks more closely at evaluation and research as part of aid cooperation.

In Chapter 12, we examine the debate on the impact of foreign aid in recipient countries. We focus on some of the new analyses of and impact on project and society levels as well as on poverty.

Chapter 13 summarizes some of the pressing and current problems and challenges in development cooperation with Southern states. Finally, in Chapter 14 considers the new forms of international cooperation that go beyond traditional foreign aid.

## Central Themes

A number of themes are discussed throughout the book. They can be grouped under six headings.

*Isolation of foreign aid policy in donor countries* While the tendency earlier – especially in the large industrial countries – was to incorporate aid policy under foreign policy as a whole, the end of the Cold War created a tendency to isolate aid from donor countries' other international relations. Foreign aid is associated with poor, marginalized countries and people in distant corners of the world. It is therefore less interesting for economically and politically powerful decision-makers, who instead leave development cooperation to more marginal groups in donor countries. Foreign aid policy becomes isolated as a separate – and in financial respects often residual – aspect of the total policy of donor countries. This applies much less to countries such as Denmark than, for example, to the USA and Japan, but the tendencies appear to be very widespread.

*Change and expansion of the goals for development cooperation* Development goals for foreign aid have vacillated back and forth during the past decades, but with a clear tendency towards constantly formulating more goals and including still more areas of social life. The expansion of goals since 1990 has not, however, gone so far as to formulate a new, comprehensive development paradigm that combines human development, democratization, sustainable resource management and the elimination of poverty. The aim of foreign aid has been expanded from changing the economic and social conditions to including institutional development and political reforms. These tendencies can be seen as an indication of increased intervention by donors. They can also be partly justified by the importance for the impact of foreign aid of the macro-economic and political-institutional framework. In any case, this development requires delicate balancing to avoid paternalism on the part of donors and to maintain respect for the right of recipient countries to self-determination.

*The role of the state as a major actor under pressure* A conflict exists between the basically state-based and state-supporting aspects of official , however, cooperation on the one side, and the widespread resistance to the state as the major actor in the development process on the other. This resistance is strong, both in the private, commercial sector and in civil society, but is based on different considerations. In the private sector, many see continued control and intervention by the state as an obstacle to economic development based on market forces and free enterprise. Among civil society representatives, the state is often considered to be repressive, inhibiting development that would benefit groups that are weak in resources. For the large Western bilateral and multilateral donors, this conflicting attitude towards the role of the state manifests itself in development cooperation that is both dependent on the state and, at the same time, attempts to find alternatives to replace the state as the major actor in the development process. In recent years, many actors have acknowledged, however, that there is a need for political regulation on both national and international levels.

*Marginalization of foreign aid as a consequence of economic globalization* The tendency towards globalization of the economy places foreign aid in new contexts in relation to trade and investments. The far greater openness for transnational economic cooperation, which some developing countries have chosen and others have been forced into, reduces foreign aid's significance as a means of furthering donor countries' commercial interests in the South. Foreign aid's importance is also reduced in countries that enjoy increasing trade and transfers of capital. An opposite tendency makes foreign aid of greater importance in the many poor countries that are not benefited, but rather slip further behind as marginalized areas in the global economy. These tendencies work together with the tendency towards isolation of foreign aid policy, so that if foreign aid is further concentrated on the poorest countries and resource-weak groups, it also becomes less interesting for the powerful decision-makers in donor countries and the better-off developing countries.

*Foreign aid's lack of acknowledgement of power relations and conflicts* The predominant foreign aid philosophy, even on the part of many NGOs, is based on the idea that the development process is free of conflict and primarily involves mobilizing sufficient resources and finding the best strategies and solutions. There is often no recognition that unequal power relations can be the greatest obstacle to economic, social and political change, and that progress, especially for the resource-weak groups, requires that these groups be strengthened politically in relation to those in power. In a broader context, there is no recognition that conflicts can function both in destructive ways and as a driving force in the development process and in international cooperation. The absence of a recognition of the importance of power relations and the conflicting character of the development process can contribute to weakening the impact of foreign aid, because the work becomes organized on the basis of unrealistic and rather naïve premises. Several official aid organizations have recently become more aware of this, and some Southern NGOs, including trade unions, work on the basis of an understanding of the development process as being conflict-filled and a power struggle. With stronger focus on aid in the process of solving violent conflicts, the belief in conflict-free development has become less dominant than it was, even among official donors.

*No recognition of differences and diversity* In formulating foreign aid policy and planning development strategy, the official donor organizations often do not recognize the enormous diversity that exists in recipient countries. Instead, it is assumed that these countries, or at least groups in them, are basically homogeneous. In addition, their problems and potential for development are stereotyped in social models that focus mainly on economic factors. There has been a tendency here, as mentioned above, to broaden the perspective to include social and political structures, but seldom in ways that have integrated understanding of the special societal conditions in recipient countries, or of culture in the broad sense. Some international NGOs have been inclined to simplify or homogenize differences in a similar way, but non-governmental organizations have usually shown more awareness of the special national and local conditions. In recent years there has been a tendency towards increased recognition of poverty's various forms and causes on the part of official donors such as the World Bank. There has been far more emphasis on variations from country to country. The main problem today, therefore, is that the strategies and proposals for solutions to poverty problems continue to be quite standardized.

It is not our intention that these six themes should be allowed to determine the form of the presentation in an effort to try and confirm our contentions. They clearly express some general conclusions that we have arrived at over the course of time; nevertheless, we consider it one of our chief aims to show where, in what ways, and to what extent these conclusions hold true. We can consider them as working hypotheses, and throughout the book we will try to define the limits of their applicability where relevant. Several of the themes will also be included in the discussions in Chapters 13 and 14.

CHAPTER 2

# Motives and Interests

§ THE motives for giving and receiving development assistance vary from country to country and from actor to actor. Motives have also changed significantly during the last fifty years. This is the subject of this chapter. First, we go back in time to examine the original reasons for starting foreign aid programmes in the USA and other industrial countries. Then the most important motives for giving development assistance are described and critically discussed. This description of the various types of motives is important for the later analyses in this book, because the motives behind participation in aid exert a strong influence on how this participation is carried out. A special section is devoted to the theoretical arguments for giving – or not giving – foreign aid to the poor countries of the world. We also examine recipient countries' motives for becoming engaged in international development cooperation. The chapter concludes with a discussion of the significant changes following the end of the Cold War.

Analytically, it is possible to separate the motives and arguments for development assistance from the development goals to be realized. The motives can of course be connected with the development goals in the sense that the arguments for initiating development cooperation originate in a wish to achieve the stated goals. But there can also be many other motives that are not directly related to the development goals, such as national security policy or commercial motives in the donor country. Therefore, we divide the discussion so that this chapter focuses on motives and arguments for and against foreign aid, while the next chapter examines the various development goals that have been formulated for foreign aid.

Strictly speaking, the motives and arguments are not necessarily consistent. Thus a country's government can give foreign aid that is mostly motivated by considerations of national security or special commercial interests, but at the same time tell their taxpaying citizens that their motives are altruistic. In the following, both aspects are considered.

## Historical Background

The earliest comprehensive proposal regarding development assistance was made by the USA's foreign minister, George C. Marshall, in 1947. His basic idea was to give massive aid to the European countries in order to rebuild them economically after the Second World War. The Marshall Plan was initiated in 1948 at the same time as the Organisation for European Economic Co-operation (OEEC), the predecessor of the Organisation for Economic Co-operation and Development (OECD). Simultaneously, special aid programmes were established for Greece and Turkey, which were not members of the OEEC.

At his inauguration the following year, President Truman presented the first plan for the expansion of American foreign aid: it was to include developing countries threatened by communism, either from outside or from within. Truman's proposal was included in the so-called Act for International Development, which was approved by Congress in 1950. Among the countries that especially benefited from this law were South Korea and Taiwan, which received considerable transfers of resources from the USA starting in 1954.

Support for Western Europe's reconstruction was phased out in the mid-1950s. At the same time, development assistance was increased to countries in the Middle East and Asia and after that to countries in Latin America and Africa.

The official motives for the Marshall Plan were based on both national security and commercial considerations. These had to do with the USA's national interests in strengthening the Western European countries against the expansion of communism in Eastern Europe and the Soviet Union, and the benefits of the reconstruction of a free Europe for American business. Commercial interests also played a role in arguments for American aid to developing countries, but here the national security motives were clearly dominant. From the time of his inauguration Truman had emphasized that the aim was to support countries threatened by the communist powers and stop the spread of communist movements within the recipient countries. The strongest argument in the latter connection was that an improvement of the population's living standard would make them less receptive to communist propaganda.

The motivation based on considerations of national security remained central in American foreign aid thinking all the way up to the beginning of the 1990s. Since the end of the 1950s, however, the government has increasingly emphasized for the American people that it is the USA's moral and humanistic obligation to help poor countries develop economically (Griffin 1991). Under President Kennedy, and especially after 1961, emphasis was also officially placed on the moral and humanitarian motives, even though the distribution of foreign aid in practice was dictated to a great extent by national security considerations (see Chapter 5 and the section on American foreign aid in Chapter 6).

Among the other countries that emphasized national security interests, the Federal Republic of Germany had a special status for many years. On the basis of the so-called Hallstein Doctrine, the Federal Republic demanded until the 1980s that all countries receiving German foreign aid had to refuse to recognize the German Democratic Republic.

In comparison, the official motivation in other large industrial countries such as Great Britain and France was based from the start more on moral considerations, but also on a kind of veneration of their own former colonies. This was especially true in the case of France. The governments of the former colonial powers appealed in general for people's support for development assistance by referring to their moral obligation to support the former colonies in their efforts to achieve economic and social progress. Accordingly, the former colonial powers also concentrated their foreign aid on their former colonies in the Third World. Unofficially, however, this priority was also based on promoting their economic and commercial interests, including continued access to natural resources, raw materials, and markets in the former colonies.

The Nordic countries established their foreign aid programmes with clearly expressed reference to moral and humanitarian obligations. The basic view was that rich countries ought to help poor countries. This was the same way of thinking that inspired the development of the Nordic welfare states, where the goal was to improve conditions for poor and resource-weak groups in their own populations.

From the start, since the end of the 1940s, it was characteristic that medium-sized and small industrial countries emphasized the importance of channelling a share of foreign aid through the UN. The motivation for this was connected with the idea that the UN could be a guarantee for peace and stability during the post-war period. Since then, some of these countries, including the Nordic countries, have continued to give high priority to the development work and humanitarian aid carried out by UN organizations.

Instead of going into more detail about the specific motives and arguments that have been officially formulated by governments in the individual donor countries, we will now examine the different types of motives that have influenced the foreign aid debate. The aim is to discover the ideas, interests and arguments that lie behind them.

The most important types of motives relate to moral and humanitarian principles, political and national security considerations, and economic and trade considerations. As mentioned above, the former colonial powers also have special motives for giving foreign aid to their own former colonies. Furthermore, during the last ten to fifteen years, the emphasis has been on motives that spring from wishes to sustain and improve the global environment; to limit international migration; to stop the flow of narcotics; to reduce the risk of epidemics such as HIV/AIDS; and to fight terrorism.

## Moral and Humanitarian Motives

The basis for moral and humanitarian arguments for foreign aid is the idea that a person who is well endowed and well situated has a definite obligation to help people who are poor and have poor access to resources. The same moral obligation applies to the relationship between rich and poor countries. Many variations of the idea exist – from the message of brotherly love in Christianity to the demand for solidarity in socialist ideologies or Mahatma Gandhi's principle that rich people ought to see themselves as trustees for their poor fellow citizens. As inherent in both Christianity and Islam, the emphasis can be on foreign aid as a kind of charity for the poor where the goal is to do one's duty. But the emphasis can also be the opposite: the poor have a right to a larger share of society's or the world's resources. Closely related to this is the principle that all human beings have a right to development, which was widely supported at the World Conference on Human Rights at Vienna in 1993 (see Sengupta 2000).

In the international foreign aid debate, purely moral and humanitarian arguments are rare. Most often, this motivation is combined with some form of enlightened self-interest on the part of the givers. An early and now classic formulation of this is found in the so-called Pearson Report of 1969, where the moral obligation to give foreign aid is stressed, but where it is also stated that development assistance to poor countries will benefit the rich countries in the long run (Pearson 1969). This thinking was carried further by the Brandt Commission, among others. It emphasized that countries in the North and South are so inter-dependent that large resource transfers to the poor countries would benefit these countries and in the long run also be a prerequisite for continued welfare and growth in the rich industrial countries (Brandt Commission 1980, 1983). Similar ideas are found in the South Commission's report from 1990 (South Commission 1990: Chapter 5).

In recent debates, the combination of moral obligation and enlightened self-interest has been labelled human internationalism. The Norwegian development researcher Olav Stokke has characterized human internationalism as the universal acceptance of the obligation to fight global poverty by promoting economic, social and political development in the South. This concept of obligation is further connected to an assumption that a more equal distribution of global resources is in the industrial countries' long-term vital interests (Stokke 1989: Introduction, 1996: 23 ff.). According to Stokke, human internationalism understood in this way has been a determining factor for shaping foreign aid policy and for mobilizing popular support for it in the Scandinavian countries, Canada and Holland.

The British development researcher Roger C. Riddell, in what is now considered a classic study of the arguments for and against development assistance, claims that narrower moral arguments have periodically set the agenda for the foreign aid debate in both Great Britain and France, in addition to the countries named above (Riddell 1987). But Riddell also points out that the strength of the position of the neo-classical economists in the 1980s, and the swing to the right in the USA, Great Britain and Germany, put the moral arguments for foreign aid under pressure. Riddell divides the critics into three categories. The first group completely rejects the idea that rich countries have any moral obligation at all; the second group partially rejects it; and the third group claims that since foreign aid has not worked, or will not, a possible moral obligation is irrelevant (Riddell 1987: Chapters 4–6). Rejection of the moral obligation will be discussed briefly here. The other criticism of foreign aid relates more to the section concerning theoretical arguments for and against foreign aid.

One of the most prominent critics of the moral obligation to provide foreign aid is Peter Bauer, whose basic view is that neither individuals nor states have any moral obligation at all to help others (see, for example, Bauer 1981). Only if wealth is accumulated in an unjust way can a moral demand be made for redistribution. But according to Bauer, this is not the case in relation to the global distribution of wealth. Therefore, Bauer completely rejects the idea that the rich industrialized countries originally based part of their growth on the transfer of resources from the colonies. He also asserts that the rich countries should in no way be responsible for poverty in developing countries. On the contrary, the differences in living standard and access to resources arise from the differences in what countries and populations have 'earned' as a result of their own efforts and those of their forebears. If individuals wish to change this by giving up part of their well-earned property, there is nothing to prevent it, but no one is obligated to do this. In regard to states, however, Bauer finds it morally unacceptable for them to use taxes, which their citizens are required to pay, for foreign aid. The state has no right to do this, because taxes belong to the citizens and must be used for their benefit. To allot part of the state's taxes to poor developing countries is a violation of inalienable property rights. Bauer also rejects any notion of giving foreign aid to the poor on the basis of the argument that it is their right as human beings to be able to satisfy their basic needs. No one has a right to more than he deserves and earns by lawful means.

Bauer's views have been supported by more broadly founded moral philosophical arguments, such as those formulated by Friedrich Hayek and Robert Nozick (Hayek 1976; Nozick 1974). These arguments especially consider social justice to be in conflict with the individual's inalienable right to freedom and property and give precedence to the latter.

It is not the intention here to discuss this moral philosophical issue further. It has been described and convincingly refuted by Roger C. Riddell, who questions the universality of the basic premises and shows instead that it is a more open question of whether there is a moral obligation under certain conditions (Riddell 1987: Chapter 4). It can also be pointed out that the recent debate about the use of the earth's limited resources has further weakened the position of Bauer and other such theoreticians. It is now obvious that further accumulation of wealth in the industrial countries is very much at the expense of developing countries' long-term possibilities for material development, because this accumulation is based on exploitation of exhaustible natural resources, both in developing countries and globally. With regard to the rich states' obligations, it should also be noted that regardless of the scope and character of the moral obligations, these states have accepted political obligations by agreeing to the UN Convention on Human Rights. And this convention also includes socio-economic rights that can be seen as a kind of universal right to development. Furthermore, the citizens in these states, through democratic procedures, have imposed the obligation upon their governments to give foreign aid to developing countries.

Moral and humanitarian motives have played an especially prominent role in connection with multilateral cooperation through the UN. While most bilateral foreign aid has been and continues to be based, to varying degrees, on national security and economic interests, multilateral aid through the UN has from the start been rooted in moral, humanitarian and global security motives. When donor countries have wished to channel part of their foreign aid through the UN's development organizations, it has basically been from a wish to contribute to real multinational cooperation and well-ordered relations between states. The motives behind channelling large foreign aid funds through development banks and the EU have been more mixed, however. They contain significant elements of the donor countries' own national interests (see Chapter 5, section on multilateral foreign aid, and Chapter 7).

Moral and humanitarian motives have also dominated most NGO aid, although the differences here are great. We discuss this in Chapter 8.

## Political and Economic Motives and Interests

Foreign aid policy has seldom been the central instrument used by donor countries to safeguard their political and national security interests. In this sphere, the establishment of military and political alliances in connection with military aid has usually been much more important. Moreover, officially, development assistance has seldom, and decreasingly, been based on donor countries' narrow interests of national security. However, this does not change the fact that the large industrial countries in particular have administered and distributed a large part of their development assistance in accordance with political and national security priorities. The same applied earlier to the development assistance provided by the Soviet Union, and it still applies to aid from India and China, which has much to do with promoting political and military strategic interests in these countries' neighbouring regions (see Chapter 5).

The same factors are valid for economic and commercial interests. Officially, these have been of secondary importance for foreign aid policies in industrial countries and have been only a modest motivating factor for providing foreign aid. Nevertheless, these interests have often formed the tacit basis for choosing recipient countries and methods. The former colonial powers have not only concentrated their foreign aid in their former colonies because of feelings of veneration and a special kind of community. They have also done this to maintain privileged access to resources and markets in the decolonized areas. The USA, Canada, Australia, Germany and Japan have not played major roles as colonial powers, but they have allowed their foreign aid policy to be determined by considerations for their commercial interests. The same is true, although on a significantly smaller scale, of the smaller and middle-sized industrial countries.

The debate about the involvement of business has taken very different forms in the different DAC countries. In Japan, domestic business interests have been included from the start in the official goals for foreign aid but have gradually been played down (see below and in the section on Japan in Chapter 6). In the USA, the interests of both agriculture and industry have played a dominant role in practice, and much of the official argument for giving foreign aid to developing countries has had to do with advantages for American business. In smaller industrial countries, such as the Nordic countries, it has been difficult for the representatives of business to win acceptance for their interests as legitimate guidelines for the administration of foreign aid. In reality, however, broad concessions are made to national business interests, including those of the Nordic countries.

One of the ways in which business interests in donor countries are taken care of is through tied foreign aid. In principle, there are several ways in which foreign aid can be tied: to specific projects, for example, or to implementation of certain policies or institutional reforms. But in the debate, tied aid normally refers to a donor's demand that grants or loans must be used to buy goods and services from the donor's own country.

Bilateral donors tie a certain amount of their aid to the purchase of goods and services from their own country due to pressures exerted by both employers and employees. The owners of enterprises emphasize receiving as large a share as possible of the orders connected with foreign aid, not just in order to increase sales of goods and services, but also in the hope of gaining access to markets in recipient countries through participation in development projects. The trade unions' reasons for supporting a certain amount of tied aid is similarly based on expectations of increasing employment as a result of orders connected with foreign aid.

It can be difficult to make a precise assessment of the significance of tied aid. One reason for this is that in addition to the formal limitations regarding purchases, unofficial or tacit agreements are often made; and such tied aid agreements for certain services or goods actually create derivative ties. This may occur when consultant firms from a given donor country, for example, design infrastructure projects according to specifications that favour equipment manufacturers from their own country; or when delivered equipment must be maintained by future purchases of parts also from the same country.

On several occasions, the DAC has adopted guidelines for untying foreign aid to a certain extent, and reducing the negative effects for recipient countries. For example, public tenders should be open to other countries, especially in the Third World, and not only in the donor country. Most DAC countries have agreed to these guidelines and also follow them to some extent. This applies especially to Japan, where foreign aid has previously been very much tied to purchases of Japanese products. In contrast, Great Britain and to some extent Holland have shown little interest until recently in untying much of their foreign aid. The newest figures from the late 1990s show that both Great Britain and Holland are now above average for total untied aid for DAC countries; at the same time, countries such as the USA, Spain and Canada still have over two-thirds of their aid tied to purchases in the donor country (OECD/DAC 2000: 211).

In recent years, the majority of DAC countries, with the USA in the lead, have proposed to give completely untied aid to the poorest countries. At first glance this seems to be a correct and progressive proposal, and this has placed any countries opposing the approval of the new principle in a precarious situation. One such country is Denmark, which usually supports reforms within DAC that benefit developing countries. The explanation is thought-provoking. Supporters of more untied aid are mostly countries that only give a modest amount of foreign aid in relation to their GNP, and only a very small share of this to the poorest countries. Countries such as Denmark, on the other hand, give extensive foreign aid and most of it to the poorest countries. Untied aid to the poorest countries, therefore, would not significantly affect most countries behind the proposal, but it would especially have a marked effect on Danish foreign aid. The Danish government does not find this reasonable, but has in principle agreed to untie more of its aid.

Figures for how much aid is tied must be viewed with strong reservations. The uncertainty is even greater when trying to calculate how much less foreign aid is worth for the recipient countries as a consequence of the ties. A study published by the OECD in 1991 estimated that the real value of the total DAC foreign aid was reduced by somewhere between 15 and 30 per cent in relation to a situation in which the recipient countries could freely choose their suppliers in their own country or on the world market (Jepma 1991). The same study points out that there were also some indirect costs connected with tied aid – for example, in the form of preferences for equipment-heavy projects requiring large imports, and biases in favour of sectors and project types that are of special commercial interest for businesses in donor countries.

Many problems and costs are evident in comparison to the ideal situation as seen from the point of view of developing countries, but it must also be emphasized that there is no negative connection between how much foreign aid is tied and its development impact. Tied foreign aid can very well promote development in recipient countries, and, under certain conditions, it can simply be an advantage that business enterprises in the donor countries are involved in some way in the development processes in poor countries. It can also be necessary, in order to gain broad support for a high foreign aid percentage in donor countries, to create opportunities for increased sales and employment in connection with foreign aid transfers – even though when viewed realistically only marginal amounts are involved in comparison with the industrial countries' total exports and employment.

We will return to the influence of business interests on foreign aid policy in selected countries in Chapter 6, in connection with other factors that have influenced the implementation of bilateral aid.

## Environmental Considerations

In addition to conventional national security and commercial interests, environmental policy considerations have come to play an increasing role since the mid-1980s for the foreign aid policies of both bilateral and multilateral donors. The linking of environmental and development problems in a global perspective has a long history, at least as far back as the publication of the Club of Rome's *Limits to Growth* in 1972 (Meadows et al. 1972). But in relation to the foreign aid debate, it was only with the publication of the Brundtland Commission's report in 1987 that this problem was seriously placed on the agenda (Brundtland 1987). This report underlined the common global interests and the inter-dependency of the world's many countries. It also argued that environmental problems had now become so great that the global community must join forces in a common strategy for growth and development based on sustainability. An important element here would be an increase in the rich countries' foreign aid to developing countries to support the implementation of their environmental policy.

The South Commission's report in 1990 followed up these considerations by emphasizing that the continued and very widespread poverty in developing countries is a strong contributing factor to the degradation of the environment, both in developing countries and globally. The report also notes that the cause of the large population growth and increasing pressure on limited resources is to be found in mass poverty. Families living in poverty and uncertainty are prompted to have many children so that they can contribute to family income and create a social security net for their parents in connection with both illness and old age. On the basis of such considerations, the South Commission found that it was in the long-term interests of the rich countries to reduce poverty worldwide (South Commission 1990: Chapter 5).

At the UN Conference on the Environment and Development (UNCED) in Rio de Janeiro in 1992, consideration for the environment was further emphasized as a global obligation that should also be a motive for giving foreign aid. Since then, most industrial countries have considered development assistance to developing countries as an important means by which to sustain and improve the global environment.

In the report from the Commission on Global Governance in 1995, environmental considerations are taken up together with a proposal for a changed motivation for giving foreign aid. It is argued that the idea of foreign aid as a form of inter-state charity ought to be replaced by an understanding of foreign aid as a payment for delivered services – for example, when developing countries act as protectors of animal and plant species and biological diversity, or as growth areas for tropical forests (Commission on Global Governance 1995: 158 ff.). Such views have created a basis for completely new motivations and arguments for giving foreign aid, which we will return to in Chapter 14.

In recent years, following the introduction of environmental considerations, the foreign aid debate has presented arguments for a broader concept of national security as motivation for giving foreign aid. The EU countries in particular have emphasized that foreign aid should also be used to reduce migration and the flow of refugees from the Middle East and Africa to Europe. A special version of this way of thinking suggests using foreign aid to reward states that agree to receive refugees who have been refused entrance to EU countries.

In the USA, the discussion of a broader national security concept has led to linking foreign aid and regional conflicts involving American soldiers. Foreign aid policy has also been designed, in part, as an element in the fight against the production and trade of narcotics (for further discussion of these newer motives, see Chapter 14).

## Summary of Motives for Giving Development Assistance

On the basis of the presentation in the preceding sections, it can be useful to summarize the main motives that lie behind development assistance. This can be done with the help of a simple figure that presents the different types of motives as dimensions. Figure 2.1 can be used to place a specific donor organization, during a specific time period or in general, on the four axes: far from the centre if the motive has great importance or close to the centre if the opposite is the case. As an example, the USA in the 1960s scored high on the national security dimension, a little lower on the economic, and low on the remaining two dimensions. Similarly, bilateral aid has generally tended to give priority to environmental considerations as the basis for giving foreign aid, and decrease the importance of national security considerations, especially after the end of the Cold War.

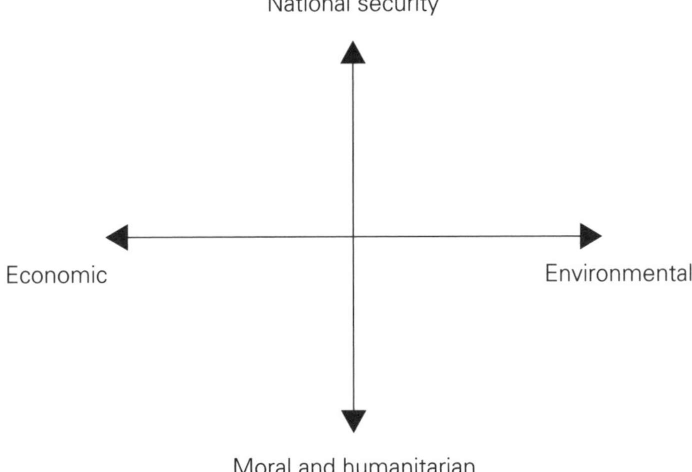


**Figure 2.1** Main motives for giving development assistance

As indicated above, there can be significant differences between declared motives and real ones, especially in official bilateral foreign aid. In general, it seems that the moral and humanitarian motives are exaggerated in official statements and in authorities' appeals to taxpayers to support foreign aid transfers, whereas the national security and economic motives in this context are understated. This depends to a great extent, however, on the context – for example, which target group the authorities direct their appeals to. There are thus many examples of political programme declarations that emphasize the benefits that businesses in donor countries can achieve through international aid.

The decreasing importance of national security considerations since 1990 must be welcomed for many reasons, but this change has also contributed to isolating foreign aid policy in several of the large industrial countries (see Chapter 1, p. 3). Whether this will change fundamentally in the aftermath of the terrorist attacks in New York and Washington on 11 September 2001 is yet to be seen.

## Theoretical Arguments for and against Foreign Aid

In the preceding discussion, we have examined different motives for giving foreign aid, including both moral motives and those based on interest. In this section, we discuss aid from the perspective of development theory. The central question is whether aid to developing countries can be justified theoretically. Can it be claimed on the basis of existing growth and development theory that foreign aid promotes development in some more narrowly defined way?

This question has been debated in detail since the beginning of the 1950s without achieving consensus (see Tarp 2000 for comprehensive reviews). It would be too great a digression to discuss all facets of the debate here. Our more limited aim is to point out some of the main positions that are used later in the book as guides for the more detailed discussion of the effects of foreign aid.

It should be clear from the start that development assistance is neither a necessary nor sufficient condition for growth and development according to the theories concerned with this question. National economic growth, and development in a broader sense, can be achieved without foreign aid, and foreign aid does not necessarily result in growth and development. Both depend on several other circumstances and potential incentives, as well as barriers and conditions that have a restrictive influence on development. The theoretical problem is thus both to formulate foreign aid's general effects and to reveal the circumstances that cause the effects (for a concise overview see Thorbecke 2000).

The first economic theories that supported development assistance were mainly based on analyses of the role that capital formation played in growth. Much simplified, the basic thesis is that investment of more capital creates growth. How large an investment is necessary to create a certain increase in national income depends on many factors, but a positive correlation is to be expected under all circumstances (see Martinussen 1997: especially Chapters 5 and 6). Aid in the form of capital transfers was considered a possible supplement to other forms of capital formation stemming from private and public investments in recipient countries.

In the further argumentation, the early economic growth theories pointed out that it was precisely capital formation that was a basic problem for developing countries in general. Their private and public savings were insufficient to finance large investments, for example, in the economic infrastructure necessary to start growth processes. Private foreign investments were also much too modest to be able to undertake this task, and very few developing countries were at all attractive for private investors in rich industrial countries. Under these circumstances, it was crucial for the rich states to support capital formation in the South through official foreign aid transfers.

Several economic theorists argued for capital aid's possible beneficial effects on the basis of a two-gap model. The developing countries had a double problem. They mobilized too few resources internally to cover the need for investments; and at the same time, they mobilized too few resources in the form of foreign exchange that could finance imports of machinery and other capital goods that they had to buy on foreign markets. If foreign aid were given in the form of either foreign exchange or direct financing of the necessary imports of the means of production, etc., it could contribute to closing both gaps. This was – compressed into a few sentences – the main message of the leading economic growth theories in the 1950s and 1960s.

Furthermore, according to the theories, the side effects of the investments financed by foreign aid – the multiplier and accelerator effects – could have the potential to start self-reinforcing growth. Thus foreign aid – using Rosenstein-Rodan's and Rostow's metaphor of an aeroplane – could help developing countries to gain so much speed that their growth processes could take off. For a more detailed and sophisticated argument, we refer to a now classic article by Chenery and Strout (1966; also Rosenstein-Rodan 1957; Rostow 1956).

It should be added that the reason for giving foreign aid that is formulated in the two-gap model does not only involve capital transfers as grants. Aid can also take the form of loans, if the loans are given under soft terms. The basic point here is that most developing countries have such low creditworthiness that they are able to take loans only at interest rates significantly higher than the level that applies internationally for the industrial countries. Therefore, taking foreign loans has not been an attractive alternative to aid in the form of grants or loans when developing countries have had to supplement their capital formation.

In the subsequent theoretical debate, doubts were raised about several assumptions behind the two-gap model. Some critics claimed that in practice capital aid had rarely, or only to a limited extent, supplemented domestic savings. Instead, there had been a tendency for capital transfers to replace public savings in particular, so that the beneficial effects of the aid were very limited – perhaps even negative (e.g. Paldam 1997: Chapter I.5).

Other critics questioned more fundamentally the model's strong emphasis on the amount of capital as an engine for growth. Instead, they stressed the qualitative aspects as being far more important. In other words, the decisive factor is how money is invested or how capital is used. Still others argued that the effects of capital investments very much depend on the conditions in recipient countries. The Swedish economist Gunnar Myrdal was one of the first to present a more comprehensive theory arguing that capital is only one among many factors determining total production and thereby national income (Myrdal 1968; see also Martinussen 1997: 78 ff.). Several economists during the past thirty years have argued that the effects of capital transfers depend to a high degree on other factors, especially including the economic policy of the recipient country (e.g. World Bank 1998b). Many neo-classical economists have strongly emphasized developing countries' own policies. It is in extension of their theories that some of the argumentation is found for the so-called structural adjustment programmes, which – with the World Bank in the lead – held such a central position from around 1980 in international development cooperation (see Chapters 3 and 4).

We will return to these problems several times, not only as theoretical but also as empirical questions (see especially Chapter 12). For now, the aim, as already mentioned, is limited to a brief introduction to some of the main positions. The theoretical arguments and criticisms referred to so far relate mostly to aid as capital transfers and, with regard to its possible effects, to national economic growth. Aid also has other forms, however: for example, transfer of technical knowledge and skills, which can influence the development process in ways completely different from capital transfers through improving the qualifications of the labour force. Exactly such a possible effect belongs to arguments for foreign aid among theorists who place special emphasis on human capital as the driving force in development processes. This way of thinking can be traced back to Joseph Schumpeter, who found that the main problem for developing countries was not the lack of capital but the lack of industrious and clever entrepreneurs and innovators in the broad sense (Schumpeter 1934).

## The Micro Level and Arguments for Aid to the Poor

So far, the discussion of arguments for and against foreign aid has focused on the macro level. Much of the theoretical debate, however, has also been concerned with the micro level. Here, the arguments for giving foreign aid have often been based on the fact that many investments in projects and activities that otherwise have high priority have not been attractive for private investors, while the public authorities could not afford to make them. There can be several reasons why it is not attractive to invest under commercial conditions. The investments can be connected with too-great risks or a too-long turnover period – the period from the time the investment is made until it provides returns. A special problem can be that the investors cannot ensure themselves full profit, because it is too difficult or impossible to demand payments from users. Investments in education involve such problems. The same applies to investments in roads and other forms of physical infrastructure. But this does not mean that such investments are unprofitable from a social-economic point of view. On the contrary, investments in education and many forms of infrastructure have proved to be highly profitable and are in fact often necessary prerequisites for economic growth and development. Therefore, strong arguments exist for giving foreign aid when authorities in developing countries lack the financial means to make such investments.

There are special arguments for aid to the poor in recipient countries and to groups among the population that have few resources. The basic view here is that neither transfers of capital nor other forms of aid that are given to authorities in developing countries necessarily also benefit these segments of the population. The same can be claimed more generally in regard to the effects of national economic growth. If the development goal, therefore, is to relieve poverty, this can be an argument for special initiatives that aim to improve living conditions for the poor. Theories about this are not in themselves arguments for foreign aid, but follow logically if and when help to the poor is given political priority as a major development goal.

It should be emphasized, however, that there are good theoretical arguments for giving priority to increasing income for poor citizens in order to promote national economic growth. This applies especially in countries where the industrial sector's growth is impeded by too limited a domestic market and difficulties in competing on export markets. Exactly such limitations exist in most African countries and many other small developing countries. Here, income increases for those who are better off will typically lead to increased imports, partly because these social groups demand goods that are not produced locally, and partly because they often prefer imported goods. Such increased imports can in themselves give the poor countries further problems with balance of payments. On the other hand, income increases for poor groups in the population mainly lead to increased demand for locally produced goods and thus act as an impetus for the country's own productive sectors, including industry. At the same time, it has been a general experience that increased incomes for the poor almost automatically have a 'trickle-up' effect on the social hierarchy, so that those who are better off also benefit. The opposite effect – trickle-down – occurs, however, only under specific and rare circumstances. Even the World Bank has acknowledged this in recent years (World Bank 1999: 1, 13 ff.). In other words, and in greatly simplified form, one can thus argue theoretically for giving aid to the poor in most developing countries on the basis of common national economic interests.

It can also be argued in a somewhat similar way to concentrate efforts especially on poor women. Not only do they play a central role in production processes, but they have also proved to a greater degree than men to have a tendency to share any increased incomes with the rest of the family – or else they have been forced to do this due to the division of power in the household.

## Recipient Countries' Motives for Receiving Foreign Aid

In the previous sections, we have described the various motives and arguments for giving foreign aid. For a complete picture, we must examine the motives of governments and those in power in the developing countries for receiving aid.

The official motives are to a great extent based on the theoretical arguments outlined above. Governments in the South want aid to promote economic and social development. The South Commission, which in many ways reflects dominant official viewpoints, especially in poor countries, notes that significantly larger transfers of resources are necessary to support development efforts. The Commission also points out that private, commercial transfers in the form of loans, export credits, portfolio investments and direct investments are not real alternatives for the large number of very poor countries. It is difficult for them to attract such transfers in larger amounts and on reasonable terms. Also, these countries are so weak economically and so vulnerable that it is difficult for them to manage the often significant changes from year to year in private financial flows.

In addition, the Commission does not feel that the most necessary development investments – in social and economic infrastructure – are commercially attractive. The reasons are similar to those named in the section above. It is not possible for poor countries themselves to finance these investments through increased export. Therefore, instead, the great majority of poor countries have a great need to have their debts to DAC countries reduced or completely written off, as a first step. The next step should be to guarantee these countries a stable flow of official aid, preferably at a somewhat higher level (South Commission 1990: 225 ff.).

Another motive is connected with the economic and political power interests of those in power in recipient countries, who see aid as an opportunity to maintain and strengthen their positions. Not all forms of aid are equally attractive in this connection. Most in demand is untied aid in the form of grants and loans on soft terms without any restrictions attached. But project aid can also be of interest for those in power, if they can arrange it in such a way that projects can be used to reward selected and defined target groups and thereby serve to build up political support groups in the population.

People in donor countries have often received the impression that developing countries and their citizens want aid at almost any price – and that they should also be grateful. However, this is not always the case in the real world, where well-consolidated regimes have refused many forms of aid. This is true of the governments in the former British colonies, for example, who find that development cooperation with Great Britain carries the risk of maintaining the colonial relation of dependency. But there has also been a more general tendency in many developing countries to prefer multilateral rather than bilateral aid. One of the reasons for this has been that multilateral aid, especially through the UN's development organizations, is given without ties to the specific national security and commercial interests that often influence bilateral donors' foreign aid policy. Also, countries in the South have better opportunities to exert political influence on the UN organizations' aid due to their membership of these organizations. In this connection, the difference is not between bilateral and multilateral aid, but rather between aid received through the UN and other aid. The latter includes both bilateral aid and aid from development banks and the EU, where developing countries have little influence.

After many years of experience with the various forms of aid, strong pressure groups have been formed in many developing countries, which want foreign aid either phased out or radically changed. In many places, there have always been oppositional groups that appeal to donors not to support their governments through aid. But in addition to this, groups have increasingly arisen that wish aid to be stopped because they believe that it generally renders recipient countries dependent on donor countries. These viewpoints are similar to those on the theoretical right, such as those of many neo-classical economists. They also resemble the views of dependency theorists and the political left, who have long considered aid to be a means of maintaining dominance over countries in the South.

## Foreign Aid after the End of the Cold War

The communist regimes' fall and the dissolution of the Soviet Union have crucially affected international aid in several respects.

One immediate effect has been the disappearance of a whole group of donor countries. Although the Eastern European countries have never given anywhere near as much aid as the DAC countries (see Appendix 1), it has been important – and both good and bad – for a small group of developing countries for many years. These include (in alphabetical order) Afghanistan, Angola, Cambodia, Cuba, Ethiopia, Nicaragua and Vietnam. Following the end of the Cold War, these countries joined the queue of recipient countries and created a new and greater demand for aid from the DAC countries. The Eastern European countries' requests for aid have had the same effect on a considerably larger scale. In other words, the result has been not only the disappearance of a group of donor countries, but also the addition since the early 1990s of a large group of recipient countries. Thus further pressure has been placed on the limited resources that are earmarked for development cooperation.

Another effect of the end of the Cold War has been reduced motivation of many DAC countries to give foreign aid. The formerly crucial national security interests that motivated foreign aid as part of the rivalry with the Eastern countries for allies, resources and markets in the Third World have lost a great deal of their importance. This applies especially to the USA, but also to Canada and other large industrial countries. National security interests played a significant role in maintaining the level of foreign aid. With their reduced importance, the way was opened for significant budget reductions. These were further encouraged as a result of the rich countries' own problems, for example, with increasing unemployment and increasing demand for care of the elderly.

The weakening of foreign aid's importance in relation to national security has strengthened the position of conservative critics of foreign aid, especially in the USA, where they were led by prominent politicians such as Newt Gingrich and Jesse Helms. Their mission has actually not had especially much to do with aid but consists more of a total attack on the welfare state, which they wish to replace with a 'society of opportunity', where citizens have greater freedom. The thinking of this 'New Right', as the conservative tendency in the USA is often called, is related to the argumentation of Peter Bauer already described. The consequence of this attitude is that just as the American state is not obligated to care for the country's own poor, it has no obligation in relation to poor countries in the Third World. Therefore, the New Right has demanded sharp cuts in both bilateral and multilateral aid (see Watkins 1994).

A third consequence of the end of the Cold War has indirectly been more frequent outbreaks of national and ethnic conflict. Such conflicts had earlier been kept under control by the two great powers, sometimes by oppression that could be legitimized by the global rivalry between East and West. The new conflicts have put further pressure on aid funding, because they have demanded peace-keeping operations, emergency relief and humanitarian aid (see Chapter 10). Furthermore, these conflicts have increased the stream of refugees to the rich countries. This also requires aid funds because many countries have chosen to use these funds to finance refugee programmes and support for those applying for asylum. Funds spent on humanitarian aid and refugees can be included in the official figures for aid from DAC countries. The decrease or stagnation in the total amount of aid means that the funds that are available today for actual development cooperation with countries in the Third World have been markedly reduced.

The impact of the changes that followed the Cold War on the amount of aid and its distribution is analysed in Chapter 5.

# CHAPTER 3
# Development Goals

§ MUCH foreign aid is given to further the interests of donor countries, as discussed in the previous chapter. All donors, however, have also emphasized the promotion of specific forms of development in recipient countries. In this chapter, we examine the formulated goals more closely and see how they have changed up to the present time.

There are significant differences from one donor to another, of course, but since most DAC countries and the large international organizations have changed their development goals and their priorities at almost the same tempo, it is possible to distinguish different periods. Variations and conflicts among donor organizations regarding priorities do exist within each of these periods, but a dominant discourse or rhetoric can be identified for each period. The World Bank has set the agenda to a great extent, but also of significant influence are the shifting policies in the large industrial countries. The theoretical development debate and research have also influenced these shifting priorities (see as background Martinussen 1997).

It should be added that the periods discussed in the following do not cover development goals for either Soviet foreign aid or aid from OPEC countries, India or China. Nor does it cover NGOs' development goals, which are discussed in a separate section at the end of the chapter.

Defining development goals in relation to the strategies used to achieve them can often be difficult in practice. A series of sub-goals often lead to realization of the end goal. Promotion of national economic growth will thus require development of human resources and strengthening of the political-institutional framework for economic activities. In the following, the main focus is the final goals. The next chapter discusses the strategies in connection with various development goals (see also Thorbecke 2000; Hjertholm and White 2000).

## Development Goals of Foreign Aid Organizations: Historical Background

To the extent that donors formulated development goals for their foreign aid in the 1950s, the focus was almost always on economic growth in the form of increased production and consumption in recipient countries. Behind this lay ideas similar to those of the Marshall Plan: the important thing was to give developing countries an injection of capital so that they could set their own growth processes in motion. If this succeeded, the people in recipient countries would experience a general improvement in their living conditions. This assumption that national economic growth would spread out and trickle down, also to the poor groups in the population, was the basis of American foreign aid, which during this period aimed to a great extent at improving the living standard of the large groups of poor so that they would be less receptive to communist and socialist ideas. The World Bank's development goals were not connected with national security interests in the same way, but were otherwise the same. The Bank also stressed the importance of helping developing countries create the prerequisites that would allow their markets to function better, since it was felt that the under-developed and poorly functioning markets were a central development problem.

Towards the end of the 1950s and the start of the 1960s, expectations of quick results from capital transfers were gradually given up, and the donors adopted a more long-term aid effort in developing countries. Growth was still the central goal, however, for most donors until around 1970. At this time, an adjustment was started that included special development goals for the poor. Due to the influence of many analyses that showed that growth did not automatically benefit the poor segments of the population, still more donor organizations formulated goals about giving special aid to these groups. Also during this period, increasing attention was directed towards the situation of women. There continued to be faith in the notion that stronger market forces would promote national economic growth and through this also reduce developing countries' dependence, but it was widely acknowledged that market mechanisms in themselves could not relieve poverty or resolve the special problems of women in developing countries. Therefore, development goals were specifically formulated about social distribution, including distribution between the sexes.

The World Bank adjusted its goal formulations around 1972, so that they came to include growth, 'redistribution with growth' and special help for the poor. The president of the World Bank at that time, Robert McNamara, introduced the newly formulated goals in connection with arguments for giving special priority to meeting the basic needs of the large groups of poor. This viewpoint was further developed, especially by the ILO, but also by UNICEF and other UN organizations (see Martinussen 1997: 298 ff.).

Around 1980, new discussions arose concerning development goals, especially as a result of the political shift in power in large industrial countries such as the USA, Great Britain and the Federal Republic of Germany. The shifts of government that brought Ronald Reagan, Margaret Thatcher and Helmut Kohl to power led to radical changes in economic policy in these countries and to demands for changes in the aims of international cooperation. These changes were fundamentally a reduction of the state's economic role and a stronger reliance on so-called free market forces. For foreign aid goals, this meant that the main focus was moved back to national economic growth, but now connected to a structural transformation of developing countries' political economy.

The World Bank's version, which quickly came to reflect the new political tendencies, was the sweeping structural adjustment programmes that mostly aimed at limiting the state's involvement in economic development. The state was to withdraw from the production sphere, stop its regulatory intervention in the private sector, and generally reduce its expenditure, including that on health and education. Foreign aid to relieve poverty remained on the agenda, but since the structural adjustment programmes did not include any considerations worth mentioning of their effects on the poor, the result was a strong toning down of poverty-alleviation measures.

This also influenced foreign aid from Nordic and other donor countries that otherwise maintained that poverty reduction was a major goal. Structural adjustment programmes became so dominant in international development cooperation that almost all bilateral donors accepted working within this framework. The dominant discourse that emerged in this regard, and the priorities of goals and strategies that belonged to it, are sometimes referred to as the 'Washington consensus' (see Stiglitz 1998). This term reflects the fact that the organizations that endorsed this consensus to the greatest extent all had their headquarters in Washington DC (the IMF, the World Bank, USAID and the Inter-American Development Bank).

The use of structural adjustment programmes as a framework for foreign aid also meant a basic change in the dialogue between donors and recipient countries. Now, very clearly formulated demands were made of recipient countries to implement a specific economic policy according to the recommendations of the 'Washington consensus'. In a historical perspective, these demands can be seen as the first generation of donor conditionalities (conditions for receiving foreign aid). The next generation of conditionalities came in the 1990s, and these are discussed below in the section on democratization and good governance.

## Poverty Eradication and Other Development Goals for Foreign Aid Since the 1990s

Even though in the 1980s most donor organizations, both multilateral and bilateral, accepted the World Bank's leading role – often together with IMF – in deciding the general priorities, many of them remained critical, especially about playing down poverty reduction. UNICEF in particular focused on the unfavourable consequences for poor groups in the population (Cornia et al. 1987), and the Scandinavian countries, Holland and Canada kept poverty reduction high on their agendas and continually criticized the Bank's narrow approach. This was one reason that towards the end of the 1980s high priority was again assigned to social and economic development for the poor, especially women, within the World Bank, which in the 1990 edition of the *World Development Report* took up the theme of poverty problems and the strategies for solving them. The report emphasized as special goals for foreign aid (a) growth with equity and the creation of better earning opportunities for the poor; (b) improved access to education, health services and other social services; and (c) direct assistance to those living under the worst conditions (World Bank 1990).

Parallel with the renewed priority to social development goals, development cooperation was becoming increasingly characterized by environmental considerations, both as a motive for giving aid and as a goal for these efforts. In this connection, the central concept became 'sustainable development', which was thus defined in the Brundtland Report of 1987: development that fulfils present human needs without endangering future generations' possibilities for fulfilling these needs. In the same report, the needs discussion is closely linked to poverty problems, and it is argued that fulfilment of poor people's basic needs must be given higher priority than more demands for increasing consumption in rich countries (Brundtland et al. 1987). This strong emphasis on poor people's rights did not win undivided support in the international foreign aid debate. The principle of considering environmental sustainability, however, won great popularity during the course of a few years. Most donor organizations today have formulated development goals regarding improved utilization of the given natural resources and limitation of harmful effects on the environment.

## Women and Gender Equality

In addition to poverty eradication as an overall development goal, and often as part of it, most donors have formulated goals with focus on women and gender equality. Initially, the emphasis was on women as a vulnerable group – as a passive category of clients that had to be assisted and offered relief through special development assistance. This later changed to a perception of women as active human beings who, as producers and in other roles, could contribute significantly to development. Some donors have also shifted emphasis from women to gender and gender equality. A distinction is often made between two main positions and associated strategies: Women in Development (WID) and Gender and Development (GAD) (Rathgeber 1990; Young 1993: Chapter 8).

The WID approach focuses solely on women and attributes the inferior status and social position of women chiefly to their exclusion from the spheres of the state and the formal economy. Proponents of the WID approach were among the first to point to women's invisibility and to the lack of data on their living conditions and activities.

According to the WID approach, women suffer because of their roles in reproduction, work within the household, and production outside the home. Poor women are also doubly marginalized, as poor and as women in male-dominated households.

Proponents of the WID approach argue further that women in general have been excluded from development processes and that they have not benefited from economic growth unless the whole process was shaped with a view to specifically improving the conditions of women. The core of the strategy for change implies a 'mainstreaming' of women – the integration of women into the mainstream of economic, political and social development. They should be ensured greater access to services, a wider range of occupations and the opportunity to achieve positions of power. Women should be treated on equal terms with men. At the same time, women are looked upon as a formerly untapped potential that could be incorporated into local and national development efforts and contribute to increasing the effectiveness of aid. The WID approach has been criticized by many researchers and practitioners (e.g. Young 1993; Richey 2000). They have argued that by focusing exclusively on women, the WID approach fails to understand how gender relations work and how they impact upon women in civil society and within the household. They have further criticized the WID approach for giving far too much attention to the public spheres: the state and the formal economy.

The alternative GAD approach is constructed around a set of key propositions. Women are actually incorporated into the development process, but in very different ways; women are not a homogeneous category, but are divided by class, colour and creed; the totality of women's and men's lives should be taken into account, not merely their productive or reproductive activities; and women are not passive or marginal, but active subjects of societal processes. The GAD approach implies less emphasis on correcting gender inequalities through special assistance to women, and more emphasis on attacking the structures and processes that give rise to women's disadvantages. It implies attention to culturally specific forms of social inequality and divisions with a further view to dealing with how gender is related to and interlocked with other forms of inequalities and social hierarchies.

Proponents of the GAD approach often do acknowledge that the previous focus on women as a social category and the accompanying aid strategies were probably necessary in the initial stages. But they also argue that a genuine understanding of the gender question depends on holistic analyses of the social and cultural systems where gender identities are created and reproduced, and where conflicts between men and women exist on different levels. Gender awareness in development cooperation is not about 'adding women' but about rethinking development goals and strategies as a whole in gender terms.

The GAD approach has become increasingly influential in the discussions of development goals since the mid-1990s. However, most official donors have retained goals – and practices – that are more in line with the WID approach (Richey 2000: 263 ff.).

## Democratization and Good Governance

After the end of the Cold War, most bilateral donors added more development goals concerning the political situation in recipient countries. These goals were primarily concerned with promoting democratization and respect for human rights, but in a broader sense also involved good governance. Sweden defined democratic development of society as the goal for development already in 1978, but for many years most other bilateral donors specifically avoided reference to political development goals. The official explanation for this was often that using foreign aid to change the political situation in recipient countries would be intervention in internal matters and thus in conflict with respect for these countries' sovereignty. Since the beginning of the 1990s, this argument has all but disappeared from official aid rhetoric and has been replaced by explicitly formulated wishes to influence political development in developing countries. In some contexts, the argument for this is that a democratic form of government and good governmental practices promote economic development, and that respect for human rights is an integrated part of poverty orientation. But in reality, many donors have gone considerably further with independent goals involving changes in the political systems in recipient countries.

It is also characteristic of the situation since around 1990 that the bilateral donors, in order to promote political development goals, also use them as conditions for giving aid. In this way, what could be called second-generation conditionalities have been introduced. Donors now make demands of recipient countries not only to carry out specific economic policies but also to adopt a specific form of political system.

It is thus a widespread demand that authorities in developing countries obligate themselves to initiate a democratization process and take initiatives to improve compliance with human rights. In regard to the latter demand, President Jimmy Carter passed legislation in 1977 requiring American aid to be reduced or terminated if a government was guilty of serious and systematic violations of human rights. This legislation did not have much practical significance, however, as long as the USA and the Soviet Union were rivals for influence and allies in the Third World. But since 1989, such political conditionality has played a more important role, also for American aid.

DAC countries have adopted declarations several times since 1989 in which they maintain that there is a connection between democratic and accountable regimes, compliance with human rights, and an effective and equality-oriented economic policy. This connection justifies DAC countries intervening in recipient countries' political relations and making demands for administrative and political reforms in order to ensure a better use of economic aid. Several of the DAC member countries have included similar formulations in national policy declarations (for a review, see IDS 1993; Stokke 1995: 21 ff.).

It should be added that while DAC countries have formulated demands to the recipient countries, they have also approved declarations that in principle recognize these countries' own right to lead development cooperation. For example, in a joint declaration in 1996 entitled *Shaping the 21st Century: The Contribution of Development Co-operation* (OECD/DAC 1997: 12 ff.) future cooperation is called a partnership characterized by mutual respect and led by the governments in recipient countries. But it is also evident from this slightly vague document that the same governments are presumed to involve the citizens to a great extent and to promote people-oriented development. The document does not explain how eventual disagreements between donors and recipients about development goals and the methods for realizing them should be solved. We will return to this question (see for example Chapter 13).

The World Bank and the UN's development organizations do not have a mandate to intervene in developing countries' political relations in the same way as bilateral donors, especially not in regard to the form of government. They cannot therefore directly formulate democratic development as a goal. However, they can do this – and have done so – a bit more indirectly: the World Bank by emphasizing good governance as both a goal and a pre-requisite for effective implementation of economic policy; the UNDP by making human development for all the major goal.

According to the World Bank, good governance as a development goal involves political reforms that ensure that the government is made accountable to its citizens. The Bank's official conception is that this happens best through adhering to regular free elections, but it does not reject the idea that other arrangements may also be found. Emphasis is also placed on citizens' freedom of expression and right to organize themselves freely according to their interests and opinions; institutional protection of citizens' rights through an effective and independent judicial system; and open and responsible administration. Openness, transparency and predictability – together with equality before the law – are crucial from the point of view of the citizens. At the same time, the administration must be accountable to the government and the legislators, who are in turn accountable to the citizens (Landell-Mills and Serageldin 1991).

The World Bank, in 1997, went a step further in formulating goals for political-institutional development in developing countries, first in the *World Development Report 1997*, and thereafter during the joint annual meeting with the IMF in Hong Kong. In this report, which had as its theme 'the state in a changing world', the major goal is formulated as development that is sustainable, shared and poverty-reducing (World Bank 1997a: 4). What is interesting in this context is that the report argues that the state is responsible for crucial tasks in promoting such development. Therefore, a special sub-goal is to support and strengthen the state. In the short term, the state must limit itself to doing the things it has the capacity to do, but in the long term, the state's capacity must be increased within several areas. This approach to the state is undeniably different from the one the Bank represented in the 1980s. Faith in market mechanisms and the private sector's potential to develop poor countries still exists, but there is also a renewed faith in the necessity of the state's participation and in the state's ability to speed up economic growth and development if it possesses the necessary capacity. The capacity of the state to help build institutions for markets was emphasized in the 2002 *World Development Report* (World Bank 2002).

## Human Development and Focus on Poverty

Good governance is also one of the goals the UNDP recommends and attempts to realize, but of special importance for this organization is the promotion of human development. The UNDP understands this as development that is measured not only in real income but also in increased welfare. Increased income is one of the prerequisites for increased welfare, but in this way, increased income becomes a means rather than an end in itself. Thus, in its first *Human Development Report* in 1990, the UNDP formulated the principal development goal that all development assistance should work to fulfil as a process of enlarging people's choices. To start with, it focused on three dimensions of opportunities and welfare: (a) the opportunity to live a long and healthy life; (b) the opportunity to acquire knowledge; and (c) the opportunity to have access to resources needed for a decent standard of living. The subsequent annual reports on human development added consideration for political freedoms and human rights; human development for women and men respectively; and citizens' security and opportunity to participate in political decision-making processes.

With the *World Development Report 2000/2001*, the World Bank incorporated to a great extent the development goals the UNDP introduced in the 1990s.

## Foreign Aid to the Private Sector

The strong criticism of the state's role that characterized the 1980s led to discussions of how foreign aid could directly contribute to development of the private sector in developing countries. The aim was also to reduce development cooperation's strong bonds to recipient states, which in many contexts were now considered to be part of these countries' development problems rather than actors that could help solve them (see p. 4).

As a result of these discussions, several donor organizations adopted special goals for development of the private sector in recipient countries. The further aim is usually to contribute to comprehensive growth and improved living conditions for the population. Support to the private sector is taken up here, however, because this form of aid cannot only be considered as a means of realizing the final goals but also involves a specific formulation of these final goals. Giving priority to the private sector, partly at the expense of the public sector, involves taking a position regarding the character of the economic system one wishes to foster through assistance.

Support for development of the private sector in agriculture has held a central position in most donors' foreign aid strategy for many years. It is not this form of economic development that interests us in this section, but rather support to the private sector comprising businesses in the cities, especially industry. It is in relation to businesses in the cities that changes have occurred since the mid-1980s.

Most donor organizations that have formulated a policy for private sector development have put the main emphasis on enterprises' environment. The point of departure is that enterprises must manage on their own. Direct aid to existing firms is considered to be anti-competitive and to constitute interference in the market mechanism's highly esteemed mode of operation. This is the basic attitude behind the World Bank's and USAID's support to the private sector. Therefore, aid is given in the form of advice about deregulation by the state, support to privatization of public enterprises, and support to establishment of a good institutional framework for private enterprises and free markets.

In this connection, it is interesting that Denmark has gone considerably further in the direction of direct support to private enterprises through the so-called private sector programme (PS programme). This programme is based on the idea that there is a great need for strengthening the productive sector in developing countries. More specifically, the programme aims to achieve this goal through modernization and rehabilitation of existing private enterprises. Danida is not directly involved, but offers co-financing if a binding partnership can be established between a Danish enterprise and an enterprise in the selected developing country. The idea behind this is to involve Danish enterprises in a more long-term cooperation with enterprises in recipient countries and so support development of the private sector in these countries. It is expected that by these means some of Danish business's commercial interests can be united with Danida's foreign aid policy goals and developing countries' development needs. The strategic methods used by the PS programme are discussed in more detail in Chapter 6 (in the section on Danish foreign aid policy).

## Foreign Aid to Institutional Development

As shown by several examples already mentioned, donors have given high priority to strengthening and developing political and administrative institutions in recipient countries. Actually, the goals in this area go all the way back to the 1960s. At that time, foreign aid was greatly influenced by arguments of modernization theories concerning the need for developing countries to imitate the industrial countries in creating particular political and administrative organs as well as a judicial system and legislation more generally. Many of the goals from that period are repeated, but it is characteristic that today the formulations are more open. Donors, including the World Bank, generally refrain from recommending a definite organizational model for all developing countries. Instead, the existing organizational structure and institutional situation in the individual country are to a greater extent taken as the starting point (see Moore 1995: Chapter 3).

The background for the renewed and expanded interest in institutional development includes a larger number of evaluations and studies indicating that many development efforts have failed because the responsible governments in developing countries did not have the necessary capacity to carry them out and manage them. Other studies indicate that reforms of economic policy have failed because governments are not sufficiently prepared to implement these reforms and carry out a changed economic policy in practice.

In spite of acknowledgement of this situation already in the 1980s, there was a tendency during this decade to de-emphasize institutional development in the public sector because the dominant view was so critical of the state. But since the beginning of the 1990s, increasing emphasis has been put on aid that also strengthens state organs. A striking example is the World Bank's African Capacity Building Initiative. Since 1991, this initiative has aimed to develop the African states' capacity to shape and carry out their economic policy – or perhaps rather the economic policy that the Bank and IMF mean that they should carry out (see World Bank 1991). Another example is the UNDP's increased interest in supporting capacity-building in recipient countries' state administrations so that they are better able to use public funds efficiently, especially to promote human development.

Seen in a broader perspective, the focus on institutional development and capacity-building involves a shift of attention from transferring resources to ensuring a better and more efficient utilization of the available resources. If we examine donor organizations' general policy, it becomes clear that this shift is not limited to the central state governments. On the contrary, at least three main areas can be identified in which institutional development appears as a central element in both goal formulations and aid strategies. The three main types of goals can be summarized as follows:

1. Strengthening of the central governments' ability and capacity to shape and implement their development policy, including their possibilities for a more efficient administration of foreign aid;
2. Strengthening of the local governments' ability and capacity to carry out resource management at the local level; and
3. Strengthening of the civil society's organizations and the institutional framework and procedures for citizens' participation in economic and political life.

A fourth goal, which seems to be in the process of being given increasing importance, could be added: strengthening of the public authorities in general so that they are better able to collect taxes and in other ways mobilize resources for development purposes.

Some bilateral donor organizations have as their special declared goal the promotion of decentralization – or more precisely the devolution of the authority for development policy to the democratically elected local governments. The idea is that in this way increased resource mobilization and more effective use of resources can be achieved in accordance with local priorities. A further argument for promoting good and effective government at the local level is that local governments' behaviour and way of working are often more important for the poor than government on the national level. The UNDP, and especially the small organization under it, the United Nations Capital Development Fund (UNCDF), have formulated similar goals, whereas the World Bank has been more reserved in relation to decentralization as a general goal (see World Bank 1997a: 120 ff.).

In addition to the named reasons for concentrating on institutional development and capacity-building, most donors also see these forms of aid as supporting national and local ownership and control of the resources that are transferred as part of development cooperation. The extent to which this goal is also attributed great significance in practice is discussed separately in Chapters 13 and 14.

## Development Goals in NGO Cooperation

The many hundreds of NGOs in industrial countries that are involved in one way or another in international cooperation differ so much from one another that it is difficult to generalize about their development goals. For many, their primary interest is to give humanitarian assistance to the needy, while the more long-term development goals are secondary and vaguely formulated. For some organizations, missionary work plays a significant role. Others belong to political movements or international interest organizations. The list of the different categories of organizations that call themselves non-governmental is long.

In order to say something more general, it is therefore necessary to focus on the more limited group of NGOs that could be called primarily development-oriented. The literature published in English often refers to these as the Non-Governmental Development Organizations (NGDOs). In the following, we discuss this group, but we use the more common name, NGO.

In relation to goals of official development aid, a common tendency for these NGOs is to emphasize the poor and especially poor women. Since the mid-1980s, the environment has also been high on the agenda. It is a further characteristic that whereas official aid sees citizen participation primarily as a means of promoting other development goals, many NGOs see people's participation as a goal in itself. In the more extreme version, NGOs do not have any other development goals at all, since they believe that their partners in the South must formulate their wishes, priorities and goals themselves. NGOs from the North can then either fully support these or select the ones that fit with their own ideas about a development worth working for. The latter is the most common, because most Northern NGOs – regardless of their declared respect for their partners' priorities – also base their work on certain ideologies and political ideas. These include, for example, the basic understanding that men and women are equal, and more generally that all people should be treated equally and their basic rights respected.

The strong emphasis on people's participation means that NGOs typically focus on civil society in their work. It is outside the state's and the commercial private sector's domains, among the people themselves, that NGOs typically work to support and strengthen the capacity for people to take development into their own hands. The aim can be to help poor target groups achieve a better life by offering them education, training, health care or other services and benefits. The aim can be to help start income-generating activities for the target group. But a further goal can also be to strengthen the poor

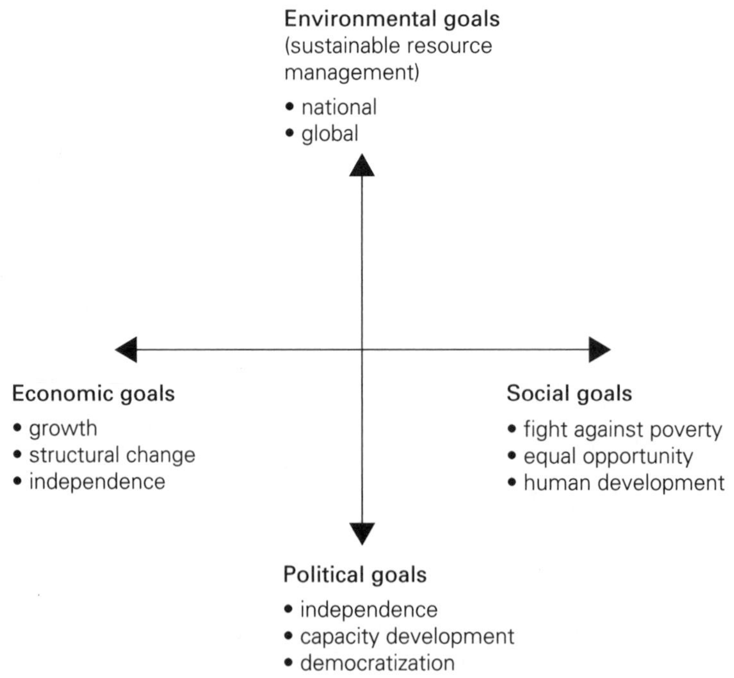


**Figure 3.1** Development goals of foreign aid

groups' own organizations and thereby their power in relation to other groups in society or the government. It is common in this context to speak of empowerment, which basically means strengthening certain groups and their organizations so that they are better able to safeguard and promote their own interests.

Many NGOs are so small that they must limit themselves to setting goals for and possibly together with local target groups in a village, a slum, or other form of local area. Historically, such focus on small local societies has usually had as its motto 'Small is Beautiful'. However, here the tendency is to connect with broader goals for development in the given country, partly through cooperation with other NGOs, partly through cooperation with governments in recipient countries or with official aid organizations. NGOs often consider themselves in such contexts as representatives and lobbyists on behalf of the poor. They also typically see it as a goal to contribute to democratization of the political systems and to promote respect for basic human rights (see Hulme and Edwards 1997b).

In addition to their development goals for their target groups and partners in the South, NGOs often wish to create bonds of friendship between people in the North and South and promote global responsibility and solidarity in their own countries. Emphasis can be put on appeals for economic support for the organization's own work, but also on creating broad public support for both official and private foreign aid.

## Summary of Development Goals

As in the description of the principal motives for giving foreign aid, the main types of development goals can be summarized by Figure 3.1, which presents the different goals as dimensions. It must be emphasized that this is a great simplification, because each of the four dimensions covers many sub-dimensions. This is also evident from the preceding sections and from the text in the figure. But with this reservation, the figure can be used to characterize the goals that a given donor seeks to realize through development assistance and possibly to designate the relative importance assigned to the different goals. Development goals that especially aim to involve women in the development process are designated in the figure as 'equal opportunity' under the social goals.

Viewed over a longer time perspective, it can be said that development goals of foreign aid have generally increased in number and complexity (see p. 4 and Chapter 4). Goals formulated earlier are seldom replaced by new ones. Rather, the tendency has been for donor organizations to continue to add more goals for development cooperation – and most often without giving any indication of their priorities. The economic development goals have existed from the start for the official donors, but over the course of time, they have been given varying emphasis in relation to the social goals.

Environmental and political development goals have become increasingly prominent during the last decade. For NGOs, the social goals have generally been in focus, but combined with an increasing interest in promoting democratization and empowering the resource-weak groups as well as supporting sustainable local resource management.

CHAPTER 4

# Aid Strategies

§ INTERNATIONAL development cooperation has always been based on the belief that government interventions supported from outside are necessary in order to promote development in the poorest countries. This belief directs focus towards two main actors (see p. 4): governments in developing countries and donor organizations. In order to achieve their aid objectives, donors have had to develop strategies that have two main aims: to make the governments in developing countries act in ways that promote development; and/or to 'replace' these governments in acting to promote development (SIDA 1994). Donors' use of changing strategies to achieve foreign aid's formulated goals led to an almost military, or in any case interventionist, way of thinking: after formulating foreign aid goals, the donors developed a set of strategies and instruments that would allow them to achieve these goals. One term used, for example, is targeted poverty eradication.

The target group and governments in developing countries have had very limited influence on goals, strategies and forms of intervention. It was only in the 1990s, when donors began to speak about national ownership of development efforts, that the term 'partnership' took on any meaning. In other chapters, we examine foreign aid on the basis of the interests of the various actors in developing countries, including the needs of the target groups. In this chapter, we discuss how donors have attempted to develop foreign aid strategies in agreement with both the changing goals and the experience harvested by donor organizations along the way.

We define first the most important forms of foreign aid, or the most important types of intervention: development assistance and emergency relief; state and voluntary aid; financial, technical and commodity assistance; assistance in the form of grants and loans; bilateral and multilateral aid; and programme and project aid. Then we describe how the dominating aid strategies since the 1960s have changed from one decade to the next. The situation in the new century will be discussed in Chapter 14. We see how the four decades have been characterized by certain pendulum-like swings in foreign aid strategies but within a basic framework of constant expansion of the areas included in the goals for foreign aid (see p. 4). Figure 4.1 illustrates how aid now addresses issues at all levels of society, and in this chapter we describe how additions of issues, levels and partners have been the underlying

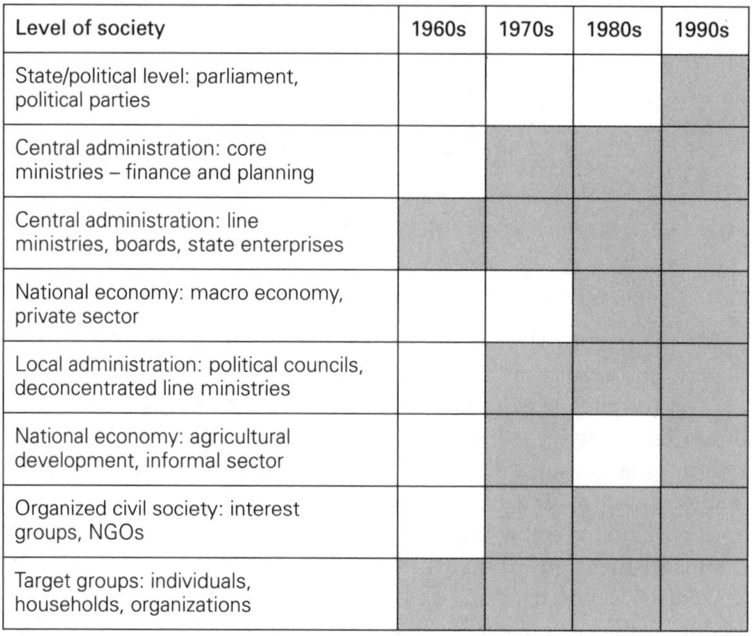

| Level of society | 1960s | 1970s | 1980s | 1990s |
|---|---|---|---|---|
| State/political level: parliament, political parties | | | | |
| Central administration: core ministries – finance and planning | | | | |
| Central administration: line ministries, boards, state enterprises | | | | |
| National economy: macro economy, private sector | | | | |
| Local administration: political councils, deconcentrated line ministries | | | | |
| National economy: agricultural development, informal sector | | | | |
| Organized civil society: interest groups, NGOs | | | | |
| Target groups: individuals, households, organizations | | | | |

**Figure 4.1** Expansion of the object areas for foreign aid to all levels of society

strategy of the international aid community since the 1960s. Still, there are differences among the main donor types. We conclude with a discussion of the main differences in aid strategies among large and small bilateral donors, UN development agencies and programmes, multilateral development banks, international NGOs and the EU.

## Intervention Types, Aid Forms and Levels of Society

When foreign aid began, donors distinguished between financial aid, which originally consisted of subsidized credits and loans; commodity assistance, which included food and capital goods; and technical cooperation or technical assistance, which is the transfer of knowledge in the form of advice, training and concrete problem-solving. Some technical cooperation is aid in the form of personnel, including experts, volunteers, advisers, and so on, financed by the donor.

These aid forms were all delivered in the form of projects, that is, efforts that were limited in time and space and had clearly defined goals. Around these projects, donors developed a comprehensive arsenal of planning and implementing tools gathered together in a so-called project cycle that stretches over identification, analysis and approval, via implementation and monitoring, to evaluation (Squire and Van der Tak 1975). After a while, the individual projects became so large and had so many subordinate goals and strategies that they began to be called programmes (Mosley and Eeckhout 2000). The programmes also grew from above, that is, as a way to extend aid to developing countries' total economies in the form of support for balance of payments and structural adjustment programmes, or to whole sectors in society in the form of sector programme aid to agriculture, health, education, and so on. This came to be known as policy-oriented aid.

Parallel with the partial change from projects to programmes (see Chapter 9), the dialogue between donor and recipient changed from being mostly a technical dialogue about capital, technology and organization, to an all-encompassing political dialogue about the structure of society and management of society's development processes. Almost all economic, social, cultural, even religious and identity aspects of life's dimensions were placed on the foreign aid agenda.

Development assistance has for the most part been an inter-state affair, that is, aid from a government in the North to a government in the South (Adelman 2000; Thorbecke 2000). If aid is given directly, it is bilateral aid; if it is given through international agencies, it is multilateral aid. Large countries such as the USA and the former colonial powers have always given most of their aid bilaterally, primarily for political and commercial reasons, while small countries, such as the Nordic countries, have started with multilateral aid and gradually developed considerable bilateral aid programmes. In the grey zone between bilateral and multilateral aid, there are some mixed forms: bilateral aid to regional organizations; bilateral aid to limited multilateral programmes (eloquently termed multi-bi aid), and so on.

Finally, non-state aid has grown in that the aid provided by NGOs and other volunteer organizations (see Chapter 8) has been financed by funds collected from the public or interest groups or by a share of state foreign aid funds. Similarly, state aid has been channelled through the private sector, but the amount of aid given by private enterprises themselves directly to partners in developing countries has been very limited. Transnational companies have to a limited extent attempted to represent their technology transfers in connection with direct investments as a form of aid.

Parallel with development assistance, donors have extended emergency relief in response to direct human suffering caused by natural catastrophes, extreme poverty, wars and other conflicts. Distribution of emergency relief resembles a military operation, because fast and effective initiatives to save human lives have had the highest priority. During the great famine and hunger catastrophe in Ethiopia in 1984, the television media introduced a situation where emergency relief agencies fight to come first to the TV screen in order to demonstrate an effective presence – very briefly – in all corners of the world where TV journalists manage to turn up. International organizations with efficient central leadership such as Médecins Sans Frontières and the Red Cross/Red Crescent are most successful at this. An example of this so-called CNN effect occurred in the mid-1990s, when the international church associations felt the need for a breakthrough to compete for attention and resources. For their campaign, they chose a logo that was easy to see on the TV screen and that demonstrated that the power to act had first priority: Action of Churches Together, ACT.

In order to mitigate the unfortunate picture of needy and helpless people, donors gradually began to speak about humanitarian assistance, which in addition to emergency relief comprised protection, integration and repatriation of refugees; support for those who are politically persecuted; minesweeping programmes; human rights activities, and so on. In recent years, the borderline between humanitarian assistance and development assistance has become more vague. At the start of the 1990s, donors began to speak about the grey zone between development and emergency relief. The concept of development-oriented relief was used to focus aid on the structures and institutions that can survive even the worst catastrophes and that can therefore be used both to distribute emergency relief and to improve subsequent development (European Commission 1996).

Similar changes in ideological language took place in relation to development assistance. Donors spoke of aid, then assistance, cooperation, and finally, partnership. Thus, in general, aid concepts reflect a constant use of some types of intervention and some development in the use of aid forms and strategies (Cox et al. 1997). This is shown in Table 4.1, which summarizes both the aid forms used constantly during the last four decades, and the development of new aid concepts and forms.

The most important general tendencies in the development of aid forms thus reflect the donors' wish to focus on the whole structure of society and people's opportunities for development and self-realization. Figure 4.1 illustrates how aid developed from the 1960s to the 1990s to concern itself with development problems and processes at eight levels of society:

**Table 4.1** Most important types of intervention and forms of aid, 1960–2000

| Constant aid forms | Development of aid concepts and forms |
|---|---|
| Inter-state cooperation | States → international organizations → NGOs |
| Interventions and strategies | Aid → assistance → cooperation → partnership |
| Phases in a project cycle | Project → programme → policy |
| Bilateral and multilateral aid | Technical dialogue → political dialogue |
| Financial, technical and commodity assistance | Emergency relief → humanitarian assistance → development-oriented emergency relief |

- The state/political level: aid is basically state-supported (see p. 4). Of interest here is the transition from accepting national sovereignty as the basis for all cooperation to a significant questioning of this sovereignty combined with the donors' wish to influence the state and the political level and even to create a society in the donor's own image.
- Central administration in most developing countries comprises core ministries with responsibility for the state's finances and development plans. The balance of power between finance and planning ministries has changed several times during the last four decades, which is reflected in cooperation especially with the World Bank and the UN's Development Programme, the UNDP.
- Central administration in most developing countries also comprises line ministries (agriculture, health, education, etc.), boards (tax, customs, etc.), and state enterprises (utilities, trade, etc.), which have been deeply involved in implementing aid projects within the physical and social infrastructure together with support for production and international trade management. Foreign aid has influenced and financed a large share of the institutional changes at this level of society in many developing countries.
- The national economy at the macro level: although aid has focused on the state's roles and functions, it has both directly and indirectly influenced most developing countries' international economic relations; macro-finances; sector balances (urban/rural; industry/agriculture/mining/services); business structure, and so on. The private sector, however, has only been a direct partner with aid agencies to a limited extent.
- Local administration: most developing countries have local administrations at the regional or provincial level and at the district and local community level, except for the large federal countries (such as India, Nigeria and Brazil), which also have states. Whether decentralization has taken the form of deconcentration of central state power or delegation of decision-making competence to local political authorities varies from country to country and from period to period. Through local administrations, aid has come into direct contact with both political and administrative structures.
- The national economy at the local level comprises, for example, the peasantry and other agricultural development as well as the informal sector, which in many developing countries is of great importance for employment, commodity supply and services. It is a natural target area for aid that attempts to create economic growth combined with income distribution.
- Civil society is defined in this context as the organizations (trade unions, volunteer organizations, religious organizations, cooperatives, etc.) and institutions (media, academic institutions, etc.) that lie between the state and citizens, and which do not only have an economic purpose. Civil society thus consists of organized units that are possible partners in aid efforts.
- The target group for aid consists directly or indirectly of the poorest

and/or most oppressed and marginalized groups in society: as individuals; as households with children, women, and men; and in economic, social, cultural and religious organizations that are the basic elements in civil society and in the national economy at local level.

We use this simple model of society to describe changes in the dominant aid strategies. The idea that outside intervention is necessary to *generate* development has existed throughout the history of foreign aid. This was even the case during periods (especially in the 1980s) that embraced an ideology that reduced the role of the state and allowed market forces to lead development (Engberg-Pedersen et al. 1996; Kayizzi-Mugerwa et al. 1998). We describe below how changes in aid strategies have gone through quite clear phases characterized by a mixture of pendulum-like swings and gradual expansion of aid's target areas so that they encompass the whole of society's structure and development.

## The 1960s: Trickle-down

The dominant development theory in the 1950s and 1960s focused, as described in Chapter 2, on the need of developing countries for investment capital and modern technology to close gaps in their economies and give them a boost so that their economic growth could take off. In accordance with this, the most important donors, the World Bank, the USA, Great Britain and France, developed their aid strategies within a very simple framework: financial assistance and experts to improve and implement projects with modern technology, especially for the development of physical infrastructure (roads, ports, telecommunications, and electricity and other forms of energy). Donors supported the establishment of effective and isolated project organizations to build up the institutional infrastructure and state boards to plan and manage the infrastructure and other economic development. The key positions within the state boards were often filled by experts from the former colonial powers and were financed by them.

These simple aid strategies did not correspond to the overall development strategies. For example, not much emphasis was placed on creating economic exchange of commodities and services between urban and rural areas, and between agriculture and industry. Aid could in principle support both an export-oriented development strategy and a strategy based on import substitution. The expectation was that modern technology and organization forms would trickle down and spread like modernizing rings in water to the surrounding traditional society.

Figure 4.1 illustrates the limited working area for aid in the 1960s, when donors typically concentrated their projects within developing countries' line ministries, boards and state enterprises. The figure understates the spreading effect that was achieved, since investments in infrastructure naturally influenced the national economy, including the private sector. The aim is just to illustrate the limited target areas for the dominant bilateral and multilateral aid in the 1960s.

During the 1960s, dissatisfaction with the dominant aid strategy's limitations began to spread. There were not many signs of automatic trickling down of modern technology and organization; large segments of the population missed out on both aid and the economic growth that actually followed in the wake of decolonization; and foreign aid did not benefit all parts of the state-bearing elite. It was during these years that tendencies towards a dual economy – a division between a modern, urban-based economy and the traditional peasant economy – led to considerable self-criticism among donors. At the same time, the 'white elephants' began their wandering in developing countries. This was the term applied to projects that were obvious fiascos and to the flagships of modern technology that were not adapted to local markets and the surrounding infrastructure, the existing management and maintenance capacity. The main criticism of the aid strategy was that the poor got very little out of resource transfers, and technology was not adapted to local conditions in developing countries (Baum and Tolbert 1985).

## The 1970s: Integrated Rural Development Projects and Fulfilment of Basic Needs

At the beginning of the 1970s, aid strategies were changed in important ways. Among donors, the World Bank led the way with a new focus on poor people as a productive force that should be utilized to spread and deepen international capitalism's continuous growth during the post-war period. Similarly, the ILO led the way in arguing for fulfilment of basic needs (food, water, housing, health, education, work, and so on) as a prerequisite for economic and social development (ILO 1977). The idea was both to fight increasing poverty in the Third World and to include the whole world's populations in one world economy, which should reach all corners of the world.

The dominant aid strategy took the form of integrated rural development projects. Figure 4.1 shows that the strategy was aimed at large parts of the local economy, especially small farmers; involved much of the central and local administrations (especially the ministries of agriculture, health and education as well as district administration); and tried to reach out to large parts of the broadly defined target group of poor people. Within the core ministries of the central administration, planning units were involved in an attempt to coordinate the multi-sector and geographically limited projects. Organizations within civil society began to play a role in foreign aid, partly because international and local NGOs began to function as channels for aid, and partly because the Nordic countries and others hoped that the cooperative movement could carry out both economic and social functions as a channel for fulfilling basic needs and as advocates for the poor.

The large and complex aid projects covered many productive and social sectors, and often had the following structure. They were linked to a national board (for example, the Bangladesh Rural Development Board) that organized all cooperatives in the country from above. They involved several line ministries from the central via the regional to the local level. They included attempts to organize the target group in the form of a mass education programme that combined literacy with social consciousness-raising. They demanded coordination committees at all levels of society as well as the constant presence of many foreign experts within project management, cooperative and sector development, and eventually local government capacity-building.

The aid strategy of the 1970s ran into many problems both within and outside its own rationale. First, the integrated development projects were institutionally extremely complex. Their demand for coordination of integrated services was most often unrealistic in relation to the administrative capacity in most developing countries. There were cases where more resources were used in coordination among ministries, boards and levels than in ensuring efficient delivery of public services to the target group.

Second, the development theory behind this strategy comprised an exaggerated faith in central planning's possibilities and necessity. The aid strategy assumed that an integrated project organization could be established where the donor and the state together could analyse and plan the composition and sequence of the target group's needs and deliver the necessary services. For example, expansion of agricultural production requires a certain amount of seed, irrigation and chemical fertilizers; this requires special organization of the target group, which demands a specific level of education and health and a certain amount of available labour, and so on. This top-down planning approach proved ineffective in all parts of the world. It was of course most difficult to implement in the rural areas of the poorest developing countries, where knowledge about local needs is not easily obtained. Neither the development theory (a slightly adapted form of modernization theory) nor the aid strategy allowed for the possibility to build on local knowledge about development needs, resource conditions or capacity (Berg 1993).

Third, the strategy was influenced by the economic development optimism of the 1960s, including the success of the welfare state in many industrial countries. Such a strategy requires a national economic surplus, which after 1973 (and again after 1979) was undermined in the oil-importing developing countries just about the same time as the strategy was being developed and implemented. Since the strategy acknowledged that the automatic spread of 'progress' was hardly likely, its inner logic demanded that the integrated packages of economic and social services for the fulfilment of basic needs should be delivered to the majority of the poor in rural and urban areas. The aid strategy contributed to building the institutional framework (in central and local administrations as well as organized civil society) for its broad implementation in developing countries, which, however, lacked both the capacity and the resources to implement the development strategy. Many developing countries had to tackle the heavy administrative consequences of the strategy – greatly expanded central and local administrations and co-operatives as well as numerous project organizations – without any other financial base than foreign aid.

Fourth, the strategy's focus on the poorest people in rural areas was considered by the elite in many developing countries as an attempt by the Western world to undermine the demand of developing countries for a New International Economic Order. According to this view, access to markets, investments and technology was judged to be more important than the needs of the poor. States and researchers in the Third World argued that aid agencies transferred the struggle for distribution of resources into the rural areas in developing countries in order to avoid changing the international distribution of resources under the existing world order.

Thus the way was opened for a new swing of the pendulum with regard to the dominant aid strategies, even though most bilateral aid agencies focused on integrated local development projects far into the 1980s. As late as 1988, the authors were involved in a comprehensive study to assess whether Danida should launch a new integrated local development project in Patuakhali, Bangladesh, similar to the Noakhali Rural Development Project, which Danida had supported since the mid-1970s. The conclusion was that an integrated local development perspective was still relevant and necessary, but that an institutionally much simpler and more split-up project was needed, based on the target group's need and actual demand for public services (COWIconsult 1988a).

## The 1980s: From Projects to Structural Adjustment Programmes

The shift in the dominant aid strategies from the 1970s to the 1980s was quite strong if one looks at the ideology and formulated strategies that were presented, especially by the World Bank. A combined wish to 'roll back the state' (see p. 4) and to create order in the macro-economic balances (balance of payments, debt, inflation and state deficits) in developing countries led to the demand for liberalization and the removal of state control within as many areas of the national economy as possible (Ray 1996; Caufield 1997). In order to achieve this, the IMF and the World Bank developed structural adjustment programmes to provide aid to governments in developing countries in exchange for promises of liberalization.

Structural adjustment programmes were initiated because of the risk of more debt crises such as the one that hit Mexico and other countries and the private international banks at the beginning of the 1980s. As mentioned earlier, the swing to the right in donor countries (Reagan, Thatcher, Kohl) led to ideologically based demands for privatization of state enterprises, state-managed trade companies, cooperatives, and so on. The state should limit itself to creating ideal conditions for the private sector's activities at the global, national and local levels. At the same time, still more donors tried to involve civil society in health and education programmes through channelling aid through international and local NGOs (see Chapter 8).

Since there were clearly limits to these aid strategies, the contrast with the 1970s was lessened considerably. First of all, the World Bank and others set a ceiling for structural adjustment programmes' share of total loans. At least two-thirds of the Bank's activities were still projects that mainly targeted physical and social infrastructure, and most often their direct partners were still the state authorities, in project implementation too. Part of the reason for this was pressure from the Nordic countries, which insisted on continuing the projects that directly aimed at reaching the target group of poor people. Another important reason was pressure from the directly involved actors: line ministries in developing countries, international consultants, entrepreneurs, suppliers and traders and not least the World Bank's own staff, which was still dominated by project-oriented engineers and sector-oriented economists (Branson and Jayarajah 1995; Ferreira and Keely 2000).

Second, many bilateral donors and UN organizations were relatively unaffected by structural adjustment programmes and continued working with the familiar forms of aid from the 1970s. To a great extent, a division of labour existed where, for example, the Nordic donors exploited the amount of freedom that the IMF's and the World Bank's structural adjustment programmes provided to concentrate on more socially oriented projects. This was also necessary in order to ensure support for foreign aid in the donor countries. At the same time, there were actual political differences (summarized well by Cornia et al. 1987). For example, in relation to aid to Tanzania, the Nordic countries wanted to continue support to President Nyerere's socially oriented policies, whereas the IMF and the World Bank, supported by the USA and Great Britain, pressed for political and economic liberalization.

The 1980s turned out to be the Cold War's last decade. This affected the distribution of foreign aid. Governments in Western-oriented developing countries received most of the aid from the OECD countries and the multilateral organizations, with only limited concern about the extent of poverty in these countries or how democratic their governments were. The West defined the conditions for receiving aid, which comprised the introduction of liberal economic systems that were open to the world economy with regard to both exports and imports and the flow of capital. The UN system, the Nordic countries, Holland and Canada were partial exceptions. They distributed foreign aid with more regard for poverty, but still within the framework of structural adjustment programmes and thus the logic of global capitalism.

## The 1990s: Political, Economic and Institutional Society-building

After the turbulence that occurred in the Soviet Union and Eastern Europe around 1990 and the rapid economic growth in East and South Asia, developing countries anticipated new opportunities in the new world order talked about by George Bush, then president of the USA, the only remaining superpower. Their optimism did not last long: the Gulf War showed that this superpower would not refrain from using military force against difficult Third World countries. The OECD countries shifted the focus of their aid to a significant extent towards Eastern Europe and the so-called transition countries, which consisted of the former socialist countries with centrally planned economies. The total amount of aid funds fell quite markedly and, most importantly, demands for political reforms increased strongly (Kenen 1994; Sandler 1997; Killick 1998).

Figure 4.1 shows that, at this time, the political level and its relationship to both the national economy and civil society were added to the aid agenda (see p. 4). The donors made explicit demands for democratization in the form of multiparty elections, observance of political human rights and good governance. The latter meant inclusion of civil society in political decision-making processes; open and transparent political-administrative systems that were accountable to the citizens; control of corruption and misuse of power; and a certain degree of decentralization of power to the local authorities. Finally, aid was aimed directly at strengthening the resources and power of special target groups, or rather at reducing their powerlessness and marginalization (Stokke 1995; Hopkins 2000).

All this demanded several new aid strategies and instruments (Berg 1997). We will mention them only briefly in this section, since they are discussed in more detail in other chapters. Since fewer aid funds were available even while the target areas for aid were becoming increasingly more inclusive, it was necessary to use more inexpensive forms of intervention and to concentrate aid more. The following are some of the ways donors strove to achieve this in the 1990s.

*Sector programme support* Aid to comprehensive programmes for the development of whole sectors, such as health, agriculture and education, was introduced towards the end of the 1980s, when it became apparent that structural adjustment programmes reduced public services in the social sector and were not able to do much about the increasing poverty in the poorest countries. For the World Bank, the sector programmes were an ideal meeting place between the macro-economic programmes and the projects that the Bank continued to finance (Jones 1997, 2000). For the bilateral donors and, to some extent, the UN agencies, the sector programmes were a necessary way out of 'projectitis' (see Danida 1991) – the spreading of aid to countless projects that gradually became a serious burden for the weak administrations and public finances in developing countries (see Chapter 9).

Sector programmes could be seen as both reducing costs and concentrating aid, since the donor could either become involved in several sector programmes with technical assistance but without large investments, or could concentrate all its aid in few sectors in few countries. The taxpayers in industrial countries could be informed of a considerable effort, for example, for agricultural development in several African countries, or the donor organization could gain considerable influence on, for example, weak health ministries in selected countries.

*Policy dialogue* In the 1980s, the most important aid-related policy dialogue took place between the IMF/World Bank and the governments in developing countries, and it was concentrated on economic policy. In the 1990s, all the most important donors strove to carry out their own dialogue with governments in developing countries, and the agenda now also comprised political aspects of the structure of society. The strategy of setting conditions on economic policy proved to be ineffective, because many donors continued to give aid regardless of whether the demanded policies were carried out or not (Collier 1997a, 2000; Collier et al. 1997). Nor did donors get very far with attempts to condition aid – under the heading of good governance – on democratization and changes in the political-administrative structure.

*Selectivity* Gradually, attempts were made to change aid policy's *ex ante* conditions to *ex post* conditions: more and more donors wanted to increase foreign aid only to those countries that could document that they had formulated and implemented 'correct' policies, which corresponded to a great extent to the Western model. This aid strategy was first developed towards the end of the 1990s, officially as a result of increasing concern about foreign aid's effectiveness (see Chapters 12 and 14). In 1997–98, the USA formulated legislation concerning cooperation with and aid to sub-Saharan Africa, for which President Clinton tried to gain support during his tour through Africa in March 1998. The philosophy was very simple: a few favoured African states would receive trade benefits, investments and aid, so that they could stimulate their economies and thereby serve as 'role models' for the African countries that continued with other economic policies and society models. Aid should thus be used as an incentive to those in power to change the structure of their societies.

This strategy suffers, however, from several weaknesses that are discussed further in Chapters 12 and 14. Ranking countries on the basis of economic and political criteria presents a major problem. The strategy builds on the assumption that aid is effective only when national policies are 'good and correct'. What would happen if social criteria were also used, asking how good countries were at reducing poverty? If developing countries were required to fulfil all three main criteria (economic, political and social) at the same time, only very few countries would qualify. This is the situation that has emerged since 1999 in connection with the emphasis on 'poverty reduction strategy papers'. On the other hand, if countries had to fulfil only one of the three criteria, then probably so many countries would qualify that aid would be neither concentrated nor effective.

In spite of these problems, strong forces in recent years, including representatives of the World Bank and the other large Western donors, have defended such selectivity in the distribution of foreign aid because it makes it possible to concentrate and document results (World Bank 1998b). This argument involves a challenge to the Nordic countries, for example. They have chosen a higher degree of continuity in cooperation with the countries receiving their bilateral aid, but they must be able to document results, including results in the countries that do not immediately have the 'correct' policies.

*Capacity-building and development* As foreign aid increasingly aimed at all aspects of recipient countries' social structure, it became necessary to enable developing countries' own organizations to manage and carry out development. This was also in accordance with donors' political goals for aid and development. Donors therefore expanded the target areas for the share of their technical assistance that was aimed at supporting national capacity within all social structures (Berg 1993).

In the 1960s, 1970s and to some degree the 1980s, donors supported organizational development within and around the organizations carrying out aid projects. This involved concrete problem-solving and training of personnel to carry out the necessary operating and maintenance functions. During the 1980s, this was expanded to building capacity in finance ministries, central banks, customs departments, and so on in order to manage the demanded economic liberalization. The IMF and the World Bank, however, were satisfied with the establishment in many countries of effective, isolated economic management units staffed by foreign and gradually by local economists, many of whom had received PhDs from American universities.

Capacity-building, understood as strengthening national organizations (and their interaction) in carrying out their normal functions, was placed on the agenda in the 1990s, when both donors and recipients demanded new cohesion between politics and economic and social development (OECD 1991, 1996). It was no longer sufficient for individuals to be well educated. Demands were now made for well-functioning, simple and transparent procedures and systems (UNDP 1997a, 1997b). Capacity now involved political legitimacy, economic resources, technical solutions and administrative procedures. Therefore, aid to capacity-building involved all the relevant actors in joint problem identification, formulation of solutions and political implementation. This presented both donor and recipient organizations with new demands for qualifications and expertise – demands that according to most actors and observers are still only rarely fulfilled (Arndt 2000).

## 1960–2000: Constant Elements and New Challenges

Development of the target areas for foreign aid strategies has thus *added* new aspects of social development rather than replacing old with new.

Since the 1960s, most donors have retained aid to development of physical infrastructure, although this has varied in regard to whether the focus is on modern or adapted infrastructure (e.g. feeder roads), and whether support has been for new investments or operation and maintenance. In a few developing countries private investments, both local and transnational, have been made in infrastructure development, but in the poorest countries the amount of investments has not lived up to market supporters' expectations. Since the 1970s, foreign aid has continued support to the social sectors, agriculture and broad rural development. In the 1990s, this was rarely in the form of integrated projects and more often in the form of sector programmes as well as support for decentralization of public administration. Since the 1980s, the structural adjustment programmes' focus on macro-economic balances has been retained as well as considerable NGO involvement in providing public services. The ideological attack on the state, however, which was based in Washington (the US government and Congress, the IMF and the World Bank), has been replaced by more constructive attempts to strengthen the capacity of developing states to fulfil the functions that are better carried out by the state than by the private sector (World Bank 1997a).

At the same time as the target area of aid strategies was expanding during the last four decades, there were signs of pendulum-like swings, especially in donors' relationship to the state in developing countries. This is seen most clearly in the World Bank's shifting strategies.

In the 1960s, the World Bank took the lead in enlarging the role of the state as the provider of modern infrastructure. The Bank supported the establishment of state boards and enterprises within trade, services and even production. In the 1970s, the Bank contributed to extending the state's institutional presence into all corners of society through support to the line ministries' coordinating role and to establishing integrated project organizations with close links to administration at local, regional and national levels. The Bank contributed to expanding the state's control of prices on agricultural inputs such as seed and chemical fertilizers, and production prices on local markets and exports. The Bank insisted on building up an extension system for small farmers that demanded a size and regularity that could rarely be provided by the weak agricultural ministries in many developing countries.

In the 1980s, the World Bank's pendulum swung over to an attack on the state with demands for liberalization (abolishment of price control on both local markets and in foreign trade), privatization (sale of the state boards and enterprises that the Bank itself had often contributed to establishing), and cutbacks (firing of public employees, especially those lowest in the hierarchy). Finally, in the 1990s, the Bank contributed to 'rehabilitating' the state, both ideologically (see World Bank 1997a and Chapter 13 below) and in the form of sector programmes via line ministries, credit programmes via special organizations and management of NGOs and local communities via local administrations.

## Foreign Aid Strategies and Donor Groups

Foreign aid thus involves an increasing number of aspects of society's development in developing countries. This expansion of aid's target area applies to all six of the most important groups of donors: large bilateral donors (the USA, Japan, France, Germany and Great Britain); small 'like-minded' donors (Denmark, Norway, Sweden, Holland and, to some degree, Canada); the UN system's development programmes (especially the UNDP and UNICEF); multilateral development banks (the World Bank and regional development banks); international NGOs with their bases in donor countries; and the EU, as a regional organization and independent donor.

Since all donors work with almost all aspects of development, there has been a tendency towards convergence in the aid world (Mahbub ul Haq 1995). In Chapter 9, we discuss what convergence means in the form of overlapping, and to some degree collisions, between the many aid actors in developing countries. Here, we examine how these six donor groups have, from different starting points, moved closer to the elements of a common aid strategy. However, the donor groups also represent different aid models. We use the following indicators to evaluate the aid models: choice of country, choice of sector, form of aid and balance between development assistance and emergency relief.

The large bilateral donors distributed their aid during the first decades on the basis of political criteria (colonial history and East–West competition) and to sectors that ensured alliance with the West: economic infrastructure and state-building. They used both financial and technical assistance organized in independent projects, and they extended development assistance and emergency relief that were organized separately. Since the 1980s, they have spread aid to more countries (as the threat from the East gradually disappeared); the social sectors (among them, projects to reduce population growth) have received more emphasis; and projects have been supplemented by broader programmes that exploited (without replacing) the frameworks established by the structural adjustment programmes. In the 1990s, the large donors pressed hard for political liberalization (especially in the form of multiparty elections) to follow the economic liberalization of the 1980s.

The small, like-minded or progressive donors started by giving most of their aid multilaterally. Thereafter, they chose few bilateral partner countries (Stokke 1989). The early aid focus was on a combination of infrastructure and agricultural development, often organized in projects that directly transferred experience from the donor countries' own development (in the case of Denmark, the cooperative movement). Since the 1980s, these donors have exploited the degree of freedom allowed by the IMF and World Bank's structural adjustment programmes to maintain a progressive profile with aid focused on the poorest countries and the social sectors. In the 1990s, they attempted to expand demands for political liberalization so that it included both political and economic human rights. They also experimented with development-oriented emergency assistance.

The UN system's development programmes have only to a very limited extent selected recipient countries on the basis of political criteria. The UNDP and UNICEF had two very different points of departure: the former played a central financing and coordinating role, and the latter focused on a role similar to that of emergency relief, targeting children and mothers. Each organization's development during the 1970s and 1980s was also different: the UNDP was gradually sidelined in the aid world as the World Bank became increasingly involved in technical assistance, and the UN's many specialized agencies increasingly received resources from elsewhere. UNICEF, on the other hand, expanded and refined its aid within health services and took on the role of advocate and lobbyist on behalf of poor people suffering from lack of development and structural adjustment programmes. In the 1990s, the UNDP moved towards a role as advocate in relation to human development, while UNICEF moved into central government in developing countries. Thus the two organizations have moved closer to each other (Childers and Urquhart 1994).

Multilateral development banks – especially the World Bank – have consequently carried out most of the strategy changes described in this chapter: from infrastructure projects in Western-oriented developing countries to projects and programmes at all levels of society, in all sectors, and in almost all types of developing countries (including transition countries after the collapse of the Soviet Union). The regional development banks for Latin America, Asia and Africa have (in this order) attempted to supplement the World Bank's strategies and programmes with independent initiatives, for example, within sub-regional cooperative projects. All the banks are limited by their mandates regarding involvement in political questions. This has led to considerable activity (especially on the part of the World Bank) involving institutional development and reform of the public sector (Stiglitz 1998). They often try to present such reforms as being related to economic questions, because a participatory state and an effective administration are seen as prerequisites for economic development (Culpeper 1997).

International NGOs typically took their point of departure in emergency relief to people in crisis in all developing countries (with emphasis, however, on Western-oriented countries), or in solidarity work with people in socialist-oriented developing countries, or sometimes in both. Their aid was therefore naturally concentrated in the social sectors, including health and education, where voluntary actors contributed to spreading experience from the NGOs' countries of origin. Throughout the 1990s, well-defined projects continued to be their primary work form, but at the same time, they moved up to the society level through lobbying and partnerships with national movements and organizations belonging to civil societies in developing countries. They contributed to a significant expansion of donors' work with political and social aspects of social development.

The EU, with respect to choice of countries, started with a narrow focus on the former colonies, which led to the comprehensive Lomé partnership with seventy developing countries in Africa, the Caribbean and the Pacific. It then moved towards a differentiated aid strategy with programmes for the poorest countries in Africa (primarily under the Lomé and the subsequent Cotunou agreements); for the poor and politically important countries in Asia and Latin America; and for close neighbours in the Mediterranean area and Eastern Europe. Since the 1970s, the EU's Lomé aid has focused on food security and development in rural areas. As a regional organization, the EU has used aid politically and commercially (especially in regard to trade), but at the same time, much of it has been progressive, with policies that are similar to those of the small, like-minded donor countries. Poverty orientation, respect for human rights, democracy and sustainable development are now written into the EU's treaty as the goals and requirements for aid. The links between trade and aid and between development and emergency relief are central elements in the EU's strategies and are typically headlined as policy coherence, but here the results have lagged far behind intentions: there are typically too many special interests connected with the individual policy and aid instruments to make it possible to ensure cohesion and mutual support.

There have been and still are great variations in the aid objectives and strategies within each of these six donor groups – and even within the EU as a 'group'. At the same time, these groups are the closest we come to typical ideal aid models. This underlines the fact that the most important explanatory factors behind the various aid models are:

- donor countries' size and political weight – large countries have other interests and use aid politically in a completely different way than small countries that have a greater degree of freedom;
- differences between bilateral state and international actors – bilateral aid is still narrower in its political orientation, whereas multilateral aid is directed more towards global systems, and non-state NGO aid has more long-term humanitarian objectives; and
- differences among the multilateral actors – the UN system, World Bank, and the EU still play very different roles, as we discuss in Chapter 7.

## CHAPTER 5

# Size and Distribution of Foreign Aid

§ THE size of development assistance is calculated on the basis of various definitions, which have been agreed upon by the most important donor countries, that is, the members of the DAC. Since these definitions have great significance for the resulting figures, this chapter begins with a brief description of the most important concepts in official aid statistics. The subsequent sections then discuss the large amount of data available and attempt to find marked tendencies and patterns in regard to the total foreign aid, its origins and distribution among regions and countries, and its distribution among sectors. We also discuss the role of NGOs and, in a separate section, examine more closely aid's importance in relation to other transfers between North and South.

## Official Development Assistance

In order to be included in the figures for official development assistance (ODA), the transfers from donor countries to developing countries or multilateral institutions must live up to three requirements:

- they are undertaken by the official sector;
- the main objective is promotion of economic development and welfare; and
- they are provided on concessional financial terms (if a loan has a grant element of at least 25 per cent).

In addition to financial transfers that meet these demands, technical cooperation is also included as ODA. Other financial transfers with a development goal but with a grant element of less that 25 per cent are included in DAC calculations as other official flows. Technical cooperation and transfers via NGOs are included in ODA with respect to the part that is financed by official aid organizations, whereas NGOs' own contribution is defined as private flows together with direct investments and other commercial transfers. Humanitarian aid is included in ODA to the extent that the purpose is judged to be long-term improvements and not just emergency relief. The dividing line here is somewhat vague, however, and varies from country to country.

It is worth noting that official development assistance is defined on the basis of the declared goals and not the actual effects. No consideration is taken of whether the transfers actually contribute to economic development and welfare; the only criterion is whether the respective donors wish their aid to contribute to such development. In practice, the tendency has been that all transfers from North to South with a grant element of 25 per cent or more are included, with the exception of direct military aid. The breadth of the definition became especially clear in 1990 and thereafter, when the USA included in its figures for official aid the amount of cancelled debt on loans originally given for military purposes. This was especially the case for loans to Egypt for its involvement in the Gulf War (Raffer and Singer 1996: 5). This method of calculation was changed again in 1993, however, when the DAC insisted on moving this form of debt cancellation to the category of other official flows. However, the DAC approved cancellation of debts originally resulting from export credits as ODA (OECD/DAC 1998: 115).

Since 1979, the costs of administrating aid in donor countries could be included as ODA. It is of greater significance, however, that since 1991 many donor countries have included expenses for refugees and people seeking asylum in the donor countries themselves as ODA. According to DAC's rules, such expenses may be included only for the first year after arrival, but since the greatest expenses are incurred during just this period, the consequence has been an increase in the formally registered amount of aid. There are no official figures for how large a share of aid is actually used in the donor countries themselves, but the DAC has estimated that expenses for refugees and those seeking asylum, for example, in Canada in 1993 amounted to about 8 per cent of the total aid. In the case of Denmark, a similar share for the same year was about 5 per cent. In 1996, this share had fallen to a little less than 3 per cent.

These conditions imply that calculations of the size of foreign aid must be read with critical care. In principle, the definition has not changed since the 1970s, but it has been interpreted differently by the DAC in different periods. In addition, several of the large donor countries, such as the USA and France, have attempted to inflate the amount of their aid by including expenses for activities that lie on the border of what is normally understood as development assistance.

The picture is further complicated by the fact that the definition of ODA also contains a definition of recipient countries that is not quite identical to that of developing countries, and this definition has also been changed several times. The DAC divides countries receiving ODA into two categories – Part I and Part II countries. The first category includes developing countries and territories that can receive ODA, and only transfers to these countries can be included. Transfers to Part II countries are termed official aid, but without the adjective 'development'. The same requirements apply to the nature of the transfers as for ODA; the only difference is which countries are recipients.

A list of the recipient countries in Part I and Part II is found in Appendix 1. It shows that Part II includes most of the former communist countries in Eastern Europe and the former Soviet republics, in addition to what are called the 'more advanced developing countries'. Part I countries are divided into the sub-groups named below. They are introduced here because later in this chapter, we refer to the distribution of aid among these categories of countries (see Appendix 1).

- Least developed countries (LDCs). The UN has recognized these countries as especially vulnerable. They all belong to the low-income group.
- Other low-income countries (LICs), that is, countries with GNP per capita of less than US$765 in 1995.
- Lower middle-income countries (LMICs) with GNP per capita up to US$3,035 in 1995.
- Upper middle-income countries (UMICs) with GNP per capita up to US$9,385 in 1995.
- High-income countries (HICs) with GNP per capita over US$9,385 in 1995.

As mentioned, changes have been made on several occasions in the placement of some countries, not only in the Part I category, but also regarding placement in Part I or Part II. Shifts of special importance will be mentioned in connection with analyses of the data, but it can already be noted that Israel was moved from Part I to Part II as of January 1997. Due to the large amount of aid Israel has received from the USA until now, the statistics reflect this shift as an extra fall in both the American and the total DAC aid to Part I countries. Thus it is clear that caution should be exercised when interpreting the statistical data. Changes and fluctuations must continually be corrected in relation to the shifting methods of calculation; after that, it may be possible to draw conclusions about tendencies and patterns over a period of time.

## The Size of Development Assistance

The debate about foreign aid's actual size had its point of departure in evaluations of need or demand. Several economists in the 1950s and early 1960s tried to calculate how much capital should be transferred to developing countries to fill the gaps between their savings and their investment needs, and between the foreign exchange available and their need for imports. In both contexts, the analyses assumed that the goal was a specific growth rate, which varied, however, from one calculation to another.

Such need estimates never won general acceptance among bilateral donors. They were more interested in assessments related to supply: how much should, could, and would donors contribute in relation to their national product? This approach to the problem was connected to a great extent with an interest in the division of the burden among the different countries. The calculation of developing countries' needs in itself did not provide any guidelines for how much the USA and the other countries should each contribute. It was in America's interests to discuss this more thoroughly in the 1960s, when the USA contributed about half of the total official aid.

In any case, it was the goal concerning the size of the transfers in relation to the GNPs of the donor countries that came to dominate the international agenda. The first time such goals were formulated officially was in 1960, when the UN General Assembly approved a declaration about making annual capital transfers to developing countries amounting to 1 per cent of the industrial countries' GNP. This goal was proposed by the World Council of Churches in 1958 at a meeting in Denmark. UNCTAD approved a similar declaration in 1964, supported in principle by the DAC countries. It must be stressed that these goals referred to all forms of transfers, including private investments. It was in 1969 that precise goals for the size of official development assistance were first proposed. This occurred with reference to the definition of official aid that the DAC countries adopted in the same year (see the preceding section). The proposal, which set the goal at 0.7 per cent of the donor countries' GNP, came from a commission under the leadership of Lester Pearson, former Canadian prime minister (Pearson 1969). This goal was passed by the UN General Assembly in 1970 and accepted by the DAC and all members of the committee with the exception of the USA and Switzerland. Most member countries, however, are very far from realizing this goal, which is evident in the following. But first, in Figure 5.1 we present some figures for the total official development assistance since the mid-1950s.

Figure 5.1 expresses the development over time in the DAC countries' net disbursements to developing countries, both bilaterally and via multilateral

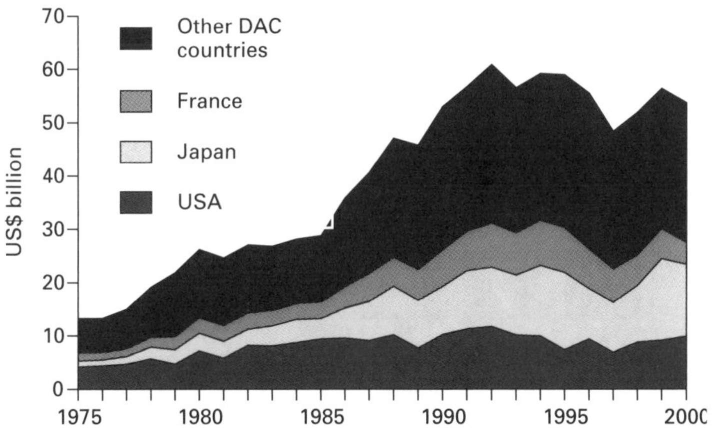


**Figure 5.1** Net ODA from DAC countries to developing countries and multilateral organizations, 1975–99

organizations. The total official aid in 1956 was US$3.2 billion. The flows went up slightly until the beginning of the 1970s, when the rate of growth increased. As shown in the figure, there was marked growth during the second half of the 1970s and again from 1985 to 1992. Recent years have been characterized by stagnation, and even a slight decline when the calculations are in current prices and exchange rates as in the figure. In real value, foreign aid has fallen since 1992 with a slight rise in 1998. As percentage of DAC countries' GNP, the fall has been marked: from 0.33 per cent to 0.24 per cent. If the 1992 level had been maintained, the total annual foreign aid in 1998 would have been US$73 billion instead of the actual figure, US$52 billion (OECD/DAC 2000: 14).

Figure 5.1 also shows the importance of the three largest donors during the period. At the start of the 1970s, the USA contributed almost half of the DAC countries' total aid, while Japan was of less importance. As can be seen, Japan's foreign aid rose during the period much more than that of the United States. The same applied to France's aid, which for a brief period in the mid-1990s reached the same level as that of the United States. Also Germany's foreign aid increased significantly during a certain period and for several years was higher than that of France or at the same level. The amount of German aid fluctuated so much, however, that the country's total aid for the period was somewhat less than that of France. The smaller DAC countries, especially Holland, Sweden, Denmark and Norway, contributed to the marked increase in foreign aid that is shown from the mid-1980s. We will return to this.

The absolute figures for the amount of official aid is in itself interesting

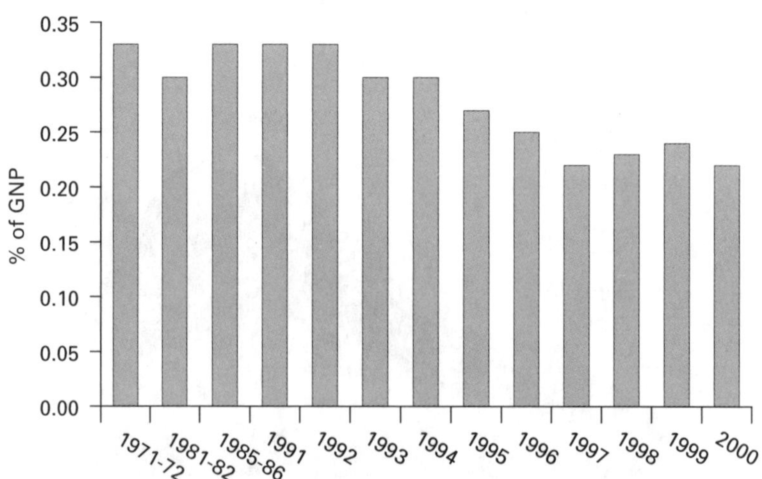


**Figure 5.2** Net ODA as a percentage of the DAC countries' total GNP (*sources*: OECD/DAC 1994: 162, Table 7; OECD/DAC 1998: A4 f., Table 4; OECD/DAC 2001: 185, Table 4)

as an indicator of how many financial resources were transferred from the industrial countries to developing countries. But to give a proper picture, they must be compared to at least three other factors: (1) the donor countries' own economies and growth; (2) recipient countries' economies and growth; and (3) other resource transfers between the North and South. In the following, we will touch on all three comparisons: first, comparison with the donor countries' own wealth and growth, which can be presented in simplified terms with the help of figures for their GNP.

In the 1970s and 1980s, the level of the net total of official development assistance was almost 0.35 per cent of GNP for all the DAC countries together. This share declined after 1992, and in 1997, fell all the way to 0.22 per cent – the lowest level since the DAC began to make such statistics. The percentage rose slightly the following year – to 0.24 and then fell again. Figure 5.2 shows the tendency since the beginning of the 1970s.

There are large differences in the relative contributions of DAC countries to the total foreign aid. This is shown in Figure 5.3, which shows the amount of aid in relation to DAC countries' GNP for 1999. It is noteworthy that most of the DAC countries reduced their aid in relation to GNP from the mid-1980s to the mid-1990s, some countries even quite markedly. The only country that increased its foreign aid in both absolute and relative terms from an already high level was Denmark. Only the three Scandinavian countries and Holland contributed more in 1999 than the UN goal of 0.7 per cent of GNP.

There are several reasons why the official aid from DAC countries was

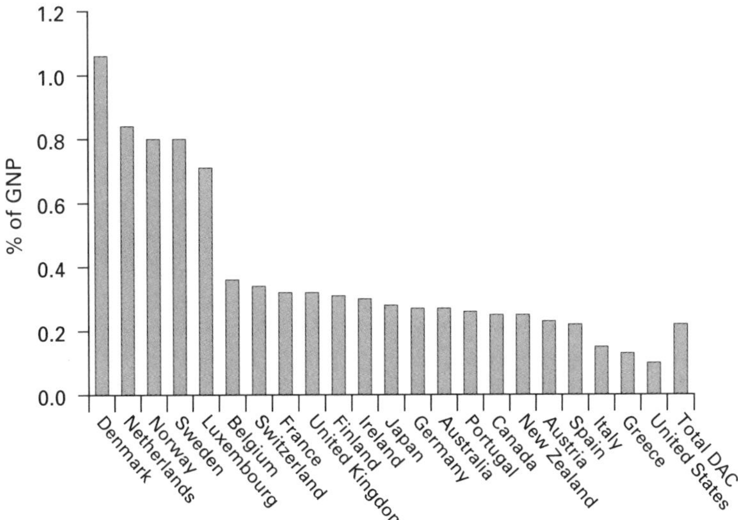


**Figure 5.3** Net ODA in 1999 from DAC countries, as a percentage of their GNP (*source*: OECD 2001: 97)

reduced. The influence of the end of the Cold War has already been discussed (see Chapter 2). Other causes can be found in the pressure on public finances internally in most DAC countries. This pressure can be also be attributed to at least four important factors. First, the distribution of age groups in the population had changed so that expenses for the aged had increased considerably. Second, most industrial countries had experienced periods with growing unemployment and the increasing public expenses this incurred. Third, repayments with interest on public debts in many DAC countries demanded a larger share of state incomes. Fourth, the cost of education had increased.

The DAC had estimated that these factors together demanded 25 per cent of the GNP in DAC countries around 1994 as compared to around 15 per cent in the mid-1980s (OECD/DAC 1998: 55 ff.). In comparison, resource transfers from North to South have completely different proportions, but this does not change the fact that the relatively modest expenses for development assistance are more vulnerable when the political decision-makers must find short-term savings. Therefore, one DAC country after another experienced cutbacks in their foreign aid budgets as part of the efforts to create better balance in state budgets. But on average, aid budgets have been cut more than public expenditures in the DAC countries (OECD/DAC 2000: 16).

The fact that aid has so often been affected by budget cutbacks is probably related to the widespread notion that aid incurs a considerable drain on the rich countries' resources. It is difficult, however, to find data to support this, as is evident in the figures already referred to for the total aid percentage, which is now only 0.2 in relation to the donor countries' GNP.

Another way to understand the proportions involved is by comparing the aid percentage with the rich countries' expenses for social measures. This is a comparison that is implied by many critics of aid cooperation when they refer to the fact that donor countries themselves have poverty and social problems that should be solved instead of helping developing countries. The UNDP has calculated expenses for social measures to be about 15 per cent of the industrial countries' GNP. A total dismantling of all foreign aid would, in other words, only make it possible to increase this percentage from 15 to 15.2, which could hardly be considered crucial seen from the donor countries' perspective (UNDP 1994: 75 ff.). On the other hand, the modest official aid is of great importance for very many recipient countries, although conditions here vary markedly, as will be discussed in a later section.

## Development Assistance from Eastern and Southern Countries

DAC countries are not the only countries that have given and still give development assistance, even though this group of donors has contributed over 90 per cent of total official aid to developing countries since the beginning of the 1980s and over 95 per cent at the end of the 1990s.

In the 1970s, however, the Soviet Union and the Eastern European communist countries did play a role. It is difficult to calculate development assistance from these countries precisely, because the statistical documentation was poor. At the beginning of the 1980s, the Soviet government itself claimed that during the period 1976–80, the country had contributed an average of 1 per cent of its national product to foreign aid. This figure was rejected, however, by the DAC countries, which instead set Soviet aid at a lower level than that of the USA. Researchers who have studied the figures carefully have rejected the Soviet figures as unreliable, but they have also ascertained that the Western figures are incorrect and seemingly a result of conscious manipulation. The most likely purpose of this manipulation was to convince Third World countries how little the Soviet Union actually was interested in supporting them economically (see Raffer and Singer 1996: 65 ff.).

For the relatively few developing countries on which Soviet aid was concentrated, however, the amount was so significant that Western propaganda had no effect. This was especially true of Cuba, which in addition to receiving direct economic transfers also benefited greatly from special trade agreements containing large grant elements. Of special importance was the fact that the Soviet Union imported Cuba's surplus production of sugar at favourable prices. Other countries, such as Vietnam and India, benefited similarly from both direct grants, soft loans and indirect support to their balance of payments. During the course of the 1980s, however, Soviet aid decreased in all areas and stopped completely after 1989. Since then, the former Soviet republics themselves have become net recipients of aid from DAC countries and multilateral organizations.

Foreign aid from some countries in the South to other developing countries has been of greater importance in some periods than aid from Eastern countries. In particular, the oil-exporting Arab countries and a few other OPEC countries have contributed sizeable amounts of economic development aid, and China and India have played important roles in this connection.

Foreign aid from OPEC countries increased markedly after the first big increases in oil prices in 1973–74, fell gradually after that, and increased again after the second increase in oil prices in 1979. This has been interpreted as a kind of compensation extended especially by the rich Arab oil states in the form of aid to the developing countries that experienced increases in the cost of oil imports on these two occasions. The increased aid was supposed to ensure recipient countries' support for OPEC's more aggressive price policy (see Raffer and Singer 1996: 123 ff.). The geographic allocation of aid from Arab OPEC countries also indicated that the wish to support other Arab states in the fight against Israel was even more important. The greatest share of aid was given to Egypt, Syria, Jordan and the Palestinian areas throughout most of the 1970s. After the Camp David agreements in 1979, support to Egypt fell markedly as an indication of the opposition by Arab oil states to what they considered to be a sell-out to Israel.

No matter how important the considerations of economy and national security were, it is notable that aid from the OPEC countries during the second half of the 1970s comprised almost 30 per cent of all official aid. It is also notable that several of the Arab oil states contributed relatively much larger amounts than the DAC countries. Saudi Arabia's aid in 1975 was thus 7.6 per cent of the country's GNP. The percentage for Kuwait was 6.9, for the United Arab Emirates 10.4, and for Qatar as much as 14.2. Foreign aid from these countries fluctuated greatly from year to year, but the aid percentages remained considerably higher than for the DAC countries until the beginning of the 1990s. Since then, most OPEC countries have mostly stopped giving development assistance. This was true of Algeria, Iraq and Libya, but Kuwait gave 1.5 per cent of its GNP in 1996 to help other countries, and Saudi Arabia's aid for the same year was 0.25 per cent of its GNP – the same level as the DAC average. After that, aid from the two countries decreased further.

No comparable figures are available for the aid given by China and India during these years, because both countries are extremely reluctant to make such information public. There is no doubt, however, that the countries that have received aid from China and India in the form of technical cooperation have received much more value in real terms than the modest total indicates. This is because wages for Chinese and Indian aid workers are considerably lower than those for Western workers. In this connection, it is notable that most aid from DAC countries to technical cooperation is used to pay foreign experts. The UNDP estimated in 1994 that this comprised 90 per cent of the US$12 billion that was used at that time for technical assistance (UNDP 1994: 80). The corresponding percentage for China and India is not known, but sporadic information about larger projects in which these countries were engaged – for example, the Tanzania–Zambia railroad or the large Indian infrastructure projects in Nepal and Bhutan – indicates that foreign expertise was delivered to the recipient countries at a modest cost.

Because of insufficient statistical information from these donor countries, we must base the following analyses on information about foreign aid from the DAC countries alone.

## Multilateral and Bilateral Aid

Part of the total aid from DAC countries is channelled through development banks and other multilateral organizations. Since 1980, transfers to these organizations have amounted to 30–35 per cent of the total ODA, with the trend slightly decreasing. During the last half of the 1960s, the corresponding share was 12–13 per cent (OECD/DAC 2000: 58).

There are big differences in how individual countries divide their foreign aid between bilateral and multilateral cooperation. France, Japan and the USA are among the countries that give the least aid, in relative terms, through the multilateral organizations – less than one-fourth – while the UK and Denmark, with 40–45 per cent, are among the countries giving the most.

It is also characteristic that the large industrial countries give their contributions to the World Bank (IDA) and the other development banks, while the Nordic countries and Holland give most in relative terms to the UN development organizations. The three Scandinavian countries give about ten times as much per capita as the USA to UN agencies. The marked difference probably reflects the large industrial countries' preference for channelling funds through organizations in which they exert great influence on decision-making. But one reason, of course, is greater confidence in the World Bank, especially in regard to effectiveness, than in the UN system.

The total net transfers from the multilateral organizations to developing countries are somewhat greater than the contributions from DAC countries to these organizations, partly because the multilateral organizations receive contributions from member countries outside DAC, and partly because they have their own resources. But contributions from DAC countries are of crucial importance. Thus, in 1996, they amounted to almost 86 per cent of the total multilateral aid.

Figure 5.4 gives an idea of how the multilateral transfers are divided among the different types of organizations, with emphasis on the largest contributors of aid and loans in 1994–98 (average). It shows that the World Bank Group's IDA alone contributes to over one-third of the total multilateral transfers with its loans as concessional aid. It also shows that the EU has now become an important donor, with over 30 per cent of the total multilateral transfers. The EU's foreign aid grew considerably throughout the 1980s and 1990s, both in absolute figures and in relation to the other multilateral transfers. Aid from UN agencies peaked in 1993 and has since fallen to the same level as in 1991. It should be added that since 1990, the UNDP and other UN agencies have revised their data to include only regular budget

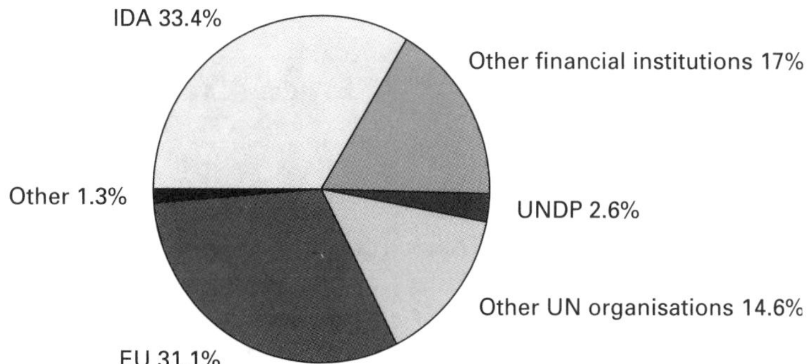


**Figure 5.4** Concessional flows by multilateral organizations, 1994–98 (*source*: OECD/DAC 2000: 64, Table III-3)

expenditures. If the voluntary contributions to UN agencies from DAC countries were added, the UNDP's share would be over 7 per cent and the other UN agencies about 20 per cent, in relation to a larger total than that shown in Figure 5.4 (see OECD/DAC1998: A42).

It should be added that multilateral organizations, in addition to the ODA, also extend a significant amount of loans that do not fulfil the demand of a grant element of 25 per cent. It is characteristic for development banks that the emphasis has been shifted in recent years from physical infrastructure to the social sectors with focus on developing human capital and relieving poverty. For a more detailed discussion of multilateral aid and loans, see Chapter 7.

## Distribution Among Regions and Countries

The geographic distribution of foreign aid varies considerably from donor to donor. Bilateral aid from the former colonial powers in Europe continues to a great degree to be concentrated on former colonies; American foreign aid is mostly allocated on the basis of considerations for national security; and Japanese aid goes mostly to regions in Asia of special commercial interest (see Chapter 6). The smaller DAC countries and the multilateral organizations have the widest distribution. The overall distribution to regions is shown in Figure 5.5. It shows that sub-Saharan Africa received most aid in 1997–98. Aid to this region has increased in absolute figures, but it is noteworthy that Africa's share of the total official aid at the end of the 1990s was the same as in the mid-1980s in spite of many donors' declared intentions of giving higher priority to this region. Transfers to the poor countries in South and

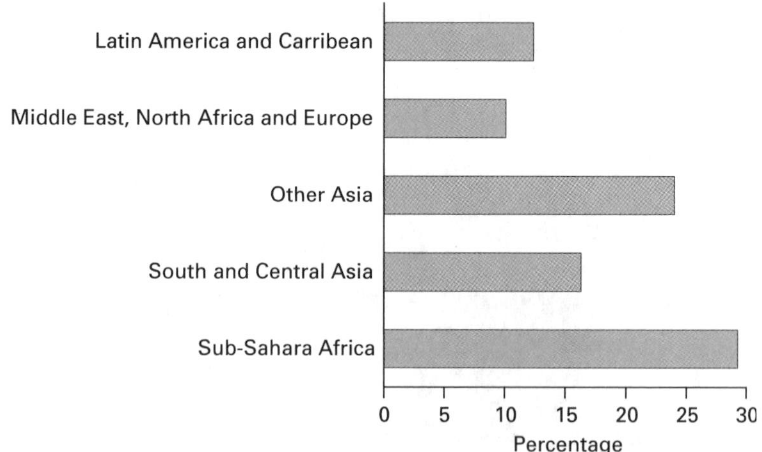


**Figure 5.5** Regional distribution of ODA, 1989–99
(*source*: OECD/DAC 2001: 263, Table 237)

Central Asia have fallen during the last twenty years, whereas those to the rest of Asia have increased significantly in relative terms. This increase has primarily been concentrated on China.

The donor countries and multilateral organizations have formulated several development goals for development cooperation (as discussed in Chapter 3) that generally give priority to aid to the poor. Therefore, it is reasonable to especially examine whether the distribution among regions and countries also reflects this goal.

According to the UNDP's calculations for 1992, no clear priority was given until then to the countries where most of the poor people in the world live (UNDP 1994: 74 ff.). Less than 10 per cent of the total aid went to the ten most populated countries where two-thirds of the world's poor live. Another calculation shows that the 40 per cent richest developing countries receive double the amount of aid per capita as the poorest 40 per cent. Since 1992, aid to Africa has fallen in real value. The same applies to India, which is the country in the world with the largest number of poor people in absolute terms.

If we use the categories of recipient countries described earlier, the DAC's own figures also show that since 1990, there has been a reduction in aid in real value to both the least developed countries (LDCs) and the other low-income countries – in spite of the fact that China has been given higher priority and is included in the latter category. As a share of total aid, transfers to the least developed countries fell from 37 per cent in the mid-1980s to 32 per cent at the end of the 1990s.

The conclusion is that there are clearly weighty considerations that influence especially bilateral donors' choice of countries other than the goal of fighting poverty where it exists the most. In the next chapter, we will examine this more closely for selected donors.

## Distribution by Sector and Type of Aid

Calculations of the distribution of foreign aid by sector are difficult to interpret precisely, because reports from the various donors differ. Criteria vary from country to country within the DAC group. In addition, the DAC's calculations cannot be compared directly with those of the World Bank or with figures from UN development organizations. Therefore, one must be careful when drawing firm conclusions about distribution by sector.

Viewed over a longer time, however, it is certain that bilateral transfers of aid have been concentrated more on social sectors such as education, health and water supply. The allocations from DAC countries to these sectors increased from about 20 per cent in the 1970s and 1980s to almost 30 per cent at the end of the 1990s. Among the social sectors, education receives the largest share, but it is remarkable that only a modest share of these funds is for primary education. Thus, in 1998, allocations to education were almost 11 per cent of total DAC aid, but primary education received only 1 per cent – in spite of the fact that DAC countries generally acknowledge that primary education is of greatest importance in the fight against poverty. In line with this same consideration, it is notable that only one-third of the aid to the health sector goes to primary health services.

All in all, it is estimated that DAC countries – in spite of the high priority given to the social sectors as a whole – give only 10–12 per cent of their total bilateral aid to the basic social areas of special significance for the large groups of poor people. According to calculations from the World Bank, allocations from the IDA to these areas are actually larger in relative terms. But in any case, these allocations are far from the goal of 20 per cent of aid to the basic social areas that won broad support at the social summit in Copenhagen in 1995. However, it should be added that as usual there are great differences from donor to donor (see OECD/DAC 2000: 206 ff.).

Parallel with the relative growth in aid to the social sectors, allocation to economic infrastructure and production has fallen. Particularly in areas such as energy supply and industrial production, aid has decreased in relative terms, but this also applies to agricultural production. The change is most marked for bilateral aid, whereas development banks continue to give up to half of their loans to these major sectors.

The distribution of aid transfers by sector gives an indication of donors' priorities, but it does not necessarily tell us very much about how the total resources are allocated in recipient countries. It is well known that many developing countries give low priority to the social sectors and investments in human development, even though they receive significant aid for these areas. Therefore, donors have also urged adoption of a so-called 20-20 agreement. Under such an agreement, donors would obligate themselves to allocate at least 20 per cent of their aid to the social sectors in order to promote human development, while recipient countries would obligate themselves to allocate the same share of their public budgets for the same purpose. Among the multilateral organizations, especially the UNDP has supported this type of agreement, and at the social summit in Copenhagen, the idea proved to enjoy broad support – at least verbally.

For many years, in the debate on distribution among sectors, there has been a special interest in aid in the form of food. This is part of the broader category of 'commodity aid', which in principle is different from financial or technical assistance. Back in the 1950s and 1960s, food aid was a very large part of bilateral aid, especially because the USA placed much emphasis on it. Since then, food aid decreased to 15 per cent at the start of the 1970s, and at the end of the 1990s, it was down to about 5 per cent.

Criticism of food aid has stressed that the grant element is too modest and that recipient countries often risk a directly negative effect. The official definition requires a grant element of only 25 per cent in terms of current trade prices. In addition, the criticism has noted that food aid has been designed to help the industrial countries dispose of their surplus production of agricultural products – a surplus production that is also due to public subsidies and comprehensive agricultural support arrangements, especially in the USA and the EU. The products that are offered through food aid have thus been selected according to what the rich countries have too much of, and not necessarily according to what the recipient countries especially need. This means, for example, that wheat has played a disproportionately large role. Earlier, a great deal of food aid even consisted of surplus animal products that in relation to their nutritional value were far more expensive than the vegetable products that now dominate this form of aid.

There was criticism that food aid pressed prices down on local markets, hurting domestic producers. Such negative effects have been limited in many developing countries, however, where transfers of food products have been used to replace commercial imports. In practice, such aid has more the form of support to the balance of payments. It has made funds available to be used according to the governments' own priorities.

In other words, there can be arguments both for and against food aid, and the picture varies greatly from country to country depending to a great extent on the government's agricultural policy. But there is no doubt that food aid for many recipient countries is a less valuable form of aid than financial or technical assistance. Nor is there any general assurance that food aid especially benefits the poor. In any case, food aid in itself does not address the central development problems for the poor in agriculture, for whom the problem is that they lack access to land and opportunities to cultivate sufficient land themselves. For the poor in a broader sense, the major problem is that they lack the necessary purchasing power to acquire the food they need. Therefore, good food aid requires that it is a supplement to much broader efforts (see Raffer and Singer 1996: Chapters 5 and 6; Colding and Pinstrup-Andersen 2000).

## Foreign Aid's Significance for Recipient Countries

Recipient countries are so different and their share of the total assistance varies so much that its quantitative significance must necessarily fluctuate considerably. First, there are great differences from region to region and country to country. The total official gross aid in the mid-1990s was about 2.5 per cent of the GNP in developing countries as a whole, but the variation was considerable – from 0.3 per cent in Latin America and 0.7 per cent in India and China to 11.5 per cent for sub-Saharan Africa (World Bank 1997c). Since then, foreign aid's relative significance has decreased in all regions (see also Table 5.1). Second, it can be noted that the size of aid does not clearly correlate negatively with decreasing average income. It is true that there is a tendency for most very poor countries to receive aid in an amount that corresponds to a high percentage of their GNP; however, there are also

**Table 5.1** Indicators of foreign aid's significance, selected countries and regions, 1998

| | ODA per capita in US$ | ODA per cent of GNP | GNP per capita in US$ |
|---|---|---|---|
| Mozambique | 61 | 28.2 | 230 |
| Burkina Faso | 37 | 15.5 | 240 |
| Bangladesh | 10 | 2.7 | 370 |
| India | 2 | 0.4 | 450 |
| China | 2 | 0.3 | 780 |
| Bolivia | 79 | 7.5 | 1010 |
| Egypt | 31 | 2.3 | 1400 |
| Brazil | 2 | 0.0 | 4420 |
| Sub-Saharan Africa | 21 | 4.1 | 500 |
| South Asia | 4 | 0.9 | 0.7 |

*Source*: World Bank, World Development Indicators (CD-Rom).

*Note*: Figures for the shown regions are weighted averages.

poor countries, primarily India, that receive very little aid in relation to the size of the population and the economy. Also, there are relatively well-off countries that receive disproportionately large amounts in foreign aid. Table 5.1 gives an indication of the great variation. Foreign aid per capita does not decrease evenly in relation to increases in GNP per capita, either in Table 5.1 or in the total data for developing countries. This reflects the limited influence of poverty orientation on allocation of foreign aid.

If we look at the weighted averages for the various regions, it is notable that foreign aid per capita is larger for the lower category of middle-income countries than for all the low-income countries together. If China and India are excluded from the latter group, however, the picture changes. It is also notable that foreign aid has considerably greater significance for sub-Saharan Africa, measured both as aid per capita and as a percentage of the recipient countries' GNP.

These different indicators for foreign aid's significance for recipient countries give only a first superficial impression. More in-depth analyses are required to get to the bottom of this question. We will return to this in Chapter 12.

## Foreign Aid and Other Transfers Between Industrialized and Developing Countries

The transfers that are defined as development assistance comprise only part of the total transfers between industrialized and developing countries. The other types of transfers to developing countries consist of export credits and other short-term credits, loans on commercial terms from private and public financing institutions, direct foreign investments and portfolio investments (purchase of securities). In addition, there are special types of credit in the form of rights to draw on the International Monetary Fund. Transfers in the other direction consist primarily of interest and repayments on loans and repatriation of profits from foreign investments.

In principle, all capital transfers to developing countries can contribute to financing development activities, but usually recipient countries benefit most from direct investments, long-term loans and foreign aid in their development efforts. Therefore, our attention will also be focused on these elements. However, it must be added that the effects of long-term resource transfers can be undermined in practice, or completely eliminated, by capital flows in the opposite direction consisting of short-term credits and speculation-oriented investments. When developing countries experience economic or financial crises, foreign investors typically begin to sell their securities and the reserves of their countries' foreign exchange, which usually further reinforces the crises.

Here, however, we will concentrate on the long-term transfers and distinguish between official aid (ODA), other public financing, and private transfers.

Private financial transfers to developing countries rose at the end of the 1970s and the beginning of the 1980s, both in absolute figures and relatively, but the Mexican debt crisis in 1982 reversed this tendency. It was not until

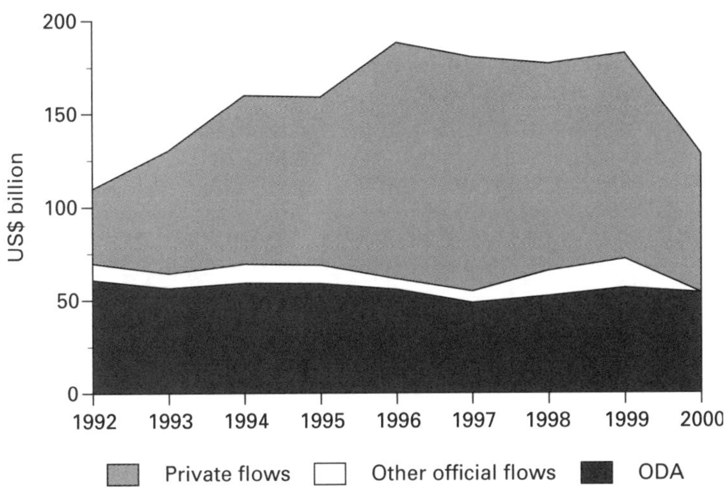


**Figure 5.6** Total net flow of long-term financial resources to developing countries and multilateral organizations (*source*: OECD/DAC 1997: A3, Table 2; OECD/DAC 2001: 180, Table 2)

ten years later that private transfers again reached the same nominal level, and they did not rise above the level for 1981 in fixed prices until 1994. As a result of these violent fluctuations, official development assistance came to play a large role in developing countries as a whole for several years. In 1981, aid comprised about one-third of total transfers. With the falling private transfers during subsequent years, this share increased to about 50 per cent in 1986–88. After 1993, aid transfers fell or stagnated, whereas private transfers rose markedly. As a result, the share of foreign aid had a clear falling tendency, and in 1998, it was down to 29 per cent. In 1999, the share was 30 per cent.

The marked increase in private transfers, both in absolute terms and in comparison with foreign aid, is generally explained by referring to the increasing globalization of production and intensification of transnational economic transactions. These followed in the wake of the extensive liberalization that many developing countries had carried out after the end of the Cold War. The literature also points to the growth potential that became more apparent, especially in the Far East and Latin America, and the reduced costs of transportation and improved communication systems. These changes have inspired many in foreign aid circles to consider whether the time is ripe to rely more on private transfers and concentrate development cooperation on measures that can promote and support these transfers.

In some contexts, this can be relevant, but the private resource flows are definitely not evenly divided among recipient countries (see p. 5). This applies especially to direct private investments, which comprise the greatest development potential among the private transfers. According to the World Bank's figures for the total net private transfers in 1996, 140 of the 166 developing countries, together, received only 5 per cent (World Bank 1997b: 14). Direct private investments were even more concentrated: only nine developing countries received in total almost 68 per cent of the total investments (World Bank 1998a: 20). Table 5.2 shows how large a share of the direct foreign investments each of these nine countries received in 1997.

**Table 5.2** Direct foreign investments in the most favoured developing countries, 1997 (in percentage of total private investments in developing countries)

| | | | |
|---|---|---|---|
| China | 37.0 | Argentina | 3.8 |
| Brazil | 15.8 | Chile | 3.5 |
| Mexico | 8.1 | India | 3.1 |
| Indonesia | 5.8 | Venezuela | 2.9 |
| Malaysia | 4.1 | | |

*Source*: World Bank, *Global Development Finance 1998*: 20.

With regard to the regional distribution of direct foreign investments, there was a strong concentration in the Far East and Latin America, whereas

South Asia and especially sub-Saharan Africa received only modest shares. Generally, primarily middle-income countries benefited, especially those that are most well off. Among the low-income countries, only China received large investments in relation to its GNP, varying between 4 and 7 per cent in the 1990s. The other low-income countries received investments amounting only to about 1 per cent of their GNP during the same period, and many of these countries, especially in Africa, did not receive any foreign investments that show in the statistics. There was, however, also an increase in foreign investments in sub-Saharan Africa, especially in South Africa.

Against this background, we can conclude that even though private transfers have gradually received greater significance in recent years for developing countries generally, we cannot say that they can take over the role of foreign aid for the majority of these countries. In fact, the situation is rather that the poorest countries, which are the countries mostly in need of resources supplied from outside, are also the countries that have been least able to attract private capital, especially direct long-term investments. Therefore, they have at least just as much need for foreign aid as they did earlier.

## CHAPTER 6

# Official Bilateral Assistance

§ IN this chapter, we examine more closely bilateral aid for five selected countries: the USA, Japan, France, the United Kingdom and Denmark, in order to show how great the variations are with respect to the amount of aid and its management. The aim is also to give concrete insight into the foreign aid policy implemented by the four large donors and by Denmark, which in relative terms is the country that has given the most development assistance in recent years. Before discussing the individual countries, we will comment briefly on the cooperation among the donor countries within the framework of the OECD's Development Assistance Committee (DAC).

## Cooperation Among the DAC Countries

The first forum for consultations, which was established within the OECD in 1960, was the Development Assistance Forum. The following year, this became a permanent committee called the Development Assistance Committee (DAC). The twenty-two countries that are now members of the committee are listed in Appendix 1, along with the date when each country joined the DAC.

Members of the DAC have in principle declared themselves willing to work for an increase in the amount of foreign aid and also in the effectiveness of development efforts. As shown in the preceding chapter and in the country examples in the following, not all member countries have taken these formal obligations equally seriously. In practice, the debate in the DAC has just as much been about dividing the burden in absolute terms as about the will to increase aid in relation to each country's economic capacity. But there can hardly be any doubt that the very existence of this forum for consultations and cooperation has had a positive effect on the quality of bilateral aid. It has also been of great importance that the DAC has defined common guidelines for documentation of the amount of aid, its composition, distribution, etc. The annual reports on international development cooperation prepared under the chairman's auspices present an authoritative summary of the comprehensive documentation. These reports also contribute to setting the agenda for the international foreign aid debate through revised goal formulations and proposals for revised strategies.

In 1996, the DAC approved a joint policy paper entitled *Shaping the 21st Century: The Contribution of Development Co-operation*. The idea here was to set a new agenda for future development co-operation, with stronger emphasis on relieving extreme poverty, promoting human development instead of just material improvements, and emphasizing partnership between donors and recipient countries. Unfortunately, the document is formulated in such vague terms – for example, 'locally owned and people-centred development' and 'partnership approach' – that it is difficult to translate it into operational guidelines or standards for evaluating the future initiatives of each donor.

More interesting are the DAC chairman's follow-up reports for the following years. They indicate the new conditions for aid that took form around 2000. The reports argue especially that the role of foreign aid as financial gap-filler is declining, because forms of private financing exist that can take over larger shares of the demand for capital and foreign exchange. Foreign aid should therefore be used to a greater extent to create the prerequisites for larger private capital transfers, improved mobilization of domestic resources and improved exploitation of resources. This demands a 'healthy policy regime', primarily a stable macro-economic framework; larger investments in human capital; more effective institutions in both the public and private sectors; and more involvement of civil society's organizations in development efforts (see e.g. OECD/DAC 1998: 48). In the 1999 report, special emphasis was given to aid that would support integration of developing countries in the world economy (OECD/DAC 2000: Chapter 2).

The DAC chairman's reports also stress that more policy coherence should be brought about. Two types of policy coherence are discussed. One involves creating better coherence in donor countries' various forms of foreign policy. The situation for most and especially the larger industrial countries is that there are obvious contradictions between aid and development policy goals on the one hand, and goals within such areas as national security, guidelines for weapon exports, trade and investment policies, agricultural policy and environmental policy on the other. The other form of policy coherence involves seeing developing countries' development problems as a whole, and this requires that donors – including the multilateral ones – try to adjust and coordinate their various policies in relation to the total problems of recipient countries (see Forster and Stokke 1999).

The DAC contributes to the debate in the individual countries, especially with reports about member countries' foreign aid policies and programmes that often contain direct evaluations – both positive and critical – of the implemented policy and management of international development cooperation. In these reports, the DAC evaluates to what extent member countries live up to the principles to which they have committed themselves as members of the development committee. The reports are available to the public and are usually translated into the national language when this is not English or French. In pace with the DAC's broadening of its perspective from foreign aid policy to include, in principle, all forms of foreign policy of significance for developing countries, the periodic reviews have also become broader. They now include evaluations of policy coherence and donor countries' policies for areas such as international trade and international investments. Emphasis in recent years has also been placed on how DAC members attempt to counteract corruption in aid cooperation.

In the following sections, the foreign aid policy of each selected country is discussed. The aim is not to give a thorough presentation of each country's policy, but rather to illustrate the great variation in patterns and tendencies in bilateral aid cooperation. The headings of each section indicate to which other aspects of its foreign relations the country's foreign aid policy is mainly related.

## The USA's Foreign Aid and National Security Policy

When the USA, in the first half of the 1950s, became engaged in rebuilding Europe, its foreign aid, from any point of view, was generous. For many years, it amounted to over 2 per cent of the country's GNP. Such generosity has not characterized American development assistance in the rest of the world. After Marshall aid was phased out, the aid percentage fell to less than half. But measured in absolute figures, American foreign aid to other countries, until 1968, was actually at the same level as all other DAC countries together. In the mid-1980s, American aid fell, in relative terms, to 25 per cent of the DAC countries' total. This share decreased further in the mid-1990s. At the end of this decade, the American contribution was around 16 per cent. During the same period, aid fell from 0.5 to 0.1 per cent of the USA's GNP, the lowest among all DAC countries and considerably below the average for other countries. In more illustrative terms, this means that while each Dane pays annually more than US$316 for development assistance, an American pays US$29 – less than one-tenth. Expressed in still another way – as the DAC chairman did in his 1999 report – the USA gives the same in foreign aid as the four front-runners (Denmark, Norway, Sweden and Holland), which together have a population equal to that of California.

At the same time, more than any other DAC country, the distribution of American foreign aid has been decided on the basis of the interests of national security. It is possible to identify five periods with especially dominant national security interests, each with a corresponding imbalance in the distribution of foreign aid. This is shown in Table 6.1, where the distribution of foreign aid to different countries and regions is presented for one year within each of the national security periods. The USA's Overseas Development Council selected the years.

The table shows shifts in geographic priorities that are so significant that they justify the claim that national security policy strongly influences aid cooperation. The concentration in Vietnam and the rest of East Asia of 71

**Table 6.1** National security periods and distribution of American foreign aid (in per cent)

| | Marshall Plan 1949–55 | Vietnam mobilization 1964–73 | Vietnam settlement 1973–79 | Camp David agreements 1979– | End of the Cold War 1989– |
|---|---|---|---|---|---|
| | 1950 | 1964 | 1973 | 1979 | 1990 |
| Israel, Egypt | – | 3 | 5 | 68 | 47 |
| Remainder of Middle East, South Asia | 8 | 36 | 13 | 13 | 17 |
| East Asia | 12 | 25 | 71 | 6 | 4 |
| Latin America | 1 | 23 | 6 | 4 | 17 |
| Africa | – | 8 | 4 | 6 | 8 |
| Europe, Canada | 80 | 5 | 1 | 2 | 7 |

per cent of the total official aid in 1973 is especially notable. The same applies to the concentration of 68 per cent in 1979 in only two countries, Israel and Egypt. Also after 1990, Israel remained the largest recipient of American aid, followed by Egypt, but at the same time, there was a relative increase in aid to the rest of the Middle East, South Asia and Latin America (OECD/DAC, USA 1995. For a more detailed analysis, see Zimmerman 1993.)

In the beginning of the 1990s, the American government began increasingly to untie development assistance from narrow national security interests around the world. The development-oriented goals were placed higher on the agenda. At the end of the 1990s, the goals were grouped in the following six categories: (a) achieve economic growth and agricultural development; (b) build sustainable democracies; (c) build human capacity through education and training; (d) stabilize world population and protect human health; (e) manage the environment for long-term sustainability; and (f) promote humanitarian assistance (see USAID 2000).

The goals for American foreign aid continue to be much broader, however, and in ways that are difficult to figure out they are integrated with the country's foreign policy as a whole. One of the problems in this connection is that changing majorities in Congress continually make new demands for the use of foreign aid funds. Another problem is that American presidents often use foreign aid and emergency relief as part of their foreign policy. The situation has become further complicated by the fact that several ministries are involved in the administration of foreign aid, even though USAID is clearly the most important government authority in this respect.

The continuing connection with national security interests is also reflected in the list of the largest recipients of foreign aid around 2000: Israel, Egypt, Russia and Bosnia-Herzegovina (Israel and Russia are not at present recognized by the DAC as foreign aid recipients). African and other low-income countries receive considerably less from the USA, in relative terms, than from DAC countries as a whole.

The total of grants to foreign aid and emergency relief in fixed prices was cut back several times in the 1990s. A considerable cutback of almost 20 per cent from 1992 to 1993, however, was due to new methods of calculation. Since 1993, in calculations of official aid, the DAC has no longer accepted the inclusion of cancellation of military debts. In 1996, foreign aid was again reduced by not less than 15 per cent, and this time there was no connection with changed methods of calculation. This lower level was maintained in 1997 but again increased markedly in 1998. In relation to GNP, however, there was no considerable change. In the meantime, the central organ for the USA's bilateral aid cooperation, USAID, was ordered to make considerable administrative cutbacks, which led to the closing of country offices and programmes in a large number of smaller developing countries. Such cutbacks, over a period of years, must be seen against the background of the USA's marked economic growth during the 1990s and the large surplus in the national budget.

Parallel with cutbacks in bilateral aid, the USA has continued its boycott of part of the payments to several UN agencies and the IDA and the soft loan programmes under the regional development banks, especially for Africa. The total amount owed by the end of the 1990s was more than US$1 billion, which for the organizations involved represents a considerable amount of money. The American Congress had offered several times to pay this debt, but usually the promises were related to demands for a revised distribution of the burden, especially to the detriment of the other large DAC countries. In 2001, after the terrorist attacks in New York and Washington, however, Congress agreed to begin paying the debt to the UN, possibly as a reflection of the USA's need for more international support to combat terrorism.

The official US opposition to giving more foreign aid is sometimes claimed to reflect the attitude among the great majority of the country's citizens; however, there is no support for this notion. The problem is that Americans generally are so poorly informed about how large foreign aid is that their expressed attitudes are difficult to use as a basis for drawing conclusions. A large opinion poll from 1993, which the DAC has referred to on several occasions, shows that a majority of those asked believed that the USA gave foreign aid of more than 20 per cent of the federal budget. The correct figure was far less than 1 per cent. Another survey in 1996, in which the interviewers first explained how much foreign aid was, indicated that only about 10 per cent felt that it was too much. It is also notable that private contributions to the USA's many NGOs is larger per capita than in most other DAC countries. This can be interpreted as greater confidence in the work of the private organizations than in USAID and other public authorities. But since these authorities to a great extent work together with and finance NGOs, we remain uncertain about the American public's more precise attitudes towards the various forms of aid cooperation.

There are several elements in American foreign aid that have provoked heated debate and continue to do so. One of them is the considerable share that directly or indirectly supports the military in several cooperating countries. With the revised methods of calculation mentioned above, this subject is no longer so central in the debate. On the other hand, the US military's direct involvement in emergency relief is now the subject of criticism from several sides. Military persons are concerned about the combination, because it can weaken real military preparedness. Civil emergency aid organizations are concerned, because aid in this way is linked too closely with American national interests. In any case, it is part of American foreign policy to combine military operations with emergency aid, as for example in connection with interventions in north Iraq with the aim of ensuring the return of exiled Kurds after the Gulf War and in Afghanistan in 2001.

Another controversial element is food aid, which as far back as 1954 comprised a considerable share of the total aid. This share decreased during the 1990s but continues to be 12–14 per cent. Food aid is given under a special law, PL480 (from 1954), which stipulates three types of aid: (a) Title I, which covers subsidized sale of American surplus production; (b) Title II, which covers emergency relief and deliveries to the World Food Programme (WFP); and (c) Title III, which covers food deliveries from state to state, with special emphasis on the poor countries. The American Ministry of Agriculture administrates the first type, and USAID the other two.

The subsidized sale has caused particular criticism, because the grant element has been too modest, and because it has not benefited poor people in recipient countries. The governments that have purchased American surplus production – either for their own national currency or for low-rent loans from the USA – have under the arrangement just sold the food on the domestic markets. If it is sold at usual market prices, it does not benefit the poor, who lack purchasing power, and if it is sold at subsidized prices, it undermines the earnings of local producers. Therefore, this form of aid, according to the critics, has confirmed the worst notions about food aid's lack of poverty orientation and its potential harmful effects (see Raffer and Singer 1996: Chapters 5 and 6). More generally, aid under PL480 has also been criticized for actually being used as a means of pressure and reward in connection with the USA's foreign policy, especially until the end of the Cold War (see e.g. Lappé et al. 1987: Chapter 4).

## Japan's Foreign Aid and Foreign Economic Policy

Japan's involvement as donor in international aid began in 1954–55, that is, at a time when the country was itself a foreign aid recipient. The first aid was given as part of the so-called Colombo Plan, which aimed to support economic development in South and Southeast Asia. An important part of the aid went to repairing damages caused by Japan during the Second World War. Therefore, special emphasis was placed on the physical infrastructure, and concentration on countries in Asia and physical infrastructure came to characterize Japan's foreign aid until the 1990s. For many years, the Japanese government considered foreign aid an integrated part of the country's economic cooperation with other countries. Even though Japan had become a member of the DAC in 1961, it was not until the end of the 1960s that aid was formally separated from other foreign economic measures such as export credits, investment promotion and trade policy. In comparison with other DAC countries, foreign aid since then has also remained more closely tied to the country's total foreign economic policy.

The official motives for giving aid are very complex and have been changed several times since the 1950s. Originally, great emphasis was placed publicly on repairing war damage and creating an image of Japan as a responsible partner in international economic cooperation. At the same time, the explanations internally were connected with national economic and political interests. The aim was to create growth in the neighbouring Asian region and open its markets for purchases of growing Japanese exports, develop better conditions for the country's foreign investments, and contribute to the region's political stability. These considerations remained central for Japanese foreign aid as a basic reflection of the country's pronounced need for access to resources and markets in other countries (Yanagihara and Emig 1991; Rix 1993: Chapter 1).

Since the 1970s, however, an increasingly more global perspective has been added, partly as a result of pressure by the USA, which wanted Japan to contribute still more to the USA's allies in the Third World as part of its policy of containment of the Eastern bloc. Japanese aid has never been based to the same degree as the USA's on ideological considerations and national security interests, but its close alliance with the USA led to a geographic distribution of foreign aid that to a certain extent reflects these considerations and interests. To begin with, Japan's preferred recipient countries were Taiwan, South Korea and Indonesia. The choice of these countries was primarily motivated by Japan's own foreign economic goals, but was also in complete agreement with American national security interests. With the spread of aid in the 1970s and 1980s, especially to Pakistan and countries in the Middle East, the USA's influence became even clearer.

Japan has continued, however, to give high priority to the neighbouring Asiatic region, with about one-third of the bilateral aid to ASEAN countries alone and a total of about 60 per cent to East, Southeast and South Asia. It is in these areas that Japan continues to have the most important foreign economic and political interests (see Koppel and Orr 1993; Rix 1993: Chapter 5). For several years, five Asian countries have received more than half of the bilateral aid: China, Indonesia, the Philippines, India and Thailand. The largest recipients of Japanese aid in 1998 were China, Indonesia, Thailand and India – in that order. Sub-Saharan Africa received about 18 per cent of Japanese bilateral aid, while the average for DAC countries was over one-third. Bilateral aid from Japan was about 80 per cent of the total foreign aid.

With regard to the distribution among countries according to average incomes, Japanese aid became more poverty-oriented during the 1980s and 1990s. Aid to Africa has increased considerably since the 1960s, in both absolute and relative terms (Inukai 1993). In 1969, only about 1 per cent went to sub-Saharan Africa – in contrast to 18 per cent at the end of the 1990s. The increased interest in Africa, which can also be seen in Japanese initiatives in multilateral cooperation, can be understood as an expression of the government's efforts to place Japan in the role as leading donor globally.

Even though Japan has given higher priority to low-income countries, it is doubtful whether its aid can be characterized as poverty-oriented. According to official statements, it is, but these also imply that all foreign aid policy is based on the idea that national economic growth is both a prerequisite and a means for relieving poverty. The focus continues to be on physical infrastructure, with 40–45 per cent of the bilateral aid (as compared to an average of 20 per cent for DAC countries). High priority continues to be given to supporting export-oriented industrial development, which follows models that the Japanese decision-makers claim have functioned so well in many East Asian countries. If we examine more closely the slightly more than 19 per cent of bilateral aid, which according to the official figures is used for education, health and other social infrastructure (1999), we find that this covers very broad definitions. Thus many factors indicate that the amounts used for what the government itself calls meeting elementary human needs are considerably more limited (Takayanagi 1997).

After 1993, Japan was the largest donor in the world. Its official aid in 1999 was 27 per cent of all DAC countries' total aid. In relation to the country's GNP, it was 0.35 per cent, considerably more than the average for DAC countries as a whole (0.24 per cent). In 1996, the total net transfers to recipient countries were drastically reduced. Calculated in yen, aid fell that year by almost 25 per cent in relation to 1995, which measured in US dollars after devaluation of the yen amounted to no less than 35 per cent. Part of the explanation for this was increased payments on loans incurred earlier by recipient countries, but considerable budget cuts were also made. Later, aid was increased again, especially as a reaction to the financial crisis in the East Asian recipient countries. From 1998 to 1999, Japanese aid increased markedly (by 28 per cent) followed by new cuts.

According to an ODA Charter approved by the Japanese government in 1992, foreign aid should aim to protect the environment while promoting economic development. Also, as expressed somewhat vaguely in the document, 'full attention' should be paid to efforts towards democratization and the introduction of a market-oriented economy; the situation regarding securing basic human rights; and the level of freedom in the recipient countries. Furthermore, it makes clear that Japan does not give aid for military purposes, and also that recipient countries must limit their military expenses and refrain from producing weapons of mass destruction (see OECD/DAC, Japan 1996: Annex 1).

Foreign aid is given in three main forms: as grants, yen loans and technical assistance. Many ministries are involved in managing aid, but two authorities have especially prominent roles, the Overseas Economic Cooperation Fund (OECF) and the Japan International Cooperation Agency (JICA). The former is responsible for providing loans, which are the major part of Japanese aid, while JICA is responsible for technical assistance. Grant aid is administered mainly by the Japanese foreign ministry, which since the 1990s has also had the authority to coordinate all foreign aid. The strong emphasis on yen loans means that the grant element in the total Japanese foreign aid is less than for other DAC countries. In the mid-1990s, the grant element was thus less than 80 per cent compared to the norm for DAC countries of 86 per cent.

This is one of the aspects of Japanese aid that has been criticized, but an even stronger criticism was directed towards the fluctuating quality of the aid. The DAC, both in its review in 1993 and again in 1996, criticized the quality and referred in particular to insufficient staffing, regarding both quantity and quality, in the organs that administrate foreign aid. The DAC welcomed the fact that Japan would move a little from supporting physical infrastructure and equipment-heavy forms of aid and more towards support for social development. But at the same time, the DAC pointed out that this would demand a considerable expansion of staff in the responsible agencies and recruitment of other types of expertise than the technical-economic experts that at present dominate completely. The DAC has also criticized the decision-making processes for being so centralized in Tokyo, and the staffing in recipient countries for being so modest, that adjustment of the aid programmes to the conditions in the individual country is undermined (see pp. 5, 6). This criticism was repeated in the DAC's review in 1999 (OECD/DAC, Japan: 1999).

Japan was criticized earlier for its high degree of tied aid. At the start of the 1970s, over 70 per cent was tied to purchases in Japan or consisted directly of deliveries from Japan. Other DAC countries claimed that in this way Japan promoted to a great extent its own products. Through technical advisers, Japan also recommended its own technical specifications and standards, presumably to a greater extent than other donor countries. Both practices changed markedly up through the 1980s, and around the mid-1990s the extent of Japanese tied aid had decreased to 15–16 per cent – compared to an average for DAC countries of about 33 per cent. Suppliers from recipient countries in Asia benefited in particular from untied aid. This made critics in other donor countries question whether these other suppliers were actually just local branches or daughter corporations of Japanese firms. However, several investigations showed that few of the suppliers in developing countries had any form of partnership with Japanese firms (OECD/DAC, Japan 1996: 38). Untying must therefore be characterized as real and extensive – and as an expression of the fact that the earlier relatively direct use of foreign aid to promote Japanese commercial interests has decreased markedly.

Unlike that of most other DAC countries, Japanese aid has not been characterized by greatly increased involvement of NGOs. There are tendencies in this direction but to a much more modest extent. This is related to the fact that Japanese law makes it very difficult to achieve official recognition as an NGO. At the same time, the centralistic structure makes it difficult to give support directly to NGOs in recipient countries. Also these conditions have been criticized in the DAC's reviews with the addition of a recommendation to create better conditions for establishing NGOs in Japan and including such organizations in recipient countries.

## France's Foreign Aid and Foreign Policy

For many years, France was the third largest donor, after the USA and Japan, and was in second place for a single year (1995). After making considerable cuts in the mid-1990s, the country dropped to below Germany, but in recent years has again taken third place. In a longer time perspective, France certainly belongs among the heavyweights in international development cooperation. France has also given considerable foreign aid in relative terms, for many years more than or about 0.6 per cent of the country's GNP. In 1999, however, this was cut to 0.4 per cent, and from 1995 to 1999, French aid decreased 32 per cent in current prices.

It is characteristic for French aid that it is strongly concentrated in the country's own former colonies, especially in Africa and also, in recent years, Indochina. The weight is also mostly on low-income countries, which receive considerably more than half of the total foreign aid. Part of the aid (13–15 per cent), however, goes to French overseas territories that belong to the group of high-income countries and territories. The two largest recipients of French aid are French Polynesia and New Caledonia. This places France as the country that clearly gives most, after the USA, to high-income countries and territories.

French foreign aid policy has traditionally been closely integrated with foreign policy as a whole, especially in relation to francophone Africa. Shifting French presidents have often been involved in the geographic distribution of foreign aid and used ODA transfers as rewards to the governments that were loyal to Paris (Cumming 1995). Immediately after the end of the Cold War, President Mitterrand declared that in the future foreign aid would not be given to countries unless their governments initiated democratization processes. However, this statement was mollified in 1991, when it was added that recipient countries themselves must decide the tempo for political reforms. After that, France continued its development cooperation with most of the traditional partners in Africa, regardless of whether they implemented political reforms or not. Thus, French aid differs in relation to the general tendencies among DAC countries, which have been moving towards still clearer demands for political and institutional reforms as a condition for foreign aid. France also differs from most DAC countries by having maintained a relatively high level of aid to Africa, including North Africa, since 1989.

Both these special characteristics of French aid should be seen against the background of France's long involvement on the African continent as a regional big power. During the Cold War, France seldom sided with the USA in its rivalry with the Soviet Union. Shifting French governments have consistently rejected American leadership in relations with Africa. Instead, they have tried to play the leading role and made great efforts to weaken both superpowers' influence in the francophone countries. France has not defined its sphere of interest in this way only through development cooperation, but has also connected these countries closer to it through special trade and investment agreements as well as monetary cooperation.

The latter in particular has ensured the protection of French economic interests in the many former colonies, which retained their connection to the French franc after independence. The French government guaranteed these African states a fixed exchange rate. In return, this special franc-zone currency (Communauté financière africaine, CFA Franc) had to follow the French franc when it decreased in value. For several years, because of this monetary union, France opposed the IMF's and the World Bank's proposal for a separate devaluation of the CFA Franc in connection with structural adjustment programmes. Even though, during the first half of the 1980s, France accepted implementation of the other elements in structural adjustment programmes, it was not until 1994 that the government in Paris – for the first time since 1958 – agreed to a devaluation of the CFA Franc.

Another area where France has followed a different policy from other DAC countries is with respect to direct military intervention in former African colonies. On many occasions, French troops have been sent in to support shaky regimes as a supplement to the support these governments received in the form of foreign aid and cancellation of debts.

Further evidence of the integration of French aid as part of the country's foreign policy as a whole is the emphasis placed on the spread of the French language and culture. In Africa alone, more than seventy cultural institutions and about seven hundred libraries are financed by foreign aid funds.

In several reviews of French aid (1997 and 2000), the DAC has in careful terms observed that it lacks a comprehensive strategy for development. This weakness can partly be attributed to the use of aid as an instrument for the rest of the country's foreign policy and for the promotion of commercial interests. The DAC has also especially criticized France for giving social aspects too little weight, especially aid to women. French aid programmes do not comprise any special initiatives to improve women's welfare or their participation in the development process (OECD/DAC, France 1997). The fight against poverty received higher priority during the 1990s, but it is not an explicitly formulated principal goal for French aid, although this is now the case for many bilateral and multilateral donors.

A third important criticism in the DAC's earlier reviews concerned the splitting up of administration that characterized French aid until the end of the 1990s. In addition to the Office of the President and the Ministry of Cooperation, the Ministry of Foreign Affairs and various funds and other public authorities were involved in decision-making processes that were not always transparent and properly coordinated. According to the DAC, a reorganization in 1998–99 improved the situation (OECD/DAC, France 2000). As a result of this reorganization, the Ministry of Cooperation came under the Ministry of Foreign Affairs, which thus comprises one pillar in the administration of French foreign aid. The other comprises the Ministry of Economic Affairs, Finance and Industry. The French Development Agency is responsible for implementation. Together with the establishment of an inter-ministry committee for coordination of foreign aid and the creation of the High Council for International Cooperation, which advises the prime minister, more cohesion was created in French foreign aid and development policy. But the DAC's most recent review in 2000 observes that three aid cultures still exist: that of the Ministry of Economic Affairs, Finance and Industry, which has as its central concerns macro-economic equilibrium and commercial penetration; that of the Ministry of Finance, which is centred on cultural outreach and development of Francophonie; and that of the French Development Agency, where the focus is on developing infrastructure, human resources and institutional capacities (OECD/DAC, France 2000).

In contrast with the United Kingdom and Denmark, for example, France has not shifted its strategy towards sector programmes, but has maintained the project form as the central instrument. However, the projects are often planned within the framework of sector-wide approaches. The need to work with country strategies is increasingly recognized, but it seems strange that the proposals for shaping such strategies do not make any provisions for country strategies to be discussed with recipient countries. They are to remain internal government documents. The same applies for the evaluation reports on French foreign aid.

The last aspect of French aid to be stressed is the relatively strong emphasis on humanitarian aid through the French international solidarity organizations, of which Doctors without Borders (Médecin Sans Frontières) is one of the best known. However, only a very modest share of foreign aid is channelled through development-oriented NGOs, which, until the establishment of the High Council for International Development Cooperation in 1999, were not consulted or included in the formulation of foreign aid policy to any significant extent.

## The United Kingdom's Foreign Aid and Development Policy

The United Kingdom established a form of foreign aid to overseas areas during the colonial period – for example, under the Colonial Development Act of 1929 and the Colonial Development and Welfare Act of 1940. Gradually, as the British colonies achieved political independence, they were offered continued aid. Both the large political parties, Labour and the Conservatives, supported for many years a considerable aid effort, which at the end of the 1970s reached over 0.5 per cent of GNP. Foreign aid was also extended to countries other than the former British colonies, but by far the largest share continued to be given to the Commonwealth countries. It was part of British policy to give preference to countries with close historic bonds to the UK.

In the 1960s and 1970s, British governments placed considerable emphasis on supporting developing countries' interests, also in regard to trade policy and other affairs.

With Margaret Thatcher's election as prime minister in 1979, the UK's aid and development policy was radically changed. Foreign aid was cut from over 0.5 per cent of the GNP to 0.35 per cent in just one year (from 1979 to 1980). Further cutbacks were carried out after 1983. The changes were so marked that the respected British Sunday newspaper, the *Observer*, wrote an editorial under the headline, 'Thatcher – Aid Snatcher', which in addition to this unflattering play on words strongly criticized the Conservative government's policy. A few years later, in 1983, the UK also became the first donor country to link its bilateral aid closely with the IMF's and the World Bank's often extensive conditionalities. This applied especially to programme aid, the principal goal of which was 'to help achieve economic reform and provide funds to relieve foreign exchange constraints', but the funds were primarily available to governments that followed the recommendations of the Bretton Woods institutions (see Healy 1996).

In the more general policy for developing countries, the Thatcher government was close to the Reagan administration in the USA and thereby broke with the earlier British tradition of supporting the demands of many developing countries in international negotiations. Until the beginning of the 1990s, the official British view was that for the most part the poor countries themselves must solve their own problems by adopting sound economic policies and creating conditions that would attract foreign investors and trade partners. Furthermore, the Thatcher government stressed that what was most important was not the amount of aid extended by the UK, but the total transfers from the UK to developing countries, especially Commonwealth countries, towards which the government felt a special obligation. With the benefit of hindsight, this argument does not seem very convincing, because the official statistics show that the total net transfers actually decreased under Thatcher (1979–90), and in 1990 were even negative, mainly because of the large repayments of loans that developing countries had previously received from the UK.

The new Conservative government that came to power in 1990 initiated a revision of foreign aid policy. Development goals in particular were adjusted, with a stronger emphasis on helping the poor and the addition of a new goal for promoting good governance – in addition to economic reforms. Population problems, the situation of women and the environment were assigned greater importance. In addition, several initiatives were taken on debt relief, both bilaterally and through international forums (see OECD/DAC, United Kingdom 1994).

Radical changes in British policy were first implemented, however, when New Labour took over government in 1997. The general principles were presented in a White Paper later the same year (DfID 1997). This document represented the first attempt in twenty-two years to make a comprehensive presentation of British aid and development policy. The new secretary of state for international development, Clare Short, has since stressed that the White Paper 'focused all our work on eliminating poverty' (DfID 2000: 6).

The new British policy, with the further adjustments carried out since 1997, maintains that elimination of poverty is the principal and long-term goal. In a shorter time perspective, the aim is to contribute to cutting in half by 2015 the share of the people in the world who live in extreme poverty. Similar operational goals are formulated for some other areas of importance for human development and conservation of the environment (DfID 2000: 11; see also Chapter 3 above). The new policy marks a shift towards a rights-based approach that recognizes development as a universal and inalienable right and an integral part of fundamental human rights – in accordance with the consensus that was achieved at the World Conference on Human Rights in Vienna in 1993. The international development goals that British aid should contribute to realizing can be summarized in three categories: (a) sustainable livelihoods; (b) better education, health and opportunities for poor people; and (c) better management of the natural and physical environment (ODI 1998). It was already stressed in the White Paper that the development goals could only be realized if strong partnerships were established, both with other donors and recipient countries.

The strategies for development cooperation have also been changed in recent years. Sector-wide approaches are used much more, as well as comprehensive strategies for each cooperating country. In principle, Country

Strategy Papers are to be prepared for each cooperating country, but as pointed out by the DAC, it was unfortunate that these strategy papers were internal DfID documents. Only summaries were made available to recipient countries, NGOs and the broader public (OECD/DAC, United Kingdom 1997: 26 ff.). NGOs in particular have criticized this practice, because it made it difficult for them to propose activities to be integrated with or supplement official aid. It should be added, however, that publication of summaries represented progress in relation to earlier practice, when even shorter versions of the country strategies were not freely available.

The size of British foreign aid increased by almost 8 per cent during the first year after the change of government in 1997. In relation to GNP, however, there was only an increase to 0.27 per cent – far from the earlier level of 0.5 per cent and even further from the official goal of 0.7 per cent. Three-fourths of the bilateral aid was given to low-income countries in 1998/99. The three largest recipients of aid were India, Guyana and Tanzania, in that order. A relatively large share of the total aid – about 45 per cent – was channelled through multilateral organizations.

In connection with adjustment of British policy, the administration was also reorganized. Overseas Development Administration under the Foreign Ministry was changed to a separate Department for International Development (DfID) under the leadership of a minister with cabinet rank, whereas the minister had earlier been subordinate to the secretary of state. The DfID received a much broader mandate and was included in coordination of policy for developing countries generally. This reflects the new and far stronger emphasis on policy coherence. The DAC has judged that the UK is among the member countries that have come furthest in the direction of linking foreign aid policy with the other policy areas of importance for developing countries (OECD/DAC, United Kingdom 1997: 18 ff.). This does not mean, however, that the various policy areas have been harmonized with development goals. Basic contradictions still exist between, on the one hand, the idea that market forces and globalization benefit developing countries and should therefore be promoted, and on the other hand, the rights-based approach with emphasis on poverty reduction, partnership and sustainable human development.

Although British NGOs are the largest and many of them the most effective among DAC country NGOs, they have not benefited from the same broad official support as in the Nordic countries. The British government first began to channel large amounts through NGOs from the mid-1980s, and only with contributions equal to the amounts NGOs could raise themselves. Volunteers sent out by Voluntary Service Overseas (VSO) and other NGOs have been financed mostly by state grants, however. The New Labour government has continued this rather reserved attitude towards NGOs, and Clare Short is not especially enthusiastic about small projects or NGO aid in the form of service provision.

## Denmark's Foreign Aid and Development Policy

In comparison with the large industrial countries and also the majority of the smaller DAC countries, Denmark's aid and development policy differs in important ways. For many years, Danish aid policy has been clearly poverty-oriented and has given considerably higher priority to multilateral cooperation. Danish policy since the mid-1980s has also differed in that it continued to increase the amount of aid, in both relative and absolute terms, whereas the tendency for most DAC countries has been stagnation or decline.

Furthermore, Danish policy has been firmly based on international humanism and strong preferences for universal international cooperation, whereas considerations of national defence and security have been given little emphasis. However, Denmark is not unique in this respect. Similar principles have been the basis of foreign aid in a small group of countries that we have referred to as the like-minded DAC countries or front-runners. In addition to the Scandinavian countries, this group includes Holland and, to some extent, Canada.

Danish aid policy has been revised several times since the Act on International Development Cooperation was approved in 1971. The most recent major changes were made in 1989 and 1994. New adjustments were carried out in 2000. Changes have also been made several times in the administration of Danish aid. While the term Danida is now an acronym for Danish International Development Assistance, it also refers to the department in the Foreign Ministry that administers foreign aid – despite the fact that the department's status in the ministry has been changed during the period under discussion.

The policy adjustment in 1989 confirmed the principal goals up to that time and the quite equal division between bilateral and multilateral aid. Within these frameworks, the plan introduced two important adjustments: a geographic concentration of the foreign aid effort; and phasing out aid in the form of loans. In addition, the plan consisted of a stronger decentralization of aid administration to the cooperating countries and emphasis on respect for human rights as a cross-cutting consideration.

Before the approval of the plan of action, Danish aid had been spread over no fewer than sixty-six countries, but about 95 per cent went to a total of twenty-seven countries. The plan's proposal to concentrate on between twenty and twenty-four programme countries was therefore not quite as extreme as it might seem at first glance. Actually, it even proposed an expansion in the sense that a far larger number of so-called programme cooperation countries were added to the traditional group of four major recipients (Tanzania, Kenya, India and Bangladesh). Therefore, it was more important that the formal country concentration was accompanied by new guidelines for formulating more concrete goals and strategies for cooperation with the selected countries. This contributed to creating better cohesion of the initiatives.

In regard to the phasing out of loans in favour of aid in the form of grants for all future programme countries within the bilateral area, changes here were in accordance with the general tendencies in DAC countries, although Denmark went further than most. The motivation was that state loans had proved to be inappropriate, especially in the poorest developing countries, and that they weakened possibilities for that flexibility in aid work that had otherwise been given increasing priority.

The adjustments in 1994 – summarized in a paper on strategy for Danish development policy until 2000 (Danida 1994a) – clarified poverty orientation and emphasized that Denmark would give foreign aid amounting to 1 per cent of the country's GNP. In addition, it stressed three cross-cutting considerations in foreign aid in connection with women's participation in the development process; protection of the global environment and sustainable use of natural resources; and promotion of democratization and respect for human rights. Furthermore, policies were formulated that concerned population, trade with developing countries and debt relief. Since 1994, Danida has increasingly replaced traditional project efforts with sector programme support.

In 1994, the number of programme cooperation countries was set at twenty, but it was not decided more precisely how much of the total bilateral aid should be given to this group of countries. Calculations for recent years show that about 61 per cent goes to the selected countries. Officially, Danida judges that further concentration would hardly be realistic, because a strong need continues to exist for transitional aid to other countries, aid through NGOs, and also allocation of funds for mixed credits, personnel assistance and research. This is a plausible viewpoint, but the fact that Danish aid continues to spread out over so many activities and countries can weaken the possibilities for achieving the desired effects.

Seen in a broader context, the policy changes in 1994 represented an adjustment of Danish aid policy to the situation after the end of the Cold War, both globally and in recipient countries. Danish policy also differs in important ways from the general tendencies in DAC countries in regard to this adjustment. It is especially notable that Danish aid to the poorest developing countries has been maintained or increased, even though new recipient countries have been added in East and Central Europe as well as in Central Asia, and even though large amounts have been given to transitional and humanitarian assistance. This broadening of Danish foreign aid has not caused a reduction in aid to the poorest developing countries, because the aid funds available have increased along with the increasing national product. Also, humanitarian assistance and initiatives in Europe and the former Soviet Union have been mostly financed by a new appropriation for the Environment, Peace and Stability Fund. This appropriation should increase until 2002, when it would have reached 0.5 per cent of Denmark's GNP. A large share of this new grant goes to environmental initiatives in Southeast Asia and Southern Africa. The total amount of Danish grants for development assistance, environment, peace and stability must be described as unusual in comparison with other DAC countries – a total of 1–1.5 per cent of the GNP compared with, especially, the USA's 0.1 per cent.

The adjustments made in 2000 were less wide-ranging than earlier. Mostly, they comprised a stronger emphasis on sector-wide approaches and respect for developing countries as partners in cooperation. However, in comparison with France and the UK, for example, Denmark has for a long time shown greater respect for partnership in connection with the formulation of country strategies – recipient countries have been consulted during the process and the central documents made public, also in English. A more important change is possibly the tightened policy towards multilateral organizations (introduced already in 1994). This is reflected in the adoption of a principle favouring organizations that give priority to the areas that Denmark emphasizes most. These adjustments can be seen as an attempt to give Denmark influence on the basis of the amount of aid and voluntary contributions, and not on the basis of the size of the country.

Poverty orientation in Danish foreign aid policy has manifested itself in the choice of partner countries: about 47 per cent of bilateral aid goes to the least developed countries and a further 40 per cent to other low-income countries. In regional terms, great emphasis is placed on sub-Saharan Africa, with 55 per cent of Danish aid. Poverty orientation is also reflected in the high priority given to the social sector and initiatives of direct relevance for poor and resource-weak groups in society, especially women. Furthermore, Danida has channelled large amounts through NGOs, both from Denmark and in the developing countries, based on the view that NGOs are in a particularly good position to reach the poor and their organizations in civil society.

Along with the increased emphasis on support to civil society organizations and institutions, Danish aid also aims to strengthen the private commercial sector in developing countries, especially through the Private Sector Programme mentioned in Chapter 3. The programme supports establishment of commercially promising cooperation between Danish enterprises and enterprises in selected developing countries. Danida extends counselling and grants for identification of partners, mutual visits and studies during the preparatory phase. During the project phase, grants are given for leadership advice, start-up phase, training, sending out experts, export promotion and measures to improve the working environment and ensure environmentally sound production. An important element in the programme is the support given to establishing commercially sustainable partnerships. The intention is not to maintain partnerships but to function as a catalyst for establishing and then phasing out public support. In this way, the PS programme gives Danish firms better opportunities to become established in relation to distant markets. The advantages of this cooperation with Danish firms for firms in developing countries are that they gain access to less environmentally destructive and more advanced technology and expertise within many areas. The further perspective is to achieve a lasting improvement of their ability to compete through cooperation with Danish firms, also after the phasing out of Danida's support.

The transition from project to sector aid in cooperation with public authorities has been accompanied by a closer dialogue about sector-economic policy and institutional reforms. Thereby, the Danish government has moved more towards intervening in the formation of policies in recipient countries and demanding administrative reforms – in principle, in the same way as the World Bank and several of the large industrial countries. It is not new for Danida to offer aid and advice based on political and institutional considerations. Since 1989, Danish foreign aid policy has been characterized by an emphasis on democratization and respect for human rights. The new element is the expansion of the dialogue about policy and management to the sectors with special priority. We are, however, not convinced that either Danida or other donors have the necessary prerequisites to participate in this way in the concrete formulation of recipient countries' various sector policies. We return to this in Chapter 13.

## Summary of the Variations in Bilateral Aid

As shown in the discussion of the five selected countries, there are considerable differences regarding foreign aid policy and its position in relation to foreign policy as a whole. For the USA, foreign aid is to a great extent influenced by considerations of national security, while Japanese aid is shaped by foreign economic considerations. For both countries, however, there were changes in the 1990s towards a more complex shaping of foreign aid policy. At the same time, first American and then Japanese aid was also markedly reduced. French aid can best be understood as part of the country's total foreign policy, especially with respect to the former colonial areas and overseas territories. The same applied earlier to British aid, which more recently, however, has come to reflect the two big parties' differing priorities. For the UK and Denmark, especially in the 1990s, a declared goal was to create coherence in the relationship between foreign aid and other foreign policy. In practice, however, foreign aid policy received a relatively independent form based on development policy goals, whereas policy for other areas of foreign relations was more strongly influenced by national considerations.

France maintained its relatively high level of aid until the mid-1990s. The UK reduced aid considerably in the 1980s. Not until the end of the 1990s did the UK's aid increase from a relatively low level. Among the countries discussed, only Denmark maintained an aid effort at a high level and also increased it as its GNP increased. This was also made possible through an extra grant in addition to the ODA recognized by the DAC.

Foreign aid policy in the USA in the 1990s became increasingly uncoupled from national security and other central foreign policy considerations. Thereby, aid has lost some of its significance for the most powerful decision-makers and was in danger of becoming isolated and disconnected from the core areas of American policy. This should not mean that American aid will become weaker with regard to quality, maybe rather to the contrary. But as shown, its aid became more vulnerable to budget cuts. The same tendency can be seen, although not so clearly, in the case of Japan and France. For these three countries, development cooperation has become less important as economic globalization has developed, and, with it, far greater opportunities to pursue national economic interests abroad in other ways than through development cooperation (see p. 5).

For the UK and Denmark, globalization has not had the same impact on development cooperation, since it continues to be seen as an important supplement to other efforts to promote international development goals and at the same time protect national business interests.

The five countries together cannot be said to represent the variations among all DAC countries, but most of these do show similar patterns and tendencies, although in different combinations. Interestingly, the re-emergence of national security concerns, especially in US aid policies, after 11 September 2001 has not fundamentally changed the isolation of foreign aid from the high politics of global security and economic integration. This is discussed in Chapter 14.

## CHAPTER 7

# Multilateral Aid

§ MULTILATERAL aid is often considered to be an independent aid form in the same way as bilateral aid, but this is not correct. Multilateral aid is actually a channel for aid from the taxpayers in donor countries to aid recipients in developing countries. Multilateral aid organizations receive most of their aid resources from Western governments and thus from state budgets in industrial countries (see Chapter 5). Since the Western countries have chosen the multilateral organizations to channel about one-third of their aid (development and humanitarian assistance), the motives behind multilateral aid typically constitute part of the complex motives for all foreign aid (see Chapter 2). The motives behind UN aid were originally based mainly on security policy considerations, but ethical motives and international humanism also came to play a strong role after the decolonized states were admitted to the UN. The motives behind foreign aid extended via the multilateral development banks had more to do with modernization of the so-called backward or under-developed economies and their inclusion in the world economy.

The multilateral aid organizations, especially the UN system and the World Bank, are such large bureaucracies and international organizations that they have lives of their own, with goals, strategies, resources and cultures. Although the multilateral aid organizations are also instruments for the strong donor countries' aid strategies, they are assigned – and win for themselves – their own functions and roles. Thus, for the last thirty years, the World Bank has manifested itself as the dominant actor within the international aid system. The World Bank, partly due to its strongly increased lending, has increased its staff, both in number and in terms of expertise, so that today it can rightly be considered the leading development organization in the world (Eichengreen and Kenen 1994; George and Sabelli 1994; Kapur et al. 1997a, 1997b; Lateef 1995; Wolfensohn 1997a).

Theoretically, multilateral aid is often placed in one or more of the following contexts: a) international politics, where the emphasis is on the inter-state power relations and conflicts, and especially the interests of the dominating state(s); b) international political economy, where the international organizations are seen as the connecting link in globalization and management of the developing countries' integration into the world economy; and c) international organization and administration, where the focus is on functions, effectiveness and differences in relation to the national administrations in both industrial and developing countries (for different perspectives, see Abbott and Snidal 1998; Alagapop et al. 1998; Diehl 1997; Frey 1997; Griesgraber and Gunter 1995; Kahler 1995; Rittberger 1993; Ruggie 1993). In recent years, a special approach to international political economy has explored the provision of global public goods, which is of great significance for the existing and potential roles of international organizations (Kaul et al. 1999).

In this chapter, we examine all three perspectives of multilateral aid. We concentrate on the extensive UN system, including the UN's global conferences and summit meetings, as well as the multilateral development banks, especially the World Bank. The EU's aid is also considered multilateral, since it is channelled via an international (although regionally limited) organization. However, it differs from other multilateral aid in that developing countries do not participate directly in the leading organs that determine aid's goals and implementation.

We summarize first the multilateral aid system's aims and structure. Then, we analyse the political expectations of multilateral aid from the Second World War until the end of the Cold War in 1989 by using the first two theoretical perspectives of multilateral aid: international politics and international political economy. This is then followed by a discussion of the size, content and financing of multilateral aid.

The following sections analyse the structural strengths and weaknesses of the UN system, the World Bank and the EU, respectively, partly by using the third theoretical perspective: international organization and administration. The discussion of the UN system is the most extensive, partly because the UN uses so many different forms of intervention that can all be considered as aid (debates in the General Assembly; negotiations concerning international regulations; global UN conferences; technical assistance from the UN's specialized agencies; and actual development aid and resource transfers); and partly because we examine the central role of the World Bank in several other chapters.

As an example of the small, progressive donors' attitude towards the multilateral organizations in the 1990s, we discuss the 'active multilateralism' that the Danish government has implemented for Denmark's multilateral aid. Finally, we summarize multilateral aid's place in the international politico-economic system in the 1990s and discuss prospects for the coming years.

## Multilateral Aid: Complexity in Goals and Organization

The multilateral aid system is not easy to understand. After the Second World War, it developed through offshoots from two main elements: the UN and the World Bank. The UN's original purpose was to promote international security after the war's global destruction, and a great share of its activities is still politically and security oriented (Alger 1998). However, the UN system has moved towards social and economic development, and most UN agencies work either with aid in developing countries – so-called operational activities, or with promotion of values and formulation of policies and standards – so-called normative activities (Nordic UN Project 1991; Nordic UN Reform Project 1996).

The multilateral development banks primarily comprise the World Bank and the regional development banks for Africa, Asia and Latin America (Culpeper 1997). The development banks each provide resources under two conditions: concessional resources, which may be grants or soft loans (called credits), and which fall within the definition of official development aid (ODA); and non-concessional resources, typically in the form of loans on commercial terms, falling outside ODA. In the World Bank, the IDA (International Development Association) is responsible for the former. The regional development banks have special funds for soft loans extended under ODA conditions (see Chapter 5).

There have been changes in the balance between *normative* and *operational* activities throughout the development of the multilateral aid system. The normative activities comprise influence on the content of and the agenda for international relations among states, enterprises and organizations; promotion of international understanding and agreements on common values, for example, about protecting vulnerable groups such as refugees and children; and setting international minimum standards and regulations for trade and other forms of economic exchange. The operational activities comprise implementation of aid projects and programmes, including technical assistance and advice on policy; and financing development and emergency relief projects. In the interface between normative and operational activities lie partly the surveillance function that some multilateral organizations have in relation to member countries' economic and social policies, and partly the technical and political advice that the multilateral organizations extend to member countries. These advisory activities are extended through technical assistance, which means that the content is often normative, while the form is operational.

Is all this foreign aid? If we examine the multilateral organizations' mandates and way of functioning, many normative activities should not be considered aid. When the decision-making organs in the UN's specialized agencies, such as the ILO (International Labour Organization) and the WHO (World Health Organization), approve policies about workers' safety, child labour, measures and standards of health, quarantine regulations, and so on, these apply in principle to all member states. This is also the case for the whole series of UN conferences on children, women, social development, environment and development, population, urbanization, HIV/AIDS, and so on. The political decisions are not directed exclusively towards developing countries and are therefore not formally aid. However, the choice of subjects has increasingly been oriented towards developing countries, and the approved policies have been followed up with technical assistance for implementing these policies and fulfilling the norms in the weakest member countries. Thus the normative activities in the UN system have increasingly come to determine the basis for foreign aid.

The same applies to the multilateral development banks, but there are differences. Since the 1980s, the development banks have received a clearer role in determining and monitoring developing countries' economic policies. During the whole post-war period, the IMF (International Monetary Fund) has performed such a role in relation to member countries' balance of payments and debt situation. Because of the IMF's focus on short-term capital flows, this is not normally considered to be development aid. In the 1990s, however, the IMF extended a greater amount of aid than the UN Development Programme (see below). The World Bank and the regional development banks have combined long-term development financing with still more politically oriented advice, which during the 1980s, under structural adjustment, represented the views of the 'international community' on correct and necessary economic policy. In the 1990s, this role was expanded to a leading one in relation to broad political issues such as good governance and poverty reduction, which are highly normative, ideological and value-based issues. Still, in the case of the governance of the World Bank itself – where the power of capital has formal and real influence – the international community is identical with the donor community.

Taken together, the various poles in the multilateral aid system have moved towards each other in the balance between normative and operational activities: the UN system has moved from a normative mandate to involvement in more operational activities. The World Bank has maintained and expanded its involvement in operational activities, but at the same time plays more explicitly normative roles in ensuring the right economic and social policies in developing countries. This has been described as the migration of tasks from the UN system to the World Bank, but this is incorrect, partly because the World Bank is formally a part of the UN system, but mainly because both the World Bank and the actual UN system have extended their tasks.

The important factor in this process – where the development banks and the UN system seem to both approach and overlap each other – is the powers behind it. We describe the reasons for the increasing complexity in the rest of this chapter. The complexity and size of the UN system can be summarized in the following way (Bergesen and Lunde 1998). The UN has:

- Sixteen specialized agencies such as the FAO (UN Food and Agriculture Organization), the WHO, the ILO, UNESCO (UN Educational, Scientific, and Cultural Organization), and UNIDO (UN Industrial Development Organization), as well as the World Bank and the IMF. The World Bank comprises both an aid organization (the IDA) and a bank (the IBRD). The difference here lies in the loan conditions, not in the policies and

procedures. These specialized agencies are all formally independent of the UN and have their own statutes, mandates, leading organs, secretariats and budgets. Formally, they must report to ECOSOC (UN Economic and Social Council), which has the mandate but not the power to coordinate all the UN's economic and social activities.
- Eleven funds and programmes such as the UNDP (UN Development Programme), UNICEF (UN Children's Fund), UNEP (UN Environmental Programme), the WFP (World Food Programme), and UNCTAD (UN Conference on Trade and Development). These 'organizations' are formally under ECOSOC, but they have their own mandates, leading organs, secretariats and budgets.
- Eleven commissions under ECOSOC are mainly discussion forums that work with social development; population; sustainable development; women's status; renewable energy; science and technology, etc.
- Five regional commissions make socio-economic analyses and discuss development questions for each of their regions: Africa, Latin America, etc.
- Two High Commissioners, the UNHCR (UN High Commissioner for Refugees) and the UN High Commissioner for Human Rights. The UNHCR has developed a separate network of offices, programmes, and activities, but both are under the General Assembly and ECOSOC.

The complexity is enhanced by two difficult and intertwined factors: the UN's tasks and institutions have increased, but its resources have declined in real terms since the 1970s. Despite the changing world order – and hence the changing demands on the UN – practically no UN agency has been dissolved in the spirit of 'thank you for a job well done'.

## Political Expectations for Multilateral Aid

On the basis of the literature on the history of multilateral aid (see Bergesen and Lunde 1998), a number of phases can be defined for the development of the UN system and the World Bank, as in Table 7.1.

In Chapter 4, we discussed the development of the dominant aid strategies where the UN and especially the World Bank played leading roles. Here, we concentrate the discussion on the political interests that lie behind the various developments in the UN system and the World Bank and focus on the situation up until the end of the Cold War in 1989. The situation in the 1990s and beyond is discussed later in this chapter.

That the UN was established with one country, one vote as its basic decision-making principle was not originally due to a demand from the poor and marginalized developing countries. It was the victors from the Second World War and the dominant economies, with the USA in the lead, that wanted a universal organization with maximum legitimacy to integrate all the countries and states in the world in order to ensure peace and stability. At the same time, the USA and Great Britain both made sure that the victors maintained controlling power in the form of the veto right in the UN Security Council, and that economic functions were managed by three institutions as agreed at Bretton Woods in 1944: the IMF, the World Bank and the international monetary system.

The UN system was also assigned a role in economic and social development that was based on divisions according to sector and function among existing and new specialized agencies in the UN: the ILO (1919), UNESCO (1946), the FAO (1946), the WHO (1948), and several smaller organizations covering telecommunication (1865), meteorology (1873), air transport (1947), shipping (1959), and so on. In addition, the UN secretariat was assigned duties within statistics and economic analysis (also in the regional commissions) as well as economic coordination via ECOSOC, which formally has a status in the UN charter similar to that of the much more powerful Security Council.

The legitimacy of the UN system was thus originally based on universality. Inter-state conflicts were to be solved through the General Assembly's and the Security Council's political and military power, and global economic and social questions would be analysed and negotiated in the economic agencies that were divided according to sector and function, which also had the world (and not only developing countries) as their workplace. It was thus the *normative* tasks that dominated the UN system's original agenda. This was reflected by the approval of the Universal Declaration of Human Rights in 1948.

At the end of the 1940s, when the world was divided between East and

**Table 7.1** Development of the UN system and the World Bank

| The UN system | The World Bank |
|---|---|
| 1945: One country, one vote | 1945: Votes according to capital contributions |
| 1945–55: From collaboration to Cold War: abandoned aspirations of unity | 1945–48: Post-war reconstruction<br>1948–58: Infrastructure loans |
| 1955–70: Superpower rivalry over the post-colonial independent states | 1958–68: Creation of development organization, IDA |
| 1970–90: Changing world orders: New International Economic Order; neo-liberalism; unipolar world; globalization | 1968–80: Poverty alleviation<br>1980–90: Structural adjustment and policy reform; self-contained development projects |
| 1990s: Proliferation of issues and organizational reforms | 1990s: Proliferation of issues and functions; leading development agency through internal reforms |

West, and when the decolonialized developing countries began to mobilize their voting power (for example, through establishment of the Non-Aligned Movement in 1955), the USA and its Western allies chose to create their own institutions to take responsibility for both political security (NATO) and economic integration (first, the Marshall Plan and then the OEEC, which later became the OECD). It is especially significant in the context of foreign aid that the answer to decolonization in Asia and Africa, and the Latin American countries' demands for support, was the establishment of the International Development Association (IDA) in 1960, an organization under Western control in the World Bank, instead of an organization under broader international control in the UN. For several years, leading developing countries had demanded establishment of a special UN fund for economic development (SUNFED), but the West refused.

The first UN conference on trade and development (UNCTAD) in 1964 was the first global sign of developing countries' attempts to use the UN system's universality to improve conditions for their integration in the world economy. Already in the 1950s, Latin American states had used the UN's regional economic commission (ECLA) to present analyses of the unequal trade between central and peripheral countries and its consequences in the form of underdevelopment. In 1966, the UNDP was established to finance and coordinate the UN system's technical assistance to developing countries. In spite of an agreement made in 1970 between the industrial and developing countries to give the UNDP a really central role, however, the organization has never received sufficient resources and power over the UN's specialized agencies to ensure coordinated UN aid in the economic and social areas.

In the 1960s, the UN system stagnated in relation to creating a new role (Jackson 1969). The Western industrial countries had created their own institutions, including the European Coal and Steel Union, which was the predecessor of the EC and the EU. The Eastern industrial countries were busy industrializing nationally, and establishing a socialist division of labour internationally. The UN was considered to be a Western organization. The Soviet Union was not interested in assuming any responsibility for financing decolonialization and development. This was considered to be the former colonial powers' and the USA's responsibility. The developing countries had not yet begun to act as a bloc. ECLA and UNCTAD published critical analyses of the dominating international economic system, but the effect was very limited, for one reason because marked economic growth took place through increasing trade and direct foreign investments *within* the centre, that is, between the USA, Western Europe and, gradually, Japan.

The UN system thus first received renewed political legitimacy after the economic crisis within the USA-led world order (called Pax Americana) at the start of the 1970s: the formal breakdown of the monetary system based on gold and the dollar in 1971 and the dramatic increases in oil prices in 1973–74. With a suddenness that surprised everyone, the developing countries succeeded in 'G-77' – the group of 77 developing countries – in taking the initiative in the UN and calling an extraordinary meeting of the UN General Assembly to approve a programme for a New International Economic Order (NIEO): more reasonable prices for developing countries' exports of raw materials; access to industrial countries' markets for developing countries' exports; regulation of transfers of technology to developing countries and of the activities of the transnational enterprises; and increasing aid to developing countries (to at least 0.7 per cent of the rich countries' gross national product).

All the NIEO demands involved changes primarily in *international* economic conditions, so that developing countries – that is, those in power in developing countries – would receive a larger part of the profits from global economic integration. Therefore, some NIEO supporters (also in the North) considered the simultaneous demand for *redistribution* of income in developing countries to be an attempt by Western industrial countries to shift the focus from international to national conditions. The demand for redistribution lay behind both the strategy for fulfilling poor people's basic needs that was first developed by the ILO (see Chapter 2), and World Bank President Robert McNamara's speech on exploiting the productivity of the poor for global economic progress.

Seen in a historical perspective, both the NIEO demands and the basic-needs strategy gave the UN system and multilateral aid as a whole increased political legitimacy. However, this legitimacy was distributed very differently: developing countries demanded NIEO; the USA and the large Western industrialized countries demanded redistribution within developing countries and national policies in developing countries that did not discriminate against transnational enterprises; and only the new important actors on the international scene (the Nordic and other like-minded donor countries and the national and international NGOs) demanded that both demands should be partially fulfilled simultaneously.

The NIEO negotiations were without result, and this, combined with the second round of increases in oil prices in 1979 and the international debt crisis around 1980, meant that the political legitimacy of the multilateral organizations radically changed character. The Western industrial countries finally gave up on the UN as a negotiating forum in the economic area, except for the trade organization, GATT, which in 1994 was transformed into the WTO. The Eastern industrial countries considered the whole NIEO question as a matter between the West and the former colonies and maintained a very low profile in the economic and social work of the UN. And the developing countries gradually lost faith in the UN, as no results were forthcoming. However, the NIEO negotiations continued into the 1980s – for example, in the form of negotiations for international codes of conduct for the transfer of technology and transnational enterprises' activities. This was partly because of the inertia caused by the hope of the developing countries' negotiators and diplomats for even the smallest breakthrough, and partly because of the UN secretariats' wish to legitimize their own normative activities in the economic area.

We have described earlier how the IMF's and especially the World Bank's political legitimacy increased greatly in the West through their new role of solving economic crises through narrowly defined stabilization and structural adjustment programmes. These programmes were offered to or forced on governments in developing countries as conditions for new loans and debt relief. For the IMF, this was a continuation of a responsibility dictated by its mandate, whereas macro-economic crisis-solving was new for the World Bank in comparison to the more far-sighted rationale of the 1970s: accelerated inclusion of small farmers in developing countries' rural areas in an integrated world economy. The transition to crisis-solving was still not completed when the World Bank published a report in 1981, *Accelerated Development in Sub-Saharan Africa* (World Bank 1981). This report turned out to be purely wishful thinking in the light of the actual decrease in income per capita in Africa in the 1980s.

At the close of the 1990s, the multilateral organizations thus stood at a crossroads (Haq et al. 1995). Political support for the UN system was at an all-time low, because the UN did not play any central role in the three great changes in the world order: the collapse of the Soviet Union and the political changes in East Europe and Central Asia; the rapid economic growth in East and South Asia; and globalization and standardization of economic policy in developing countries through structural adjustment programmes. The World Bank played an important role in the latter change, but received considerable criticism from industrial and developing countries, as well as international and local NGOs, for the continuing increase of poverty and political oppression in many developing countries.

## Size and Composition of Multilateral Aid

Figure 7.1 shows the long-term trends in disbursements of concessional aid from the UN, international financial institutions (mainly the World Bank and the regional development banks), and the EU (aid managed by the European Commission, excluding aid from EU member states). The decline since 1995, which is carried mainly by the UN but also by the multilateral development banks, is significant, since the data are for net disbursements at current prices.

Total annual multilateral development aid has increased in current prices from about US$13.5 billion in 1990 to about US$19 billion in the last half of the 1990s. Despite the explosive increase in private capital flows to developing countries that reached a high of almost US$250 billion in the mid-1990s; despite a 16 per cent fall in real terms in total development aid between 1992 and 1996 (equal to a decrease of US$3.7 billion); despite the fact that multilateral aid was only about one-third of total development aid;

and despite the magnitude of the need for aid (expressed in the number of poor, low gross national products, enormous environmental problems, and so on), multilateral aid organizations are now engaged in 'big business' of a magnitude that is unprecedented for international organizations.

In 1999, Western countries (DAC members) channelled US$18.5 billion through multilateral organizations. Table 7.2 summarizes a number of trends in multilateral aid financing.

- DAC countries are *the* providers of multilateral aid resources, and the EU and EU member countries provide the bulk of multilateral financing. The declining EU share between 1996 and 1999 was due to extraordinary Japanese and US contributions to the Asian Development Bank (AsDB) in the wake of the financial crisis in East Asia in 1997–98.
- In 1996, three multilateral organizations were of equal size, each channelling some US$4.5 billion in concessional aid: the UN system; the World Bank (mainly IDA); and the EU (excluding aid from individual EU members). The decreasing allocations through the UN in 1999 reflect a long-term declining trend, whereas the World Bank's smaller receipts of ODA in 1999 is due more to the timing of disbursements from donor countries to the IDA.
- The large and increasing allocations to the EU as a regional channel for multilateral aid represent a long-term strategy. EU leaders, the Commission and donor countries with large aid budgets seek to turn all EU member countries into aid providers by making aid a part of regular EU activities. Aid through the European Development Fund (reserved for the African, Caribbean and Pacific countries under the Lomé Conventions) constituted

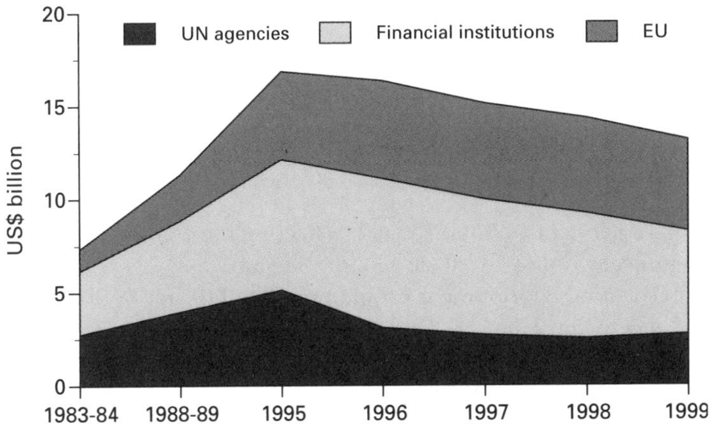


**Figure 7.1** Concessional flows by multilateral organizations (*source*: OECD/DAC 2001, Table 17)

**Table 7.2** ODA from DAC countries to multilateral organizations, 1996 and 1999. Net disbursements (million US$).

| Organization | 1996 | 1999 |
|---|---|---|
| UN agencies | 4,372 | 3,646 |
| of which: | | |
| • UNDP | 903 | 713 |
| • UNICEF | | 351 |
| • WFP | 547 | 281 |
| • UNHCR | | 330 |
| World Bank Group | 4,353 | 2,914 |
| of which: | | |
| • IDA | 3,985 | 2,834 |
| Regional development banks | 1,307 | 5,007 |
| of which: | | |
| • African Development Bank | 132 | 355 |
| • Asian Development Bank | 799 | 4,148 |
| • Inter-American Development Bank | 376 | 360 |
| EU | 4,600 | 4,978 |
| of which: | | |
| • European Development Fund | 1,184 | 1,920 |
| Other multilateral organizations | 1,715 | 1,972 |
| of which: | | |
| • IFAD | | 53 |
| • IMF | | 511 |
| Total | 16,347 | 18,517 |
| of which: from EU members | 11,303 | 9,947 |
| Multilateral ODA from non-DAC countries | 268 | 386 |

*Source:* OECD/DAC 1998: Tables 23 and 43; 2001: Tables 15 and 35. Data for 1996 are not available for all organizations.

only 30–40 per cent of total EU aid, reflecting the EU wish to be present as a significant donor in all developing regions.

- The UN's central development programme (UNDP) received some 20 per cent of aid to the UN and only some 4–5 per cent of total multilateral aid. The UNDP's declining income raises a serious question about its capacity to maintain its primary strength: its presence in all developing countries as reflected in its offices in some 120 countries. UNICEF's low share of aid from DAC countries is compensated for in part by voluntary contributions raised by national committees in donor countries.

- Table 7.2 shows concessional funding only. The UN's small and declining shares are accentuated when non-concessional lending is included. It is noteworthy that in 1999 the IMF, which is not a development organization, received US$0.5 billion for concessional aid, which could make it a more significant actor than the UNDP even in development aid.

Figure 7.2 shows in more detail the annual development aid from the multilateral organizations to developing countries. The figure demonstrates that there are not three equally large multilateral aid organizations (the UN, the World Bank and the EU), but that two organizations are clearly dominant in financial terms: the World Bank and the EU.

It should be noted that Figure 7.2 does not include the World Bank's non-concessional lending, which is almost three-fourths of the World Bank's total annual loan agreements and payments, nor does it include (for recent years) the UN agencies' extra-budgetary resources. For example, in 1978 (after the financial crisis in East Asia), the World Bank made a single loan agreement with South Korea for US$5 billion on commercial terms. This involves the World Bank as both bank and development organization, but it is not development aid. The UNDP channelled in 1996 a total of US$1.476 million, which included projects that the UNDP administered but which were partly financed by governments in, for example, Latin America. These projects cannot be considered as UNDP activities, and they are therefore excluded from OECD statistics. This emphasizes the difficulties described in Chapter 5 in gaining an overview of development aid's size and composition.

Nevertheless, the total figures for the financial flows through the World Bank and the UNDP are important in order to understand the position of

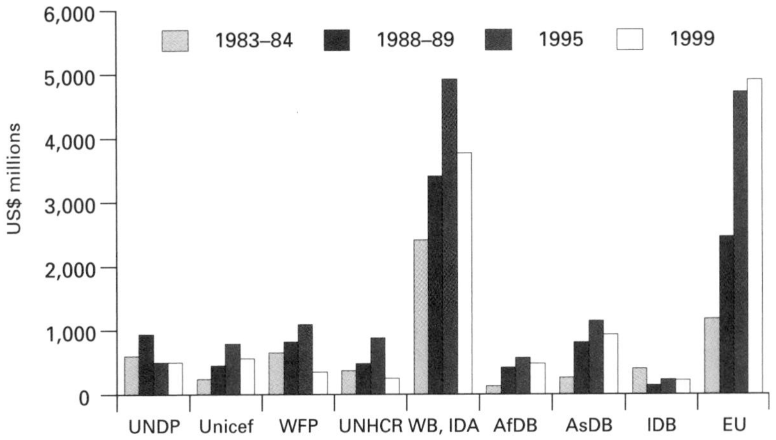


**Figure 7.2** Concessional flows by selected multilateral organizations, selected years (*source*: OECD/DAC 2001, Table 17)

these organizations in international aid. The Bank, especially, places its total organization (money and staff) behind its statements, analyses, policy recommendations, and so on – in other words, behind its demand to be considered the most important development organization in the world. The Bank's procedures for preparing and monitoring projects are the same for the IDA and IBRD projects. Another indicator of the Bank's importance is that the average size of new loan projects in 1997–98 was US$100 million (139 million for IBRD projects, and 55 million for IDA projects). If this is compared with UN projects, which have between a few thousand and at most some few million dollars per project, it is natural that most governments in developing countries relate to the World Bank and the UN with different degrees of seriousness.

Figure 7.2 shows the increasing importance of the UNHCR and the WFP within the UN until the end of the 1990s as a result of the increasing number of refugees in Africa, Asia and Europe. It is also an indication of food aid's double role: emergency relief for an increasing number of people suffering from emergencies resulting from political conflicts and from natural catastrophes, and export of surplus production of grains, especially from North America. The figure also confirms the financial crisis that has hit these humanitarian organizations in recent years as a result of the serious crises in the regions near donor countries, especially in Europe.

## Financing Multilateral Aid

Financing multilateral aid depends on political decisions about the size of total aid in the Western donor countries, as well as its distribution between bilateral and multilateral aid. The size of multilateral aid can thus be judged in relation to selected countries' bilateral aid. The Scandinavian countries (Denmark, Norway and Sweden) administrate through their three *bilateral* aid organizations (Danida, NORAD and SIDA) aid that is comparable to the total aid of the UN system. French bilateral aid is larger than the UN's and EU's aid and the World Bank's (IDA's) concessional aid (Bergesen and Lunde 1998).

Table 7.3 shows four comparable sources of aid financing for multilateral organizations: Japan, the USA, Germany and the four front-runners that have met the UN aid target of 0.7 per cent of GDP: Denmark, Netherlands, Norway and Sweden. These four sources of aid provided the multilateral organizations with two-thirds of their total income.

Despite their comparable significance as funders of multilateral aid, the four countries or groups of countries have widely different preferences within the multilateral system (see Figure 7.3). The four like-minded countries provide a disproportionately large share of the UN's voluntary funding, which is well in line with their 'small country status' and their general foreign policies. For Germany, the EU is the primary 'multilateral' partner, which

**Table 7.3** ODA from DAC countries to multilateral organizations, 1999, net disbursements (million US$).

| Countries | World Bank | Regional banks | UN agencies | EU | Other multi-lateral | Total multi-lateral |
|---|---|---|---|---|---|---|
| Four front-runners | 541 | 186 | 989 | 409 | 423 | 2,527 |
| Germany | 416 | 96 | 325 | 1,317 | 84 | 2,238 |
| Japan | 161 | 3,689 | 728 | - | 270 | 4,848 |
| USA | 800 | 435 | 594 | - | 468 | 2,297 |
| Other DAC | 996 | 601 | 1,010 | 3,252 | 727 | 6,607 |
| Total DAC | 2,914 | 5,007 | 3,646 | 4,978 | 1,972 | 18,517 |

*Source:* OECD/DAC 2001: Table 15

reflects German interests as a leading EU partner. The preferences of Japan and the USA for the multilateral development banks also reflect their global interests and international economic policies. In fact, the unusually large Japanese contribution to the AsDB in 1999 conceals Japan's increasing role in the World Bank: during the 1990s, Japan provided almost one-fourth of the funds for IDA.

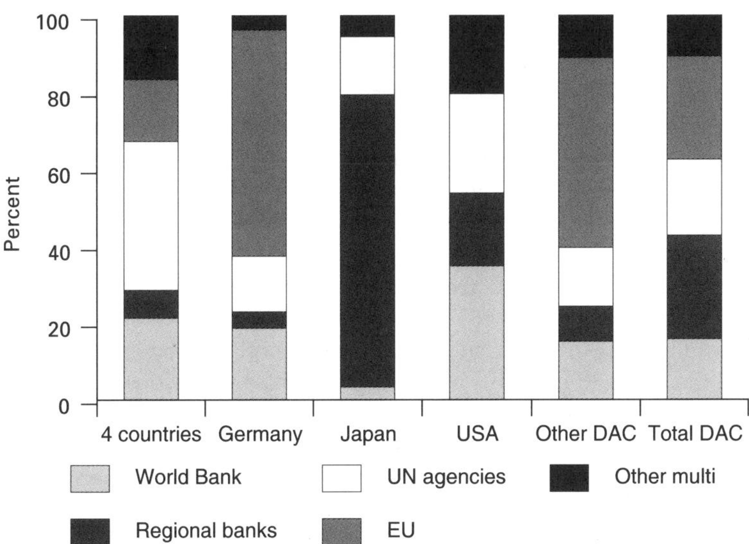


**Figure 7.3** ODA from DAC countries to multilateral organizations, 1999 (*source*: OECD/DAC 2001, Table 15)

Bergesen and Lunde (1998) have shown that the differences between the countries become clear when we look at how the core resources of the UNDP, the UNFPA and UNICEF are financed. In 1995, Scandinavia and Holland financed 42 per cent of the OECD's contribution to these three central UN agencies, whereas the total share of the large donors – France, Japan and Germany – was only 30 per cent. The differences in willingness to finance are illustrated even more glaringly when we look at the contributions per capita in the same countries. Scandinavians gave ten times as much as Americans in multilateral aid and sixteen times as much to the UN. Scandinavians gave more than Germans to the World Bank, but twelve times as much as Germans to the UN. Scandinavians gave twice as much as the French to the World Bank, but sixteen times as much to the UN. Finally, Bergesen and Lunde made a revealing though hypothetical calculation of the funds the UN system would have available if the four large countries (France, Japan, Germany and the USA) gave just as much per capita as the Scandinavian countries: US$25.6 billion annually – compared to the total of US$3–4 billion that the UN received from OECD/DAC countries annually at the end of the 1990s.

A final aspect of financing of the UN system is the balance between *core* contributions and *supplementary* contributions. The UN agencies' *aid* activities are financed mainly through voluntary contributions, primarily from governments in member countries. Decisions about the use and priorities of these funds are made by the leading organs of these agencies. Activities are also financed by fixed contributions that are used for activities that have been agreed upon. These funds are made available by member governments and others. During the 1990s, core contributions to the UN's operational development programmes (especially the UNDP, the UNFPA and UNICEF) decreased in both current and real terms, whereas the supplementary contributions increased in the beginning of the 1990s and thereafter stagnated or decreased.

The most important suppliers of supplementary contributions vary for the different agencies. For the UNDP, they consist of cost-sharing, where governments – especially in Latin America and the Middle East – contribute to programmes that are led and implemented by the UNDP. For UNICEF, they include considerable income from the sale of Christmas cards. Similarly, financing of the UN's specialized agencies consists of operational aid activities, partly from a share of their member-financed core budget (about US$300 million annually), and partly from supplementary contributions (US$600–700 million annually).

It is obvious that the possibilities for the UN to assign priorities and manage its efforts are poor when such a limited share consists of core contributions, and when resources must be divided among and used by many different agencies. All in all, there are many agencies, large demands and needs – and rather a small amount of money.

## The UN System: Strengths and Weaknesses

The UN uses at least five forums and instruments to promote development. The five types of interventions range from a global, symbolic level to operational fieldwork. The five aid forms and forums discussed in the following sections are: the UN General Assembly; UN's negotiation platforms; thematic UN conferences and summit meetings; technical assistance from UN's specialized agencies; and development aid from UN's funds and programmes.

*Debate and decisions in the UN General Assembly* Delegates from all countries in the world meet annually in New York for several months to discuss the international situation. In regard to development questions, a maximum of consensus is sought. While the UN General Assembly can perhaps be attributed a certain importance in questions of security and in normative areas, its significance in regard to initiatives in the area of development is almost non-existent. This is unavoidable with typically 150 items on the annual agenda and with a structure where the smallest and poorest countries comprise a majority. The same applies to the UN Economic and Social Council (ECOSOC), which functions as a mini-General Assembly. These large and unwieldy forums have only achieved symbolic value in international cooperation.

The UN General Assembly attempts to create the framework for the UN's development aid through analysis and decisions every three years about the 'UN's operational development activities'. The UN's operational activities should be universal, voluntary, free, neutral and multilateral. They should also meet the needs of developing countries with flexibility, for their benefit, and at their request in accordance with their own development policies and priorities. The demand for control by the developing countries themselves permeates the resolutions. Consideration of state sovereignty is also sacred. Governments in recipient countries have the main responsibility for coordinating and integrating all foreign aid. Even when UN agencies are encouraged to create a better division of labour among themselves, it should happen 'under coordination by the governments'. Formulation of a 'country strategy note' to be used for UN aid should be voluntary and led by the developing countries that wish to have such a framework. The UN can promote establishment of forums and mechanisms for use in policy dialogue between the parties involved in the development process, but only when the UN is requested to do so by the governments. The UN should support, within the national priorities, the drafting of frameworks for strengthening civil society and voluntary organizations when this is in accordance with government wishes.

The General Assembly constantly encourages simplification and standardization of the operational procedures for the UN's development system, especially through greater consistency in the budgets. Serious concern is expressed about the continuous lack of resources for the UN's operational development activities. The relation to the UN's specialized agencies is special, because these are led by their own political organs. The General Assembly can therefore only recommend that the whole UN system support the resident coordinator, who coordinates UN aid in each country. The best achievable situation is that the coordinator, who is normally the UNDP's leader in the country, be allowed to propose adjustments in the UN agencies' programmes in the country so that they agree with the country strategy note.

The General Assembly has not had an initiating function (Childers and Urquhart 1994; Alger 1998). The same is true of the elaborate procedure for approval of 'international development strategies' for whole decades attempted by the UN since the 1960s. They have been broad, non-obligating collections of items that were on the development agenda during the years preceding approval. Thus they have not had any significance during their respective decades for the implementation of the UN's own development activities.

*Negotiations about international regulations* Attempts to use the UN to negotiate binding regulations for international, development-oriented, economic relationships accelerated, as described, during the second half of the 1970s within the framework of negotiations for a New International Economic Order (NIEO). The actual attempts at regulation aimed especially at creating a code of conduct for transnational enterprises and other private actors, where the individual member states were supposed to sanction the rules by including the international agreements in national regulations. Negotiations for international codes of conduct regarding transfers of technology and transnational enterprises ended without result. This was inevitable, because the dominant states could not accept them. Negotiations between so many states could not establish effective regulations regarding so complicated and uncontrollable areas as technology transfer and the transnational enterprises' investment practices (Engberg-Pedersen 1982).

Attempts at regulation that were in the interests of the USA and Western Europe have been more successful. The UN's negotiating platform for trade (the GATT, now incorporated in the WTO, which was established outside the UN) has been used to negotiate international trade agreements (eight in all, one after the other). In contrast to the GATT, the WTO is the first real negotiating organization – in principle, universal, but clearly reflecting international power relationships (Krueger 1997). Within the framework of the GATT, the USA, the EU/Western Europe and Japan usually concluded negotiations; the result was then presented to the rest of the world for acceptance. As an international organization, the WTO is used as a platform for bilateral or regional negotiations about interpretations of international agreements and about purely this-for-that agreements.

The UN has been used more regularly in attempts at regulation through the very few UN conferences within areas where new global problems demand global solutions – for example, a convention on child labour in the ILO where the rich countries could use the UN to limit the 'freedom' of developing countries to exploit children. Another example is a WHO convention on breast-milk substitutes, also influenced by an ethical attitude that did not interfere with the national affairs of industrial countries.

Most optimism can be mobilized in relation to environmental issues, although regulatory efforts do not match the magnitude of global environmental problems. At the UN Conference on Environment and Development in Rio in 1992, the states approved two global environment conventions, one on climate change and the other on biodiversity. They have yet to be tested in relation to both precise goals and implementation of sanctions – that is, interventions beyond political declarations about goals for reducing harm to the environment. With regard to follow-up instruments, the Montreal protocol on limiting the use of ozone-destroying substances has come furthest. A fund has been established to compensate industry in developing countries for technological changes that can reduce emissions of harmful gases. The Kyoto agreement on $CO_2$ and other greenhouse gases has been engulfed in a storm as a result of the USA's negative attitude, but seems to have survived as a real regulatory effort.

International regulation as a form of intervention by the UN has thus proved useful in three main contexts: trade agreements between states where both negotiation procedures and results point to confirmation of the strong states' influence; environmental questions that are regulated by a combination of political declarations of intent and financial incentives; and special social questions where ethical considerations are allowed to manifest themselves (Desai and Redfern 1995). International state control of the transnational economic actors, however, is highly unlikely, whether it involves banks, productive enterprises or service companies. The conflicts of interest between countries are too great for this, and the US-dominated world order is based too much on neo-liberalistic principles for market-based economic integration.

*Global conferences and summit meetings* Since the beginning of the 1970s, there has been a long series of UN conferences and summit meetings. Activity was more intense during the first half of the 1990s: Children (New York, 1991), Environment and Development (Rio, 1992), Human Rights (Vienna, 1993), Population and Development (Cairo, 1994), Social Development (Copenhagen, 1995), Women and Development (Beijing, 1995), Urbanization (Istanbul, 1996), plus a series of smaller conferences in between on food security and nutrition, reform of the public sector, and so on. In recent years, these big events have been replaced by special thematic sessions of the UN General Assembly organized in New York, such as the conference on HIV/AIDS in 2001. In 2002, an unsuccessful conference on sustainable development ('Rio + 10') took place in South Africa, and a partly successful conference on financing development was held in Mexico. In almost all cases, both political goals and plans of action are prepared, primarily for implementation by states supported by the UN and other international organizations. In addition to the few attempts at regulation mentioned above, the conferences and summits have produced four types of results:

COMMON POLITICAL GOALS AND MINIMUM STANDARDS These are directly written into the plans of action and other documents approved by the conferences. The main problem with this type of result is the difficulties involved in setting clear goals, since the plans of action must apply for the whole world. It was possible to a certain extent at the children's summit, certainly because the whole world can agree to be considerate of children's interests. But this summit meeting also revealed the difficulties involved in defining measurable, quantitative goals. One reason for this is that the subsequent follow-up can come to involve goal fulfilment at any price, regardless of relevance in the given local community. This was an important criticism of UNICEF's vaccination campaigns at the end of the 1980s, when all means were used to vaccinate 90 per cent of the infants in the world.

NEW KNOWLEDGE AND INSIGHT This was an important result of the Rio summit, since it boosted environmental consciousness throughout the world. This was especially due to the great work carried out by international NGOs before (and to a lesser degree after) the summit. On the other hand, the Copenhagen summit in 1995 on social development did not produce much new knowledge: NGOs that would have been able to communicate the discussions at the summit meeting to the world at large were not involved; labour market questions were too politically sensitive, in industrial countries as well, to open the way to common insight; and socio-political subjects were generally reasonably well documented long before the summit. The HIV/AIDS conference in 2001 produced no new knowledge but did spread insight into the seriousness of the epidemic. Typically for the UN, it came to be dominated by a diplomatic fight between Western and Arab countries about whether it was legitimate to point out especially vulnerable groups (for example, homosexuals and prostitutes) and to emphasize women's rights.

NEW RESOURCES For twenty years, every UN conference was supposed to lead to establishment of a special fund to finance development aid within the relevant area. Negotiations about money came to dominate the conferences without any results worth mentioning, and almost never led to 'new' money, because industrial countries at most just reallocated the items in their development budgets. It was therefore sensible that the decision was made before the Social Summit in Copenhagen not to discuss more money, even though the Danish government actually led the way with regard to debt relief for the poorest developing countries. This realistic attitude changed, however, before the HIV/AIDS conference, when the UN secretary-general put all his prestige behind the establishment of a special fund with special criteria and procedures for resource allocations. These new procedures, which circumvent the UN's normal institutions, are an attempt to mobilize resources from countries that are critical of the UN, such as the USA, and especially from new actors in the form of the transnational enterprises both within and outside the health industry. However, it is very doubtful whether additional resources will result from this resource mobilization drive.

A COMMON PLAN OF ACTION As already mentioned, almost all UN conferences have approved a plan of action to be implemented globally. However, these plans of action may have done more harm than good. They are never actually carried out. The industrial countries usually consider them to be irrelevant for them, and developing countries are not interested if they are not accompanied by funds. It has therefore typically been the many UN agencies that have been busy demonstrating that their work is in accordance with the many demands of the action plans. At the same time, UN agencies have pressurized developing countries to make more or less relevant national plans and often to establish special institutions to manage the individual UN plans of action. This has seldom been effective and has sometimes made it more difficult for developing countries to work for a nationally cohesive development policy. The plan of action for HIV/AIDS, however, can prove to be an important instrument in advocacy initiatives taken by international NGOs and national civil society organizations.

UN conferences and summits should primarily be evaluated on the basis of the political goals that they have agreed upon, and the new knowledge and insights produced through their preparation (Singer and Jolly 1995). During the second half of the 1990s, both internally in the UN system and outside it, the expensive and demanding conferences required such an exhausting effort that they were organized only in cities with existing UN secretariats, such as New York and Geneva.

Another question is whether the consensus-seeking purposes of UN conferences are always beneficial. One could imagine that the Social Summit would have had more long-term effects if the state and government leaders who came to Copenhagen acknowledged and declared that they disagreed about many things, instead of compromising themselves to agree on an all-inclusive text. From domestic politics, we know that great political disagreements exist when it comes to such questions as labour market conditions, poverty eradication and social security. How then could the 187 countries that actually participated in Copenhagen, and whose governments each carry political compromises with them on these questions, be able to agree on a precise text that has global relevance?

In such UN negotiations, all attempts are made to limit the number of reservations made by the participating states. Therefore, the *Copenhagen Declaration and Programme of Action* (UN 1995) should be judged in relation to the political goals and the new insights that were reached. As already mentioned, there is not much of the latter, because the idea was more to see all elements in social development in an integrated perspective, which is valuable in itself. The ten commitments, which were the summit's clearest goal, are reasonable but will hardly change social development in developing countries. For example, how can a local opposition force a country's political leaders to live up to the commitment to 'eradicate poverty'? The eighth obligation is the most concrete: 'We commit ourselves to ensuring that when structural adjustment programmes are agreed to they include social development goals, in particular eradicating poverty, promoting full and productive employment, and enhancing social integration.' Around 1990, this would have been a very important obligation, but in 1995, the World Bank itself had begun to use the same terminology.

*Technical assistance from the UN's specialized agencies* The UN's specialized agencies are a mixed group that comprises large, old organizations such as the ILO, the FAO, the UNESCO and the WHO, even larger and stronger organizations such as the IMF and the World Bank, and several smaller, specialized agencies such as UNIDO and the IMO (International Maritime Organization). If we exclude the IMF and the World Bank from the analysis, the following generalizations can be made.

The UN's specialized agencies were established to function as centres of excellence – international centres of knowledge with the best global expertise within each of their sectors: agriculture, labour and employment, health, education, industrial development, shipping, and so on. They all had a norm-setting function, since their leading organs were supposed to establish internationally acceptable and mainly technical norms for making national policies and regulations. In addition, the ILO in particular had/has a special negotiating role, since states negotiate with the labour market's parties in order to approve conventions for worker safety and other elements comprising a set of regulations within international labour policy.

In the 1960s, the specialized agencies began to extend technical assistance to the increasing number of independent developing countries. The idea was that this work should be financed by the UNDP on the basis of the following model: the UNDP had offices in all developing countries. These entered into agreements with the recipient governments for five-year country programmes. The projects within this programme were implemented by the UN's specialized agencies. The Western donors should thus provide funds to the UNDP, which should plan, finance and coordinate the total UN system's technical assistance.

The system broke down during the 1970s and 1980s (Danida 1991). Technological development in individual sectors, the increasing differences between developing countries and the improved direct communication throughout the world made the role as knowledge centre unrealistic and unnecessary. Other development actors with far more money built up their own technical expertise: the World Bank had more staff members than the specialized agencies within each of their sectors. Bilateral donors employed their own specialists and drew on national consultants in key sectors. The specialized agencies sought funds directly from donors, which financed specific projects directly, and this undermined the UNDP's coordinating role.

The result was 'projectitis' – the specialized agencies in their search for financing sent experts from, for example, a project in Zambia to the next project in Nepal. The projects had unrealistic goals, which were supposed to be achieved in one to three years within a financial framework of less than US$1 million. This was used to pay expert salaries, reports of varying quality, project administration and study tours for staff members in recipient countries' sector ministries. Gradually, many fine specialists sat in the specialized agencies' headquarters in Geneva, Rome, Paris or Vienna with little opportunity to use their knowledge because few resources were provided to ensure good technical support for the small, spread-out projects.

The mass media in industrial countries often view the placement of most of the specialized agencies' staff in their headquarters as a problem, but there is nothing wrong in this – they need to be there in order to fulfil their analytical and norm-setting functions. Many superficial critics of the UN want the WHO's doctors, for example, to be out in the village clinics where people are dying because of lack of educated personnel and supplies. But the WHO and the other specialized agencies should not be in the field. Chasing after just such small projects is what has undermined their intended function.

An analysis (Danida 1991) has pointed out, on the basis of a comprehensive study of eleven multilateral organizations in four developing countries, that the UN's specialized agencies should concentrate on capacity-building in the relevant line ministries in developing countries. This would demand establishment of technically based contacts of longer duration – for example, between the health ministry and the relevant specialists in the WHO's headquarters.

Some of the specialized agencies have also experienced crises for other reasons than projectitis. In the case of the FAO, a poor and corrupt leader established a 'foreign ministry' at the headquarters. All contacts between the technical staff in Rome and their colleagues in the field had to go through this filter, which only increased the distance between field and headquarters. UNIDO, the UN's industrial development organization, experienced a special crisis when its original faith in central planning and state management of industrial development was renounced by most developing countries. Two analyses in which we were involved (Danida 1992, 1997) proposed concentration on technical assistance to the political and strategic level, as well as to the institutional framework for industrial development within selected sub-sectors. UNIDO should build a critical mass of expertise within these areas. Subsequently, we observed that UNIDO had actually succeeded in concentrating both initiatives and capacity so that more relevant advice could be offered to developing countries (Danida 1997).

The situation for the UN's specialized agencies at present is not good. The large-scale 'Nordic UN Project' proposed in 1991 (Nordic UN Project 1991) that the specialized agencies should give more emphasis to their normative role. However, this is hardly realistic, since neither the industrialized nor the developing countries are interested in giving the specialized agencies such a role, except within very specialized aspects of the agencies' efforts (for example, the WHO's work concerning the length of quarantine periods). The specialized agencies cannot be global centres of knowledge, but they could move towards becoming global centres of experience within selected technical-political areas of special relevance for the poorest developing countries. An experience centre should be based on research, gathering of information and analysis of experience with solutions within its field, and the results should be disseminated worldwide in connection with assistance in formulating policy and building capacity. This does not lie very far from the original role of the specialized agencies, but it is probably more realistic.

*The UN's development aid and resource transfers* As already described, the UN also has several funds and programmes that provide aid directly to developing countries, including the UNDP, UNICEF and the WFP. UNICEF symbolizes this aid at its best. UNICEF is a social organization with a relatively clear target group: children and women. It uses three main instruments: financial transfers to support national public services, especially within health and education; technical assistance for capacity-building, usually in connection with the financial projects; and campaigns and political advocacy for the benefit of the target group. With country offices in all developing countries, UNICEF works with all national partners in these countries: the political leadership, the state, civil society and the target group's own organizations. UNICEF works at all levels of society, and from the country's capital, UNICEF's well-known Land Rovers reach the most remote areas.

At the beginning of the 1990s, this very comprehensive approach led to an almost too omnipotent organization. It spread its resources too thinly and could not ensure sustainablity in its social programmes. The organization's image approached that of the self-assured super-actor that did not have time for capacity-building, because so many babies would die in the meantime. As already mentioned, the fulfilment of centrally defined, quantitative goals was the mantra of the organization in the 1980s. A large-scale evaluation in 1991–92 (Engberg-Pedersen and Freeman 1992) financed by Australia, Canada, Denmark and Switzerland, contributed to moving UNICEF's strategic choices towards capacity-building and empowerment of the target group.

As mentioned above, the UNDP was supposed to function as a central coordinator and financing source for all technical assistance via the UN system. Instead, it had the image of a bureaucratic manager of 100–200 small, often ineffective projects in every single developing country. Gradually, as the World Bank's role increased with regard to policy dialogue with developing countries, coordination of foreign aid and extension of technical assistance, the UNDP became more marginalized in the aid world. The organization attempted to find a new role for itself – for example, through aid to two important initiatives at the start of the 1990s.

First, as mentioned earlier, the UNDP began to publish annual reports on *human development*. By focusing on human welfare and opportunities, it gave expression to the growing theoretical criticism of economic growth as the only measure of development. It thus acquired an independent identity in the broad debate. However, the organization has not yet succeeded in manifesting this in operational activities in developing countries that would give it a clear profile and role in the field. Second, the UNDP's projects were increasingly implemented without the participation of the UN's specialized agencies. With a complex mixture of state agencies and temporary units financed by the UNDP, projects were carried out in a way that involved UNDP offices directly in capacity-building within national institutions.

An analysis of the UNDP (Engberg-Pedersen et al. 1996) tried to support these two initiatives. If its proposals were carried out, the UNDP would be able to play a very important role, with a combination of policy advice regarding human development and technical assistance for capacity-building – especially within good governance, where it could support management of public resources and establishment of institutional frameworks for people's participation in national and local decision-making processes. There is still a need for this combination in most developing countries; the analysis, however, proposed adjusting the UNDP's role to fit four main groups of developing countries. These are the small and medium-sized low-income countries, which are the UNDP's main target group; the countries that are in the midst of a transition phase from war to peace, catastrophe to development, or from central planning to market economy; the large low-income countries with relatively well-developed state structures; and the middle-income countries. It should be possible to adjust the UNDP's role in this way without breaking with the organization's universal status as part of the UN system.

The analysis of the UNDP was financed by Denmark, India, Great Britain and Sweden, but it did not lead directly to a clear concentration of the organization's efforts on capacity-building. The reason for this was a combination of a weak top leadership; a staff with capacity within project administration, not capacity-building; many developing countries' interest in using the UNDP's few resources to fill the gaps in various corners of their central administrations; pressure, also in the richer and better functioning developing countries, to maintain the right to receive UNDP aid; and inferior political leadership, since donor countries' representatives in the UNDP's governing bodies typically had limited insight and experience regarding development problems in the field. The UNDP's new administrator, Mark Malloch Brown, began to use the analysis, and during 1999–2000, the UNDP took a positive step in the proposed direction. At present, however, the organization is in a serious financial crisis that can threaten its global role.

In conclusion, each of the UN's major instruments for development cooperation has strengths and weaknesses – but the clear trend is towards dominance by the weaknesses. Despite many valuable efforts to renew and reorganize all aspects of the UN system, it still faces a vicious circle of huge objectives, half-hearted initiatives, lack of capacity to set priorities, dwindling resources, and poor quality in the delivery of existing activities. At the same time, the UN's strength in international development cooperation lies precisely in its diverse instruments and cumbersome participatory procedures. These give it legitimacy in an ever more complex world. When organizations such as UNAIDS or UNICEF manage to translate the norms and policies adopted by the UN General Assembly or UN conferences into operational activities that influence national policy-making in developing countries and have beneficial impacts for the poorest people of the world, they make effective use of the UN's structural capacities.

## The World Bank: Strengths and Weaknesses

Over the years, the World Bank has provided almost one-third of the net, official, bilateral and multilateral resources to developing countries (Gilbert et al. 2000). For this reason, we discuss the role of the Bank throughout this book. In this section, we summarize three trends that have characterized the Bank over the past forty years: expansion of its activities; changing emphasis in its roles and functions; and emerging challenges and limits regarding its delivery of a neo-liberal development model and world view.

The World Bank's original mandate was relatively narrow: to ensure financing for reconstruction and (to a lesser degree) development, partly through insuring private investors against loss, and partly by lending capital to specific projects. In these projects, the World Bank's share was to secure the necessary foreign exchange (Mason and Asher 1973). The World Bank's Articles of Agreement state that the Bank can lend only to *projects*, and that only *economic* criteria are to be used. The Bank has gone far beyond this mandate (George and Sabelli 1994; Lateef 1995; Culpeper 1997; Gilbert and Vines 2000). The constant extension of its activities can be summarized in five dimensions:

1. Size: the World Bank has become by far the largest international development organization in regard to the volume of loans, staff, expertise and organization. It includes an increasing number of country offices in low-income countries, especially in sub-Saharan Africa (Griesgraber and Gunter 1996).

2. Sector focus: the Bank has moved from physical infrastructure, via development in rural areas, to social sectors and environmental and institutional questions, including corruption and governance. In the 1960s, more than two-thirds of the Bank's loans were for economic infrastructure, especially electricity supply and transport. From about 1980, the Bank's loans to the social sectors (population programmes, health, education, and so on) were about 5 per cent of total loans. They increased to 20 per cent in the mid-1990s (Bergesen and Lunde 1998).
3. Subject and policy focus: the World Bank's starting point in infrastructure and macro economy was supplemented early on with agricultural development and gradually with all sectors and political-institutional questions. In recent years, relief efforts have also been added to the agenda, stretching from rebuilding physical infrastructure via delivery of health services to closing financial gaps in state budgets, finance systems and currency accounts (World Bank 1997g).
4. Country focus: the Bank has moved in a circle from Western Europe (1950s), via Western-oriented developing countries (1960s–1980s), to all developing countries and countries in transition from central management to market economy (1990s onwards). Extension to Eastern Europe and the former Soviet republics in the 1990s must be expected to be the last extension of the Bank's borders (Mosley et al. 1995: xxx).
5. Intervention level and type: the Bank has moved from the project level, gradually supplemented with technical assistance, to programme, policy and institutional activities on the macro and sector levels, as well as societal crisis management.

A driving force in this constant extension is the Bank's attempt to attain more goals simultaneously. In recent analyses by Bank insiders (Gilbert and Vines 2000), three roles are discussed: bank, development agency and knowledge producer. M. Naim (1994: 194 ff.) points to four different roles: (1) the Bank as bank, the intermediary between the capital market and borrowers; (2) the Bank as instrument of the large Western industrial countries' foreign policy; (3) the Bank as missionary for changes in the politico-economic behaviour of governments in developing countries; and (4) the Bank as development actor, transferring resources from rich to poor countries. We find this to be a more appropriate description of the Bank's roles, although it pays insufficient attention to the internal dynamics of the Bank as a knowledge-producing organization (Squire 2000). Some of the World Bank's problems in the 1990s can be summarized as difficulties with all four roles.

THE BANK AS BANK Many developing countries that can afford to receive loans from the Bank on non-concessional terms can borrow money almost as cheaply on private international capital markets. Here, borrowers are free of the World Bank's interference in the form of advice and conditionalities.

The financial crisis in East Asia in 1997–78 was sobering to the emerging economies, however, since commercial banks proved to be elusive partners during times of crisis. In support of IMF packages, the Bank provided US$8 billion in short-term liquidity financing to Indonesia, Korea and Thailand in 1997–98. This role as lender of last resort could, however, easily undermine the Bank's capacity to mobilize long-term concessional and non-concessional capital.

THE BANK AS AN INSTRUMENT OF FOREIGN POLICY During the first decades, the World Bank's loan policy reflected the competition between the systems in the East and West. Woods (2000) describes how the Bank was drawn into the Cold War and was under such heavy US influence in the late 1980s that it challenged the 'Bank's status as a multilateral and technical agency' (Woods 2000: 132). It is true that in the 1990s the Bank has extended a certain amount of support to integration of Eastern Europe and the former Soviet Union in the world economy, but the Bank suffers under the West's decreasing interest in the fate of the poorest developing countries and risks being marginalized together with them.

THE BANK AS MISSIONARY The Bank's missionary attitude was most strongly expressed in the structural adjustment programmes from the 1980s. Recognition of the fact that economic structural adjustment was not sufficient to solve low-income countries' problems has led the Bank into several institutional, social and political areas and partnerships where it lacks both capacity and comparative advantages (Nelson 1995). Since the late 1990s, the Bank's political and technical advocacy of *selectivity* in aid allocations in favour of developing countries with 'good' or 'sound' economic management is presented as a knowledge-based concern for effectiveness in poverty reduction. However, it represents just as much an ideology-based reward and punishment strategy that replaces the explicit political allocation criteria under the Cold War. This is discussed further in Chapter 12 on aid impact.

THE BANK AS A DEVELOPMENT AGENCY This role is separate from the bank and missionary roles in its focus on transfer of resources to the poorest countries and people. Through IDA, the Bank has achieved a higher focus on the least developed countries than most large bilateral donors, whose aid allocations are heavily influenced by commercial and political interests. During the 1990s, and especially under the presidency of James Wolfensohn, poverty reduction became the Bank's overriding goal, as reflected in the 1990 and 2000 versions of the *World Development Report* and in the recent, Bank- and IMF-driven national processes of preparing 'poverty reduction strategy papers' (Kanbur and Vines 2000). The challenge lies in mobilizing sufficient human and financial resources to achieve a reduction in absolute global poverty, which has remained stubbornly at 1.2 billion people since the 1980s. If this is not achieved for capacity, political or other reasons, the Bank will lose credibility as the world's leading development agency. This may well threaten its very existence. The Bank has increasingly tied its own survival to poor people's success in pulling themselves out of poverty.

In the 1990s, the Brookings Institution studied the World Bank's history in relation to five different functions, which are not essentially different from the four roles described above: the bank function; the aid function; technical and expert advice; the policy-changing function; and function as a forum for building consensus. The Brookings Institution concluded that the Bank's dilemma in the mid-1990s was that the scope of its substantive activities – its list of programme priorities – had been so extended as to be unrecognizable. There were all kinds of additions and expansions, such as population and gender questions, governance and public sector management, education, and trade with raw materials. The Bank as an organization was wide open for substantive offshoots. New subjects gave prestige, and the dynamics of technological and social change continued to place them on the agenda. The Bank was put on the defensive in relation to both the public and the political leadership; it felt forced to take on new subjects, since important owners of the Bank and interest organizations in the form of NGOs demanded it. The Bank's involvement in these new areas was also spurred on by an attitude of superiority towards the poor quality of the UN system's broad functions. Many in the Bank felt that it must be the responsibility of the 'world's leading development organization' to take in one new area after another.

This process led to four serious challenges for the World Bank, which can be seen as a combination of gaps, dilemmas and conflicts:

1. A gap between goals and resources: If all aspects of social development in all types of developing countries are on the World Bank's self-appointed agenda, it is unavoidable that the result will be a lack of resources for implementation. The World Bank risks catching the typical UN disease: large and ambitious goals and many too few resources. This can threaten delivery, including that of the organization's core services.
2. A gap between goals and competence: this follows directly from the first. The Bank has extended its expertise to almost all sectors and disciplines (for example, with 300–400 environmental specialists), but it is impossible to cover everything. The Bank is still biased towards economists and engineers. In the early 1990s, some 80 per cent of the Bank's senior staff had been trained in economics and finance at institutions in the USA and the UK (Woods 2000: 152). Conversely, we still see many examples of inadequate competence in political science and sociology, considering that the Bank throws itself into reforming public administrations in many different types of developing countries. This gap will become even more visible, since the World Bank wishes to become more directly involved in

implementation of projects and programmes that demand comprehensive expertise in the individual developing country.

3. Contradiction between ideology and practice: in the 1980s, there was a conflict in the World Bank between the neo-liberal ideology, which demanded giving priority to the private sector and market forces, and reality's formal and actual dependence on the state and the public sector, both as the Bank's direct partner and as necessary actor in the development process (p. 4). This conflict proved to be very pronounced in the discrepancy between the structural adjustment programmes' demand for privatization and a reduced state on the one hand, and the loan projects' constant expansion of the state's structure and functions within the physical, financial and social infrastructure and production-generating activities on the other. Mosley et al. (1995: 306) refer to an example of a structural adjustment loan to Malawi, for which the Bank demanded removal of subsidies on chemical fertilizers, which at the same time were a central element in an agricultural development programme that the Bank also supported.
4. Marginalization: the Bank faces – in the midst of its present high point – serious threats of marginalization in relation to the dynamics of the world economy. These dynamics steer capital flows and investments around the poorest countries and groups within the populations that the Bank supports – for example, through sector programmes for the social sectors. Another form of marginalization is related to the weakness of the development paradigm promoted by the Bank. In its move towards a post-Washington consensus, parts of the Bank (led by its former chief economist, Joseph Stiglitz) may have been quite self-critical of the narrowness and limited effects of the structural adjustment programmes that were pushed so strongly in the 1980s and early 1990s. However, the Bank as a whole has relatively little to offer in terms of viable strategic alternatives for development. Its poverty reduction policies are broadened to include empowerment, but the underlying strategies for economic growth are traditional and hard to distinguish from the earlier adjustment programmes. Today, Stiglitz calls for the Bank to put much more emphasis on presenting *alternative* policy options and scenarios in its advice to countries and institutions (2000: 4). But does the Bank staff have the imagination, competence, and intellectual and political space to do this?

An important element in the analysis of the World Bank's history is thus that beneath the political and ideological swings, there lies a strong organization dominated by Western-educated economists, engineers and other technicians. They have had considerable power in the development of the economic infrastructure in most developing countries, of their agricultural policies, public services within the social sectors, public administration's organization and way of functioning, and gradually the formulation of sector policies and societies' judicial-institutional structure. The World Bank's procedures and planning instruments have kept step with these processes only to a certain extent (Fox and Brown 1998). The planning-oriented project cycle was supplemented in the 1980s by structural adjustment programmes and in the 1990s by sector investment programmes. These, however, are all being continually prepared and treated as projects (Jayarajah and Branson 1995; Jayarajah et al. 1996).

For just this reason, it was a big problem for the World Bank's self-perception when a report written in 1992 by one of the Bank's vice-presidents, Willi Wappenhans, concluded that the quality of the projects supported by the Bank was a great problem. The report pointed especially at the Bank's constant preoccupation with *new* loans (World Bank 1992: iii). Prestige and career opportunities were based more on preparing, approving and paying new loans than in ensuring relevance, quality and long-term impact (Green and Toye 1996).

According to Bergesen and Lunde (1998), this represents a change from great self-confidence to acknowledgement of problems in the Bank with regard to its ability to lead projects. From 1950 until far into the 1970s, the Bank's ability within project management was largely above all criticism, which was a central element in the World Bank's image as a success. The Bank's evaluation department (OED) evaluated more than one thousand projects implemented in the 1970s at a value of about US$22 billion in Bank loans and US$67 billion in total investments. The analysis found that 86 per cent of all projects (with 90 per cent of the total value) seemed to have achieved their most important goal and were judged to have been worth the effort, with an economic rate of return (where this was relevant) averaging 18 per cent. During the next decade, the success of the Bank's projects declined, however. In the 1980s, the quality of economic analysis in projects was poor in 13 per cent and only acceptable in 25 per cent of the projects that had been through a cost–benefit analysis.

It was especially embarrassing for the Bank that serious problems with quality and results were revealed with regard to its loans for infrastructure. This was an area in which the Bank had developed a strong reputation during preceding decades: electricity supply, transport, large irrigation systems, water supply and sewerage, and telecommunication. According to Wappenhans's report, the situation, with two-thirds success and one-third fiasco in the Bank-supported projects, was due to a combination of conditions inside the Bank, rapid growth in the project portfolio, and decreasing capacity of recipient countries in crisis.

The World Bank has had great impact on developing countries, both directly through loans, technical assistance and policy advice and pressure, and indirectly as the leader of the international donor community since the 1970s (Ayres 1983). At the same time, the World Bank has received the 'honour' for far more than it actually can take responsibility for. This applies to both praise and criticism. Since the demonstrations against the World Bank in Copenhagen in 1970 and Teresa Hayter's classic analysis *Aid as Imperialism* (1971), many politicians, researchers and NGOs from both industrial and developing countries have accused the World Bank (often together with its sister organization, the IMF) of being responsible for harming the environment, unemployment, rising food prices and so on.

In the 1990s, this changed slowly to a more realistic evaluation of the Bank's influence, which in spite of everything is limited (Adedeji 1995). Mosley et al. concluded in *Aid and Power: The World Bank and Policy-based Lending* that the Bank had a certain amount of power and influence, 'but not as much as the Bank hoped' (1995: 305). Likewise, an analysis of the structural adjustment programmes in sub-Saharan Africa supported by the World Bank concluded that they had limited impact on both economy and poverty seen in relation to other economic forces and processes (Engberg-Pedersen et al. 1996). This realism stands in contrast to the speeches by President Wolfensohn in which he says that the Bank is the most important development organization, having all the poor people in the world as direct clients and coordinating the world's development efforts both in real life through country-specific 'comprehensive development frameworks' and in cyberspace through a 'global development gateway'.

At the conclusion of this chapter and in Chapter 14, we discuss the future prospects for the World Bank in the light of the gap between goals and self-perception on the one hand, and capacity, resources and legitimacy on the other. Is there a future for the World Bank as a global development knowledge bank and/or as the global poverty reduction agency? Can these roles fulfil all of the functions hitherto assigned to the Bank, or will it have to find a specialized role within the international development community in order to safeguard quality and make ends meet? The Bank seems to be facing a dilemma in relation to at least three trends:

- The internal and partly external push for the Bank to become an omnipotent development agency for all categories of developing and transition countries in need of poverty-reducing economic recovery and growth. This would be the logic of a global development and crisis management agency operating within a 'neo-liberal-plus' development paradigm – that is, with basis in neo-liberal economic growth supplemented by democratization and empowerment of the poor.
- The demand for efficiency and effectiveness in a world of scarce ODA. This requires selectivity in the Bank's aid allocations, concentration on the 'good performers' among developing countries, and hence the risk of leaving the troubled countries to their own devices. This is the logic of a Western development agency operating safely within a neo-liberal development paradigm.
- The demand for development as freedom (Sen 1999). This requires a

transformation of the Bank to address poverty reduction in all its dimensions in direct collaboration with people's organizations and national and international social movements. This would require a new development paradigm incorporating some post-modern, anti-development critique of the neo-liberal development discourse.

The Bank president's talk of the poor as clients and NGOs as equal partners points in the latter direction, but the Bank's political masters and its competencies and resources push it towards hard choices between the two first trends.

## The European Union: Strengths and Weaknesses

The 1970s saw the emergence of the European Community (now European Union) as a large, new, independent actor in the donor community. The European Commission represents the EU member states. It was first with the Maastricht Treaty of 1992 that development cooperation was written into the constitutional framework as a legitimate function of the Community. As we have seen, EU aid, combined with the bilateral and multilateral aid of the EU member states, makes 'Europe' the dominant aid donor in the world. Three features have characterized EU aid over the past thirty years: ambitious and often innovative attempts to combine political, trade and development concerns into one cooperation scheme; a desire to use aid to present the European Commission as an international actor in its own right in all developing and transition regions; and a considerable gap between a set of progressive aid and development policies and instruments on the one hand, and the reality of persistent weaknesses in the implementation of EU aid on the other. The latter feature implies, of course, that the EU in general has had limited success in relation to the two former features.

The EU is a potentially omnipotent aid donor in terms of the comprehensiveness of its objectives, the multitude of its instruments and the distribution of its aid. The diversification of EU aid is seen in the following characteristics of its allocation. The EU has large separate aid programmes for the ACP countries (Africa, Caribbean and Pacific); Central and Eastern Europe and the New Independent States (the former Soviet Union); the Mediterranean and Middle East; and other Asian and Latin American countries (see Figure 7.4). In recent years, EU aid to the two first groups has been of almost equal size, indicating that the alleviation of extreme poverty is not the overriding EU objective. The diversification also includes special programmes for NGOs and the private sector (including the European Investment Bank) as well as sizeable food aid and humanitarian aid components (some 20 per cent of total aid) (Wolf and Spoden 2000).

The most striking feature of EU aid is the persistence of its problems of securing efficiency, effectiveness and overall quality. In 2000, the European

Centre for Development Policy Management (ECDPM), which specializes in EU aid matters, launched an internet discussion with the following presentation of the key question of quality:

> European cooperation is insufficiently founded on realistic and appropriate cooperation strategies. Policies are guided by legal and financial instruments instead of clearly defined objectives, cooperation priorities and adapted country-level, regional or sectoral strategies. The current system of multi-annual programming is weak, because it reduces 'strategy' to a group of projects, selected and implemented without any dialogue with local actors on the ground. Also many political priority areas (e.g. the fight against poverty, support for civil society, cooperation with conflict-affected countries, and support for decentralization) lack coherent strategies. (Lehtinen 2000)

These characteristics confirm an analysis we made a decade earlier of the EU's effectiveness at country level (Danida 1991). In an analysis of the allocation of EU aid, Wolf and Spoden (2000) concluded that aid to ACP countries in 1975–2000 had been allocated on the basis of other criteria than poverty and development needs and performance. Thus politics has been the decisive criterion, meaning that small ACP countries have received up to eight times as much EU aid per capita as large countries. The earlier, explicit preference for former French colonies in the allocation of EU aid has been modified, but it has not been replaced by explicit poverty reduction criteria.

To understand the under-utilization of the potential that the EU has had through its huge resources and many instruments, one has to look at the institutional location and the political foundation of EU aid as an entity, separately from the aid of EU member states.

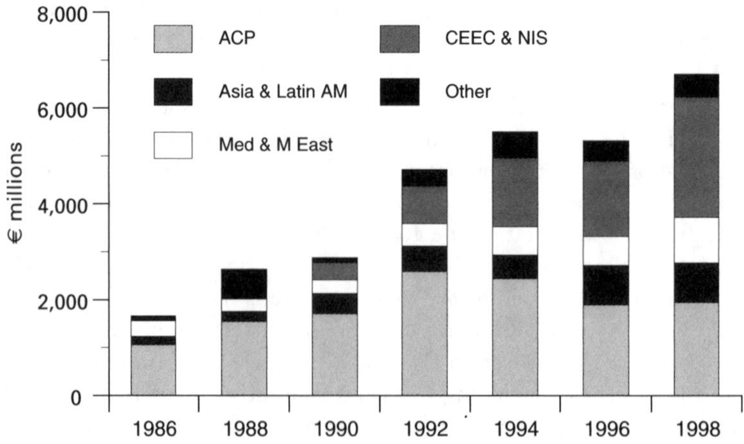


**Figure 7.4** Disbursement of EU aid to different regions, selected years (*source*: ECDPM 2001)

In the 1970s, an unusual merging of interests made it possible for the EU, to a greater extent than the UN system, to realize the ideas behind the demand for a New International Economic Order. The former colonial powers, France, Great Britain and Belgium, were interested in using the EU's resources and competence in the area of trade policy to tie the former colonies in Africa, the Caribbean and the Pacific (ACP) closer to Europe, economically and politically. These developing countries, almost all of which belong to the low-income group, were interested in the NIEO package's combination of comprehensive financial and technical assistance with the levelling of fluctuating prices for exports of raw materials and minerals and favoured access to markets in industrial countries. As a regional organization, the EU was interested in ensuring deliveries of cheap raw materials and in increasing its own role in world economy and politics.

This identity of interests led to several agreements (first made in Yaoundé and from 1975 in Lomé – at the same time as NIEO negotiations in the UN) between the EU and seventy ACP countries. The agreements contained all the above-named components. In an international politico-economic context, their two most important innovations were: the attempt to regulate and compensate fluctuations in trade between developing and industrial countries; and developing countries' entitlement to and ownership of the aid that the EU made available in five-year programmes for each country. The latter gave governments in developing countries considerable influence on the use of EU aid, including sector distribution and the tempo of implementing activities (Koning 1995). In the 1970s and the beginning of the 1980s, this system of agreements was considered by many actors and analysts as an innovation and an example for the future regulation of North–South cooperation, either in the form of globalization of the Lomé Agreement system, or in the form of establishment of similar regional North–South agreements between the USA and Latin America; Japan and South Asia; Europe and North Africa; Europe, Japan or the Soviet Union and South Asia.

Instead, neo-liberalism's breakthrough in the 1980s meant that the Lomé cooperation gradually came to resemble a niche. The regional North–South agreements made in the 1990s involve the establishment of common markets and free flows of capital, not regulation of international economic processes. In Washington (home of the USA's government and Congress, the IMF, the World Bank and the Inter-American Development Bank), the focus of the Lomé cooperation on developing countries' entitlement to aid and on integrated programmes for development of rural areas was considered after the 1970s as an anachronism that stood in contradiction to a market-based rejection of state management and central planning. The attempts that the EU made during the 1980s to expand the Lomé cooperation to include country-specific policy dialogues and aid for macro-economic reforms in the ACP countries did not place the EU centrally in structural adjustment programmes and debt relief. This was in spite of the fact that the EU in many ACP countries was clearly the largest donor, with an average of more than 10 per cent of foreign aid.

There are many reasons for the limited influence of the EU's extensive Lomé cooperation and other aid activities on structural adjustment and politico-economic reforms in developing countries in the 1980s. The EU was/is a donor that primarily seeks an expanded role for itself in the international political system. This is why aid is used more to buy legitimacy and cooperation than to force economic and political reform and standardization. The advantage of a division of labour with the IMF or the World Bank is that these are actually multilateral organizations that do not need to think so much about short-term political benefits (in contrast with the bilateral donors).

There are also extremely rational reasons why the EU continues to give aid to agricultural development, infrastructure in rural areas, health and education, and so on. Also for the World Bank, structural adjustment programmes comprised only a limited part of total aid (under one-third). Continuity in the broadly planned and goal-oriented aid was necessary to avoid a breakdown in the low-income countries' local communities, including political and social rebellion as a result of price increases on food and other necessities.

A final reason for the EU's position on the sidelines during the 1980s neo-liberalism in international aid is that the formulation of the EU's aid policies was strongly influenced by countries such as Denmark and Holland. The EU has as its aid goal emphasized the fight against poverty and food insecurity, which at the same time could serve as a framework for the EU's food aid. The EU therefore came to have quite progressive aid goals, comprehensive aid instrumentation (everything from policy dialogue and programme aid to large and small projects, technical assistance, NGO cooperation, commodity aid and emergency relief) and an aid planning process that was extremely friendly towards developing countries (five-year plans with local ownership of EU resources).

There is broad recognition that the problem for the EU has mostly been *implementation* of its fine policies and strategies (Cox et al. 2000). The NIEO-like regulatory elements proved to be both too difficult and too insignificant in size to make any great difference for most of the ACP countries that exported raw materials. The Stabex export stabilization scheme has been criticized for the following devastating reasons (Wolf and Spoden 2000: 18–20): slowness of disbursement; little effect in terms of stabilization; lack of funds; obstruction of diversification (contrary to objectives); distorting incentives; unintended recipients of stabilization funds; and biased allocation of funds. Despite preferential access to the EU and the Stabex scheme, ACP export performance has deteriorated over the last two decades. Its share of the EU market declined from 7 per cent in 1976 to 3 per cent in 1998 (ECDPM 2001).

The most important aspect in the context of this analysis, however, is the under-utilization of the EU's aid resources due to insufficient capacity in the EU system's aid organization, with poor interaction between the Commission and EU delegations in developing countries. The following aid management problems have been confirmed in various studies (Danida 1991; Montes and Migliorsi 1998), here summarized by Wolf and Spoden (2000): too many goals – lack of capacity in the Commission; weak transparency and blurred responsibilities; insufficient operational flexibility; and delays in disbursements.

The EU's greatest comparative advantage is, as already indicated, that it has all kinds of aid forms at its disposal, also grants. In the same programmes, it can support import of equipment, policy formulation, capacity development (including training and scholarships), project investment in infrastructure, operations and maintenance support, and even emergency relief. It has the potential to ensure consistency in these complex country programmes, since the EU Commission has large, permanent delegations in most developing countries (especially as part of Lomé and Cotonou cooperation). However, it still plays a limited role in development cooperation with developing countries, especially in relation to the size of its aid. There are three main reasons for this:

1. Lomé cooperation is based on the assumption that developing countries are entitled to aid. This positive aspect has meant, however, that the EU has made few strategic demands regarding the uses of aid.
2. EU staff – also for the same reason – have limited experience with development-strategic issues. The fact that there is almost no job rotation between Brussels and the delegations plays a role here. The Commission's knowledge about practical development work has been limited.
3. The EU is very dependent on private consultants in both the formulation and implementation of aid projects. Thus, delegation staff become over-burdened with 'contract management'. It is difficult for them to play a central role in the technical dialogue with developing countries and other aid organizations' sector specialists.

Partly in the context of the overall reforms of the European Commission in 1999–2000, three important initiatives were taken in mid-2000 to address some of the weaknesses identified above. First and foremost, seventy-seven ACP countries and the European Union (fifteen member states and the Commission) signed a comprehensive, twenty-year 'partnership agreement' in Cotonou, Benin. Second, a new EU 'development policy' was published, giving priority to poverty reduction in EU aid. Third, the Commission's external aid system was reformed, with the aim of integrating most EU aid under one structure, thus enabling integration of the EU's political, economic and development relations with individual regions around the world.

For the first five years of the Cotonou Agreement, the European Development Fund (the ninth EDF) was allocated €15.2 billion plus outstanding funds from previous EDFs (approximately €10 billion). The principles of the agreement include the equality of partners and ownership of development strategies by local partners. Although central government is the main partner, participation is open to civil society, the private sector and local government. Dialogue and mutual obligations are related to a set of core values – respect for human rights, democratic principles and the rule of law. Also, differentiation and regionalization are foreseen to reflect the ACP partner's level of development, needs, performance and long-term development strategy.

The two main pillars are trade and aid. The current all-ACP, non-reciprocal tariff preferences will be maintained until 2007. From 2008, a set of alternative trade arrangements is meant to replace them, compatible with WTO rules. The least developed countries (LDCs) are entitled to maintain non-reciprocal preferences. However, even before negotiations on the Economic Partnership Agreements (EPAs) were set to start in 2002, the EU took a new trade initiative for the LDCs: from March 2001, 'Everything But Arms' (EBA) extended duty- and quota-free access to all imports from LDCs, with the exception of bananas, sugar and rice, which will be liberalized more gradually. While this is a positive step for the forty ACP countries that are also among the forty-eight LDCs, it is more problematic for the thirty-seven ACP countries that are not LDCs. All existing sub-regions of the ACP, which are supposed to negotiate EPAs with the EU, comprise both LDCs and non-LDCs (ECDPM 2001).

The aid under the EDF is meant to finance national and regional indicative programmes in sectors where EU aid is said to have comparative strengths, viz: economic development (including structural adjustment), social and human development (including promotion of social dialogue), and regional integration and cooperation (where the EU is said to have special expertise). Gender, environment and institutional development are meant to be thematic or cross-cutting issues in all activities. An ACP–EU Private Sector Business Forum and a new investment facility will strengthen the private sector, partly through local financial institutions. Reflecting an attack on the earlier 'entitlement to aid' approach, the EU now reserves the right to adjust allocations to individual countries through rolling, 'pluri-annual programming'.

Thus, the four innovations in the Cotonou Agreement are: (1) a broader political dialogue between the EU and ACP countries or regions dealing with development cooperation, peace and security, the arms trade, migration etc.; (2) a broader partnership, which also includes non-state actors and local authorities in consultations and planning of national development strategies, aided by EU financing; (3) the Economic Partnership Agreements with a mixture of regions and countries; and (4) flexible resource allocation with a preference for 'good performers'. These measures do not hide the fact that ACP countries are of declining importance on the EU's geo-political agenda, so it may not help to expand the issues under dialogue; nor the fact that, although a legal commitment by both sides, the role and inclusion of non-state actors are vaguely defined; nor that the EPA and other trade agreements tend to become highly complex in management terms and possibly divisive among ACPs. Also, the Commission headquarters and its 128 delegations around the world face an uphill battle to develop the necessary development-strategic, substantive and management capacity to ensure implementation that is fair, effective and of high quality in terms of poverty reduction and development impact.

From January 2001, the EuropeAid Co-operation Office has had the responsibility to manage some 80 per cent of EU's external assistance, amounting to more than €9 billion annually. Its responsibility is to manage the project cycle of EU aid projects from identification of projects in most regions of the world through implementation to monitoring and evaluation. Pluri-annual programming remains the responsibility of the Commission's Directorate General for External Relations and Development. EuropeAid's Management Board is chaired by the External Relations Commissioner, which reflects the desire to integrate and use development assistance in EU's regional presence. The EuropeAid Co-operation Office will have 1,200 staff members, half of whom should serve abroad. Other elements of the reforms of EU external assistance (decided in May 2000) include: deconcentration of responsibilities to the field, that is, the 128 Commission Delegations, and decentralization to partner institutions; reinforcement of programming and evaluation (country strategy papers and national indicative programmes); streamlining procedures (avoiding EU member states' 'micro-management' of projects); introduction of a 'sunset clause' (to uncommit unused money three years after a political commitment).

Will this work? Will it increase the quality and impact of EU aid? Bossuyt et al. (2000) suggest that this will depend on at least three critical dimensions of the reform process:

1. Will the development perspective, and poverty reduction as the overriding objective, be safeguarded under the new 'collective management' of EU assistance, where general external relations and trade are likely to be dominant?
2. How can the 'management logic' that has characterized the reforms (in order to speed up aid delivery) be reconciled with other forms of logic aimed at making a difference, ensuring local participation, and enhancing quality?
3. Will the EU finally be able to strengthen the human resource base for its aid, not just in terms of more staff but also in terms of new competencies to address the ever more complex development agenda?

## Active Multilateralism by Small Countries

Small donor countries tend to provide a higher share of their aid through multilateral channels. We showed earlier how the front-running, like-minded donors (Scandinavia and the Netherlands) in both absolute and relative terms are highly significant donors for the UN and other multilateral agencies. Historically, the reasons have been a mixture of small country support for the UN (in the midst of superpower rivalry), a desire to reach all developing countries, and a concern about cost savings through the use of multilateral as opposed to bilateral channels. The small donors have therefore provided much of their multilateral aid as untied core grants to the multilateral agencies.

At the same time, the small front-runners have had to accept the large countries' blatant disregard for the idea of multilateralism. In particular, the USA has used its power in the various multilateral organizations despite its low and declining contributions. In the World Bank, the USA had a voting share above the 20 per cent needed to block changes of the Bank's constitutional articles. When the US share dropped to 17 per cent in 1989, the majority required for constitutional amendments was increased to 85 per cent (Gilbert and Vines 2000: 20). The US president has appointed the World Bank president and has either appointed or been able to block the appointment of the heads of the major UN agencies and regional development banks. To their credit, the US administration and Senate have always been honest, transparent and direct about their foreign policy objectives for the multilateral aid system (Ruttan 1996; Schraeder et al. 1998).

The small, progressive donor countries have reacted in different ways to these explicit attacks on multilateralism. Gradually, their pursuit of national interests has become more open and a normal part of national politics at home. We illustrate this with a case study of Denmark's active multilateralism (covering some US$600–700 million annually). The Danish foreign ministry published in 1996 a *Plan of Action for Active Multilateralism* (Danida 1996b) that was based on three principles: maintenance of a significant multilateral engagement with an approximately equal distribution between bilateral and multilateral aid; a wish to influence and strengthen the international system in accordance with the goals of Danish aid policy and with respect for the organizations' different mandates; and use of political pressure, professional inputs and varying financial contributions to influence the organizations in accordance with the goals of Danish development policy.

This comprised a break with original Danish policy for multilateral aid, which until the end of the 1980s left it to the organizations' governing bodies to decide priorities. This was based partly on the philosophy that developing countries' especially strong position in the UN should be supported. The action plan formulated a number of goals, which may be summarized as follows:

1. The fight against poverty should be the central goal for the multilateral development organizations' activities.
2. Multilateral organizations must implement the action programmes adopted at key UN conferences and summits on sustainable development, women,

population, social development, and so on. Greater transparency and improved division of labour within the multilateral system should be secured to improve overall effectiveness.

3. Debt relief initiatives should be launched in the wake of the 1995 Social Summit in Copenhagen. Multilateral agencies should promote good governance throughout the world, in part through capacity development assistance. Multilateral agencies should improve humanitarian assistance through the linking of relief and development assistance and through greater emphasis on preventive measures in relation to both human and natural disasters.
4. Multilateral organizations should employ more Danes in high-level positions and should buy more goods and services in Denmark.

This level of goals for active multilateralism is doubtless quite realistic. The goals are not all so general that they lose meaning, nor are they so narrow that both Denmark and the multilateral organizations would lose flexibility in maintaining that the multilaterals are, in spite of everything, multilateral. Denmark formulated four means to achieve active multilateralism:

1. Alliances with other member countries: to be effective this must reach further than to the Nordic and other like-minded donor countries. Danish efforts to reform UNIDO, for example, were carried out in close cooperation with Argentina and Great Britain. In analyses of the UNDP, India was an important partner.
2. Political and technical dialogue with the multilateral organizations on three levels: the governing bodies, secretariats, and activities in developing countries. We have participated in several analyses of multilateral organizations' effectiveness and performance at both the field and headquarters levels that seemed to have some influence on policies, priorities and procedures in these agencies.
3. Allocation policy – described as the financial body language by the minister of development at the time. The multilaterals should be penalized and rewarded in relation to fulfilment of the Danish goals. The aim was a more differentiated, politically managed, financing policy, so that organizations would have to make special efforts to maintain their share of Danish multilateral aid.
4. Increased interaction between Denmark's bilateral and multilateral aid, for example, by utilizing bilateral experiences in multilateral aid, and financing special multilateral efforts in Denmark's twenty main bilateral cooperation countries.

Paradoxically, the financial body language is the least effective means. The multilateral organizations are unusually clever at demonstrating a widely embracing fulfilment of goals for the benefit of different donors. They are also good at moving funds around so that it appears that, for example,

Danish earmarking helps. It is unfortunate that financial body language works better on UN agencies, which depend on voluntary annual contributions, than on development banks, which depend on negotiated replenishments every few years, or the EU, which to an increasing degree finances development aid through its ordinary budget.

The other means used in active multilateralism function best through a rather closed and bureaucratic process. The political and technical dialogue with the individual multilateral organizations, supported by political alliances with other states, demands thorough preparation by civil servants, consultants and researchers in donor countries. The analyses must be puched through the governing bodies in interaction with the multilateral secretariats. This demands continuous efforts by the donor countries' diplomats. If active multilateralism is to be effective, there is not much room for broadly mobilizing political discussions in the donor country. This is unfortunate in regard to ensuring the necessary understanding and support, for example, for the large Danish multilateral aid.

Active multilateralism demands thorough preparation and hard work. It would be destructive, for example, in relation to Danish credibility in multilateral organizations, if the launching of active multilateralism were to attract a great deal of attention without the necessary resources to follow it up. The Danish Foreign Ministry did not receive new staff for this work, but tried to manage with the help of a system of 'yearly negotiations' between Denmark and the individual multilateral organization.

It is difficult to evaluate the experience with active multilateralism so far. It has proved difficult to use the financial body language actively, because it affects only few organizations (especially recipients of voluntary contributions in the UN system). Changes in the distribution of Danish aid are not new, however. The active use of earmarking has more 'political signal value' than actual effect in changing organizations' priorities, due to aid's fungibility: an organization can use contributions from one donor to meet the earmarking demanded by another.

International bureaucracies and active states together have considerable space to manoeuvre, because multilateral aid is politically marginal, operationally oriented, and under constant change and adjustment to very turbulent conditions. On the other hand, the special organizational culture in the UN system, which includes both bureaucrats and diplomats, means that there is a long, rough road to any changes that will have any lasting effect in developing countries.

In a revision of its active multilateralism policy in 2000, Denmark introduced a new instrument in the form of thematic funds to promote particular policies and programmes across the multilateral system. For a small country, it is easier to promote particular pet policies than to penalize large multilateral organizations through financial body language. Thematic priorities are more amenable to substantive policy dialogues with the multilaterals (as opposed to the focus on organizational performance inherent in the earlier multilateralism) and to mobilization campaigns in the home country. Thus Denmark decided to focus on HIV/AIDS and violent conflicts as the two initial themes of active multilateralism.

A 'thematic multilateralism', however, has to be large and systematic to have any impact on the multilateral agencies beyond symbolism and political campaigning at home. Denmark allocated only a small share of its multilateral aid to the thematic funds. It decided that these funds should be used primarily in a few selected developing countries (for example, Ethiopia and South Africa) that Denmark wanted to support outside its bilateral aid programmes. It is laudable that Denmark recognized the need for the bulk of its multilateral aid to continue in the form of untied core grants to multilateral agencies, but it tends to defy the objectives of active multilateralism.

## Multilateral Aid Since the 1990s

The political support for the multilateral aid organizations has been threatened since the end of the Cold War in 1989 by the interaction of several factors: the USA's unchallenged position of leadership, which reduces the opportunities for manoeuvre of independent international actors; growth in the global flow of private capital (for both speculation and investments); change in the way in which conflicts manifest themselves, from between states to inside the states that formally comprise the international organizations' member basis; the tempo of the international exchange of knowledge and of communications that circumvent the formal channels in, for example, the UN's specialized agencies; reduction of aid in general and of multilateral aid in particular; and the long series of problems with internal effectiveness in both the UN and the development banks, as discussed above. In this section, we summarize the global challenges for multilateral aid after the end of the Cold War. Then, in Chapters 13 and 14, we examine the overall challenges for aid in the new century.

*The UN system* For the UN system, 1990 started out most positively. The US president at the time, George Bush, appeared to be willing to give the UN a new role in solving military conflicts for the purpose of establishing a new world order based, among other things, on the peace dividend resulting from the reduction of the superpowers' weapon race. After the Gulf War in 1991 and the USA's unsuccessful intervention in Somalia, it quickly became clear that the UN did not receive any share in the peace dividend, and that the USA made use of the UN Security Council only when it was sure of getting what it wanted (Alagapop et al. 1998). In addition to the UN's financial problems, the most glaring being the USA's continuous refusal to pay its billion-dollar debt, the UN has faced two fundamental challenges to its role as aid channel and actor.

First, new changes are on the way regarding the sovereignty and universality of the nation-state, which is the UN's fundamental building-block. This is manifested partly in the spread of political and social conflicts within state borders, and partly in the huge differences that characterize the Third World. There is no longer much meaning in speaking of developing countries as a group, since there are such extreme differences between, for example, South Asia, the Middle East and sub-Saharan Africa, and between large and small countries. However, UN negotiations continue to define the West and developing countries as groups. The analyses made by the UN (and the World Bank) that are produced as a basis for the multilateral organizations' normative activities (such as advice about correct national policies) continue to talk about Botswana and Indonesia, for example, in the same breath. In recent years, the World Bank's economists have also relied to a great extent on regression analyses of indicators such as 'state behaviour' as a basis for quite dogmatic policy recommendations (see Chapter 12). If the UN took the consequences of the increasing differences between developing countries and focused on the low-income countries that need aid the most, this could lead to a simultaneous marginalization of the UN and the low-income countries from what is called 'high politics'. It would be easy for the rich countries and states that are also concerned with economic growth (and eventual crises) in North America, East Asia and Europe to put together a double survival kit for the UN and Africa. It becomes more difficult when India and China, which house the great majority of the world's poor, demand both aid and equality in international politico-economic relations, and when the multilateral organizations struggle to give themselves roles as economic and social watchdogs and problem-solvers, also in the middle-income countries.

All in all, the positive consequence of the local challenges to the sovereignty of nation-states is that the UN system intervenes more directly in internal conflicts and oppression of rights within a new understanding of human security and development. The negative consequence can be that the UN loses legitimacy as an inter-state and universal organization.

The other fundamental challenge to the role of the UN as aid channel and actor is the spread of knowledge and decentralization of decision-making that influence the whole world (Weiss and Gordenker 1996). The UN is still influenced by a belief in state-led development, central planning and official control of knowledge and information, which characterized the UN system's establishment during the post-war period. The developing countries took over this belief from the Soviet Union, and it became the basis for formulation of the NIEO demands in the 1970s. Two examples of this are UNDP's planning model, which still speaks about central financing of country-specific five-year plans, and UN's specialized agencies' attempt to be fixed centres of knowledge within their respective sectors and areas – in spite of the spreading access to internet and the tempo of technological innovations. In addition, UN aid continues to have governments in developing countries as the primary target group in spite of the explosive growth in both transnational enterprises and non-state actors in the so-called civil society.

UN Secretary-General Kofi Annan, in 1997, presented proposals for reform of UN activities within the economic and social fields with political goals for modernizing the UN to be able to meet the demands of the day. At the time, this was called the most comprehensive and extensive reform in the organization's fifty-two-year history. The reform proposals, however, were mostly about merging the field activities of several UN agencies (UNDP, UNFPA, UNICEF) under one roof (UN Development Assistance Framework, UNDAF) in the individual developing country; ensuring a stronger co-ordination of these organizations at the headquarters level (UN Development Group); and merging some of the departments and offices in New York (Annan 1997). This all has more to do with rationalization and cutbacks than with reform. Unfortunately, the Nordic countries' proposal for reform of the UN system was influenced by the same faith in rationalizing, merging and centralizing (Nordic UN Reform Project 1996).

*The UN and global governance* There were three more forward-looking answers to the crisis in the UN system's position in the world order(s) of the 1990s. The UN agencies themselves, together with progressive states and NGOs, attempted to use the UN as a platform to promote *common international values*: human rights, democratization, social development, participation, eradication of child labour, discrimination etc. (Alger 1998; Desai and Redfern 1995; Weiss and Gordenker 1996). As discussed above, the UN organized eleven global conferences and summits during the first half of the 1990s for this purpose, including the Social Summit in Copenhagen in 1995.

The second joint forward-looking proposal was made by the independent Commission on Global Governance under the leadership of the Swedish prime minister at the time, Ingmar Carlsson. This was a proposal for the establishment of an Economic Security Council under the UN for governance of economic interdependence. The council was supposed to be more representative and democratic than the Bretton Woods Institutions and the G7 meetings of the world's largest economies, and more effective than the UN system (Commission on Global Governance 1995: 274). The Commission proposed that if this council were established, then ECOSOC should be abolished together with other agencies that could no longer be justified on the basis of objective criteria, among them UNCTAD (UN Conference on Trade and Development) and UNIDO (UN Industrial Development Organization).

The Carlsson Commission's analysis and proposals were based on interdependency theories and idealistic international political theory (Keohane 1998). They lack a good deal of political realism and insight in the international organizations' ways of functioning. Until now, no UN agencies have been either established or abolished as a result of these proposals. The main reason seems to be the slowness of the UN system and marginalization of the UN within the politico-economic arena. The WTO was established outside the UN, and reform negotiations in and around the UN have hardly come further than to initiate considerations about expanding the political Security Council to include the defeated countries of the Second World War (Germany and Japan) and the largest developing countries (India and Brazil, among others).

The third forward-looking, comprehensive reform proposition builds to a large extent on the proposals of the Commission on Global Governance. Before an International Conference on Financing for Development (Mexico, March 2002), the UN secretary-general appointed a High-level Panel on Financing for Development, led by the former president of Mexico, Ernesto Zedillo. The Panel addressed 'systemic issues' in the following way:

> It is clear, however, that the challenges of globalization today cannot be adequately handled by a system that was largely designed for the world of 50 years ago. Changes in international economic governance have not kept pace with the growth of international interdependence. The Panel endorses the proposal of the Commission on Global Governance to create a global council at the highest political level to provide leadership on issues of global governance. The proposed council … would not have legally binding authority but through its political leadership it would provide a long-term strategic policy framework to promote development, secure consistency in the policy goals of the major international organizations and promote consensus-building among governments on possible solutions for issues of global economic and social governance … To pave the way, it supports a Globalization Summit to discuss this issue …
>
> Despite its youth, WTO is in urgent need of reform and support in certain critical aspects. The necessary changes are unlikely to be achieved from within … The issues of labour and environmental standards need a stronger focus in the international arena than they currently have … In the environmental domain, the sundry organizations that now share policy responsibility should be consolidated into a single Global Environment Organization with standing equivalent to that of WTO, IMF and the World Bank. (UN General Assembly, A/55/1000, 26 June 2001)

The panel urges the conference 'to obtain a commitment by the industrial countries to implement the aid target of 0.7 percent of GNP'. It recommends a carbon tax, both to raise resources for development and to reduce $CO_2$ emissions; the possible establishment of an International Tax Organization; the launch of a Development Round by WTO; the launch of a campaign for the UN's Millennium Goals etc. All in all, the Commission on Global Governance and the high-level panel represent a social democratic view of governance reforms to create a progressively modified neo-liberal world order.

The UN system's survival as a key actor in international development cooperation and humanitarian assistance therefore seems to depend on the following questions. Will the world's dominant nation-states and the increasingly diverse developing nation-states agree on the need for a universal organization that can serve both as a platform for norm-setting for global development and as an instrument of capacity-building, monitoring and operations to ensure application and implementation of the globally agreed norms and policies? Will the UN organization (with all its disparate components) be able to overcome the image and reality of inefficiency and poor quality from which it suffers in all parts of the world?

The answer to the first question depends to a large extent on the future of equitable development and poverty reduction as rationales for international cooperation – in competition with likely rationales such as: humanitarian relief and political trouble-shooting; global integration and standardization; or international problem-solving and management of global public goods. The answer to the second question depends on the likelihood of a 'cultural revolution' in the UN system and international diplomacy, which would require political leadership and effective pressure from international civil society and the private sector. We return to these critical questions in Chapter 14.

*The World Bank* For the World Bank, the challenges of adjustment to the world orders of the 1990s can be summarized as three risks that can almost be characterized as UN diseases.

- the risk of being overtaken by other actors (in the case of the World Bank: private finance and investment capital) and thus become isolated as problem-solver in the poorest countries and social security net in the rapidly growing developing and transition countries;
- the risk of exaggerated self-importance and narrow-mindedness in pressing for just one development model and one development discourse, which cannot capture the world's diversity and the social movements' demands and ideas for alternatives; and
- the risk of being overburdened with responsibilities (covering all development sectors and themes in all types of developing and transition countries) with a diminishing capital base, which almost unavoidably will lead to the over-extension and diminishing quality that has characterized the UN system since the 1970s.

It would be fate's irony in the international aid world, if many years' expansion of the World Bank's responsibilities and resources, which indirectly have been at the expense of the UN system's planned central role in multilateral aid, should lead to a contradiction between functions, resources and capacity that is just as great as that which has undermined the UN system since the promising NIEO period in the 1970s. The World Bank risks catching the UNitis disease.

The World Bank has grown from being a centralized, top-managed, businesslike bank and development organization, staffed by economists and engineers, and responsible to its political 'masters', the USA and its allies. It has become a more open, decentralized, many-headed development organization, staffed by increasing numbers of soft technical specialists, and cooperating with NGOs and the private sector both globally and locally. The World Bank's President Wolfensohn went so far in 1997 as to say that the Bank's customers were not 150 governments, but 4.7 billion people, including especially the 1.3 billion poorest and the marginalized and excluded people in all societies in the world (Wolfensohn 1997a, 1997b).

As already mentioned, the USA's votes in the World Bank were reduced by half, from 35 per cent in 1947 to 17 per cent today. The USA has also in recent years sharply reduced its financing of IDA, which has led to attempts to change the sharing of burden among donor countries. However, there is no sign that the USA's influence on the World Bank's development and loan policies has been reduced. The World Bank is therefore today in an identity crisis, which neither Wolfensohn's progressive statements nor several organizational changes during the 1990s can solve.

The underlying questions are: can the World Bank manage the omnipotent role as the world's leading development agency (in terms of knowledge, resources and implementation) that it has been given and has taken upon itself? Is there a viable alternative to this omnipotent role, that is, can the Bank retreat into a more focused role, and if so, what would it be? What are the implications of the omnipotent role for the Bank's immediate competitors in the multilateral development system, that is, the regional development banks, the UN's operational agencies, and the EU?

The answer to the first question depends not so much on whether the Bank hires additional staff with 'soft' qualifications. It depends, of course, primarily on whether the Bank is given sufficient ODA to play a significant role in all countries with major poverty problems. It also depends on whether Bank management can control the expansionist tendencies of its own bureaucracy and the demands of many external stakeholders that the Bank should be more directly involved in implementation in all corners of the world. The Bank cannot be the world's leading development organization, both in Washington and in individual developing countries – not even if these are only the low-income countries (LICs) or poverty-ridden middle-income (MICs) and transition countries. Finally, the answer depends decisively on whether the Bank can open up to alternative development discourses and paradigms and learn how to listen to the poor, to social movements, and to civil society organizations.

The possibility of a viable alternative to the omnipotent role of the Bank hardly lies in a retreat to a role as a bank that provides loans and credits for infrastructure development. Other multilateral and bilateral agencies (regional development banks, the EU, Japan etc.) and private national and transnational enterprises can easily challenge the Bank's role in such traditional support for economic development. Reducing the Bank's omnipotence by reducing its 'geographic scope' is currently being attempted in three ways:

- pulling or pushing the Bank out of MICs that can borrow from private international banks – this strategy was dealt a significant blow in East Asia when the crisis-ridden MICs needed the Bank to compensate for the short-term nature and volatility of private commercial flows;
- pulling the Bank out of transition countries and other countries affected by political conflicts and crises – this may have some potential, provided that the affected regional powers (for example, EU, Japan, USA, Australia, Russia) have the will and capacity to step in with both conflict resolution and economic recovery assistance; and
- concentrating Bank resources on the 'good performers' among low-income countries, and assigning only policy advice, technical assistance and humanitarian assistance (by other agencies than the Bank) to the 'bad performing' and crisis-ridden LICs. We find this latter option highly problematic as a way of reducing the omnipotent role of the Bank and discuss this at some length in Chapters 12 and 14.

*The World Bank and the multilateral system* The implication for the Bank's immediate competitors in the multilateral system seems to place the burden of finding specialized roles on these agencies.

The regional development banks (AfDB, AsDB, IDB and even EBRD) cannot compete with the World Bank in its knowledge-based links between socio-economic analysis and advice, macro-economic, structural and sectoral development programmes. The regional banks have comparative strengths in two fields that can be mutually supporting: regional collaboration and economic integration; and economic and social infrastructure rehabilitation and development, including related policy-making and institutional capacity-building. The regional collaboration issues include conflict and crisis prevention through joint problem-solving and confidence-creating institutional interactions. They also include region-specific and sub-region-specific aspects of global economic integration related to market access, technical trade barriers, technology development, and so on. The work still to be done in infrastructure sectors obviously differs between regions (Africa vs Latin America) and within regions (East vs South Asia), but many countries and sub-regions are still in need of simple, well-founded infrastructure policies and programmes. These sectors also give the regional development banks a logical role in post-crisis and transition countries.

The UN system cannot compete with the World Bank as an omnipotent development agency, because the many UN agencies cannot function as a system. In fact, the UN would strengthen its effectiveness and its legitimacy if it stopped trying to operate as a coordinated system at either global or national levels. Its strength lies in its diversity of normative, policy-making bodies, operational and protective agencies. Still, the UN can and should maintain an overall, common perspective founded on human development, human rights and human security. The UN has the legal instruments, the democratic procedures, the institutional platforms and the political legitimacy to provide an ideological alternative, correction, or at least supplement, to the economic governance by IMF, the World Bank and WTO. The UN will continue, however, to lose legitimacy and resources if it does not manage to translate these norms and perspectives into effective operations of relevance to poor people and developing societies. This applies to countries struggling under all types of conditions: development, conflicts, emergencies, recovery, and so on. Creating and strengthening links from equity norms to effective operations is the essential challenge for the UN as a system. Emphasizing the differences between the UN and the World Bank is likely to be more successful than efforts to democratize the Bretton Woods Institutions. The demands on the World Bank and IMF by progressive states and international civil society should be focused more on the quality and relevance of their advice and services than on the democratic deficit in their constitution and operations.

The EU should be recognized as a regional body with clear politico-economic interests, rather than as a multilateral agency. Its strength should be that it represents a region with strong historical ties with – and political obligations towards – many of the least developed and most marginalized countries in the world. The EU should be permitted to link politics, trade and development through inter-regional collaboration, but this should not be at the cost of development assistance from a humanitarian, social-democratic perspective. The EU has relevant experience from structural funds aimed at developing poor regions within the Community, and the EU ought to be able to launch innovative programmes to develop sub-regions among developing countries. The EU, however, still faces an uphill battle to prove its own ability to perform in the international development community.

With such specializations in the multilateral community 'around' the World Bank as the leading development organization, a tendency would exist for a technocratic management approach to be allowed to dominate development cooperation. This is most explicitly the logic of the country-specific 'comprehensive development frameworks' promoted by the Bank (see Chapter 9) as well as the call for performance-based selectivity in the allocation of aid. Recipient countries, civil society organizations and social movements have to counter these tendencies at two levels: by demonstrating through global advocacy the ideological foundation and implications of such management approaches; and by creating space for political debate about development alternatives in the context of national and local democratization in individual developing countries and regions.

## CHAPTER 8

# The Role of NGOs in Development Cooperation

§ IN the aid debate, NGOs are sometimes termed the third sector – the others being the state and the profit-driven private sector. This division between the NGO sector and other sectors does not completely correspond to the theoretical division between civil society on the one hand and the state, market and private enterprises on the other, but it does come close in relation to NGOs' roots. The divisions are less clear, however, with regard to NGOs' activities and ways of working. Development-oriented NGOs have increasingly attempted to become involved in other areas of society, especially through lobbying in relation to both local and central political authorities.

This chapter discusses the role of NGOs in international development cooperation, with special emphasis on the changes that have occurred in recent decades. No clear definition of NGOs lies at the basis of this presentation, but it is assumed that the organizations we are interested in play some kind of role in development processes. They influence the distribution and utilization of resources and power, or at least attempt to achieve such influence. This means, for example, that sports and recreational clubs are not of much interest, but on the other hand they should not be disregarded completely. When a boxing club for scheduled caste Hindus in Katmandu, or for slum inhabitants in Nairobi, contributes to members' greater self-confidence, it also contributes to consciousness-raising processes that can be important for young men's lives in a broader context. Therefore, in concrete terms, it is relevant to include this kind of organization in our discussion.

Generally, however, in the following sections, we examine private volunteer organizations that focus on economic, political and cultural development for specific groups of people (see discussion of development goals in Chapter 3). This does not mean that we have thereby arrived at a definition of a homogeneous group; on the contrary, the next two sections show that within this slightly narrower conception, NGOs are very different with regard to more specific goals, ways of functioning and organization.

## Four Generations of NGOs and Their Strategies

A first general idea of NGOs' various roles can be found by using as our starting point David Korten's classic attempt to divide them into four generations (Korten 1987, 1990: Chapter 10). Originally, Korten presented the idea of generations in the mid-1980s while working for USAID, but it has since been developed further in close dialogue with many NGO representatives and in this way has become rather more widely known. Division into generations does not mean that all NGOs have gone through, or are in the process of going through, changes in their goals and strategies represented by the four generations – on the contrary, all four generations continue side by side – but one of Korten's points is that an increasing number of NGOs, both in the North and South, have moved from the first to the third generation and some are on their way to the fourth.

The goal for first-generation NGOs is to help people in acute need. This is done by giving emergency relief to cover an immediate need for food, medical aid, shelter or similar basic necessities. Religious organizations have traditionally played a central role in this work, but many secular humanitarian organizations also belong in this category. Many of these organizations started their work at the time of the reconstruction of Europe after the Second World War: Oxfam in the UK, for example, and CARE (Co-operative for American Relief Everywhere). A few of the large international relief organizations can date their origins from the period following the First World War: the Save the Children Fund, for example. As Europe was rebuilt during the 1950s, these organizations gradually began moving their work to countries in the South, where many missionary organizations had long been actively involved in a combination of emergency relief and development aid. This was especially the case in Africa.

The thinking behind NGOs' emergency relief efforts was not only to meet immediate needs. The organizations also had the idea that in this way they could help needy people to help themselves. Missionary organizations were among the first to follow such ideas by providing education and primary health services. Similar initiatives became increasingly widespread as NGOs gradually shifted from first-generation to second-generation strategies in which the emphasis changes from giving help to self-help. The aim is to strengthen the target groups' own capacity so that, in the long term, they are able to take care of themselves. A popular comparison between first and second generations distinguishes between giving a man a fish to satisfy his immediate hunger and giving him a fishing rod and teaching him to fish so that in the future he can take care of himself.

The transition to second-generation strategies means that NGOs ideally enter into cooperation with the target groups or their representatives and carry out activities together with them. In practice, however, close cooperation has often been difficult, since many Northern NGOs have functioned more as service providers offering education, training, health services, credit, and so on. But in any case, the basic idea is to support the efforts of the target groups themselves to become self-reliant. Therefore, emphasis has also been placed on consciousness-raising activities and support for self-organizing within target groups.

It is a characteristic of NGOs of the second generation that they work locally, in one or a few villages, slum areas, or other specific local communities. Thus, because they can utilize their knowledge of the locality, these NGOs can avoid taking on projects that demand more than they can deliver. Behind this strategy also lies the idea that it is useful to work with small projects that contribute, both in the short and long term, to improving conditions for the target group.

It is exactly on this point that criticism comes from NGOs that have moved on to the third generation. They recognize the usefulness of working locally but, at the same time, they often find that other factors in society at large present such serious barriers for development in small local communities that it is necessary to attack problems on a larger scale. An illustration from David Korten shows that NGO staff members, often from big cities, have less insight into fishery technology than the local fishermen, whose major problems are often quite different: for example, how to gain access to good fishing areas and to markets where they can get a proper price for their catches. Such problems demand broader strategies that both aim to help people to help themselves in a local context, and at the same time to do something about the external conditions that block improvements for the poor in target groups.

Third-generation NGOs, in other words, combine their initiatives at the micro level with initiatives at the macro level. They do not only help the poor improve their living conditions directly, but also aim to change the structures and institutions in society that keep large groups of the population in poverty. In regard to the latter, this type of NGO tries to influence development policy and the whole public system in ways that benefit poor and marginalized groups, especially women, and in most cases with special consideration for the environment. This generation's NGOs also emphasize influencing official donor organizations and international finance institutions towards the same goals. These NGOs typically combine concrete development initiatives with advocacy on behalf of the poor and marginalized groups. A further characteristic of Northern NGOs in this category is that they place very great emphasis on building the capacity of their partner organizations in the South so that they themselves can carry out development work and act as advocates for weak groups.

If such NGO strategies are implemented as part of national, and perhaps also global, networks and popular movements, then Korten places the organizations involved in the fourth generation. Some of the largest international NGOs must be considered today to be fourth-generation organizations. The same applies to networks established by many smaller NGOs in both North and South. One example of this is the campaign organization, Jubilee 2000, which, with support from a very large number of NGOs, demanded debt relief for the poorest countries. In the wake of growing economic globalization, a special variety of NGOs has emerged that concentrate their efforts around advocacy and lobbying for the benefit of the world's poorest countries and groups of people without being directly involved themselves in development work in the South. One example is ATTAC, which demands a tax on financial transactions, partly to prevent speculation and resulting crises, partly to liberate funds to promote development (see www.attac.org).

Figure 8.1 summarizes and illustrates some of the NGOs' possible choices regarding areas of activity and strategies. It applies to NGOs in both South and North, but the national macro-level relates only to developing countries.

The following sections discuss in more detail how NGOs are organized and what strategies they use in cooperation with official aid organizations, governments in recipient countries, and grassroots organizations representing the target groups.

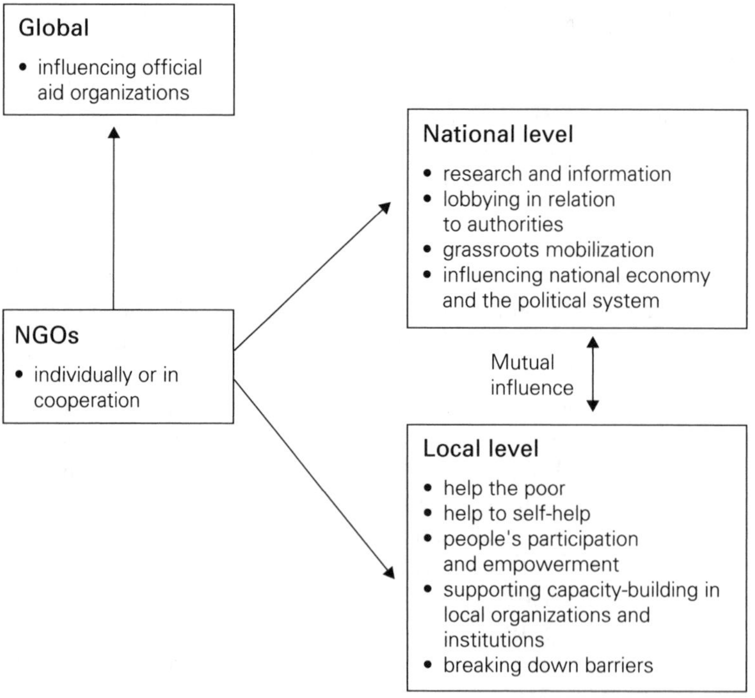


**Figure 8.1** NGOs' areas of activity and strategies

## Third-party and First-party Organizations

Descriptions of organization forms often distinguish between third-party and first-party organizations. It is characteristic of third-party organizations that they consist of members or supporters who in principle do not benefit from the work of the organization. Rather, this work is directed towards outside target groups in an attempt to improve conditions with some form of strategy. Oxfam and CARE are examples of such organizations among NGOs in the North. First-party organizations, on the other hand, work on behalf of their members or supporters. Trade unions in developing countries are examples of this type of organization. In addition to working with rights within the narrow area of their trade, they are also involved in development work for the benefit of their members. A broad variety of grassroots organizations, which are typically based in small local communities, also belong to this category, as well as organizations based on common economic interests: for example, joint utilization of wells for irrigation or forest areas. Other variants are cooperatives and cooperative enterprises.

In practice, the border is often blurred between the two organization types. On the one hand, activists and staff in third-party organizations do benefit from their involvement. On the other hand, leaders and staff in a first-party organization normally work much more than they are paid for, both directly and indirectly. Nevertheless, such a distinction can be useful as a general characteristic. It can also be useful in describing the widespread forms of cooperation between various types of organizations. Inspired by

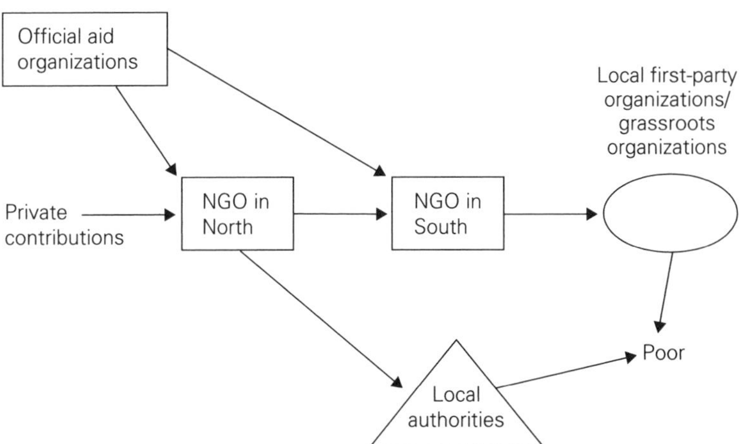


The arrows in the figure indicate resource transfers or other forms of assistance. NGOs in both North and South also use their own resources in their work

**Figure 8.2** NGOs' choice of partners and forms of cooperation

Alan Fowler (Fowler 1997), Figure 8.2 illustrates the typical cooperative relations between North and South.

NGOs in the North can be in direct contact with selected target groups. This is generally true of first-generation NGOs and also many second-generation NGOs; among others, missionary and other humanitarian organizations that are directly involved in education and health projects. As mentioned in the preceding section, though, there has been a widespread tendency for Northern NGOs to withdraw from direct aid to the poor. Instead, they have begun to cooperate with small local organizations – most often first-generation organizations – either directly or through national NGOs in the South. The large Northern NGOs most often use a many-stringed cooperation strategy that, in addition to cooperation with Southern NGOs and small local organizations, involves cooperation with local governments on specific development activities.

## Choice of Partners and Forms of Cooperation

Since the 1970s, it has been common in NGO circles to speak about, and to attempt to establish, partnerships between organizations in the North and South. Another topic has been a concern with replacing aid with cooperation based on equality, where NGOs in the South play a leading role in determining development priorities. A large international symposium held in 1987 with NGO representatives from forty-two countries declared that this was the agenda for future cooperation (*World Development* 1987).

Ideas about partnerships based on equality and Southern NGOs' primary responsibility for development efforts in their own countries have been accepted to a certain extent as the goal for cooperative relationships. However, this does not apply to all larger NGOs from industrialized countries. Many consciously wish to continue direct management of projects in developing countries. Even Northern NGOs supporting these ideas in principle find it difficult to realize them in practice. Cooperation is seldom based on organizations in equal need of each other. Northern NGOs need partners in the South, of course, if they are not going to manage projects themselves, but this does not imply equality with the Southern NGOs, which generally have a more fundamental need for transfers of resources, knowledge and skills either from official aid organizations or Northern NGOs. In addition, the latter are generally much larger organizations than the ones they cooperate with in recipient countries. It is true that large and well-functioning NGOs are found in countries such as India, Bangladesh and the Philippines, as well as in several Latin American countries; but this is not the case in most of Africa or in poor Asian countries such as Nepal. Therefore, attention is focused on large Northern NGOs – often with close connections with the official aid system – that cooperate with small, resource-weak Southern NGOs (for a critical discussion see Fowler 2000).

Inequalities are further reinforced by the fact that large NGOs in the North usually have bureaucratic structures with fixed routines and formal procedures for managing their aid work. Moreover, bureaucratization and formalization have increased as Northern NGOs receive increasingly larger shares of their total resources from official aid organizations that, in their turn, demand specific formats for applications, accounts and reports. If NGOs in the South wish to cooperate with such organizations, they thus have to accommodate themselves to the formal demands. Many leaders of Southern NGOs have experienced this as considerable erosion of their independence, but they nevertheless are forced to accept it for economic reasons.

In this context, they have not been able, as an alternative, to apply for support directly from official aid organizations, because such support is connected with similar demands. Also, Southern NGOs often meet opposition from Northern NGOs when they try to achieve direct grants from official aid organizations. A survey by the British government in 1995 revealed that 80 per cent of NGOs surveyed opposed aid being channelled directly to Southern NGOs (Wheat 2000). The list of reasons given included the following: Southern NGOs lack experience to manage, monitor and evaluate projects; they are more vulnerable to donor influence; they are likely to respond to availability of money rather than need; they will fill a void created by a retrenching state in many poor countries; and they are susceptible to manipulation by donor agencies and political groups. Representatives for Southern NGOs who know of the survey have reacted sharply and interpreted these findings as expressing a combination of distrust and protection of organizational interests. We agree with this interpretation. It would have been more convincing if the British NGOs had stressed their role as partners in capacity-building in the South – a role that can hardly be fulfilled by official donor organizations.

A general problem, from the point of view of Southern NGOs, is the strong preference for project financing among many official aid organizations; this is often carried further by NGOs in the North because they receive grants for their activities based on the same principle. Expressed rather pointedly, the demand to describe and carry out activities as limited projects involves an artificial division of complex problems into smaller parts suitable for external financing and management. This makes it especially difficult for organizations attempting to pursue a broad strategy, since they achieve external financing only for smaller parts of it. In this context, it can be mentioned that many NGOs in the South find it troubling that during the last decade official support has focused so much on micro-credit, that is, loans for the poor. This type of loan can easily receive external support, whereas it is difficult to finance other activities that NGOs consider to be at least as important.

From the viewpoint of Northern NGOs, it can be difficult to find suitable partners in recipient countries, even when they are prepared to compromise on equal partnerships. This is partly because there is often competition between the many organizations in the North trying to establish connections with the relatively few real development organizations in the South. There might seem to be a very large number of NGOs in most developing countries, but further investigation shows that most of them belong to other categories that are not development-oriented. Alan Fowler, in a rather polemic way, counted fifteen different types of NGOs whose principal goal does not include contributing to economic, social or political development for the benefit of poor segments of the population (Fowler 1997: 32). In the following, we name the most common types and, as illustration, add some comments about Nepal:

- Political front organizations, which have the primary goal of mobilizing support for a specific party or politician. After democracy was established in Nepal in 1992, many of the newly elected members of parliament established or took over NGOs in their constituencies in order to use them to gather more political support.
- Semi-public organizations, which aim to increase or regulate citizens' participation in official development work. Several ministries in Nepal have established such organizations and registered them as NGOs.
- Commercially-oriented NGOs, which ensure income for the 'owners'. In Nepal, many registered NGOs are actually consultant firms that earn money (usually tax-free) working for foreign donors.

Aside from these and other types of NGOs that are not actually development-oriented on behalf of either poor members or poor segments of society, the number of NGOs in many developing countries is relatively modest. For the many foreign NGOs seeking partners, this means that there are too few to make one-to-one, twinning arrangements. Instead, it is typical that 'good' and 'attractive' local NGOs are asked to cooperate with Northern NGOs. This can strengthen the local NGOs' independence on individual external partners to a certain extent. However, because of the bureaucracy already described, the result in practice is more often that Southern NGOs are exposed to considerable outside pressure and extra stress in their working conditions.

A further aspect of the forms of cooperation that create difficulties for Southern NGOs is the imposition of norms and values by outside partners, as well as fluctuations in priorities influenced by what is 'in'. Since the mid-1970s, and with special force after 1989, NGOs in the North have exerted pressure on their partners to make them live up to increasingly comprehensive demands, both regarding development goals and their internal organization. Thus, in addition to existing goals concerned with improvements for the poor, there are now goals involving special initiatives for women and the environment. As for internal organization, Southern NGOs are not only expected to be politically independent, effective and have great impact, but they are also required to do all this in accordance with democratic procedures and with equal participation by men and women. Alan Fowler believes that NGOs in the South are in this way subject to expectations and demands that few NGOs in the North could live up to (Fowler 1997: Chapter 5).

In practice, it can be extremely difficult to reconcile all the goals that many Northern NGOs impose on their partners in the South. Political independence, for example, can mean poor impact in relation to local authorities and the powerful elite. Southern NGOs' internal democracy is often connected with inefficiency and a slow pace in practical development work. On the other hand, a strong, charismatic leader with good political connections can ensure both impact and efficiency. Examples of this are provided by three large NGOs in Bangladesh: Grameen Bank (and Grameen Enterprises), BRAC (Bangladesh Rural Advancement Committee) and Savar Gonoshasthaya Kendra (within the health sector). All three organizations, which are among the most successful in the Third World in regard to the impact of their work for the benefit of poor segments of society, are led by prominent individuals who are in no way accountable to their members or supporters through democratic procedures. These same three men established these NGOs at the beginning of the 1970s. This is not a general argument for Northern NGOs to disregard democratic values in their choice of partners, but a recommendation to include further considerations and carefully evaluate what is most important.

## Catalysts for Development

The dominant conception among NGOs today, both in the North and South, is that alleviation of poverty and promotion of development are primarily the responsibility of the poor themselves and almost completely dependent on their own efforts. What NGOs and their staff can do is to function as a kind of catalyst, or even only as advisers, in relation to the poor, and also attempt, together with them, to change the structures and institutions in society that cause oppression and the marginalization of large groups in society.

One of those who earlier tried to give a systematic description of NGOs' role in a democratic development process was Guy Gran (Gran 1983; see also Martinussen 1997: Chapter 24). According to Gran, there are so many social conditions and internalized norms among the poor themselves that there is usually a need for a catalyst in the form of one or several persons who can help start their self-organization and development efforts. The best method would be to select members of the local target group for training and education and then let them return to function as such catalysts in their local society. But Gran also finds that volunteers from industrial countries can be of great use by working together with and among the poor. In this connection, he proposes procedures similar to the empowerment strategies described below. The central idea is to start by raising the consciousness of the poor about their common problems and available options for action, and from this platform support their self-organization.

Other writers, for example, Robert Chambers, believe that Gran's strategies are based on a much too optimistic evaluation of how much development workers from outside can accomplish. The most widespread conception among NGOs today probably lies closest to Chambers's more pessimistic and careful judgement about what volunteers from industrial countries can accomplish if poor people have not already organized themselves and taken a minimum of responsibility for their own development. This is also reflected by the strong emphasis on the necessary cooperation with first-party organizations that we have discussed earlier in this chapter. Nevertheless, Northern NGOs continue to send out their own staff members or volunteers to work in projects and organizations in developing countries. A considerable change in the expectations of these people's abilities can be observed, and their roles in development work are gradually being redefined, but it continues to be characteristic of most NGOs in the North that they maintain a presence in recipient countries in the form of their own employees from industrial countries.

During the last twenty years, there has been a strong tendency towards a marked change in the primary role of development workers coming to recipient countries. As indicated in earlier descriptions, by no means all NGOs in the North have changed their strategies and thereby the functions of their staff. There continue to be some first-generation organizations that send staff members out to solve the immediate problems of groups of poor people. There are also many organizations where staff members place the main emphasis on participating directly in solving technical problems. But the general tendency has been towards drawing development workers away from doing things by themselves to working instead as catalysts for the target group's self-organization and own initiatives – and further to supporting local organizations in their work by functioning as advisers. Expressed in rather simplified and schematic terms, development workers' primary role has changed from being action-oriented to assisting in building capacity in partner organizations, for example, through training. Many also work with advising established organizations on how they can plan their activities.

This description of development workers' various roles can also be used to describe the phases of cooperation between an outside NGO and local organizations. According to Alan Fowler, these phases are entry, integration and consolidation, and withdrawal (Fowler 1997: Chapter 5). He also proposes procedures for NGOs in the North to use in these different phases. The central elements here are thorough preparation and in-depth discussions with partner organizations in connection with entry, in order to formulate common understandings and goals.

In this first phase, development workers from outside can become involved directly in activities relating to the target group. The ideal, however, would be to contribute to building the partner organization's own capacity and to support integration in the organization of the activities being financed by the Northern NGO. In the consolidation phase, it is crucial that responsibility and decision-making competence are gradually transferred completely to the partner organization, so that development workers coming from outside really become advisers. This is a prerequisite for being able to carry out withdrawal at a later stage without thereby terminating the activities. Or, in other words, strengthening the partner organization's capacity and its assumption of responsibility for and control of the use of resources and implementation of activities is a prerequisite for achieving sustainability.

The strategy described for the consolidation phase, with its emphasis on capacity-building within the partner organization in the South, often meets difficulties in practice. Most donors prefer to extend financial support to activities that are directly related to target groups. Official aid organizations are extremely reticent in funding current expenditures of NGOs in the South, even though this is what they need most during the consolidation phase. As a result, organizations are often not able to continue activities when their grants from outside are withdrawn.

## Empowerment Strategies

Today, most development-oriented NGOs aim their work to a considerable extent towards support for economically poor groups that are excluded from political decision-making processes. The goal is empowerment, which comprises both immediate improvements in poor people's material living standards and a psychological–social dimension. This latter aspect can be characterized briefly as a stronger feeling of self-respect, to be achieved by uncovering internalized norms and feelings of inferiority that have contributed to their oppression. Empowerment is also considered by most organizations to be relational and relative. It involves ensuring poor people's right to have their most elementary needs satisfied as well as their right to participate on equal footing in decision-making processes that affect them. This typically requires empowering them in relation to better-off and politically stronger groups and especially in relation to a locally or nationally dominant economic and political elite.

Many NGOs are reluctant to involve themselves directly in conflicts and power struggles. Instead, they base their strategies on the assumption that they can strengthen their partners without confrontations with other groups. In this respect, they follow the thinking that prevails among official aid organizations (see p. 5). Many Southern NGOs, however, have gradually acknowledged that economic and social development for the poor often involve conflicts and struggles for political power. This group includes civil rights organizations, which both criticize authorities for violating human rights and draw attention to social oppression in civil society – for example, oppression of the scheduled castes in India.

To describe the empowerment strategies further, it can be helpful to distinguish between at least five types of efforts, each with a specific aim:

1. Support for improving living conditions by offering education, training, health and other services, or through entrepreneurial benefits in a broad sense, including job-creating and income-generating activities.
2. Consciousness-raising of members of the target group about their rights and possibilities for action.
3. Encouragement of self-organization and participation in development work and political decision-making processes.
4. Support for expanding and strengthening established organizations so that they are better able to safeguard the interests of their members and supporters.
5. Support for the breaking down of barriers that block this safeguarding of interests – or, formulated positively, creation of political and institutional frameworks that promote and benefit people's self-organization and political participation.

A better framework for self-organization and participation can be achieved by governments with or without guidance and support from NGOs or others. The other elements in an empowerment process, however, basically depend on the poor and marginalized groups' own efforts. NGOs and other outside actors can help, but it is impossible for outside actors to empower target groups; rather, these groups – as co-operating partners – must receive assistance in order to take root and grow stronger.

Empowerment strategies can start with the individual and move from there to establishing small groups and then still larger and stronger organizations. They can also start with households and likewise move towards social networks, social and cultural organizations, and further to political organizations. John Friedmann is one of the authors who strongly emphasize households as the basic unit in civil society (Friedmann 1992: Chapters 3 and 4). His strategies for empowerment therefore focus on strengthening households that are excluded from the economic life of society and political decision-making processes.

If these households are to improve their conditions, the process must start from below. They must ensure they have physical space, free time to act in relation to society, relevant knowledge, skills and other human resources. Only then will they be able to involve themselves in the social networks and social organizations that are the prerequisites for political influence. Friedmann also emphasizes access to resources, credit and so on. Although the household is the starting point, Friedmann acknowledges – as do most development theorists today – that family relationships are characterized by inequalities, especially related to gender and age. Therefore, an empowerment strategy that aims to create greater equality in society also implies special initiatives to support poor women's empowerment (Friedmann 1992: Chapter 6).

More feminist-oriented strategies go a step further, based on the conviction that all women must be included, not just the poor. Women in general need to develop self-confidence and the capacity for collective action in order to transform the processes and structures that reproduce women's subordinate position. For Kate Young, for example, it is not enough that poor women receive better earning opportunities, greater access to resources, and more opportunities to participate in political decision-making processes; the more ambitious goal is to achieve equality between genders in all areas of life in society (see Young 1993: especially Chapter 9). Here lies the source of conflict about priorities in aid cooperation between organizations that place the main emphasis on gender-related inequality, and those that have poverty-orientation as their starting point and only within this framework concern themselves with inequalities between men and women. In practice, the latter approach is followed by most NGOs.

## Multi-pronged Strategies

The types of empowerment strategies enumerated above can be seen as levels of escalation, starting with the small and near and gradually moving upwards to the level of society. But they can also be considered as a series of mutually supporting elements in a comprehensive strategy. In NGOs' actual planning of their work, it is seldom clear on which of these conceptions their strategy is based. Furthermore, the individual organization rarely has a strategy for all the mentioned dimensions. Seen as a group of actors, however, there is no doubt that NGOs together play a role in all dimensions. Individually, very few NGOs have any great influence in regard to empowering the poor and marginalized groups in society, but in societies where many NGOs have been involved in such work for longer periods of time – for example, in India and Bangladesh – results are visible.

Another experience is that the most visible results have been achieved when NGOs have cooperated with clearly defined groups of people with common interests, and when they have also combined the various strategy elements in a comprehensive effort. In connection with the former, it is a general experience that an empowerment process is easier to initiate in relatively homogeneous groups, where the members themselves experience a sense of belonging and community. Women with the same social background and same (lack of) education can be such a homogeneous group. The second point – about the importance of combining various strategy elements – especially concerns tackling concrete and visible problems while proceeding with consciousness-raising, education and organization. It has proved to be very positive for empowerment processes when participants can continually observe concrete results – for example, in the form of joint construction or maintenance – while they also experience greater self-confidence.

An illustration can be found in the work that the Indian NGO, SEWA (Self-Employed Women's Association), carried out in the 1980s for and together with a group of women street vendors in the city of Ahmedabad. One of the group's greatest immediate problems was that they often had to pay both the regular shopkeepers and the police for permission to sit on the pavement with their wares. SEWA initiated its cooperation with the women in order to solve just this problem and took the case to court to ensure them the right to 'two yards of pavement'. They won the case, thus establishing the basis for further cooperation. SEWA first taught the women reading and arithmetic. The latter increased their earnings immediately, because wholesalers and customers could no longer cheat them so easily. The next step was to offer the women credit schemes on considerably better terms than they could obtain from wholesalers or moneylenders. These credit schemes could easily be combined with savings schemes. This model, with a combination of various empowerment strategies that also included legal aid, has been used since by SEWA and other organizations throughout South Asia.

Special versions of empowerment strategies have been used to considerable effect by the international labour movement (and ILO) to strengthen trade unions in developing countries (see Martinussen 1996). A broad variety of support forms have been used, such as technical and financial assistance for existing trade unions' internal courses, shop steward training, and membership campaigns through information disseminated at the workplace. These activities have been further supplemented by national and regional seminars in which trade union leaders and shop stewards have had the opportunity to discuss common problems, exchange experiences and develop common strategies. Special campaigns have been aimed at a stronger inclusion of women in trade union organizing, and others have been aimed at improving the working environment.

The best results have been achieved when these assistance activities have been planned in close cooperation with existing trade unions in developing countries. Local ownership and adaptation to local conditions have been extremely important for the long-term impact. Another experience is that such local ownership has been further strengthened when outside experts have gradually withdrawn from actual teaching and training activities as local people have become educated. In this way, training activities have become integrated in local trade unions' own programmes, although they have required continued financial support from outside. A third experience is that programmes can support trade union cooperation in a far broader sense through creating a national and regional network for trainers and trade union leaders. In this way, a scaling-up of empowerment activities has been achieved, from workplaces and the local organizations to national trade unions and regional associations. Programmes can thereby also support adjustments in official labour market policy and legislation that are important in relation to workers' rights.

Of course, not all these experiences can be generalized to all organizations concerned with empowering selected resource-weak groups in society; the most successful results are achieved among relatively well-organized male industrial and mine workers. The results are much more modest, for example, among female plantation workers or self-employed small producers. On the other hand, there is little doubt that some of the fundamental ideas can be used by NGOs other than international trade unions. In the terminology of Fowler referred to above, programmes for assistance to trade unions in the South give a concrete idea about how the phases of entry and consolidation can be tackled. It can be added that some of the most comprehensive workers' education activities, for example, in India, have been continued even after international assistance has been withdrawn. Thus, these programmes are also an example of a successful withdrawal phase or conclusion of the cooperation.

## NGOs' Comparative Advantages Under Debate

It has been mentioned several times that NGOs since the mid-1980s have come to play an increasingly prominent role in international development cooperation as a whole. This is not so much because these organizations have been able to mobilize more resources directly from the people, but more because official aid organizations have increased their financing of NGO activities (see Chapter 5). One of the reasons for this has been growing scepticism, especially in the USA, towards states in the Third World. This scepticism has in turn been connected with the desire to use more resources to support the private sector as well as to support organizations and institutions in civil society. This has increased the interest in channelling public funds to NGOs in both the North and South. Moreover, the change can be related to the increasing recognition of NGOs' advantages when compared to official aid organizations.

Among the comparative advantages often stressed are the following (comparisons are implied with both bilateral and multilateral official aid organizations in general):

1. NGOs have more flexible forms of organizing and working. They are less bureaucratic and better at adapting to local conditions. They also react more quickly when conditions change.
2. NGO staff members are motivated less by serving their own benefits and more by idealistic principles about benefiting poor people in the South. This makes them better able to cooperate directly with target groups and to promote genuine people's participation.
3. Due to close cooperation with local groups, NGOs are also better able to

gain necessary insights into problems and the possibilities for solving them. They are able to learn from partners and can in this way be innovative and experimental.

4. NGOs are not biased towards the capital city and areas of economic growth, but on the contrary are motivated to work in remote regions.
5. NGOs can work within politically sensitive areas where official donors must show caution. This applies, for example, to direct assistance to society's marginalized groups in struggles for their rights.
6. NGOs can create alternative development models and experiment with other forms of assistance and cooperation inspired by partners in the South.

To these it can be added that NGOs, compared to private commercial firms, are generally considered to be much cheaper. They do not need to be paid for their efforts in accordance with market conditions.

It is immediately apparent from this list of comparative advantages that they are all related to efforts in civil society and especially to poor groups in society. There is also a tendency for the advantages to be primarily associated with work in local society and on a small scale. Therefore, one of the first critical questions to be asked is whether third-generation NGOs risk losing their comparative advantage when they place greater emphasis at the macro level. Critics of this strategy like to emphasize this risk. Supporters, on the other hand, claim that NGOs continue to maintain their strengths at the micro level, and that they are also able to take advantage of their independence from special economic and political interests when they attempt to influence authorities and official aid organizations at the macro level. Their information and advocacy activities benefit from the confidence NGOs inspire in most parties who see them as unselfish actors.

For the most part, these views seem to be plausible, but it should be added that perhaps they do not refer so clearly to comparative advantages when compared with official aid organizations in general. Many UN agencies (for example, UNICEF) and some bilateral organizations (including not least those in Nordic countries) enjoy the same respect for independence and neutrality. Therefore, the dividing line is not so clearly between NGOs and the official aid organizations, but rather somewhere within the latter group.

## Convergence and Competition Between NGOs and Official Aid Organizations

It can be questioned whether all or even most NGOs have been able to maintain their comparative advantages, even at the micro level. The large NGOs in the North in particular have found it necessary, with the aforementioned increasing financing from official aid organizations, to organize themselves more bureaucratically and introduce less flexible procedures. They have also been under pressure from funding agencies that want NGOs to focus on their core competencies and thus enter into a kind of division of labour. This can undermine people's involvement and lead to further professionalizing of NGOs. As project-makers for official aid organizations, NGOs have had to imitate them in many respects. The same tendency applies to many Southern NGOs that have been integrated into official aid systems in a similar way. On the other hand, there has been a tendency for many years for UN development organizations and many bilateral organizations to imitate the NGOs' working methods. The ones that especially emphasize poverty orientation – and by now this includes most bilateral and multilateral UN agencies – increasingly work in remote areas and in closer contact with representatives of poor target groups.

Recruiting staff members for projects in developing countries has also changed, so the typical profiles resemble one another more closely. The official donors want employees who are not only technically qualified but also motivated to work closely with local residents far from national capitals. On the other hand, NGOs look for more professionalism and expertise in their personnel.

Not many studies have been made that expressly compare NGOs with official aid organizations, but one such confirms these tendencies towards convergence. This is an evaluation of the Norwegian Sudan–Sahel–Ethiopia Programme, where the organizations carrying out the project included both NGOs and multilateral organizations (see Marcussen 1996). The evaluation indicates that NGOs were generally less bureaucratic and more flexible in methods of working, but the difference was not marked, because multilateral organizations had decentralized some decision-making competence to their local staff. It also showed that there was no decisive difference in regard to cooperation with target groups. Both types of organizations were committed to following participatory strategies, and NGOs' results in this respect were not more convincing than those of multilateral organizations – for one reason, because NGOs worked with relatively large areas and vaguely defined target groups. Furthermore, multilateral projects were just as often in remote areas as NGO projects. There was no clear tendency that showed that NGOs were better at learning from their local partners than those responsible for multilateral projects, who seemingly had better procedures for gathering experiences than NGOs did.

It is clear that no general conclusion can be drawn from one such study. It was concerned with areas in northern Africa with special problems that forced NGOs to act more relief-oriented than development-oriented – something that seemingly also corresponded to the more general approach of the Norwegian organizations. Furthermore, it concerned areas with weak organization of civil society in comparison, for example, with South Asia. This confronted the Norwegian NGOs with special problems concerning contact with target groups. Nevertheless, it is thought-provoking that, in practice, such relatively small differences could be observed between the working methods of NGOs and multilateral organizations. This should serve as an incentive to further debate about how NGOs can generally ensure that they sustain some of the important comparative advantages that contribute to justifying their major role in international development cooperation (see Fowler and Biekart 1996).

## Long-term Effects and Sustainability

As public grants to NGOs have increased, more demands have been made regarding results. Several studies made during the last ten years agree that NGOs are relatively good at achieving immediate goals. A comprehensive study carried out at DAC's request concluded in 1997 that the immediate goals for the examined NGO initiatives had been realized in 90 per cent of the cases (Riddell et al. 1997: x). It is more difficult to document positive long-term effects for the poor and impact in a broader context. The same is true in regard to sustainability (see also Fowler and Biekart 1996).

A comprehensive evaluation of the work of Danish NGOs completed in 1999 can be used to illustrate the results of impact studies made in recent years (see Oakley 1999). The evaluation shows that the studied organizations together with their partners in the South generally had made relevant and effective efforts. Projects within the social areas had great immediate effect on the living conditions of poor people. The results were more mixed in relation to income-generating projects. Impacts in a broader context were difficult to ascertain. The study noted that NGOs' strengths lay more in relieving the terrible effects of poverty on poor people than in removing the fundamental causes of poverty. Therefore, it was also difficult to identify the long-term impact of the initiatives.

The study further criticized Danish organizations for doing too little to ensure sustainability, but it also stressed that in NGO work with such poor people in such poor societies, it is difficult to imagine how they could manage without financial assistance from outside. Danish organizations were praised for their strong support of partners in the South but criticized for not setting this support in a broader context as part of aid to democratization and ensuring poor people their rights and access to resources. NGOs were criticized for not thinking and working strategically – for not seeing their activities in relation to local development processes and ongoing conflicts. NGOs' own evaluations were described as too narrowly linked to immediate results and not sufficiently related to improvements in society and lasting progress for target groups. In several contexts, they were also criticized for not documenting actual and good results. This applied especially to effects on women, which NGOs presumably underestimated because they had not systematically observed these effects.

If we cut to the bone of this comprehensive and many-faceted study, four important conclusions emerge:

1. When everything is taken into consideration – the size of the problems, the costs etc. – Danish NGOs have done a good job for the immediate benefit of poor target groups and strengthening of partner organizations.
2. NGOs' own documentation of achieved results, however, is weak and too narrowly linked to immediate goals. The organizations have done too little to investigate and document things that have functioned well.
3. NGOs had often not been able to plan work strategically and innovatively. They were inclined to do things in the usual way.
4. Efforts were generally too modest to create *visible* changes in society for the lasting benefit of target groups, but it is possible that the Danish organizations had actually contributed to such a development.

A lesson to be drawn from the study is that NGOs should analyse their own work better and see it in a broader context, and that, with this as a starting point, they should develop more comprehensive country strategies. They should place more emphasis on building capacity in developing countries to enable them to solve problems themselves, and less on achieving immediate project objectives.

Although this study of the work of Danish organizations can in many ways be considered representative of recent impact studies of Northern NGOs' efforts, we also advise against generalizing. More in-depth studies of selected organizations and their projects, also in connection with the Danish evaluation, show great variation in the results. There are thus many examples showing achievement of lasting results and economic sustainability, especially in cases where the partner in the South has been a strong and well-functioning organization (see Sultana and Folke 1999).

In addition, any evaluation of the effects of NGOs' work contains a considerable element of discretion. At the very start, there is the question of whether only lasting changes should be included or whether NGOs should also be credited with bringing about significant improvements in living conditions, even though the improvements do not have a long duration. Furthermore, there is the question of how much of the improvements can be attributed to NGO efforts. This problem of attribution applies to assessments of all forms of aid (see Chapter 11), but applies to a greater extent to the work of NGOs because their aid is on a smaller scale than that of large bilateral or multilateral donors.

Considerations of this kind play a large role in a research project that Oxfam in the UK and Novib in Holland initiated several years ago (Roche 1999). For the same reasons, less emphasis is placed on concrete conclusions about long-term impact and more on learning from experience and improving methods for evaluating impact. The project pointed out five things NGOs ought to strive for: (1) increased recognition of the need to develop institutional learning and impact assessment processes; (2) development of strategic alliances with other NGOs and other sectors, including state structures; (3) deepening engagement with social and political processes in NGOs' own countries of origin; (4) development of new forms of accountability; and (5) further development of professional norms and standards within and across agencies (Roche 1999: 278 ff.).

If NGOs succeed in making improvements in all these areas, their efforts will have greater impact, but there will also be a basis for a more differentiated and humble assessment of what NGOs have accomplished.

These proposals illustrate how NGOs can progress from acknowledging lacks and weaknesses to adjusting their strategies. In this connection, it is also important to avoid a one-sided focus on impact that can be documented for those who finance NGOs' work. This could result in ignoring innovative and risky activities, which are often those that are most needed in cooperation with, and in advocacy for, the most vulnerable groups in poor countries. We return to some more elements in the above-mentioned proposal later in this chapter.

## NGOs' Development Education and Advocacy Activities

In addition to the tasks NGOs carry out in recipient countries, it is generally agreed that they play decisive roles in forming opinion in their own countries in support of foreign aid in general, and aid that is oriented towards poverty, women and the environment in particular. The many volunteers and activists who participate in NGO work typically function as opinion-makers in their local communities. They disseminate information about their experiences, insights and attitudes, and in this way create understanding for foreign cultures and for the need for international solidarity and cooperation. Similar results are achieved through many Northern NGOs' development education activities, which at the same time contribute to creating more realistic and differentiated images of poverty in developing countries than those that are often presented in the written press and the electronic media.

These development education activities in the North are highly valued by many Southern NGOs. Time after time at international meetings, they emphasize how important it is that their Northern partners speak out on behalf of poor countries. This applies not only within the area of foreign aid, but also regarding debt relief, more reasonable trade conditions, and the right to work in rich countries. Within all these areas, Northern NGOs can play important roles as pressure groups that contribute to placing problems of poor countries on the agendas of not only official aid organizations but also of politicians and decision-makers within private enterprises. The campaign 'Jubilee 2000' for debt relief for the poorest countries is considered by many as a good example of how Northern NGOs can build up pressure on political decision-makers. The same applies to the many information campaigns of recent years about globalization's negative consequences for most developing countries. Advocacy and lobbying have been central aspects of the total strategy of many development-oriented NGOs in the rich countries, but both have been given still higher priority in recent years.

Southern NGOs also stress that problems in their countries should be presented properly and in context, and not focus only on human suffering and deprivation – often illustrated by pictures of seriously ill or dying children. This subject is also a source of conflict between NGOs. The Northern NGOs focusing on emergency relief have fewer reservations about using what critics call the 'pornography of misery'. Experience confirms that making misery visible gives better results in campaigns for collecting funds than more factual information. For these organizations, this method is therefore justified in that it makes it possible to extend more help to the needy. Other NGOs argue sharply against this method, especially those organizations that are not engaged in emergency relief and at the same time are not so dependent on private contributions because their activities are mostly financed through state grants. We examine this dependency on state grants in the following section.

## NGOs' Relationship to States in the North

The increasing role of NGOs in administrating funds from official aid organizations has made many ask whether these private organizations have become too financially dependent on their own states, and whether they have become too strongly integrated in official aid systems (see Hulme and Edwards 1997a). A further question is whether they have also thereby lost some of their political independence and special character and instead come to resemble official aid organizations with respect to objectives and strategies. This is the opinion of many observers also within NGOs themselves. They point to the tendency in recent years for private organizations, as well as NGOs in the South, regardless of their original starting point, to concentrate on micro credit because this aid form enjoys a great deal of attention from state authorities. Critics also point to the growing tendency for NGOs to implement state development projects instead of exploiting their comparative strength to initiate their own projects in close cooperation with partners in the South.

This concern is not new. It was clearly voiced by the international NGO association ICVA (International Council of Voluntary Agencies) in the first half of the 1980s. In 1985, the ICVA formulated a set of guidelines for receiving public funds (Heijden 1987), noting that public financing could lead to a situation where, in practice, NGOs give priority to goals and development strategies other than their own, simply in order to attract state funds. ICVA was also worried that NGOs would tone down their criticism of donor countries' policy towards developing countries in order not to offend grant-awarding authorities. Moreover, ICVA pointed out that extra burdens not relevant to development work would be required of NGOs in order to fulfil the demands of public authorities regarding reports and accounts.

During the same period, some large NGOs assessed the risks connected with receiving public financing to be so great that they decided to refuse them. This applied to Oxfam's branch in the USA, for example, while most large organizations in Canada and Europe either set a ceiling on the share of expenses they could accept to be covered by the state, or formulated guidelines about conditions for accepting state support.

It is also interesting that several DAC countries' official aid agencies in the mid-1980s began to consider how they could avoid weakening NGOs' independence and their ability to function as political grassroot organizations. Judgements in DAC countries varied. The USA, France and the UK concluded that financing could at most amount to one-half of the cost of each NGO project or programme. Private organizations should finance the other half through other sources such as fund-raising and membership dues. Sweden and Norway were ready to finance all the way up to 80 per cent, and Holland and Denmark felt that full public financing did not necessarily weaken NGOs' independence. The decisive factor was that NGOs were able to determine their goals, priorities and strategies themselves, and that grant conditionalities were not linked to agreeing with official policy but only to demands for quality.

Since the mid-1980s, NGOs have often debated the correct attitude towards state funds, but the general tendency has clearly been for still larger shares of private organizations' activities to be financed by grants from official aid agencies, as well as the multilateral ones. For many NGOs, it has been an important factor that in this way they could increase their efforts within areas neglected by official aid donors.

From the viewpoint of NGOs, the ideal arrangement would be to receive a share of public funds with no strings attached and in such a way that stability and predictability in regard to incoming resources would be ensured over a period of years.

These ideal conditions have not been realized in very many DAC countries, but Holland and Denmark in particular have developed forms of cooperation that closely approach NGO wishes. In Holland, the government introduced a scheme in the last half of the 1980s that enabled the state to approve grants for a period of three years with a looser agreement for ten-year periods. In Denmark in 1991, framework agreements for financing were made with large NGOs for four-year periods. Within the framework of approved budgets, organizations can initiate projects and activities without first applying for approval from Danida.

Although examples exist of NGOs maintaining considerable independence even while receiving most of their financing from official donor agencies, there is still reason to be concerned when the problem is viewed in a larger perspective. David Hulme and Michael Edwards argue strongly for concern on the basis of several studies of the relationship between NGOs and state donors (Hulme and Edwards 1997b: 275 ff.). They stress that the tendency is not clear, but that it applies to an increasing number of NGOs in both North and South. They have been caught in a process where the first step is entering into an agreement with official donors about receiving grants. The next step is reorganization of NGOs' procedures for project design, implementation, monitoring and reporting so that they come to resemble those of official donors. The third step is changing recruiting policy for NGO personnel so that – as the two authors express it – English-speaking experts in logical framework analyses are given preference. At the same time, connections to grassroots organizations and the poor in developing countries become weaker so that the latter are reduced from being the primary partners to becoming clients and consumers of NGO services.

Developments have not yet come this far within leading NGOs in the North, and maybe they do not need to go this far, even with increased financing from official aid organizations. But to stop this process requires a consciousness of the risks and a structuring of cooperation based on NGOs' comparative advantages (see Fowler 1997: Chapter 6).

## NGOs' Relationship to States in the South

It is not possible to say very much in general about the relationship between NGOs and public authorities in developing countries. The countries are much too different for that. The same applies to NGOs. It is possible, however, to point to certain systematic differences between domestic and foreign NGOs. The following is an attempt to describe various types of relationships and the problems involved, as well as the possibilities for cooperation that promotes development. In this connection, we refer to some examples from different countries and regions.

It is possible to make a somewhat simplified division into three types of relationships between authorities and NGOs:

- Confrontation: NGOs are in opposition to authorities, and authorities try to limit NGOs' work.
- Co-opting: only NGOs that allow themselves to be integrated into the state system are permitted to work.
- Cooperation: both authorities and NGOs are committed to a constructive dialogue. Cooperation can consist mainly of a division of labour, or working together directly to solve problems, or a combination of these.

It is difficult for NGOs from the North to act in open conflict with the authorities when they are working in foreign countries, but they can focus their support on groups in society not favoured by these authorities. General support to the poor in this context is rarely controversial in itself, but if the poor target groups belong to a certain religious or ethnic group, for example, this can raise problems with the authorities, as can giving support to women in a strongly conservative Muslim society. But it is more often NGOs from recipient countries themselves that are in sharp opposition to the authorities, and may be subject to coopting by the state.

Many NGOs have in practice taken on the role of gap-fillers in relation to public authorities. This is especially true of NGOs that focus on the provision of social services to neglected target groups. During the last two decades, NGOs in many areas have experienced pressure to assume such a role, because the state has narrowed its functions due to economic decline or pressure from development banks and other donor organizations. This has often disadvantaged the poorest groups in society and in remote areas where NGOs have felt a special responsibility. This tendency has given rise to intense debate in NGO circles, and increasing numbers of NGOs have arrived at the conclusion that gap-filling as an independent strategy is unfortunate. It frees states from responsibilities that rightly should be theirs. Therefore, it is important to combine provision of social services with advocacy, and support the rights of marginalized groups in society to education, health services, access to pure drinking water and other basic necessities. This is also important because NGOs are seldom able to carry out these tasks in the long term, and because they usually can reach only small, limited groups among the many people who have been left in the lurch by authorities.

## Variations Regionally and Over Time

During the long periods when many Latin American countries were ruled by military dictatorships, NGOs functioned to a great extent as both social and political opposition. Many of them developed and worked under the protection of, particularly, the Catholic Church; others were supported by the Protestant churches and the trade unions. There was little or no cooperation with state authorities which were considered repressive. It would have been impossible to cooperate to achieve the NGOs' chief concerns – improvements in living conditions and greater freedom. Latin American NGOs saw themselves as representatives of the citizens and civil society in the struggle against the state.

This attitude of confrontation has gradually been replaced by constructive dialogue as many countries have achieved democratic forms of government. However, some of the tradition of maintaining distance and independence in relation to the authorities remains in many places in South and Central America (Bosch 1997). This has been expressed in recent years in a debate among NGOs about how they should react to the new political agenda with its emphasis on democratization and liberalization of the economy. It is a paradox that democratization presents many NGOs with their greatest problem, because it demands that they produce documentary evidence to show that they have their roots among the people, and that they actually represent the groups in society that they claim to work for. Democratic political culture demands that conflicts about distribution of resources and power are open and that they are finally decided through democratic decision-making processes – that is, through state institutions that organize citizens' political participation. This is not a natural thing for many of the older NGOs in Latin America, which are also criticized for undermining the emerging democratic institutions and procedures by keeping themselves outside as a kind of extra-parliamentary opposition (see Pearce 1997).

Coopting NGOs and subordinating them as client organizations in the public system have for many years characterized the situation in countries such as China and Indonesia. Here, authorities do allow NGOs to function in small local communities both in cities and rural areas, but a basic condition has been that they refrain from manifesting any opposition to the government in power. In China, NGOs have been forced to cooperate with the Communist Party and its front organizations. This applies to embryonic initiatives among the Chinese to establish independent citizen associations as well as to foreign NGOs (see, for example, Howell 1995).

In the Middle East, NGOs in almost all the Arab countries were under direct state control until the beginning of the 1980s. NGOs mostly functioned as front organizations for one-party and military governments. Since then, control has been eased, especially in Egypt; however, NGOs have been pressured by political and religious movements that wish to see their opinions promoted. Conservative and fundamentalist Muslim organizations in particular are opposed to independent development-oriented NGOs (see Marzouk 1997).

The attitudes of authorities towards domestic NGOs in sub-Saharan Africa vary from repression to a milder form of control-orientation. However, central authorities rarely interfere in the work of private organizations at the micro level in remote regions or in city slums, mostly because they do not have the capacity to do so. However, local politicians often do interfere in NGOs' work. NGOs that have become politically involved have most often been met with suppression by central authorities. In several countries, for example, Uganda, a kind of division of labour has emerged as democratization has progressed. Authorities have actually encouraged (and sometimes paid) NGOs to take over services and development tasks in a specific area and for marginalized groups. This has further stimulated the discussions referred to above about NGOs' gap-filling role.

Among the countries where NGOs enjoy the greatest freedom of action are India, Bangladesh and Sri Lanka. There are, however, important differences from state to state in India, and the situation in Bangladesh has changed several times with shifts in government. In recent years, many of Bangladesh's large NGOs have also come into opposition with conservative Muslim groups that have strongly condemned these organizations' special assistance for women. As a whole, however, the relationship between NGOs and the authorities in the South Asian countries mentioned must be characterized as an advanced combination of cooperation, dialogue and mutual control. It is actually not only authorities that attempt to exercise control over NGOs; the opposite is also typical. NGOs exert pressure on local authorities to make sure they implement approved welfare programmes and other initiatives for the benefit of the poor and marginalized groups such as scheduled castes and tribal people.

It is interesting that the criticism referred to above of the Latin American NGOs for remaining outside the formal democratic processes is rarely made in relation to South Asia and especially not India, where the form of government has been democratic since independence in 1947. On the contrary, here it is considered a natural aspect of political culture that the struggle concerning distribution of resources and power be carried out both inside the political system and outside it, in the social sphere we loosely refer to as civil society.

These comments should not be understood as an attempt to give a comprehensive characterization of the relationships between NGOs and authorities in different countries and regions, but only as a review of a few trends and patterns to illustrate their variety (see also Clark 1997). If we look a little closer at these relationships, the picture becomes much more complex. One reason for this is that the various state authorities within a single country can behave in extremely different ways. This is the case, for example, when comparing the states in India, but also when comparing the city councils in some of the larger Indian cities or the line ministries' activities at the local level. In some cases, close cooperation exists with local NGOs; in others, NGOs and authorities are clearly antagonists.

## Variations Among NGOs

Variations are increased further because NGOs are very different. It is significant whether NGOs limit themselves to small-scale initiatives or also attempt to affect societal structures. In most developing countries, NGOs that primarily belong to the second generation are accepted by authorities, although not always with enthusiasm. There is more widespread opposition, however, to NGOs of the third-generation type, even in many formally democratic societies such as Kenya. This is especially the case for NGOs that seek to influence political development by opposing violations of human rights or corruption and misuse of power among politicians and civil servants. This is also more widely the case for the increasing number of grassroots organizations that understand their role as not only to give material assistance to the poor but also to safeguard the concerned groups' interests and rights *vis-à-vis* the authorities.

In weak states where authorities already have problems legitimizing their exercise of power, difficulties can arise when NGOs assume the role of communicating and supporting the demands of poor, marginalized and oppressed groups in society. An increasing number of organizations attempt to play just such a role. They do this in the name of humanism, solidarity and democracy, but this does not change the fact that they then question the distribution of wealth and power in their societies. No such question is raised when NGOs, often together with authorities and official aid organizations, seek to reach the poor with education, health services, job-generating activities and other forms of support. But when such forms of support are combined with building the capacity of grassroots organizations that demand a more equal division of wealth and power, conflicts are bound to arise (see p. 5).

In this respect, among NGOs (in a broad understanding of the term), the labour movement's organizations hold a special position. These organizations' primary goal is to improve members' economic conditions through collective bargaining and negotiations with employers in the public and private sectors. Many trade unions in the Third World further attempt to help members with small-scale development projects, credit schemes and so on, but these are marginal activities in comparison with collective bargaining and actions. Therefore, trade unions, much more than other NGOs, are basically organized to articulate and aggregate demands on behalf of their members. This can be done locally and in individual enterprises but, again, trade unions usually differ from other NGOs by embracing whole sectors, large regions or even whole societies.

This is also one of the reasons why many authors do not regard trade unions as NGOs, but as a special form of popular organization. We agree, but none the less include them here because, in relation to economic and political development processes, they often function in ways similar to NGOs, understood in the narrower sense. Trade unions for workers in industry, mining, plantations, fisheries – if they are strong enough and conditions are otherwise favourable – can be of decisive significance for members' earnings and welfare. Although industrial workers in particular often earn good wages, improvements for trade union members generally mean improvements for poor families as well. Moreover, trade unions can influence state policy and the role of the public sector to move towards the same goals as those of development-oriented NGOs. All this requires that they are genuine first-party organizations, that workers join voluntarily and leaders are accountable to their members. This is a description that far from all trade unions live up to. However, those that do also support, within several essential areas, both democratization and human development.

The role of trade unions is not always evaluated positively by official aid agencies or other NGOs. On the contrary, workers' organizations are often criticized for a narrow pursuit of special interests on behalf of their own members. In this context, it is sometimes claimed that these members are not poor. This view can be correct with respect to unions of highly paid industrial workers or others with good wages, but it overlooks at least two important conditions. First, the great majority of trade union members in the Third World are relatively poor in their own societies. Second, the democratic organization of workers leads the way for other forms of self-organizing based on interests or opinions. It is not typical that workers' organizations prevent other forms of self-organization. On the contrary, their demands for freedom to organize and to engage in collective action promote more widespread acceptance and recognition of these rights by the authorities.

The final question to be discussed briefly concerning the relationship between NGOs and states in the South concerns the long-term effects of strengthening NGOs and other civil society organizations. Some authors have argued that such a development could further weaken states that are already weak. Henrik Secher Marcussen has thus concluded, based on observations in West Africa, that massive donor support to local NGOs – often circumventing central authorities – has weakened both the legitimacy of the state and its ability to co-ordinate development efforts, especially within such areas as natural resource management (for example, Marcussen 1996).

Results, however, should be seen both in a broader context and a longer time frame. If civil society organizations really grow stronger and in a sustainable way – not just temporarily while they receive funds from donors – there does not seem to be any doubt that better conditions would thereby be created for mutually binding dialogue between citizens' organizations and authorities. A strong, well-organized civil society is not an alternative to a strong state, but one of its prerequisites; most likely an indispensable prerequisite, if the strong state is also to function democratically.

## 'Small is Beautiful' – Is It Also Effective?

One of the NGOs' comparative advantages that has often been stressed is that, due to their modest size, NGOs are more flexible and better than official aid agencies at adapting their initiatives to local needs and conditions. Among NGOs themselves, however, this positive judgement has been challenged since the 1990s with the view that being small also imposes considerable limitations on an organization's impact. This viewpoint is especially expressed by those who believe that NGOs should not limit themselves to working at the micro level, but should also contribute to changes at the macro level (see earlier in this chapter). The argument is that it is here most NGOs fail, because individually they cannot achieve any notable influence on either socio-economic processes or on the political system's and state's general policy. This has given rise to discussion about how NGOs, both individually and together, can adjust their strategies so that they achieve greater impact at the macro level (see Edwards and Hulme 1992; Fowler 1997: Chapter 9).

Some of the changes that are being discussed can be summarized as follows:

1. More cooperation with state authorities.
2. Increased emphasis on national and international lobbying.
3. Establishment of networks and federations of NGOs.
4. Scaling up of activities at the micro level.

Many NGOs already cooperate closely with state authorities, especially at the local level. But it is also characteristic of some organizations that they prefer as little contact as possible with the authorities. This can be because there is too much disagreement about development goals, or because the authorities' involvement can inhibit cooperation with grassroots organizations and other representatives of poor groups. The argument against this is that NGOs, by cooperating with authorities – but without working for them – can influence their policies. This applies especially in relation to many weak states in poor developing countries where both the need and the opportunities for exerting influence can be significant.

Many examples can be found of large and well-functioning NGOs, both in the North and South, that have been able to influence line ministries and local authorities to be more poverty-oriented, partly by drawing the attention of civil servants to the problems of the poor, and partly by proposing concrete cooperation within such areas as primary health services, water supply, credit and adult education. In countries like India and Bangladesh, NGOs have often experienced that in this kind of cooperation, the earlier neglect of poor groups in society has been based on lack of knowledge and resources and not primarily on unwillingness. This has opened the way for improvements beyond what NGOs could have accomplished alone.

On the basis of concrete relationships in cooperative efforts, NGOs can attempt to influence government policy within selected areas, but experience shows that this can also be done without a basis in concrete cooperation. Both foreign and national NGOs can influence the political agenda by making poverty and environmental problems visible, and especially problems for women and marginalized groups. They can point out the need for increased efforts on the part of the public sector and propose strategies based on their own work. There is no doubt that the effect will be greater if this influence is organized in networks of NGOs working together to arrange national and international conferences and carry out larger campaigns. The large NGO conferences in connection with various UN conferences on social development, women, the environment, human rights and so on have often contributed to placing new items on national political agendas.

An example of one of the more serious network cooperations among Northern NGOs established in recent years is Eurostep (European Solidarity Towards Equal Participation of People). For several years, this organization has produced a yearbook together with other NGOs, *The Reality of Aid*, which presents a critical overview of international development cooperation seen from an NGO point of view (see Reality of Aid Project 2000). This joint project can potentially be of great significance for NGO advocacy in relation to authorities in both Europe and many developing countries. There are many other examples of international cooperation among NGOs, including use of the Internet for documentation, exchange of ideas, and communication in the broadest sense. In this connection, we can especially refer to *One World*, a network of several hundred NGOs (see www.oneworld.org).

At the same time, it must be acknowledged that the situation in most developing countries is definitely not characterized by close cooperation among NGOs. Even in small local areas, competing NGOs often find it difficult to agree about a division of labour that could at the same time ensure that their resources and support benefit a broader segment of the population. Often, at the national level, attempts are made to establish national federations of NGOs, but one common problem is that NGOs frequently compete with one another. Another problem is that they generally hesitate to commit themselves to working only within NGO networks.

This lack of cooperation is seen by many as an unfortunate pattern that should be changed. This is the case among independent observers, donor representatives and representatives of state authorities. The main argument is that coordinating NGO efforts would lead to less waste as a result of overlapping activities, and perhaps also to a certain amount of synergy if the activities of various NGOs were properly linked together into consistent development programmes.

On the face of it, this idea seems appealing. It can often seem strange that small NGOs would almost prefer to fight one another rather than cooperate, but in this context it should be remembered that these organizations are also motivated by the wish to promote their own ideas about what is the best form of development. There is no single answer to this. Therefore, there is also a limit to how much NGOs can be expected to adjust their activities to those of other organizations. Another question is how far authorities and official donors can allow themselves to go, not only morally but also in regard to the fact that compulsion in relation to NGOs would easily destroy an essential part of their motivation for carrying out voluntary work.

The fourth idea mentioned above for changing NGOs' strategies is probably the one that raises the greatest doubt. A scaling-up of the individual organization's activities to include a larger area and larger groups of the population would demand considerable growth for most, and this in itself could be difficult to manage. Furthermore, as a result of such a strategy, NGOs could become further professionalized and bureaucratized, to a point where they would lose several of the comparative advantages they have had, including close contact to small grassroots organizations in recipient countries. Critics also point out that if NGOs were to assume tasks within areas such as education and health to a much greater extent, this could be used as an argument to reduce the obligations of authorities within these areas, as discussed earlier.

Clear conclusions are not to be reached here, since the effect of an expansion of the area for NGO efforts would presumably depend on the specific circumstances, including the type of NGO, the societal context, and how such a strategy would be combined with other ideas to achieve greater impact. It is important to note, however, that the overall picture we see today is of a leading group of NGOs that are not satisfied with disparate initiatives on a small scale. They aim for influencing national and global priorities in development cooperation and rich countries' overall policy towards developing countries.

## CHAPTER 9

# Actors in Aid Interaction

§ FOREIGN aid is a policy field where a great distance exists between the original suppliers of funds, for example, from taxes and voluntary contributions in donor countries, and the final users, among them the poorest people in developing countries. Furthermore, it is a policy field where ambitions exist to be equally involved at both ends of the process: citizens and enterprises in industrial countries want to be active participants in cooperation with developing countries; and aid organizations consider local participation in aid-supported activities in developing countries to be a prerequisite for success and an aid goal in itself (see the discussion of empowerment in Chapter 8).

Between the citizens and private actors in industrial and developing countries, a great many organizations work with aid as their main activity (especially on the donor side) or with aid as an important resource in their current activities (Raffer and Singer 1996). The many organizations comprise:

- voluntary and interest organizations in donor countries that mobilize resources for aid and/or participate actively in aid planning and implementation;
- political organizations in donor countries (including parliaments) that decide the goals and the amount of aid;
- aid organizations in donor countries that manage the various forms of aid (bilateral, multilateral, NGO, private sector etc.);
- private enterprises and organizations that earn their livings through aid;
- multilateral aid organizations and international NGOs that are channels and independent actors in aid;
- the political system in developing countries that formally asks for/accepts foreign aid and makes priorities for its use;
- central administrations in developing countries that integrate aid into national planning, budgeting, implementation and accounting procedures;
- ministries and organizations in central and local administrations that receive and use aid as part of their ordinary functions;
- project organizations that are often established temporarily to implement donor-financed aid;
- voluntary and interest organizations in developing countries that implement and/or receive aid;

- organizations that, on behalf of the target group, receive and use aid for development and/or emergency relief.

The unusual thing about aid as a policy field is not that so many organizations are involved on various levels; what is unusual is rather the distance and difference between the suppliers and users, and the way in which inequality is built into the relationships during the process (Mosley et al. 1995; Stewart 1995). In spite of talk about partnership, the flow is mostly a one-way process from donor to recipient, even though donor actors often speak quite honestly about being personally enriched by the meeting of cultures that results from this distance and difference. An example of another type of policy field is industrial policy in donor countries, where enterprises and interest organizations formulate goals and demands, participate in carrying out activities and receive benefits from them. Also in social policy (aid within industrial countries), users normally have influence on policy formulation, if only through elections.

In this chapter, we first describe two tendencies: professionalization and participation, which have interwoven characteristics. The analysis shows that critics like Robert Chambers (1997) are hardly correct in claiming that there are clear contradictions and dichotomies between expert-led 'from-the-top-down' aid and people-led 'from-the-bottom-up' collaboration, which are presented as two opposing development paradigms. There are also weaknesses in the ideological presentation of development cooperation, which has as its primary advocates UN agencies and to an increasing extent the World Bank. Progressive-sounding development goals (for example, people-led development) do not change the form and process of aid in any decisive way. The interaction between actors is more varied than Chambers claims, and more unequal than the UN claims.

Thereafter, we examine the support for and formulation of aid policy in donor countries. Development assistance has only seldom been a key issue in open political processes such as election campaigns. Aid policy formation depends rather on whether aid has been instrumental in overall foreign policy (as in the large donor countries) or whether it has been 'beyond politics' with emphasis on ethical imperatives and international humanitarianism (as in the small, like-minded countries in Scandinavia and the Netherlands). In either case, recipient countries are involved to a surprisingly small extent in aid policy formulation despite the increasing call for equity, partnerships and local ownership.

The next section therefore examines the institutional frameworks for aid's use in developing countries and discusses the consequences of the partial movement away from project aid, which is the most important instrument for actor interaction. We examine one aspect of actor interaction of importance in evaluating aid's impact in developing countries (see Chapter 12): co-ordination and integration of aid in recipient countries' central administrations.

Here, we further develop elements from Chapter 4 on aid strategies: the various actors and levels of society in developing countries that interact with different types of donors. In this way, the analysis of actor interaction provides a process perspective on the analyses in other chapters.

## Professionalism and Distance

The distance between aid's donors and recipients has become greater during the 1980s and 1990s. Aid was originally given through projects that were clearly identified with the individual donor with the help of logos and abbreviations in documents and on equipment, automobiles and buildings (for example, USAID or UNICEF Project '…', and even 'Aid from EU' or 'Aid from the American people'). Experts were appointed by the donor; aid was tied to purchases in the donor country; and journalists and teachers were sent out to inform about the impact of the donor's projects in developing countries.

During the last ten to fifteen years, much of this has been changed, and with good reason. The emphasis is on national and local project ownership, and projects are presented, for example, as the national health ministry's or district government's programme. The 'foreign experts' have transformed themselves into 'advisers', and the aim is to replace them or in any case supplement them with local specialists. The tying of aid has been reduced, even though very large shares of aid funds still return to donor countries. Only information dissemination still attempts to be primarily oriented towards donor-specific initiatives, in an open attempt to maintain the taxpaying citizens' identification with aid and its results.

These necessary and sensible changes have led to less direct donor involvement in aid implementation. This greater distance to the final target group of poor people is a problem for most donors (bilateral, multilateral and NGOs), since they all seek partnership with organizations in developing countries, instead of carrying out the projects themselves. The partners are sector ministries and organizations in civil society, including local groups and NGOs. The goal is to transfer responsibility to developing countries. The use of partnership, however, unavoidably introduces one or more organizations (partners) into the process from donor to recipient.

Professionalizing aid also has other aspects, connected with the desire for quality in aid. The demand for improved aid preparation has led to extension of the project cycle with more identification and formulation missions. It has also led to the production of schematic reports on development and project goals, expected results, planned activities, resource requirements, and so on (Curry and Weiss 1993). The demand to prepare and pre-plan aid implementation has led to comprehensive monitoring and evaluation procedures as well as to comprehensive training, organization-building and institutional capacity development.

The call for professionalization partly reflects an improved insight into development demands and aid complexity and partly the fear of making mistakes in the turbulent surroundings where aid is carried out. The actors' knowledge about the connections between economic growth, human development, political influence, sustainable use of resources and similar difficult issues has improved, as described in Chapter 2. At the same time, acknowledgement of the mistakes and 'white elephants' (fiasco projects) of the past has increased and become more direct as a result of the global flow of information. The media, state auditors and politicians are present in all donor countries ready to 'exploit' aid catastrophes, which are unavoidable if one takes chances in aid in an attempt to do something effective for needy and poor people.

Professionalization has thus led to the development of a specialized aid industry with a market, technological development, demands for competence, branch culture, competition, economic interests, workplace considerations, and so on (Raffer and Singer 1996). On this point, the only difference between aid and other industries is that its goals are generally ethical and its self-perception idealistic. All in all, professionalization of aid as an idealistic policy field carries with it two important risks:

- The risk of bureaucratization, because the actors feel forced into complex solutions of complex but very concrete problems of poverty and development; and because the actors must show all necessary consideration in order to avoid being criticized for idealistic reasons (for not achieving the high goals) or on the basis of effectiveness (for feeding the white elephants).
- The risk of self-overestimation, because the aid industry admits actors as active participants only if they accept and support the idealistic goals for aid, thus reducing the ability to be self-critical; and because aid achieves legitimacy through the idealistic goals just as much as through the results that can be shown.

Our assessment is that these risks are real, even though there are great differences between donor countries and between donor organizations. Many aid actors experience frustration about the institutional and procedural obligations, including the comprehensive demands for project preparation missions, each with its often mechanical reporting rituals that prevent an effective effort on behalf of people with a great need for aid. On the other hand, researchers and other participants just as often make proposals for better analytical preparation and better insight into local conditions, which makes it possible to avoid situations where aid ignores local knowledge, supports local power relations and oppression and so forth.

In an industry that recruits its personnel from the whole world and all cultures, it is also impossible to avoid examples of incompetent aid practitioners who can hide behind aid's great idealistic goals. Critical questions risk being rejected by aid administrators who claim that changes would just increase suffering. The worst examples of this are within emergency relief, where proposals to base the donor effort on existing local human resources, technology and institutions have been rejected with the argument that it would cost lives because of delayed implementation.

This combination of bureaucratization and self-overestimation, however, does not prevent many aid organizations from being open to changes and experiments with new aid forms and strategies. In fact, we often see changes in aid fashions when all donors pursue the same new plus words and strategies (see Chapter 4). Our assessment is that it is not possible to conclude clearly about these two risks – bureaucratization and self-overestimation – which result from the demand for professionalization of an industry that is so clearly based on idealistic goals and policies.

The demands to professionalize do not apply only to donor countries. All demands for extended preparation, better-planned and -led implementation, and detailed monitoring and reporting regarding aid projects have been transferred to the weakest actors: developing countries' institutions. Since donors often have their own professionalizing demands, the risk of bureaucratization has become a reality in most developing countries receiving aid. We return to this later in this chapter.

## Participation and Institutions

The demand for participation has been and is just as strong as the demand for professionalism. The main emphasis is on developing countries. Here, participation of people and institutions is a goal for many aid organizations and a means to ensure a more effective and sustainable implementation of aid-supported activities (Chambers 1997; Cernea 1991). For example, all aid organizations' strategies for fighting poverty include the promotion of people's participation and empowerment, based on the double assumption that participation in aid activities is a prerequisite for poverty eradication, and at the same time, that poor people's participation directly reduces poverty (World Bank 2001a). Some immediate reduction of poverty does follow directly from the transfer of resources, whereas there is hardly any evidence to support the assumption that people's participation in itself leads to the approval and implementation of poverty-reducing policies and programmes.

In donor countries, the main arguments for participation in aid by different groups in society are partly that this creates support among the people for aid and the willingness to finance it, and partly that donor countries can use their own development experience and transfer it – in adapted form – to developing countries. The aim has been to oppose the tendency to isolate aid, as we described on pages 3 and 4. In donor countries, this has led to arrangements for support to businesses to promote trade, investments and technology transfers from national enterprises (Schulpen and Gibbon 2001), and support for financing of national NGOs within both development assistance and emergency relief (Oakley 1999).

In developing countries, the demand for participation has embraced all levels of society, although there have been some shifts in priority given by aid actors to participation (see Chapter 4). Behind these shifts, there has been a long-term tendency to seek more participation (under the label of ownership) at a continually higher level of society, which has led to the current demand for national ownership of aid. These levels and this tendency can be summarized as follows.

*Physical participation:* already in the beginnings of foreign aid, *quid-pro-quo* morality played an important role. An active effort was required of recipients of aid projects, especially in the form of labour. In emergency relief's food aid, food for work was the central strategy, and it was also used in development projects. An important example is Bangladesh, where women under food for work were given work, income and prestige in connection with maintenance of roads and other physical infrastructure. In development projects, participation was extended to demands for physical contributions in the form of land, materials, and so on. The rationale was both Protestant morality (it is not good for people to get something for nothing) and economic effectiveness. The most classic error in the demand for physical participation was the implicit assumption that poor households – and especially women – have an endless resource of unused labour that can easily be used in aid projects.

*Local priorities:* goals about adapted technology, use of local knowledge, strengthening of local decision-making competence, and gradual empowerment of the target group have led to comprehensive attempts to include and listen to representatives of the target group when making priorities about such things as locations of schools and health clinics or the building of feeder roads and irrigation systems. In some cases, local communities were/are given the right to make priorities between sectors, that is, whether aid should go to health, roads or agriculture. Most often, however, donors allow local priorities to be made only within a sector, just as they also add quite narrow decision-making criteria to the projects. This is usually partly due to the donors' own sector preferences, partly an often justified distrust of the local authorities' ability to use aid, and partly a wish to develop local competence in analysing possibilities and making decisions on the basis of clear and understandable criteria.

In recent years, the emphasis on local priorities has moved beyond the sector-specific towards creating space for national political priority-setting processes. Ultimately, this should be the objective of the poverty reduction strategy papers (PRSPs) promoted by IMF and the World Bank, the comprehensive development frameworks (CDFs) promoted by the Bank, and the medium-term budget/expenditure frameworks promoted by the IMF, the Bank and others. These initiatives contain elements of budget support as the dominant aid form, which is related to the long-standing issue of local co-financing.

*Local co-financing:* the demand that aid recipients should participate financially in projects has taken different forms in foreign aid. The first form was planned financing by a developing country's government of part of the project investment and in any case of all operations and maintenance costs. The rationale was/is that in this way the developing country shows that the project has high priority, also in the use of national resources. This corresponds to the arguments for giving aid as loans instead of grants. Gradually, during the 1980s, when the poorest developing countries proved to be unable both to co-finance projects and repay loans, many bilateral donors moved towards giving aid only as grants and also financing operations and maintenance costs.

At the same time, experiments increased with another form of co-financing, that of user fees. Again, different arguments were put forward: users value the services they pay for; incomes would be generated for local institutions extending the services (for example, clinics); local bureaucracies could develop an economic way of thinking; competition would be developed with private enterprises offering similar services, and so on. Experience with user fees is very mixed, but there seems to be agreement that the poorest people need to receive compensation if their access to services is to be assured.

*Use of local expertise:* for many years, foreign experts attached to aid projects had an operational role while they also trained local counterparts. This has been changed so that local expertise is made responsible for leading the projects, eventually with foreigners as advisers. The problem has thus changed character. Since donors wish to attract the best local expertise for 'their' projects, they pay higher salaries than local employees can receive for similar work in the public sector. Nevertheless, the active participation of developing countries' own expertise in aid-financed activities represents progress. Normally, these activities provide better access to equipment and resources than the often deprived and under-financed state projects. The move towards budget and sector support ought to lead to full reliance on local human resources, but donors have tended not to rely fully on national staff. They continue to insist on assigning expatriate experts as advisers to line ministries, local governments and civil society organizations in charge of programme implementation.

*Institutional integration:* local participation can also be promoted through organizational means. Already in the 1970s, many integrated projects included committees that involved the relevant ministries and interest groups in project leadership and coordination. Often, this participation was more formal than effective, because the involved interests held each other in checkmate and thus almost prevented the projects from concentrating on delivering services to the target groups. This was bureaucratized participation. The same applies to the formal integration in developing countries' national plans and investment budgets. The integration was often, also formally, only symbolic, since the aid-financed project often existed in the national plans and budgets only as a title and a minimum amount of funds sufficient to claim that the project had national priority. Potentially, the current emphasis on budget and sector support implies a break with such 'token' institutional integration.

*Policy dialogue, strategic planning and institutional participation:* since the 1980s, policy dialogue between aid donors and recipients became the mechanism that was supposed to ensure national participation in structural adjustment and other aid programmes. It was often a rather special form of national participation, however, for the policy dialogue was combined with conditionality: without macro-economic and structural reforms, the governments in developing countries would receive neither loans nor the IMF and World Bank stamp of approval, which also influenced the amount of aid given by bilateral donors. This conditionality, however, proved useless in changing the formulation and implementation of reform programmes (see Chapters 4 and 12). Therefore, donors began to develop sector programmes, which combined dialogue on policy and strategy with involvement by the directly affected national institutions (especially sector ministries and local administrations), and which involved a significant amount of aid. Thus, institutional participation does exist to an increasing degree.

The combination of professionalization and institutional participation is reflected in the fact that all types of donors emphasize partnership with organizations in developing countries that receive aid for institutional capacity-building. The risk of bureaucratization is considerable, both for donors and recipients and the interaction between them. This is not the closed realm of experts feared by Chambers; nor does it ensure national and local ownership of aid, as claimed by donors and governments in developing countries. It is this balance and its consequences for the quality of aid that we examine more closely in this chapter.

## Popular Support and Aid Policy-making in Donor Countries

In 1996, the OECD Development Centre collected available knowledge about support by people in donor countries for development assistance and emergency relief. The result indicates the following characteristics, which probably apply quite broadly in Western Europe and North America (see also Reilly 1999).

*A constant high level of support – mostly for emergency relief:* opinion polls in most donor countries indicate reasonable stability on a high level (often over 60 per cent) of support for foreign aid. People's support, however, is especially directed towards emergency relief, aid to people suffering from natural catastrophes, hunger, war and conflicts. The mass media have contributed both to the amount of support and to its focus on emergency relief, with the help of the so-called CNN effect.

*Little faith that it helps:* people express great scepticism about the effectiveness of development assistance – they do not believe that it helps. The mass media's emotional pictures of continued poverty and hopelessness in Africa, the population explosion, corruption, and destruction of natural resources understandably reinforce this scepticism.

*Exaggerated ideas about the amount of aid:* many people have two factually incorrect ideas about the amount of aid being given. First, the majority believes that aid comprises a very large share of the national budgets in donor countries. In the USA, a poll in 1993 (Smilie 1996: 34) showed that a majority of the population believed that 20 per cent of the federal budget went to foreign aid (compared to the actual figure of less than 1 per cent). Secondly, the majority expected that aid in all developing countries is of considerable size (in contrast to the actual few dollars per capita), and that it finances most development activities in developing countries (rather than just some few per cent in most developing countries).

Ian Smilie pointed out that there was considerable stability in these three basic elements in people's attitude towards aid. He concluded that opinion polls gave almost the same results at the beginning of the 1980s as at the beginning of the 1990s. He considered this to be a problem for foreign aid, also considering that many state donors and NGOs invested heavily in information activities. On the other hand, it is impressive that such a large majority of people in donor countries maintain their support for public efforts to solve problems and fight poverty in distant countries. Table 9.1 shows that the average support for aid in donor countries was quite constantly at 80 per cent in the 1980s and 1990s.

It should be noted that Table 9.1 does not take the size of the individual country's aid into consideration. As indicated in Chapter 5, the aid efforts of Spain and Ireland are quite modest. Marc Stern has collected and analysed the available studies on popular support for aid. Among his conclusions are the following (1998: vi–vii): Support for ODA varies significantly from country to country. Actual aid fatigue exists only in a few countries, especially the USA. People often rank aid low in relation to other foreign policy priorities. Health, satisfaction of basic needs, emergency relief and protection of the environment are the most popular aid goals. Aid to foreign countries in need is given priority over aid to strategic allies, but there is a tendency to focus on neighbouring countries rather than poor people in distant countries. The arguments against aid refer primarily to domestic economic needs and poverty in the donor country. There is a significant amount of scepticism about aid's effectiveness and especially the consequences of waste and corruption. The younger generations generally express greater support for development assistance and multilateral cooperation as a whole. There is no direct correlation between the economic conditions in the donor country and popular support for aid. Ethical and moral considerations play a significant role in forming public opinion on aid.

Experience across the OECD countries seems to be that there are no direct links in the individual donor country between aid organizations' effectiveness, people's knowledge about development problems and their support for aid, and the size of the country's aid. The pressure to demonstrate results and effectiveness is often expressed with reference to the need to ensure people's support, but it seems to be more an ideological demand for a change in aid's design towards the use of quantitative measures. Both politicians and researchers express the demand for effectiveness, especially as an argument for greater selectivity and focus on developing countries that carry out 'correct' policies.

Gorm Rye Olsen (2001) explores the link between public support for development cooperation and humanitarian assistance on the one hand, and policy and decision-making in regard to aid in European donor countries on the other. He argues that in complex humanitarian emergencies, such as those in Somalia, Iraq and Kosovo, the media play an important role both

**Table 9.1** Popular support for foreign aid in OECD, 1983 and 1995 (percentages)

| Rank order according to 1995 figures | 1983 | 1995 | Difference 1983–1995 |
|---|---|---|---|
| 1. Spain | | 95 | na |
| 2. Ireland | 86 | 92 | +6 |
| 3. Holland | 89 | 90 | +1 |
| 4. Denmark | 86 | 89 | +3 |
| 5. Portugal | | 88 | na |
| 6. Luxembourg | 87 | 87 | – |
| 6. Italy | 81 | 87 | +6 |
| 8. Sweden | | 84 | na |
| 9. Finland | | 82 | na |
| 10. Canada | | 82 | na |
| 11. United Kingdom | 81 | 82 | +1 |
| 12. Norway | | 80 | na |
| 13. Germany | 81 | 79 | -2 |
| 13. Japan | 79 | 79 | – |
| 15. Switzerland | | 78 | na |
| 16. France | 81 | 73 | -8 |
| 17. Australia | 65 | 72 | +7 |
| 18. New Zealand | 70 | | na |
| 19. Austria | | 68 | na |
| 20. Belgium | 81 | 66 | -15 |
| 21. USA | 50 | 45 | -5 |
| DAC average | 78% | 80% | +2% |

*Source:* Marc Stern 1998: 4.

for public opinion and for decision-makers. In relation to development assistance, he suggests instead a top-down link: a relatively narrow elite, termed 'aid mafia' in Denmark and 'development lobby' in the UK, decides on the size and allocation of the aid budget with little concern for public opinion. Public support for aid is in reality lower than the above figures indicate. It is easy – and to some extent politically correct – for people to express support for aid in general (and, as noted, mainly for emergency relief and other humanitarian assistance). When people in donor countries are asked about their preferences among a large number of areas of public sector expenditure, development aid tends to land close to the bottom, together with public expenditures for culture, for example.

Olsen distinguishes between two types of policy-making. In France and the EU, aid policy-making is highly elitist – neither politicians nor civil society organizations are very much involved. In the UK and Denmark, NGOs and to some extent the private sector are involved in policy-making coalitions through 'issue networks' and 'policy communities', based in part on ethical concerns. Germany lies somewhere between these two types of policy-making. In all cases, the state bureaucracy in charge of aid administration is considered to have decisive influence on aid policy-making and the allocation of aid resources among sectors and countries.

Right-wing analyses of aid policy-making suggest that such policy communities consist of altruistic stakeholders, who all have an immediate interest in aid delivery, and who are 'paid' for their support through allocations to their respective pets. Left-wing interests were first rewarded through support for socialist experiments in developing countries and, later, through empowerment strategies. Religious and other social groups and movements are given state resources as implementers of aid aimed at their partners in civil society in developing countries. Consulting firms are given a huge and safe market in project cycle studies, monitoring and evaluation. And the industrial sector is involved through tied aid. This 'slicing-the-cake' understanding of aid policy-making in donor countries overlooks the fact that the changing aid strategies fundamentally reflect changing – and gradually improved – understandings of poverty reduction and development promotion (see the discussion of emerging aid strategies in Chapter 4).

An important lesson from such debates is that aid policy-making takes place in relatively closed circles in donor countries and international organizations. The policy communities are led by aid bureaucracies in donor governments and supported by donor NGOs (through moral and political advocacy) and multilateral organizations (through knowledge and political advocacy). The policy communities include policy-makers in developing countries only to a very limited extent. It is only after aid policies have been adopted by donors that policy implementation involves institutions in recipient countries, and then mainly the government bureaucracies. Politicians in the poorest developing countries have been conspicuously absent from aid and even development policy-making. This is unfortunate in view of the talk of partnership and local ownership during the past decade.

Significant forces, however, are trying to modify donor dominance in aid policy-making. Northern NGOs have begun to take partnership seriously by involving their Southern partners in policy-making structures and processes in the Northern countries. Progressive donor governments engage in – more or less effective – consultations with their partner governments and other stakeholders in developing countries. The UN system has always provided space for its majority of Third World member states to express their concerns and priorities, but donor influence on actual programme priorities and design remains critical. Even the IMF and the World Bank insist on government ownership of each developing country's comprehensive development framework and poverty reduction strategy paper. These, however, have to be approved by the donor-dominated IMF and World Bank executive boards within the framework of the reigning development paradigm, policies and strategies.

Fortunately, the rationale of donor actors for various aid goals, considerations and programmes is often based on analyses of actual needs in developing countries. The altruistic interests and the soft goals are related to developing countries and their problems. It is important, however, to point to the inequality that exists between donor and recipient actors. A donor organization often makes demands of the recipient government that are based on the donor's own political goals and the target group's needs and goals. Donor actors are deeply involved in the development process in the developing country, whereas recipients are largely absent as actors in the aid process in the donor country. It is here the inequality lies. And it is on the basis of the interaction between process and content that demands concerning quality and capacity should be made of the donor actors. The usefulness of broad goals and strategies for aid can, of course, be judged only on the basis of aid's impact in developing countries (see Chapter 12).

## The Institutional Framework for Aid in Developing Countries

The institutional framework for aid has some typical characteristics in most developing countries, except for large federal states such as India and middle-income countries like those in Latin America, due to a relatively small amount of aid. The main characteristics can be described as follows.

*Many donors of different sizes:* the multilateral agencies and many bilateral donors and international NGOs are found in most developing countries, except for the Soviet-supported regimes during the Cold War and 'pariah states' like Liberia, Iraq, Somalia, Kampuchea, and earlier Rhodesia and South Africa. Typically, the largest donors have included the former colonial powers, the USA, the World Bank, the EU, and also Japan in South Asia. The donor presence in the capitals of developing countries has varied from large country offices with considerable local decision-making competence to 'flying missions' with narrow project preferences.

The large donor countries usually have embassies with special aid sections. These are rather large in the respective former colonies. The Nordic countries originally had aid missions in a few developing countries, but in the 1990s these were integrated into their embassies, leading to an expansion of their institutional presence. USAID closed several country missions at the start of the 1990s as part of aid cutbacks, but the World Bank has increased the number of country offices in order to be closer to project implementation. The UNDP, with over 130 country offices, has the most extensive network, and several other UN agencies (especially UNICEF, the FAO, the WHO) have done their best to follow the UNDP's example.

*Core ministries with approval and monitoring competence:* in accordance with the principle of national sovereignty, which is the foundation of the international political-administrative system, foreign donors must be approved by the recipient country's government, which has typically established one or more departments for international cooperation within the core organizations of the central administration. At first, these departments were most often placed within planning ministries or commissions, in accordance with the common faith in central planning. Later, the departments were moved into finance ministries. In both cases, the aim was to integrate aid into the government's national plans and investment budgets. In many developing countries, aid from multilateral development banks was placed under the finance ministries, because it is financial aid. In some developing countries, such aid has been approved and coordinated by the central bank.

Departments in the central administration for coordinating aid have typically had special offices for the largest bilateral donors: for the Nordic countries, for UN aid, for EU aid, for development banks, and so on. Thus, close relations developed between the individual donor and the authorities responsible for giving approval. This has been strengthened through officials' trips to donor countries or donor organization headquarters. This donor orientation, together with serious inequality in the size of staff – one developing-country official is often responsible for several donors with both embassies and country offices – has meant that aid management is fragmented in the individual developing country. This has been reinforced by the fact that NGO aid was usually approved and managed by other offices, for example, in the social ministry or the prime minister's office.

*Line ministries, boards and project organizations:* most development assistance is given in the form of projects, which formally, and after a while also in practice, are integrated under line or sector ministries, public boards and state-owned enterprises. The projects usually have been donor-specific with a medium-long-range time perspective (from one-year technical assistance to infrastructure development over ten to fifteen years). They often have several consecutive phases if the developing country proves to lack capacity to take over operation and maintenance.

The aid-financed projects' form and content have changed radically over the years, especially in relation to their integration in developing countries' administrations. In broad terms, the process has been as follows: advanced project islands → isolated project organizations → multi-sector project institutions → policy-oriented programmes → sector programmes → budget support. The background for these changes has mainly been donors' varying strategies for achieving aid goals. The expectations directed towards sector ministries have developed correspondingly: to import modern technology → to take over operations and maintenance → to coordinate state services → to liberalize and privatize public services → to prepare and implement sector reforms and strategies → to manage public finances.

For boards and state-owned enterprises – involved with trade and public utilities, for example – donors' changed demands mostly involved privatization, in spite of the fact that these same donors had contributed to establishing these state institutions twenty or thirty years earlier. This was especially the case for multilateral development banks and to a certain extent large bilateral donors. Many small bilateral donors and UN agencies, also in the 1980s, continued to support boards and state-owned enterprises in spite of the dominance of structural adjustment programmes.

*Local administrations:* most developing countries have an administrative structure with at least three levels: central administration, region or province, and district. The province level is often only administrative, while the district level can include a political council, deconcentrated units of sector ministries, and a local administration with extremely limited resources. Local administrations have also been given varying roles and opportunities in relation to aid, but most often they have been ignored, since the donors' primary institutional partners have been project organizations, sector ministries and boards.

The local departments of the health ministries, for example, however, have been 'recipients' of countless donor and disease-specific projects. They have attempted to integrate these into the primary health services supported by both the government and the donors on the political level. In the 1970s, local administrations were included as coordinating units in many integrated, multi-sector projects – generally, without great success. During the 1980s and 1990s, local administrations were seen as donors' essential, potential partners, both directly as project-carrying organizations and indirectly as units that were strengthened in execution of decentralization programmes. This led to increasing interest in developing the institutional capacity of local administrations.

*NGOs and organizations in civil society:* during the 1970s and 1980s, donors' interest in using international and local NGOs as channels for both development assistance and emergency relief increased. This was because state institutions in many low-income countries proved to have problems with effectiveness, both administratively and with regard to financing operations and maintenance. Surprisingly, many donors found it more reasonable to finance all a project's expenses when a local NGO was responsible for the project than when, for example, a social ministry was responsible. This motivated many countries to hunt for NGOs that were capable and worthy of support. The strongest local NGOs received far more inquiries and offers of money from bilateral and multilateral donors and international NGOs than they could manage (Hulme and Edwards 1997b). At the same time, a multitude of small local NGOs burgeoned as a response from industrious politicians, businessmen and interest organizations to the many new aid opportunities. Many have no local capacity or support (see the discussion in Chapter 8).

Parallel with this market-led development of local NGOs, an institutionalized civil society of local interest organizations began to manifest itself. They represented a third path in the ideological confrontation between state management and market forces. This development, however, was not radically new, as a concept or in concrete terms, since there were hardly more interest, religious or economic organizations than there had been before this focus on civil society.

## Survival of the Project Aid Form

The most used aid form is still the project: an externally formulated intervention in local development processes. This form has a clear time perspective and a series of well-defined activities financed by a donor in agreement with a partner in the developing country. The institutional framework for 'programme aid', which includes balance of payments support, food aid, structural adjustment programmes, and even budget support, is also the project. Most programmes are organized as projects in both donor and recipient organizations. The project cooperation form has thus been able to survive the appearance of a series of new actors (especially NGOs in donor and recipient countries and local governments in recipient countries), new aid forms and instruments, and a changed aid ideology with emphasis on process-oriented aid, partnership and national ownership.

National or local administrations in industrial or developing countries prepare and carry out policies. This is done with the help of orders, bans, grants, incentives, sanctions, information dissemination, production and management of public services, maintenance of public installations, and investment projects. Donors tried in the 1990s to support their partners in all these activities through process support and aid to capacity-building. But the institutional framework for cooperation is still the project. Why?

The traditional reasons for the project cooperation form still apply: the donor supports directly only those activities that are in accordance with the goals of its development and aid policy. The donor can (with the help of technical assistance) contribute to implementing just those activities that have preference. The donor can demonstrate to the world, and especially the politicians and taxpayers at home, that aid is being used effectively on efforts of importance. Through the project, the actors can reach a well-defined target group because they are able to circumvent unnecessary administrative levels and limitations. The donor can contribute to the empowerment of the target group, because it can prevent local power holders from controlling resources. Different interest groups in both donor and recipient countries can exert pressure on behalf of just their sector, region or theme, so that it will receive resources (money, foreign exchange, jobs, higher wages, and so on) and political attention. The recipient can control the donor's influence within the project's defined framework.

There are many problematic aspects connected with the donor-specific project aid form: it is difficult for recipient countries' central political and administrative institutions to set national priorities and allocate sufficient resources for their implementation. This is because the projects, which demand both resources and attention, fragment national policies, plans and budgets. There are countless examples of developing countries' governments focusing exclusively on donor-financed projects, which is different from implementing policies. The projects taken together often create more overlapping than synergy, because they live their own lives: they are formulated independently of each other, and their success criteria vary. Projects are implemented in a cycle from identification and preparation; through agreements, contracts and implementation; to control, monitoring and evaluation. This demands comprehensive, project-specific missions and reports that often overburden weak institutions in developing countries. The projects often lead to a focus on disbursements: donors must use the resources agreed upon and planned for within the framework of the project, even though continuous monitoring perhaps shows that implementation capacity is too low, or that other activities should have higher priority. Projects obligated, formally or in practice, to buy equipment and consulting services in the donor country can be more than 30 per cent more costly than they would be if developing-country institutions could make purchases through open competition.

All in all, this has led to undermining the institutional capacity of many developing countries' public administrations and NGOs and goes against aid's intentions. Since this has been going on through all the decades of foreign aid, it must be judged to be at least as serious for governments in developing countries as the public cutbacks and privatizations that accompanied the structural adjustment programmes' ideological and actual attack on the state in low-income countries (Engberg-Pedersen et al. 1996).

In the 1990s, some people in the World Bank (the trend-setters) have been the leading critics of the negative consequences of projectitis (see Denning 1994; World Bank 1998b). The World Bank has problems in this area, however, because it is part of its mandate to work with projects, and because most of its staff are technicians and economists who specialize in project preparation and monitoring. Therefore, the Bank's proposals for a solution – that aid should concentrate on sector investment programmes (SIPs) and other sector-wide approaches (SWAps) – are also formulated and prepared within the framework of the project form. The idea is that all donors who want to support the agricultural sector in a developing country, for example, must agree with the government, the agricultural ministry and other national actors on an agricultural policy and strategy that is then translated into concrete activities. The individual donor can then choose some parts as 'its' aid.

In Chapter 12 on aid impact, we see that when projects are correctly used, they can both contribute to capacity development and to improving the target group's livelihood.

## Donor Coordination and Aid Integration

The demand for aid coordination has been put forth with almost constant force since the 1960s. The rationale is obvious: in most low-income countries, the central administration is too weak, both in technical-administrative terms and in its ability to coordinate aid from thirty to sixty bilateral and multilateral donors and international NGOs. This is especially true when this aid is given in the form of hundreds, maybe thousands, of projects. Carol Lancaster (1999) examines the institutional consequences of aid dependence and concludes that it leads to capacity destruction. This is because both donors and their immediate counterparts among recipient government institutions are unwilling to follow coordinated planning and implementation processes that might reduce the resources set aside for their particular sectors and programmes. In practice, it has only been the donors themselves that have been able to diminish the negative consequences of the donors' competition for good projects and the risk (and reality) of functional and geographic overlapping between projects.

Developing country governments have had a clear interest in receiving all the aid that is offered, also even though the donors' explicit or implicit policy preferences have often been contradictory. Examples of contradictory donor advice have been seen in all social and sector policies: centralization vs decentralization; user fees vs free services; support for agricultural cooperatives or for advanced farmers; food aid in the form of commodities or money; investments in main or feeder roads; development of universities or primary school education; support for formal or informal institutions; export-oriented or import-substituting industrialization; advanced or adapted technology, and so on.

During the first decades, the aid world discussed *donor* coordination – developing countries had not yet entered the scene. As late as the 1970s, there was an expectation that the UN Development Programme, UNDP, had a central coordinating role, not only for the UN but for all foreign aid. The

UNDP was supposed to finance and coordinate all technical assistance directly from the UN system, that is, also the aid from the FAO, UNESCO, the WHO, and the UN's other specialized agencies. In addition, the UNDP's five-year country programmes, agreed upon with governments in individual developing countries, served as a reference point for all other multilateral and bilateral aid to these countries. As described in Chapter 7, the UNDP's central role was undermined before it could be implemented, because other actors' aid increased more than the UNDP's, and because no aid organization – not even the UN's specialized agencies – wished to let itself be coordinated by the UNDP.

For the multilateral organizations, the important thing was to manifest themselves with clearly profiled projects and country programmes, so that they could attract donors' attention and resources. In the severe donor criticism of ineffectiveness in the UN system that has characterized the aid debate during the last twenty years, it should be remembered that the Western donor countries themselves contributed to making the UNDP's role impossible. Donors gave more resources to multilateral organizations outside the UN system (especially development banks and the EU), and they gave multi-bi-assistance to the UN's specialized agencies within each of their specialities. This led to a critical fragmentation of the UN's total development aid.

The UNDP has carried out several attempts to recapture the initiative in donor coordination. First, an aid coordination mechanism was developed in the form of country-specific roundtables, where governments in developing countries were supposed to conduct dialogues with donors about aid needs, problems and priorities. The large Western donors had little confidence in this system; therefore, they and the World Bank developed a system of consultative groups for the most important developing countries. Under the leadership of the World Bank, annual meetings are held where donors, on the basis of a presentation by the World Bank, discuss the size of aid needs followed by donor commitments to give aid to the individual country. To ensure that the donors are represented by leading officials (or ministers) with competence to give such a commitment, the consultative group meetings are usually held in Paris. The result is that all donors sit on their home turf and discuss a single developing country's problems with its government, but on the basis of a presentation by a donor-controlled multilateral organization. In this way, the basic inequality in the interaction between aid actors is confirmed and institutionalized.

The UNDP's other attempts comprised, among other things, implementation of theme discussions (agriculture, health, capacity development, and so forth) within the UN system for the purpose of coordination of at least the UN's limited aid. In some developing countries, this was carried out with inclusion of the relevant national authorities, but even this was not effective: individual UN agencies do not want to be coordinated, because they consider it as a threat to their independent profile and thus to their survival. The same limited success has been the fate of the attempt in recent years to establish one UN coordinator in each country and to create one UN country strategy and one UN country office. This is why in Chapter 7 we expressed doubts about the UN secretary-general's recent reform attempt, which continues to follow this coordination line on both the country and headquarter levels, through the UN Development Assistance Framework (UNDAF) and the UN Development Group (UNDG), respectively.

In two consultant studies for and on UNDP (Engberg-Pedersen and Freeman 1994; Engberg-Pedersen et al. 1996), we have argued for a change from donor and aid coordination, which has had very limited success, to aid integration, which moves the focus from the donors to the recipient institutions. To make this possible, recipient institutions, individually and together, must have the capacity to determine development and aid priorities and to demand adjustment and integration of aid in the national institutions' planning and working procedures and budgets. Therefore, a central job for the UNDP ought to be to extend technical assistance to strengthen recipient institutions' capacity to integrate foreign aid. One reason the UNDP has not carried out this proposal immediately is that the provision of capacity-developing aid to national bureaucrats to enable them better to manage other donors is not a very 'saleable' main function. It is somewhat easier, for example, for UNICEF to mobilize resources (including the sale of Christmas cards) with a message that this aid goes directly to the poorest women and children in the world!

A main element towards improved aid integration would be to move the focus and activities from the donor society 'into' developing countries. In the OECD's Development Assistance Committee (DAC), donors have negotiated improving aid procedures for many years. In some areas, it has been possible to come a long way, perhaps especially in relation to untying aid so that money for purchases is no longer automatically used in the donor country itself. In other areas, coordinating content (aid should support national priorities and the policies and programmes agreed upon) is more important than harmonizing procedures.

Another donor coordinating system is perhaps also on its way towards a similar shift. Since 1988, the donors' special aid programme for sub-Saharan Africa (Special Programme of Assistance for Africa, SPA), under the leadership of the World Bank, has coordinated especially the policy-oriented aid to Africa. An evaluation of the SPA found that coordination has been most effective in relation to untying and streamlining purchasing procedures in connection with support to developing countries' imports. Donors, however, did not succeed, for example, in creating common attitudes and procedures with regard to paying salaries to the local employees of the donor-financed projects (World Bank, OED 1998). This problem (relatively high salaries and other incentives paid by donors to developing country officials and experts connected with 'their' projects) bears a great deal of the blame for aid's fragmenting effect on central and local administrations in developing countries.

There is, however, reason for some optimism regarding aid integration. The broad self-criticism on the part of donors regarding the project aid form, and the talk of national ownership and partnership point in this direction. Concretely, the sector-wide approaches (SWAps) favoured by most donors aim at aid integration rather than aid or donor coordination. The World Bank's highly influential report, *Assessing Aid: What Works, What Doesn't, and Why* (1998b), is very critical of the effects of lack of coordination, partly because of the administrative burden on recipient institutions as a consequence of the fragmented nature of aid. More fundamentally, this report is critical of the donors' reliance on individual projects: due to the fungibility of aid, the objectives and qualities of individual projects matter less than the quality of overall policies and the capacity of national and local institutions in the developing country. We discuss this at some length in Chapter 12.

## Aid Management and Politics

In 1999–2000, the World Bank, led by President Wolfensohn, designed a new country-specific mechanism to facilitate aid coordination and integration: the comprehensive development framework, CDF (Wolfensohn 1999; Hopkins et al. 2000). The idea is to seek coordination within a development matrix of actors and sectors for each country. All national (government, civil society and private sector) and international partners (multilateral and bilateral donors and international NGOs) involved in the development of a particular country must discuss and agree on a division of responsibility in relation to national development policies on issues, problems and sectors. The CDF was intended to supplement rather than replace the World Bank-led consultative groups for each developing country. The CDF does have potential for enhancing the transparency of aid relationships and encouraging substantive discussions on development priorities, at least among government authorities and donors. To reduce the alienation inherent in the Paris location of meetings in country-specific consultative groups, the World Bank promoted the use of global country-specific video conferences in order to involve all partners in CDF discussions.

The CDF suffers from three basic weaknesses, however. First, there is little chance that individual donors are interested in accepting such a 'central planning' approach; they are likely to continue to pursue their respective non-development objectives and to invest in pet sectors. Second, unless recipient governments have adequate capacity to prepare and monitor the CDFs, these are likely to institutionalize World Bank and other donor influence on national planning rather than integrate aid into national priorities. Third, the CDFs are likely to strengthen the power of bureaucrats (national and international) in development planning and priority-setting, despite the call for national ownership and 'government in the driver's seat'; cabinets may be involved, but parliaments have a very limited role in the CDFs.

Thus, the CDF may give a good picture of the real influence of aid and donors in national development planning, but it contradicts the development community's rhetoric about respect for national policies and recipient ownership. It is remarkable how soon the CDF rhetoric, which was pushed strongly by Wolfensohn himself, has given way to the new fad in such relationships: the Poverty Reduction Strategy Papers (PRSPs). The strength of the latter lies in their inclusiveness (from IMF to local civil society groups), but this is also their potential weakness: the PRSP is becoming overloaded with a diversity of expectations, ranging from continued economic stabilization and structural adjustment, through policy-led aid coordination, to democracy and participatory priority-setting for effective poverty reduction.

Still, the most promising initiatives towards improved aid integration seem to be the PRSPs and the SWAps. The PRSP can and should reintroduce politics, including political disagreements rather than bureaucratic consensus, into the design and implementation of poverty reduction policies, strategies and programmes, ranging from governance to sector and community development. The precondition is that recipient countries dare to demand respect for national policies and that donors dare to let go and grant such respect.

With regard to sector programme support, there seems to be a need for both donors and recipients to understand better the difference between policies and politics and the distance from policies to implementation. In an assessment of the early experience of donors and their partners (Therkildsen et al. 1999: 1f.), we concluded as follows:

- Policy-making in low-income countries (LICs) is primarily about mobilization and use of resources in a process characterized by conflicts and bargaining under conditions of constant change, resource scarcity, inadequate knowledge and insufficient capacity. Sector policy outcomes are significantly influenced by the actors and stakeholders directly involved in the implementation processes. Individuals and personalities exert their influence through leadership and through formal and informal position and power.
- Implementation processes and resource scarcities determine the outcome of sector policies and related sector support. Sector policies may, and often do, change overnight. Implementation approaches, especially with respect to target groups, are much less likely to change rapidly; they are influenced more by long-term resources and capacities. Often, networks of implementing organizations have greater impact on sector support outcomes than explicit policies do.
- Through its reliance on elaborate policy documents, detailed planning procedures, formalized agreements, fixed targets, and so on, the typical approach to sector support does not capture the reality of policy-making and implementation in LICs. Policy-making, implementation and evaluation activities are typically concurrent and overlapping. The 'target' is constantly

moving. Yet donor procedures for sector support tend to follow a planning and cyclical approach similar to that of the project cycle. Sector policy assessments tend to focus on the specific contents of policies and to neglect the processes producing policy, for example, in sector-specific implementation networks and at service delivery points.

- Sector policies and support programmes are a part of and affected by the political, institutional and financial reforms that are currently implemented in all corners of the public sector in LICs. 'Reformitis' is replacing 'projectitis' as a key characteristic of donor–recipient relations. Many sector support programmes address issues such as incentives and pay, decentralization of functions, the interaction of markets, regulatory systems and political spheres – but they often do so in an uncoordinated and even contradictory manner. The result tends to be overload and de-capacity-building in the already weak public sectors of LICs.

## Actor Interaction on Different Levels of Society in Developing Countries

Earlier in this chapter, we have seen that aid policy is special, because it is to a great extent part of decision-making processes that take place in donor countries with limited participation by recipient countries. There is clearly a difference, however, between donors on this point. UN agencies like UNDP and UNICEF have always been decentralized to the country level to a significant extent, while the World Bank has both its strength and its competence in Washington. Likewise, the small, progressive, bilateral donors have generally gone further than the large ones in including governments of developing countries in discussions of country strategies, sector programmes, and so forth.

For most donors, the changes in aid relations during the 1990s moved towards their greater involvement in institutional structures and processes in developing countries and a stronger role for developing countries' institutions in the total aid process. Analysis also shows that international donors have been the driving force behind almost all these changes. If we limit the discussion to small and medium-sized low-income countries, which comprise the largest group receiving development assistance, we can summarize actor interaction during these years on eight levels of society (see also Chapter 4).

*State or political level:* the new element here is that most donors, also including the small bilateral donors, UN agencies and international NGOs, attempt to enter a dialogue with and influence recipient countries' political leaders, parliaments, political parties and human rights organizations. The aim is to promote democratization and political leaders' accountability to the people. Since donor involvement has become very intensive on this level, great humility is required on the part of donors towards differences in history and culture among developing countries. At the same time, political leaders in developing countries must be both reflective and self-conscious in order to ensure that local politics is taken seriously and is given adequate space.

*Central administration's core ministries:* also here, more donors have entered the scene, especially in connection with reform of the public sector in which multilateral development banks, the UNDP and most of the large and small bilateral donors wish to participate. In spite of greater agreement among donors, partly based on pragmatism, about the role of the state in developing societies (see the discussion in Chapter 13), there are still considerable differences in attitude among donors based on their different experience with state organizations' role, management and way of functioning in their countries of origin. The greatest challenge lies in developing countries' political leadership and core ministries, which demand that administrative reforms be based on their own countries' needs, and that they are adapted to these countries' capacity and institutional traditions. This can lead to a showdown with donor discussion groups, which – for example, within the framework of the SPA – attempt to negotiate the 'correct' administrative reform.

*Central administration's line ministries, boards and state-owned enterprises:* the interaction with donors in many developing countries has differed greatly between line ministries and state-owned enterprises. Most donors, including development banks, the UN system, bilateral donors, and many international NGOs, want stronger line ministries. This is expressed in sector programme aid and capacity development. On the other hand, development banks and to a certain extent the large bilateral donors press for privatization of state-owned enterprises (World Bank 1995). A common element is the demand for user fees and market orientation, which applies to both line ministries and state-owned enterprises. Here, however, the political differences between donors become apparent, since UN agencies, small donors and international NGOs are more reluctant to introduce market mechanisms for the delivery of public services, especially to the poor.

*National economy on the macro level:* aid involvement in macro-economic and private sector development accelerated with the structural adjustment programmes of the 1980s where the World Bank played a leading role among donors. In spite of many declarations of intent by donors, aid initiatives directly related to large and medium-sized enterprises in the private sector are still limited. They still mostly entail creating prerequisites for economic growth through physical infrastructure, liberalized economic policies and financial services such as credit systems. In these areas, most donors let the World Bank and IMF take the lead, with the exception of infrastructure investments, which are still characterized by much donor competition for good projects.

When political dialogue and aid move beyond economic policy into the areas of labour markets and education, differences between donors begin to be clearer due to differences in their experience with business development and state intervention. The relevant state institutions in the small and medium-sized low-income countries rarely take the initiative in demanding aid's subordination to national policies for these areas, which are most often 'new' political areas in these countries.

*Local administration, with political and administrative units:* decentralization plays an increasing role in the interaction between donors and governments in developing countries, although there have been earlier attempts at decentralization and giving aid directly to local administrations. Active donor involvement on this level resembles their involvement with line ministries. Donors are directly involved with the deconcentrated units delivering public services. The tendency in recent years has been for most donors to be involved in the administrative aspects of local administration carried out within the framework of sector programme aid. Thus, district councils and other political units are kept outside most aid on this level. Many donors (bilateral, multilateral and NGOs) prefer to give aid to organizations in civil society, which often compete with or are even in opposition to the formal political units on the local level. There are some donors, however, that are very active in giving aid to the political and administrative levels in the local administrations simultaneously.

*National economy on the local level:* donors have always actively given aid to development of agriculture, crafts, trade, small industry and the informal sector in the interface between rural and urban areas. In the 1990s, many donors – from NGOs to the World Bank – highlighted micro-credit as their main strategy (World Bank 1996b) without it seeming seriously to have stimulated the informal sector in many of the least developed countries. Actor interaction is made difficult by the fact that many developing countries do not have a local private sector with entrepreneurs that stand ready to invest in production.

*Organized civil society, with NGOs and interest groups:* interaction between donors and recipients is being increasingly spread out to civil society. As described in Chapters 4 and 8, this shift from the situation where the state was the only partner for donors occurred already in the 1970s and then accelerated under the wave of liberalization during the 1980s. During these decades, local NGOs were the new partners for donors. It was only in the 1990s that the whole of organized civil society, including economic, social, cultural and political interest groups, became drawn in as important direct partners for donors. This applies to most donor types, although some international NGOs have had longer experience with such direct partnerships.

For formal reasons, the multilateral organizations (the UN system and development banks) have generally been more closely connected with state governments (except for UNICEF) than the bilateral donors, which through project organizations have given aid directly to organizations outside central and local administrations. Today, even the World Bank and UNDP, which otherwise have been very focused on central administration, try to enter into direct dialogue with organized civil society. The earlier donor competition for good projects has now been replaced to a considerable degree by donor competition for effective local organizations that can also function as good partners.

*The target group consisting of individuals, households and organizations:* it is difficult to generalize about direct actor interaction between the target group and the very different donors. In spite of much talk about target group participation and empowerment, there have hardly been decisive changes in this interaction. For most bilateral and multilateral donors, the target group is still mostly recipients of public services rather than active participants in international aid.

In their analysis, *European Development Cooperation and the Poor*, Cox et al. (2000: 40–56) find that donors can play at least five types of roles in making a difference for the target group of poor people: (1) promoting economic growth and hoping for some trickle-down; (2) supporting the creation of a pro-poor, domestic policy environment that gives the poor access to resources, knowledge and rights; (3) improving domestic institutions at national and local levels to make them more accountable and responsive to the needs of the poor; (4) financing specific poverty-focused interventions to target special groups with services; and (5) taking the lead in policy, programme and institutional innovations aimed at effective poverty reduction. We return (in Chapter 12) to their findings on the effectiveness of these roles; the point here is that these roles involve donor agencies in all dimensions of societal development in recipient countries, but not necessarily in direct interaction with the poor.

All in all, aid is in a situation where the continually increasing number of donor actors (including international NGOs) have moved far into central and local administration, the political system and organized civil society in developing countries – or in any case in the low-income countries. It is difficult to imagine a way back, in the form of a swing of the pendulum, which would draw donors out of developing country institutions, unless they should withdraw completely from giving aid. The decisive question, therefore, is whether the different types of developing country institutions have political legitimacy, technical and administrative capacity, as well as financial resources, not only to act as partners but also to demand that donors give aid on their conditions. We discuss this question in Chapters 13 and 14.

CHAPTER 10

# Emergency Relief and Humanitarian Assistance

§ DEVELOPMENT assistance and emergency relief used to be two very different sets of activities, delivered by different organizations. Within the UN, the World Food Programme (WFP) and the High Commissioner for Refugees (UNHCR) were engaged in relief and humanitarian assistance, whereas the UN Development Programme (UNDP), FAO, ILO, WHO and others provided development aid. The multilateral development banks stayed out of the relief business, though the World Bank in the 1990s returned to an involvement in reconstruction and rehabilitation of post-conflict and transition countries that had been the Bank's original role in the late 1940s and the 1950s. Most bilateral donors had separate units in charge of relief, which was delivered directly or through NGOs and UN agencies. Most NGOs grew out of relief activities (such as Red Cross/Red Crescent, Médecins sans Frontières), and many moved into development cooperation (such as Oxfam, Lutheran World Federation). The EU has had the most clear separation between relief (European Commission Humanitarian Office, ECHO) and development aid (delivered by several departments in the Commission).

While many agencies since the 1980s have become involved in both development and humanitarian assistance, the organizational culture, strategies and performance criteria of the two fields have changed back and forth from closeness to separation. Originally (1950s and 1960s), development aid and relief shared the wish to do things quickly and efficiently, and all aid was delivered through projects managed directly by foreign staff. During the 1970s and 1980s, humanitarian assistance continued to emphasize rapid reaction and the achievement of immediate results on the ground, whereas development assistance – as we have seen throughout this book – paid increasing attention to integrated services; institutional capacity-building; economic, social and environmental sustainability; local participation and ownership.

Following the droughts in the Horn of Africa in the mid-1980s, there was increasing disillusionment both with the tendency towards extensive 'spoon-feeding' of refugees and disaster victims whose situation did not seem to improve (for example, Eritreans and Ethiopians living in refugee camps in the Sudan for decades), and with the continuous delivery of relief to *recurring* catastrophes. Anderson and Woodrow (1989) describe well how relief failed to reduce the vulnerability of disaster victims (whether from drought or flooding). For humanitarian assistance to reduce people's vulnerability and the risk of recurring disasters, it needed to develop a range of new approaches, strategies and instruments that reduced its distinctiveness from development assistance. Aid agencies and analysts started to explore the 'continuum' from relief, through recovery and rehabilitation, to development and prevention. New concepts were invented and tested: 'sustainable recovery', 'development-oriented relief', 'disaster prevention and preparedness', and so on.

The 1990s saw another major challenge to the separation between development aid and relief: peace-building (covering peace-making and peace-keeping) was integrated into international, coordinated humanitarian interventions in complex political emergencies (Edkins 1996). The politicization of humanitarian assistance challenged the sacred neutrality of relief workers, turning them into partly unwilling parties to the conflicts. This change, which has also resulted in personal threats to the lives of relief workers, interacts with the increasing complexity of development-oriented relief to produce a potential swing back towards a renewed division of labour between relief, development and peace-keeping. International and national NGOs recognize the capacity of armed forces (whether from the UN, NATO or the EU) to maintain order, protect relief workers and deliver services in conflict situations and complex emergencies; but they criticize the military 'takeover' of relief as expensive, of low quality and potentially traumatizing for conflict victims.

The major changes in the 1990s can be divided into two parts (Duffield 2001: 11). During the first half of the 1990s, the conflict-related focus of the international community was on humanitarian interventions: the establishment of institutions that allowed aid agencies to work in situations of conflict and to support civilians in war zones. Partly due to the limited success of these interventions (see, for example, Clarke and Herbst 1997 on Somalia), the policy focus shifted in the mid-1990s towards conflict resolution and post-war reconstruction. Today, more development and relief agencies and more political actors are becoming involved in ever more integrated human and natural disasters with a diversity of objectives, strategies and instruments that cover relief to human beings, conflict prevention and resolution, capacity-building for crisis management and disaster prevention, development promotion, and empowerment.

Despite this highly demanding set-up for relief and humanitarian interventions, the distinction between relief and development funds has not been lifted within donor agencies, which still have separate budget lines, spending limitations, implementation requirements and institutional responsibilities for the two types of assistance. Most significantly, many donor agencies, including the largest humanitarian donor, ECHO, maintain a six-month limit on their interventions, despite the fact that their assistance to individual emergencies continues for several years (IFRC 2001). Implementing agencies in continuous disaster areas such as Afghanistan, Somalia and Africa's Great Lakes region cannot plan their interventions and build local capacities; for example, they are not allowed to buy essential vehicles, but have to rent them for repeated six-month periods at much higher costs.

Below, we explore three myths about the increase in humanitarian assistance in the 1990s. We examine how the multilateral aid system has attempted to generate a system-wide response to complex emergencies, and the challenges generated to effective aid throughout the system. We discuss possible links between aid and conflict, including the links between development and security and the challenges of humanitarian interventions in existing state structures, for example, through relief provided by NGOs. We do not, however, examine peace-making, peace-keeping, and the militarization of humanitarian assistance in any depth, since this lies outside the scope of this book (see, for example, Chomsky 1999; Weiss 1999). We conclude with an assessment of the challenges facing donors in enhancing the effectiveness of emergency relief and humanitarian assistance.

## Disasters and Relief: Myths and Realities

In recent years, three interrelated trends have been taken as 'established facts', bordering on 'conventional wisdom', and as justifications for changes in the international humanitarian regime.

1. Disasters with human causes are becoming more important than disasters with natural causes. Human suffering as a result of conflicts is a greater challenge to donors than human suffering caused by natural disasters.
2. Political conflict is increasingly an intra-state issue, which demands new forms of intervention by the international community. Combined with the increasing concern for human rights and democratization, this is the direct justification for humanitarian interventions that link aid with military activities.
3. Traditional development assistance is ineffective in complex emergencies. As a consequence, humanitarian assistance is expanding and contributing to the decline of development assistance.

This conventional wisdom is challenged by both facts and theories. Figure 10.1 shows the number of people affected by different types of disasters and by conflicts during the 1990s. Over the decade, 1,442 million people were affected by floods (though the actual number is lower, since many individual human beings are affected several years in a row); 382 million by droughts and famine, and 'only' 311 million by conflicts.

The number of people affected by different types of natural disasters oscillated during the 1990s, whereas the number of people affected by conflicts *declined* from an annual average of 37 million during 1991–95 to an annual average of 25 million during 1996–2000. Thus, the evidence does not

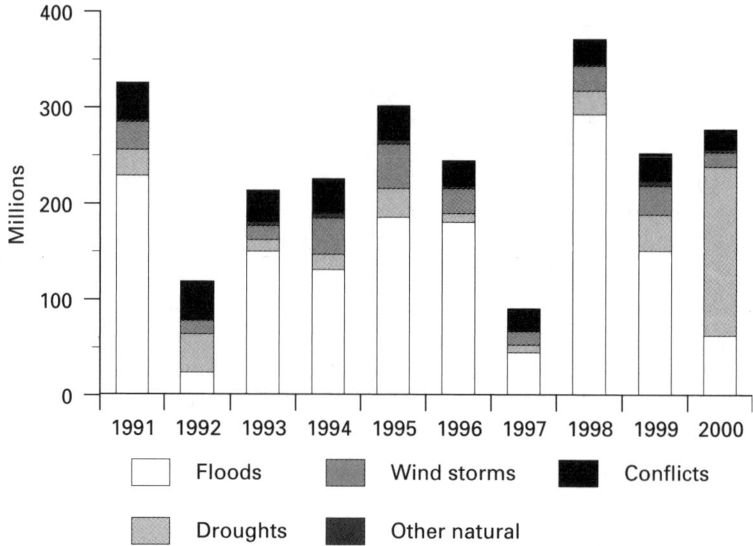


**Figure 10.1** People affected by disasters and conflicts, 1991–2000 (*source*: IFRC 2001, Tables 7 and 16)

support the claims made in recent years of rapidly increasing environmental disasters and conflict-related disasters. According to IFRC, 'towards the end of the 1990s, the world counted some 25 million "environmental refugees" – for the first time more people had fled natural hazards than conflict' (IFRC 2001: 11). It is striking that the alleged increase in conflicts and conflict-

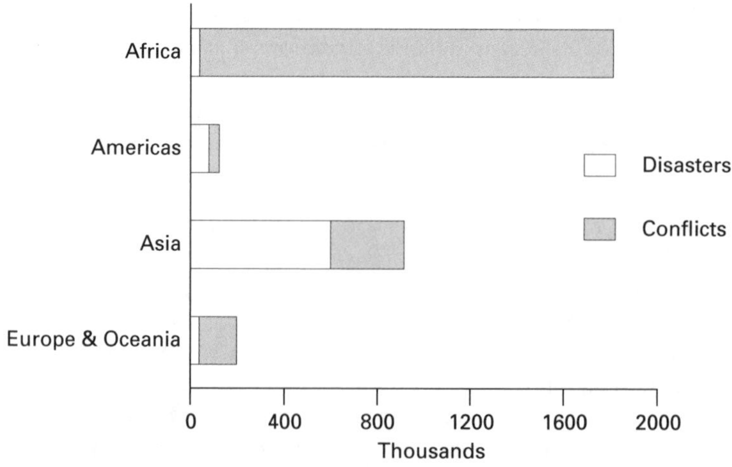


**Figure 10.2** People killed by disasters and conflicts, by region, 1991–2000 (*source*: IFRC 2001, Tables 6 and 15)

affected populations was in reality a significant fall. The number of conflicts increased from forty-six in 1991 to fifty-nine in 1995 and then fell to thirty-eight in 2000 (IFRC 2001: Table 14).

The situation is slightly different when we look at the number of people *killed*, as opposed to being affected, by disasters and conflicts. Understandably, conflicts play a larger role in these statistics, although there is great uncertainty about most of the numbers given. For example, the figures show that famine killed 280,000 people over the decade, whereas some suggest that almost 1.5 million may have died from the famine in North Korea during 1995–98 (IFRC 2001: 161).

Figure 10.2 seems to support the claim – and the media image – that disasters and especially conflicts are concentrated in the least developed countries, particularly in Africa. However, most of the reported killings from conflicts in Africa took place in the first half of the 1990s, including the 1994 genocide in Rwanda.

During 1991–2000, 90 per cent of those affected by disasters lived in Asia, and only 6 per cent in Africa. Similarly, 88 per cent lived in countries with a medium level of human development, including China and India (IFRC 2001: Table 11). Figure 10.3 provides additional data on the extent to which Africa has generated disaster-related and conflict-related humanitarian needs and problems. The total number of disasters in Africa increased from fifty-seven in 1994 and 1995 to 143 and 195 in 1999 and 2000, respectively, which resulted in a doubling of the number of disaster-affected people from 11 to 23 million (still less than one-tenth of the number of disaster-affected

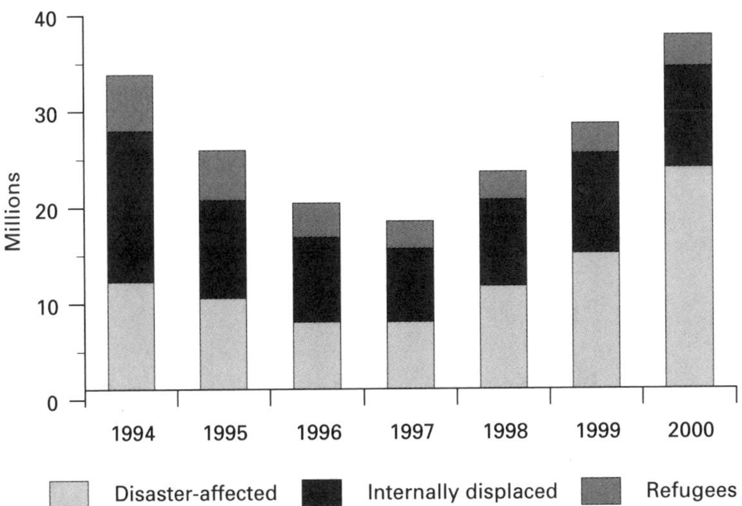


**Figure 10.3** Number of people affected by disaster and conflict in Africa, 1994–2000 (*source*: IFRC 2001, Tables 3, 20 and 22)

people in Asia). The number of internally displaced persons in Africa fell from 15.7 million in 1994 to 10.5 million in 2000, which was approximately half of the internally displaced persons found globally. Finally, the number of refugees and asylum-seekers originating in Africa fell from 5.9 million in 1994 to 3.3 million in 2000. This constituted between one-third and one-fourth of the world's refugees, depending on whether Palestinians are included or not.

All in all, fewer people suffer conflict-related problems in Africa, whereas the number of people affected by natural disasters in Africa increased in recent years. If these figures are compared with information on the number of absolutely poor, however, it is evident that structural poverty remains the main challenge in Africa. During much of the 1990s, the number of poor people living on less than US$1 a day was ten times higher than the total number of people affected by disaster and conflict in Africa. The media image of Africa as being only conflicts and disasters is not supported by the facts.

What about the tendency for humanitarian assistance to push out development aid? The answer is uncertain, partly because humanitarian assistance includes relief, refugee assistance, some rehabilitation, and individual donors classify their aid differently. Figure 10.4 shows a major increase in bilateral donors' emergency relief from 1.2 per cent of bilateral aid in the late 1970s to 9.3 per cent in the late 1990s. However, even with this increase, emergency aid took less than one-tenth of bilateral aid. Furthermore, there are huge differences in the emphasis put by different donors on relief, from 0.2 per

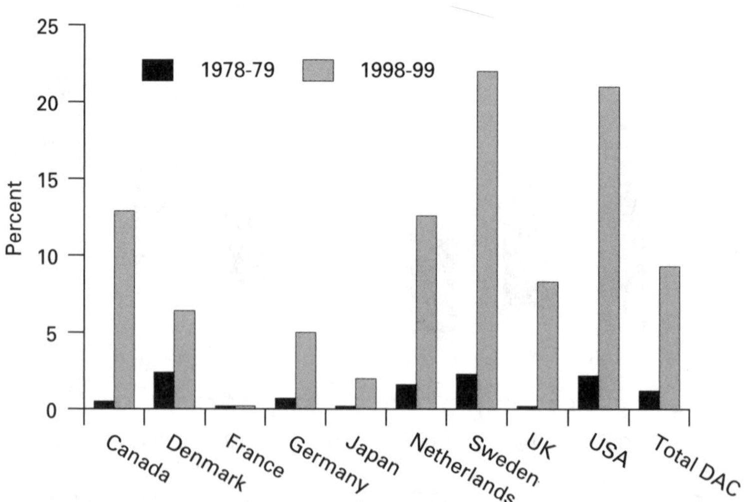


**Figure 10.4** Emergency aid as a share of bilateral aid. Selected donors, 1978–79 and 1998–99 (*source*: OECD 2001, Table 18)

cent in France and 2 per cent in Japan to 21 per cent in the USA and 22 per cent in Sweden.

Among multilateral development banks, the World Bank is the only significant player with 4.3 per cent of its funds going to emergency assistance in 1999 (OECD/DAC 2001: 223). The EU has become a major provider of emergency aid, amounting to US$500–800 annually in the second half of the 1990s, which constituted 25–30 per cent of total Western relief and was equivalent to 10–15 per cent of total EU aid. The relief is delivered through the European Commission Humanitarian Office (ECHO).

The myth about rapidly increasing humanitarian assistance also needs to be seen in the context of where the relief aid is going. The share of total bilateral emergency relief going to the least developed countries shrunk from 46 per cent in 1995 to only 28 per cent in 1999. The 'winners' were primarily the Balkans (IFRC 2001: 168). In 1999, ex-Yugoslavia received more than half of the ECHO's total humanitarian relief, which meant that the EU's long-term partners in Africa, the Caribbean and the Pacific (ACP) saw their share of ECHO aid fluctuate: 28 per cent in 1998; 15 per cent in 1999; and 35 per cent in 2000. The UN's annual global appeals for relief for humanitarian assistance fluctuated between US$1 billion and US$1.8 billion during 1995–2000, while Africa's share declined from US$1 billion in 1995 to US$0.6 billion in 1999 and 2000.

## The Multilateral Response to Complex Emergencies

The concepts of 'complex political emergencies' and 'humanitarian interventions' were coined in the 1990s, following the end of the Cold War. They refer to emergencies with political origins and multi-sectoral effects within nation-states and across borders, and involving multi-dimensional international responses. The most distinct break with past practices concerns the involvement of UN, NATO and EU forces in peace-making (-building and -keeping) in coordination with humanitarian relief by international NGOs and UN agencies.

There were several reasons behind these changes: The UN was 'allowed' by the remaining superpower, the USA, to engage directly in conflict management and resolution; NATO and the EU were, and are, seeking new roles for themselves on the international political stage; the East/West conflict was replaced by concerns in the international community for good governance; the principle of national sovereignty was supplemented by principles of human rights; questions of national security were supplemented by concerns for human security; the economic adjustment and debt management programmes of the 1980s were supplemented by human development and poverty reduction programmes; there was dissatisfaction with the effectiveness of humanitarian assistance due to the recurrent nature of disasters, and hence a desire to address the 'root causes' of natural and human disasters.

To address the new reality, which was less new than depicted by the aid agencies, first a 'continuum model' and then a 'gaps and linkages model' were coined to link conflict and disaster preparedness and prevention, relief, reconciliation, rehabilitation, reconstruction and development (Buchanan-Smith and Maxwell 1994). These were still largely seen as distinct interventions to be delivered by specialized agencies in a coordinated manner. The international aid community was looking for linkages and for gaps that needed filling in concrete emergencies. The performance of the international community in response to actual crises showed, however, that there is no neat continuum from crisis to development. It also showed that several humanitarian and development agencies used the 'gap-filling' pressures to move beyond their original mandates into the 'grey zone' of development-oriented relief or relief-cum-development, where they faced serious capacity problems. In crisis situations, any type of assistance has direct influence on the coping capacities of disaster victims and on the power and positioning of conflicting parties. With this increasing confusion in international relief, the aim was to ensure that aid agencies 'do no harm' (Anderson 1996). In particular, humanitarian action in protracted crises faced numerous dilemmas (Duffield 1998; Hendrickson 1998).

In a study for the Danish Ministry of Foreign Affairs (2000), the Centre for Development Research (CDR) and COWI analysed the multilateral aid response to violent conflict and concluded that it concerns 'more than linking relief and development'. They describe the blurring of relief and development, with relief becoming more oriented towards development (focusing on sustainability, relying on credit as opposed to grants, and engaging actively with governments and warring parties), while much development assistance aimed at conflict resolution and human empowerment rather than growth and state-building. The report analyses the emergence of human security as an overriding issue (Danish Ministry of Foreign Affairs 2000: 9 f.). New agencies are entering the stage to deal with issues such as reconciliation, electoral and judiciary reform, police and security reform, mine clearance, disarmament, demobilization and tribunals and truth commissions. All of these sectors cut across the relief–development distinction and address problems of security in the short and long term. Human security is associated with the risk presented by war, violence, epidemics, harmful international trade and global environmental phenomena. Sometimes, the complex concept of food security is included as well, which confirms the weakness of the relief–development distinction and continuum. The international community still lacks a coherent conceptual and strategic framework for its interventions in concrete crises and disasters.

The CDR/COWI report offers the following findings and conclusions on the multilateral aid response to complex political emergencies (Danish Ministry of Foreign Affairs 2000: vi–viii).

- Multilateral (and bilateral) agencies suffer from a poor, though improving, understanding of the nature and evolution of violent conflict in developing countries, both generically and within specific countries, including such dimensions as the underlying political reality, the effects of violence on social structures, the roles of elites and their supporters, and the economic factors sustaining violence.
- Weakness continues to exist in the ability to arrive at an agreed set of programming needs and priority responses before, during and after violent conflicts. This problem encompasses identification of priority needs, agreement on country-specific roles and responsibilities, burden-sharing among multilateral agencies and bilateral donors, and basic operational coordination.
- There are continuing impediments to effective aid responses in the internal operations and cultures of the UN and other multilateral agencies, which tend to isolate expertise in dealing with violent conflict. Development agencies have programming systems that highlight careful planning and are resistant to policy direction in areas such as conflict prevention. The UN specialized agencies focus on sectoral and technical issues and are reluctant to consider political issues such as protection and security. Humanitarian relief agencies optimize their programming systems around logistical competence and speed of delivery with little room for the analysis and negotiation needed in conflict situations. In all agencies, there is a scarcity of expertise in conflict analysis.
- There is persistent under-estimation and/or under-provision of the resources and programmes needed to provide protection and support human rights effectively through the rule of law, good governance, justice, and equity before, during and after violent conflicts. This inadequate response to the needs for protection in the wider context of human security has undermined aid, provided warring parties with opportunities to rearm and prepare further violence, and frustrated efforts to link relief and development programmes. As regards the latter, funding has generally been inadequate for fast disbursing, transitional initiatives in the period immediately following violent conflict.

With these persistent problems and challenges in responding to complex political emergencies, donor and agency staffs have started to question whether the international response system in its move towards more integration and coordination is reaching the point of negative marginal returns or the point of no return. It is necessary to improve the quality of conflict analysis and understanding and to establish a strategic framework for interventions in individual violent conflicts. But it may not be possible to enhance operational coordination and reduce the differences in competence, culture and policies between humanitarian, security and development agencies.

In a related study for the Danish Ministry of Foreign Affairs (2001), the

CDR and COWI examined donor response in conflict-affected countries, using post-genocide Rwanda as a case (see also Gourevitch 1998; Uvin 1998). The concept 'conflict-affected' is more appropriate than 'post-conflict', because conflicts continued after the 1994 genocide in Rwanda, which is also directly affected by (its participation in) the wars in neighbouring Congo. The study identified two critical conflict-related needs that had not adequately been addressed by the government and donors in the second half of the 1990s: managing equitable human settlement and land access; and enhancing the role of civil society in community development, stability and reconciliation. These issues are predominantly developmental, yet they involve humanitarian agencies engaged in resettlement and peace-making.

The needs related to human settlement and land were unmet in Rwanda as a result of a combination of institutional barriers, inflexible funding mechanisms, uncertainties and disagreements about land reform and settlement patterns, as well as inadequate aid management. The opportunities that have been missed with regard to civil society, including women's groups, are primarily a function of weak aid management: numerous Rwanda-specific conferences were not translated into transparent, effective and efficient implementation partnerships on the ground. At the time of writing, hopes are being vested in the PRSP process (poverty reduction strategy paper) as a framework for improved aid management and implementation partnerships. The PRSP could be the strategic framework for bilateral and multilateral agencies and their national partners, but only if the capacity for conflict analysis is improved and programmes are established reflecting such conflict analysis.

## Aid, Society and Conflict

Duffield (1998, 2001) suggests that a new development–security terrain emerged in the 1990s, and that humanitarian aid plays a key role in a new global governance. Donors are directly involved in complex tasks of conflict resolution and social reconstruction. A new political humanitarianism moves beyond relief and rehabilitation into conflict prevention and resolution, reconstructing social networks, strengthening civil and representative institutions, promoting the rule of law and security sector reform (Duffield 2001: 11). In our context, it is significant that development and humanitarian aid are seen as part of global governance, because aid is delivered by a cross-cutting governance network consisting of an increasingly complex web of government agencies, multilateral organizations and international NGOs. At the same time, aid targets a mixture of nation-states, weak 'quasi-states', civil society structures, opposition groups and even warring parties.

Duffield argues that this has led to a reinterpretation of security, incorporating conflicts, crimes and terrorism. Aid provides political legitimacy to all recipient regimes regardless of their human rights records, unless political humanitarianism is applied to country-level interventions. This leads to selective inclusion of some – and hence exclusion of others – in the liberal peace and world system. Southern governments, project partners and even populations have to perform and prove themselves fit for humanitarian assistance, in the same way as the donor demands for selectivity are based on performance in the use of development assistance.

Collier and Hoeffler (2000) share the emphasis on selectivity, although they have a different perspective on the links between aid and conflict. They explore the effects of economic assistance on the risk of civil war, either directly or through the impact of aid on policies. For the period 1965–99, they predict the risk of conflict occurring during five-year periods, based on country characteristics in the preceding period. They suggest that the average aid-recipient country had a risk of conflict of around 11 per cent, which is used as a benchmark for considering the effect of interventions aimed at risk-reduction. They suggest the following characteristics of risk-prone countries:

- Low level of per capita income → higher risk of conflict.
- Slow economic growth → higher risk of conflict.
- High dependence on primary commodity exports → higher risk of conflict.
- High population growth → higher risk of conflict.
- Excluding cases of ethnic dominance, the more heterogeneous the society is in respect to ethnicity and religion → higher risk of conflict.
- Geographically dispersed population and mountainous terrain → higher risk of conflict.

Based on these characteristics, they conclude that aid reduces the risk of conflict through the following routes:

- Aid augments government revenue and reduces dependence on primary commodities.
- Aid may raise the growth rate, conditional upon policy.
- Aid may cumulatively increase income, which directly reduces the risk of conflict and reduces dependence on primary commodities.
- Aid may influence policy and hence expand growth, incomes, and so on.
- Aid may improve policy and may then reduce social and political grievances.
- Aid may also influence policy to expand exports and hence primary commodity dependence, which could increase the risk of conflict.

Collier and Hoeffler (2000: 13) suggest that the overall effect of an increase in aid volumes to a country is to reduce the risk of conflict from the baseline case of 11.3 per cent to 10.7 per cent. If both aid and policy are improved (in their understanding), the risk of conflict is reduced to 7.9 per cent, that is, a combination of policy improvement and aid may reduce the conflict risk by around 30 per cent (from 11.3 per cent to 7.9 per cent) over a period of five years. In our assessment, such calculations cannot provide the policy prescriptions sought by the authors, but they are useful in drawing our attention to the complex interaction of aid, conflict and society-building.

To understand the risks and potentials involved in aid, we need to combine such quantitative economic analyses with political-economic, political science and anthropological analyses of aid and donor interventions in state and society structures and conflict dynamics. This can be done properly only in a country-specific and situation-specific context, and underlines the need for high-quality country strategies for each donor (covering both development and humanitarian assistance) and strategic frameworks to guide the donor community in all conflict-affected countries. Whether a donor provides humanitarian or development assistance to the current government, or tries to circumvent the current regime by supporting, for example, international NGOs in partnerships with local civil society organizations, the donor has to be fully aware of the economic, political and technical resources that it introduces into local conflicts and power struggles (Addison 2000).

Donors have a tendency to view conflict and disaster as social regression. In reality, human conflicts are part of the transformation of society, and occasionally natural disasters such as drought may be part of environmental transformation. Whether social transformations are negative or positive depends on their violent or non-violent character and on whether they tend to deepen democracy and equity. Whether environmental transformations are positive or negative depends on the productivity and sustainability of the changes and on whether they involve democratization of access to natural resources. Donors face a much more complex agenda than 'just' to contain conflicts and ameliorate their effects, as has been the favoured approach in the past. The new agenda demands strategic selectivity from donors in new and challenging ways, which we discuss in Chapter 14.

## Challenges to the Effectiveness of Humanitarian Assistance

Contrary to popular myths, humanitarian assistance has not taken over the international aid scene. In fact, it faces a number of constraints that determine its future potential and role. We see four major challenges to humanitarian assistance.

*There are limits to integration* The attempts during the 1990s to link relief, rehabilitation and development within the operational aid activities of individual donor agencies have had little success. Multilateral agencies such as the World Bank and UNHCR now seek to concentrate more on their respective 'core' activities – development and refugee protection. Moving much beyond their mandate proved to be unsustainable during a period of rapidly declining aid resources, which for UNHCR meant that its income was reduced from some US$1 billion to US$750 million a year. UNHCR has had to reduce its support for internally displaced persons and focus again on international refugees. The World Bank tries to limit its role in conflict-related and transition programmes, partly as a consequence of policy pressures to focus on the 'good performers' among low-income countries.

The European Commission has only recently (April 2001) published an assessment of its achievements within 'linking relief, rehabilitation and development'. The aim is to manage EU interventions in the 'grey zone' between relief and development assistance, but the approach is focused on overcoming the 'time gaps' between short-term relief and long-term development promotion. The Commission emphasizes the differences between humanitarian crises (with human causes), where aid agencies (bilateral, multilateral and NGOs) may operate in a political-institutional vacuum and need to focus on aid and donor coordination, and structural development crises, where aid agencies, for both formal and political reasons, work with recipient governments and focus on local aid integration and management.

The European Commission Humanitarian Office (ECHO) emphasizes speed and efficient service delivery through its many operational partners. It also demands, however, that these address long-term development problems and prospects already during emergency relief operations. The capacity of ECHO's approximately 180 implementation partners to do this obviously differs. In 2000, NGOs from EU countries implemented 65 per cent of ECHO's assistance, whereas UN agencies were responsible for 19 per cent (mainly the WFP and UNHCR, but also UNICEF). The aim of recent reforms in the European Commission has been to speed up the response time in both ECHO and the departments responsible for development assistance, while recognizing that decisions on the latter (which may be implemented by the NGOs also engaged in relief) take much longer time.

More importantly, the recent fundamental management and organizational reforms in the European Commission have kept ECHO and humanitarian relief *outside* the integration of the Commission's external relations, which were aimed at establishing an integrated EU response to global crises. ECHO is kept outside the responsibility of the Commission's crisis management team, with the alleged objective to maintain the neutrality of humanitarian assistance. Thus, there are both political and operational reasons for limiting the integration of humanitarian assistance with development cooperation and political-economic relations.

Still, quite a lot can be done at the operational level. Some success in integrating relief and development activities has been related to *food aid*, in spite – or because – of the heavy criticism being raised against this form of relief (Colding and Pinstrup-Andersen 2000; Stewart 1998): It has led to unsustainable spoon-feeding among disaster victims; it has introduced aid dependency and provided negative incentives to local farmers; it has undermined local food markets and exports; and it has provided inappropriate food packages, which reflects the dumping of surplus food rather than the meeting of essential dietary needs. The major food aid providers – the WFP, the EU, the USA, Canada and Australia – have for many years experimented with less disruptive food aid forms, particularly the monetization of food aid: food is provided to national reserves and is sold at local markets when there are shortages, and the money surplus generated (in both foreign and local currency) is channelled into national humanitarian and development programmes. At the local community and project level, the provision of relief food as hand-outs has increasingly been replaced by food-for-work. Furthermore, the activities supported by such projects have often been extended from simple road and school maintenance to broader environmental protection and natural resource management.

*Recovery requires aid* Even if there are limits to the integration of aid types, aid is urgently required to support recovery in addition to relief and development. The IFRC (2001: 12–33) discusses four ways for aid to secure and strengthen recovery.

First, the delivery of relief should support, not undermine, recovery. When relief agencies 'flood' into disaster areas, partly in competition for visibility among donors and on TV screens, they are unlikely to allocate their aid in accordance with basic needs in the disaster. Addison (2000: 401) notes that more than 200 NGOs plus several UN agencies were operating in Africa's Great Lakes region following the genocide in Rwanda in the mid-1990s. This is a problem of less than optimal resource allocation in terms of both geography and time. A few months after the disaster, many relief agencies will have left the area due to waning political and media attention and reduced aid allocation. Relief may also distort local development efforts, for example, by introducing salaries to relief workers that cannot be sustained by local administrations when the international relief agencies have left. In his analysis of the role of 'the disaster relief industry' in 'famine crimes', de Waal (1997: xvi) asserts that 'most humanitarian aid in Africa is useless or damaging and should be abandoned'.

We disagree with such assertions, but to minimize the risks of distorting effects, relief must be managed as a secure platform for recovery. This includes making use of existing institutions in the disaster area, contributing to long-term capacity-building, and providing relief plus assets (such as tools, seeds and other agricultural inputs) for the recovery of the disaster victims' livelihood. To reduce vulnerability in areas characterized by recurrent natural disasters, housing and other habitat structures may have to be modified during early reconstruction. Relief can provide breathing space and a minimum of resources from which to move towards sustainable recovery. It can lead to recovery, however, only if it is followed up by development interventions. Development-oriented relief should not be considered sufficient and be used to legitimize donor pull-out, as was the case, for example, in Somalia.

The second main approach suggested by the IFRC concerns the inclusion of risk-awareness in development promotion. In many natural disasters, speed is indeed decisive for the saving of lives, but even the most efficient international NGOs and UN relief agencies are likely to be much too late in arriving at disaster sites. This means that community preparedness is the only practical solution for poor countries located in high-risk areas. The capacity of communities and local institutions to respond to recurrent disasters must be strengthened. The IFRC suggests (2001: 20) that this is best done by agencies that have a permanent presence in disaster-prone countries and are engaged in long-term collaboration with genuine local partners.

The third approach concerns the funding gap between relief and recovery. Donor agencies are fully aware of the persistent rigidity of their budget lines, despite a decade of discussions of the relief–development continuum and development-oriented relief. Several relief donors operate with a six-month spending window on emergency funds. The IFRC makes reference (2001: 23) to a fifteen-year TB campaign in Eastern Europe, which is being run on one-half-year contracts with ECHO. Any proposal of activities that move beyond basic relief is required to strategize and to develop endless output and impact indicators and monitoring and evaluation systems. Attempts to extend ECHO's work into rehabilitation efforts with longer time perspectives and longer-term contracts have, as discussed above, been contained, partly for political reasons (to protect ECHO's humanitarian mission from EU's broader external relations agenda) and partly for efficiency reasons (ECHO lacks capacity to manage medium-term and longer-term programmes). The funding gap between relief and recovery programmes remains a real challenge to both humanitarian and development agencies.

The IFRC's fourth approach to addressing recovery concerns linking aid and the advocacy of structural changes at political and economic levels. The realization is simple: 'Aid alone will never be able to combat root causes and break the cycle of disasters' (IFRC 2001: 28). Aid cannot address all aspects of conflict, climate change, under-development, structural poverty and uneven globalization and marginalization. But relief provides an opportunity and entry-point for political advocacy by international NGOs, UN agencies and their local partners. Complex emergencies demand *concurrent* action within relief, rehabilitation, recovery, development (including risk awareness and local disaster preparedness) and advocacy. Concurrent actions differ from the continuum and integrated approaches, since they can be taken *ad hoc* by the most capable local, national and international agencies within an overall strategic framework. The days of quick-in/quick-out relief are numbered, but they should not be replaced by attempts at central planning that are clearly ineffective in the most turbulent surroundings in the weakest countries.

The IFRC concludes (2001: 32): 'Three things must happen simultaneously, if the cycle of disasters is to be broken and recovery is to take root: Inject the "risk dimension" into development in all disaster-prone regions … Programme emergency relief as the beginning – not the end – of increased commitment … Seize the opportunity for advocacy that relief provides.'

*Conflict prevention may be mainstreamed but not necessarily integrated* In 2001, the UN secretary-general published a report on the prevention of armed conflict. He reiterated his pledge to move the UN from a culture of reaction to a culture of prevention, but the report's underlying message was that the UN and its member states and partners should do more of the same in all fields. The report was based on the premise that conflict prevention and sustainable and equitable development are mutually reinforcing activities. It quotes studies by the Carnegie Commission showing that the international community spent about US$200 billion on the seven major interventions of the 1990s (Bosnia, Somalia, Rwanda, Haiti, the Persian Gulf, Cambodia and El Salvador, excluding Kosovo and East Timor), whereas a preventive approach could have cost only some US$70 billion. These figures are highly uncertain, but they undoubtedly reflect the cost-effectiveness of prevention over cure also in conflict management. Kofi Annan's recommended solution is: more resources, earlier interventions, coordinated planning, and coordinated implementation, all within a framework of respect for the national sovereignty of individual states.

Preventing violent conflict must be multi-dimensional, and it should therefore be part of all development and humanitarian aid – in aid vocabulary, it should be 'mainstreamed'. In the development of a 'toolbox for conflict prevention', SIDA has distinguished between the prevention of outbreak, escalation and relapse into violent conflict. Under each phase, she examines political, diplomatic, economic, legal and military measures – a list for the international community of a total of eighteen measures to prevent violent conflict. Almost all of these include foreign assistance for the promotion of improved governance in conflict-affected countries and for the punishment of oppressive regimes and warring parties. This is a challenge to the international community, but it does not mean that all these measures have to be delivered as integrated packages by individual agencies. The international community needs conflict-specific and country-specific strategic frameworks for conflict prevention, reconciliation and resolution, but the implementation of the individual measures should be handled by agencies in accordance with their respective capacities.

Much-improved *conflict analysis* is seen as a major requirement for the international community and for individual agencies (Addison 2000; Ramsbotham and Woodhouse 1996). The World Bank sees this as an assessment of the degree to which poverty reduction activities (1) may have a negative effect on stability and human security; and (2) are negatively affected by war-related destruction and destabilization of normal socio-economic activity as well as by the diversion of public resources from development purposes to military and other expenditures. These issues reflect the Bank's attempts to limit its involvement in conflict situations to activities within its core mandate of development and poverty reduction. Referring back to Duffield's analyses, it is evident that analyses of the links between conflict and aid must be broader and include how all forms of aid – and the donors themselves – affect local power structures and conflict dynamics.

*'Selective humanity' breaks with basic humanitarian principles* Resources for humanitarian assistance have increased, but not commensurate with the increasingly diverse use of this type of aid. Eastern Europe and Central Asia have been added to the target areas for conflict and disaster relief; the closer links between relief and both development assistance and broader humanitarian interventions have reduced the resources available for 'pure' relief; and national and international mobility has added new target groups (internally displaced persons, 'poverty refugees' and even various forms of migrants) to the recipients of humanitarian assistance.

The declining aid resources have pushed selectivity to the forefront of development cooperation. Donors aim to be selective between countries (wishing to support the good performers) or within countries (selecting the best partners and sectors). At the same time, the global situation after the terror attacks in New York and Washington in September 2001 has revived the justification of aid as a potentially powerful tool of conflict prevention, reconciliation and resolution. Humanitarian assistance, however, can help diffuse tensions and the risk of fundamentalist attacks on globalization and the Western world only if aid agencies become much better at listening to and engaging constructively and respectfully with the adversaries of the present world order. This requires that aid agencies have a significant presence in the world's actual or potential trouble spots, reflecting a development-oriented, long-term commitment.

These are requirements that contradict the emphasis on speed and top-down service delivery in the operations of relief agencies. Aid agency staff must be personally involved in local dialogues in ways that are new and alien to the operations and roles of both relief and development agencies in the past. Furthermore, contrary to the ideological emphasis on aid to the good performers, this new aid rationale calls for strategic use of aid in the countries that are affected by conflicts and are most likely to produce migration and/or attacks (political and/or terror) on international institutions and donor countries.

These developments introduce a new form of selectivity that breaks with the fundamental humanitarian principles underlying much development aid and relief. At one end, performance-based selectivity threatens the continuity needed for development cooperation based on partnership and national ownership; at the other end, conflict-oriented selectivity threatens the poverty orientation that now dominates the formal objectives of the international development community, and the priority given to basic needs fulfilment in traditional relief activities. In Chapter 14, we discuss this in terms of an ongoing 'clash of aid rationales', the outcome of which is uncertain.

CHAPTER 11

# Evaluation

§ DECISIONS about international development cooperation are not made primarily on the basis of what evaluations (or research) have taught us are the most pressing problems and the most adequate strategies. What the various major actors in the North and South find to be relevant and of special interest often have more weight. Within this framework, however, there has been significant – and growing – interest in learning more about how aid has worked.

Development theories have contributed to setting focus on the central problems, and they have pointed out important causes for under-development or non-existent development. Actors in development cooperation – with due consideration for their own interests – have been able to work out strategies for their efforts on the basis of these theories. There has been a similar growth of interest in investigations of how such strategies have worked in practice. This is true of studies that aid organizations themselves have commissioned in the form of evaluations as well as broader research on the impact of aid upon development in recipient countries. For many years, donor agencies and Western researchers have completely dominated these areas, but the authorities, NGOs and researchers in the South have gradually manifested themselves as independent actors who evaluate aid cooperation's usefulness on the basis of their own interests and perspectives.

Friction and conflicts have arisen when actors in the South have brought attention to donors' lack of understanding of conditions in recipient countries, or when they have claimed that aid is designed more in accordance with the donors' interests than the recipients' needs and priorities. The tendency, however, has been moving towards greater attentiveness on the part of donors. Furthermore, many donor agencies have actually decided to give priority to building capacity in recipient countries, so that they are better able both to evaluate the impact of aid, and decide on the basis of their own research where the main problems in the development process lie.

In this chapter, we first examine more closely how donor agencies have developed their evaluation practice as part of efforts to document aid's impact and adjust strategies so that they contribute more effectively to realization of the formulated development goals. At the end of the chapter, we discuss assistance for building evaluation and research capacity in developing countries.

## Evaluating Aid

In the broad sense, evaluation involves a systematic investigation of how a measure or intervention has worked (or not worked). Social science evaluation research differentiates between various types of evaluations. In the context of this book, two types are of particular interest: process evaluation and impact evaluation. The former aims to reveal the whole process from decision-making and planning of the intervention to impact. Impact evaluation examines to what extent an intervention achieves the desired results and thereby helps to solve the problems the intervention aimed at solving. In other words, impact evaluation examines in what respects and to what extent specific inputs and activities achieve the formulated goals.

Usually, evaluation is differentiated from monitoring. Monitoring determines only whether the planned activities are carried out, whereas evaluation also entails an investigation of whether these activities bring about the desired impact. Aid jargon in this context makes a distinction between output and impact. Output refers to the products that immediately result from an effort or activity. Examples of outputs could be delivery of a number of water pumps, or training activities carried out for a specific number of people. In relation to such outputs, impact consists of the changes created as a result of the deliveries and activities. The impact emphasized would depend on the goals, but examples could be improvement in people's health in the areas receiving water pumps, or increased income for those who have received training.

According to these definitions, monitoring entails keeping an eye on whether or not the planned resources are being used, and whether or not they result in the planned outputs. These factors are also investigated during evaluation, which then goes a step further and examines whether or not the intended impact is also achieved. Figure 11.1 illustrates the difference between monitoring and evaluation and also gives an idea of the different components involved in project- or programme-type interventions.

Systematic evaluations began to have great significance in the USA from the beginning of the 1950s. The aim was to investigate whether measures taken by the state worked according to intention in solving the societal problems that caused them to be carried out. Interest for evaluation then spread to USAID and the World Bank. Also, in 1952, independent of this development, the Indian Planning Commission had already established a separate evaluation unit to follow implementation and impact of India's five-year plans. In the 1960s, evaluations were also adopted by public administrations in Western Europe, and gradually also by bilateral aid agencies there. At the end of the 1970s and the beginning of the 1980s, most bilateral and multilateral organizations established independent evaluation units and administrative procedures for carrying out evaluations (see Stokke 1991).

The administrative organization of evaluation activities varied greatly from organization to organization, and the methods were also very different. At first, only a modest exchange of experiences took place, but with the establishment of DAC's Expert Group on Aid Evaluation in 1983, a forum was created for exchange of experience and also for drafting joint guidelines. In 1986, the Expert Group presented the first comprehensive set of guidelines for DAC countries. Here, evaluation was defined as a systematic study, as objective as possible, of ongoing and completed projects and programmes, including their design, implementation and results, in order to discern their effectiveness, long-term impact and sustainability. In addition, it was emphasized that evaluation of the relevance of formulated objectives should also be included, in relation to the problems existing in recipient countries.

The addition of this evaluation of relevance entailed an expansion that placed the DAC guidelines in a category that the literature often refers to as third-generation evaluations. The first generation consisted of narrow technical impact measurements. The second generation continued impact measurements, but in a broader sense. Both these types of evaluations took the measurements for granted and studied to what extent they had been achieved through the projects or programmes. The new element in the third-generation evaluations was to evaluate in relation to whether the formulated goals also reflected real and important problems or were just treating symptoms. At the end of the

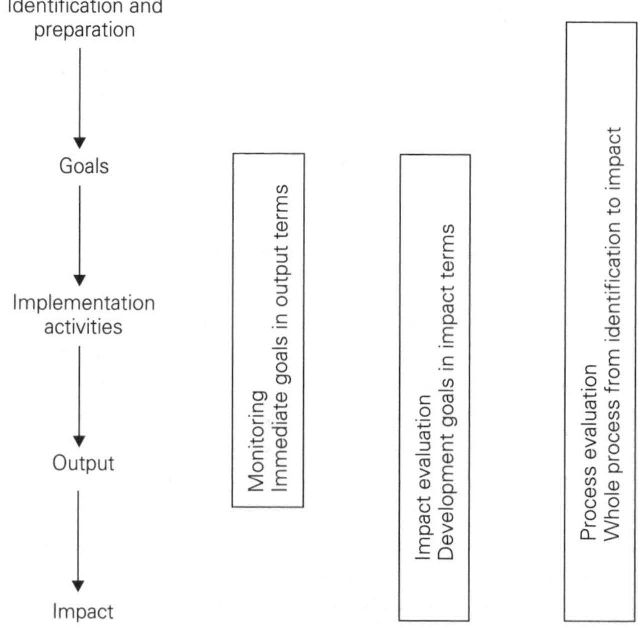


**Figure 11.1** Monitoring and evaluation

1980s, a so-called fourth generation of evaluations appeared, to which we return below.

Since 1986, the DAC has adjusted its definition of evaluation to emphasize that it should present reliable information that can be used by decision-makers in both donor and recipient countries to improve their efforts. Emphasis on the reliability of the information entails two important points. First, evaluations ought to be carried out by independent and impartial evaluators, persons who are not involved in the aid activities themselves or do not have any special interest in the project or programmes. The other point is that evaluations should be carried out by specially qualified persons who are able to use the relevant methods systematically and transparently so that in principle others can check the results.

## Different Types of Evaluations

The DAC's efforts to create common conceptions and common guidelines have not led to a corresponding uniform practice among bilateral donors, nor are multilateral organizations characterized by any great uniformity. Several basic elements have been adopted by most, however, making it possible to give a simplified presentation of the procedures that essentially apply in the practice of most official aid agencies. Such a presentation can be based on the main components that typically comprise an evaluation that examines both process and impact. These are listed below. For each component, the factors that evaluators often consider are described. The focus here is project evaluation, but the procedure is largely the same for programme evaluation. However, evaluations of broader aid forms such as sector support, country programmes and structural adjustment programmes require other procedures. We discuss these and other forms of evaluation below, but first the main components in project (and programme) evaluations.

*Project preparation – from project idea to project document* One central aspect here is to investigate who has been involved in the process and whether the problems dealt with are important and properly described. It is of special interest whether representatives of the recipient country's authorities and the target group have participated in the preparations. In addition, this component entails a thorough evaluation of the project document as management instrument, answering such questions as the following. Are the objectives clearly formulated and realistic? Are the assumptions about the conditions for implementation of the project reasonable and realistic? Have the institutional and organizational conditions been taken into consideration? Is there a reasonable relationship between budget items and inputs in the broad sense, and the planned activities and outputs?

*Project implementation and production of outputs* Some of the central questions are: Have the planned inputs been delivered on time? Have they been well suited to their purpose? Have the planned activities been carried out and the outputs produced in accordance with the project document? What is the explanation for eventual deviations? Are they due to external conditions that are difficult to anticipate, or have they been due to weaknesses in the project design or implementation? Has implementation achieved other results than those that were planned? These kinds of questions indicate what is called in aid jargon the project's *output performance.*

*Goal realization and impact* Evaluation questions here are: What development goals are formulated for the project? Are these goals still relevant? In what way and to what extent are the goals realized? What are the reasons for any deviations – conditions inside or outside the project? Which factors have been of special significance – positive and negative – for the degree of goal realization? In this context, the question is sometimes raised as to whether the project has functioned efficiently and created a specific degree of goal realization as inexpensively as other comparable projects. This part of the evaluation is sometimes characterized as an evaluation of the project's *impact performance.* The evaluation can include impacts other than those referred to in the project goals, through broader questions about whether the project has created improvements for the target group or perhaps inflicted damage of some kind. It is also common in aid evaluations today to examine sustainability, i.e. whether the project is designed so that the activities can be continued in the local context, also after the end of the externally financed project. It is furthermore of significance whether or not the achieved improvements for the target group are lasting.

*Project organization and leadership* Interest for this comes partly from the basic wish to ensure sustainability. This demands that the project not only delivers the planned services, but also builds local capacity to take over the activities and continue them. Therefore, it is of interest whether project work has been carried out as an individual effort or as an integrated part of the development efforts in the recipient country. In addition, this part of the evaluation has to do with whether or not technical, administrative and financial management has functioned properly, and whether or not resources have been utilized effectively. Emphasis is also placed on whether the target group and the local authorities have been involved.

On the basis of an evaluation, conclusions are drawn as to whether goals have been realized (documentation), and what has been learned from the experiences (lessons learned). If the evaluation entails a project that is to be continued, the main emphasis is placed on experiences that can be used to improve the project. With an evaluation of a completed project, however, interest is focused on the experiences that can be used to improve preparation and implementation of other similar projects.

It is a basic assumption of the described form of evaluation practice that it is possible to generalize about causal relationships under various circumstances so that positive experiences with a specific project design can be transferred to preparation of similar projects to be implemented under similar conditions elsewhere. It is exactly this assumption that is criticized by supporters of the so-called fourth-generation evaluations discussed in the next section.

With more and more development cooperation taking the form of broad sector support or equally broad support to, for example, democratization and respect for human rights, evaluation practice has also been changed and expanded. Many of the questions mentioned above are repeated, but within a broader framework. A sector programme evaluation examines whether and how donors' total inputs have contributed to building institutional capacity in recipient countries, and furthermore, whether and how this has influenced institutional performance and development in the relevant sector. A sector programme often includes several components, and each of these is evaluated separately and in relation to its contribution to fulfilling the goals of the whole programme. Since sector programmes are usually supported by several donors, the evaluations must also examine closely the different forms of inputs and the interaction among donors and with national authorities in the recipient country.

Evaluations of country programmes are even broader, but they usually focus on the roles a single donor plays in supporting recipient countries' policy formulation and implementation of development strategies, as well as the overall impact of the cooperation between donors and authorities.

So-called thematic evaluations study whether and how aid has promoted improvements in selected respects such as equal opportunities for men and women, institutional development, democratization and natural resource management. Although these studies mostly focus on a single donor, they evaluate the effects of this donor's efforts and cooperation with the recipient country in relation to many different aid forms in different sectors. An example of a comprehensive thematic evaluation is Danish support to promotion of human rights and democratization. This was carried out in four selected countries and in addition included reviews of experiences from a larger number of countries with focus on four selected areas. The four areas in which Danish aid's relevance and impact were investigated were 'justice, constitution, and legislation; elections; media; and participation and empowerment' (see Danida 1999).

Evaluations of aid forms typically comprise studies of aid's impact in several countries, but with focus on a single aid form, for example, balance-of-payment support, technical assistance or credit schemes. A good illustration of this type of evaluation is a comprehensive study of Swedish programme aid based on both country studies and thematic studies (see White 1999a).

Yet another form of evaluation aims to study development organizations' own relevance and capacity to realize formulated goals. Multilateral organizations in particular have been the subject of such evaluations – most often on bilateral donors' initiative. An example is a larger, Danish-initiated evaluation of eleven multilateral organizations' performance in four selected countries with a further aim to evaluate these organizations' effectiveness and ability to adapt their efforts to the recipient countries' needs and conditions (see Danida 1991a, b). Another example is an investigation of the UNDP, initiated by the governments of Denmark, India, Sweden and Great Britain in the mid-1990s (see Engberg-Pedersen, Martinussen and Freeman 1996). The aim was to evaluate whether the UNDP, both globally and in several selected countries, had focused its activities on the basis of careful assessment of developing countries' needs and the organization's special strengths and capacity. A further aim was to indicate how the UNDP could increase its relevance and effectiveness through a stronger focusing of its activities.

In addition to multilateral organizations, many NGOs have been the subject of evaluations aimed at judging their capacity to administrate public funds and achieve the lasting results that were aimed at in recipient countries (see Chapter 8). Bilateral donors have also commissioned – although in many fewer cases – such capacity studies and evaluations of their own organizational effectiveness.

## Participatory Evaluations

Supporters of fourth-generation evaluations often call the evaluation practice used for projects and programmes described above *conventional evaluation.* They also call their own methods and practice *participatory evaluation.* Supporters of the latter are especially found in NGO circles and among researchers (see Marsden and Oakley 1990). They are inspired by broader social science evaluation research that is very critical about the possibilities for identifying impact of specific measures or interventions. It is their view that it is rarely possible to establish causal explanations in relation to social conditions. Similarly, it is usually impossible to point to impacts that can clearly be seen as an effect of specific projects, programmes or political interventions (the problem of attribution that we also discuss in Chapter 12).

Participatory evaluations therefore conclude that it is not worth the effort to attempt to use conventional procedures. It is not possible to generalize experiences, because far too many different conditions and factors are involved. Instead, evaluations should be seen as part of a learning process for the actors involved in a certain development activity. Experiences can be applicable only in the same local context (Guba and Lincoln 1989). Therefore, participatory evaluations are limited to ongoing projects, and their aim is to improve them and strengthen their impact. Claus Rebien has proposed a definition of participatory evaluation as a problem-solving process where the involved stakeholders together collect and study knowledge about an aid activity and use it to adjust and adapt the activity (Rebien 1996). External evaluators' role in this connection is to function as initiators and motivators who can support stakeholders in the work of finding out how goals and results should be evaluated. However, in principle, it is the stakeholders themselves who carry out the evaluation.

Stakeholders basically include project staff, the target group, employees in the recipient country's public administration with responsibility for the area, employees in donor organizations, and others who are involved in the aid activity. Thus, the group becomes so large and complex that one of the problems in practice is to identify a representative sample.

Participatory evaluation is an ongoing activity, which in a certain sense begins at the same time as activities are initiated. Therefore, its supporters maintain, it also represents a gradual transition to the type of procedure that Robert Chambers in particular has argued for under the term 'participatory rural appraisal' (Chambers 1997: especially Chapters 6 and 7). However, Chambers himself considers evaluation more narrowly, as one among several elements in this approach. Its primary aim is to ensure the poor segments of the population full ownership of aid activities and make sure these activities are designed in accordance with their own ideas about problems and how they can best be solved.

It can be argued that completely participant-led aid activities are appropriate and correct, but it seems rather problematic to equate them with evaluation. In any case, this practice has a purpose different from that of conventional evaluation. Donor organizations and the decision-makers who must determine whether the activity should continue to receive funds cannot be expected to find it convincing when stakeholders evaluate an activity in which they participate themselves and in which they have a special interest. In addition, the group of stakeholders will usually be so complex that it would be difficult to imagine them agreeing about the evaluation, especially when so many stakeholders outside the target group are included – which by the way is not part of Chambers's approach. These are some of the reasons why the conventional evaluators are very sceptical about purely applied participatory evaluation. They do not feel that such evaluations give a sufficient basis for either decision-makers or administrators in donor organizations.

In its pure form, the participatory evaluation has not won acceptance in official aid organizations' practice, but the debate it has provoked has resulted in procedures that attempt more than earlier to involve stakeholders in the evaluation process itself. Some large NGOs – Oxfam for example – have gone quite far in this direction, and several official donor organizations have emphasized the need to involve stakeholders in recipient countries. Often, representatives for the relevant authorities participate in evaluation teams. The target group is involved in the process through interviews by evaluators. Here, the inspiration of fourth-generation evaluation is especially apparent in their greater openness. One of the basic ideas is that the target group representatives chosen to be interviewed should participate in deciding what should be evaluated and how.

## Challenges for Evaluation Work

The different goals of the evaluations can create problems when the work is being prepared. There are at least three different goals – each with its own target group.

- Evaluations aiming to improve management and leadership. Here, the target group is officials in aid organizations. The target group should also include partner organizations in the South.
- Evaluations aiming at collecting experiences that can be used to improve future aid efforts. Here, the target group is mainly the people who are involved in delivering aid, but it can also include the broad, interested public.
- Evaluations aiming at monitoring and documenting. Here, the target groups are the political decision-makers, the public and taxpayers, and others involved in financing aid. Usually, the target groups are mostly in donor countries, but documentation should also be directed towards decision-makers and the public in recipient countries.

At first, the major goal was mainly to carry out a systematic *experience collection* in order to improve the quality of aid. However, a control function was gradually added to this idea of evaluation as a management instrument. The purpose of the control function was more to *document* for the political decision-makers and taxpayers that aid worked in accordance with its intentions.

The growing criticism of aid up through the 1980s shifted the emphasis more towards the control function. Public criticism also contributed to this. In many DAC countries, the press communicated this criticism with a special preference for fiascos and the lack of any show of results. This led to pressure on evaluation teams for greater openness with regard to evaluation results and demands to present them in completely different ways. Internally, aid organizations could communicate evaluation results using inside jargon and with emphasis on technical aspects of aid. This was not appropriate for communicating with politicians or the broader public. Still, only a few aid organizations have taken the consequences of this and presented evaluation results in ways that are adapted to the needs of external target groups for information and documentation. This is probably one of the greatest challenges for work with evaluations in the future.

Another important challenge lies in making aid objectives precise and operational. It is difficult to present convincing evaluations, when the goals being evaluated are as vaguely formulated as 'alleviation of poverty'. The work is made even more difficult by the fact that today aid must contribute to realizing many goals that are not prioritized; they are sometimes contradictory;

and they are often changed over time. In addition, bilateral aid in particular is determined to a certain extent by implicit goals concerning commercial interests or national security considerations. In such cases, evaluations clearly face great difficulties from the start.

Thus, when we consider methods for demonstrating aid's impact, we are confronted with the problem referred to earlier: how to identify what effects are due to aid efforts (or joint development efforts involving both donors and national authorities) and what effects are due to other factors in recipient countries and in their international relations. In project evaluations, it is possible to define relatively precisely which donor-driven activities should be investigated; these, however, are often so modest in scope that their separate effects can be difficult to trace in the complex development processes where countless other factors are at work. In relation to the broader forms of aid cooperation such as sector support, it becomes easier in certain respects to identify effects, because they involve more comprehensive donor-supported efforts. In such cases, however, it can be difficult to isolate the contribution of a single donor from those of other donors and from the recipient countries' own authorities. This is not so decisive when seen from a broad development perspective, but it is very important for the control function that evaluations must also fulfil. It continues to be necessary, through evaluations, to be able to document the usefulness of the individual donor's efforts for the political decision-makers and the broad public. It is clearly here that the greatest challenge lies, since both multilateral and bilateral donors increasingly move towards large sector programmes and support for capacity-building in recipient countries' political and administrative institutions.

## Use of Evaluations in North and South

As for the use of evaluations, the most important goal, as already mentioned, is to document the extent of aid's benefits. If an evaluation is to be reliable, it must be carried out by external and independent experts. This procedure, however, is not necessarily the best for aid organizations' own learning processes and thus for efforts to improve quality. It is therefore often advantageous for some of the organization's own staff to participate in the evaluations so that they can ensure that experiences are used. Clearly, in principle, this can also be achieved through a proper procedure for disseminating the evaluation results and the lessons learnt. Nevertheless, concrete insight and first-hand knowledge give a better basis for management than the large comprehensive reports that external consultants usually deliver.

Formulated in another way, there are arguments to support internal staff members' participation in evaluations on the basis of the wish to ensure immediate gathering of experience and its integration into the so-called institutional memory. The risk of only using external consultants is that learning mostly takes place within their private firms. There is hardly any indisputable solution to this dilemma, but there are several aid organizations that are trying to find a balance by allowing their own staff members to participate as resource persons. They can follow the evaluations and comment on them during the process, but they are not involved in formulating the conclusions and recommendations. Own staff in this connection can be both persons from the main office, from embassies in recipient countries, and from project or programme management.

The preceding discussion has focused on feedback and learning within donor organizations, but the aim of evaluations is also to strengthen recipient countries' capabilities to improve their own efforts within broader development efforts. Therefore, results and lessons learnt should as a minimum also be made available to the authorities and organizations in recipient countries, and in a form that makes them directly usable. More ideally, the whole process should of course be carried out in close cooperation between donors and partners in the South.

Not very many official aid organizations have a positive record on this point. Much too often, these organizations carry out evaluations without real participation by recipient countries. Local authorities and organizations sometimes become involved in evaluations through the opportunity to choose members of the evaluation teams. It is moreover common for consultants from recipient countries to be assigned tasks in connection with evaluations. The whole process, however, is led from outside by the responsible donor organization and in accordance with its information needs and procedures. The final reports are of course delivered to authorities and partners in recipient countries, but the reports are seldom in a form that they can use. Therefore, many stakeholders in developing countries consider evaluations as a necessary evil that accompanies foreign aid – and not as an instrument they can use in their own work.

In relation to sector programmes, better possibilities exist in principle to adapt evaluation processes to the needs of recipient countries, because here the total efforts within the concerned sector are evaluated and thereby also the local authorities' performance. The danger, however, is that the individual aid organizations also within this area follow their own special procedures that they try to use in all recipient countries, instead of adapting the procedures to conditions in each country. The problem is real, because each donor has a need for information and evaluations that can be used for its own collection of experience and documentation in its own country. This requires uniform procedures and methods in all the countries with which this donor cooperates – also in consideration of resources. Donors, however, can in this way easily place themselves in a situation where they do not only approach evaluations in a way that is alien to recipient country authorities and organizations, but they also come to give these partners grades for their performance. This is considered to be in conflict with ideas of national ownership (see the further discussion about this in Chapters 13 and 14).

## Aid for Capacity-building in the South

As an alternative – or at least as a supplement – to the donor-led evaluation practice, aid can be given to build Southern partners' own capacity. Several official aid organizations have chosen to do this in recent years, but no clear policy for this area has emerged as yet. One of the procedures most often used is for donors to enter into closer cooperation with some few selected research institutions and consultant firms in recipient countries in order to recruit some experts to participate in the evaluation team. In addition, there is a tendency to give local institutions and firms the responsibility for the whole or parts of an evaluation or report. This makes it possible to develop an independent evaluation capacity in these institutions and firms, and because of the usually high fees paid by donors, this also provides the opportunity to engage the best expertise.

However, this procedure is not problem-free. Undoubtedly, it leads to a strengthening of local expertise within the area of evaluation, but this mostly happens on conditions set by donors and in accordance with their standards and procedures. And even more problematically, it happens to some degree at the expense of independent research in recipient countries. In several African countries in particular, there are so few researchers to draw upon that their greater involvement in evaluation work at the same time reduces research capacity noticeably. Many of the research institutions participating in donors' evaluation work are so dependent on the fees for this work that it would be difficult for them to disagree with the aid organizations. This limits their possibilities to take critical positions concerning the impact of aid.

Behind all this lies a far bigger problem. Most poor countries have too few well-qualified researchers, insufficient funds to finance even these few researchers' work, and too few independent research institutions. This applies in general within all research areas. This means that development problems in these many countries are thoroughly researched only to the extent they can attract international attention. It also means that these countries often lack capacity even to keep abreast of international research and are hence prevented from taking independent positions about whether and how they will use the results of this research. It is therefore most welcome that in recent years several donors have increased support for building and strengthening independent research capacity in the South. Some of the funds go to institutions and researchers in donor countries, but most go directly or indirectly to strengthening research capacities in developing countries.

Since the introduction of sector-support programmes, more donor countries, for example the Nordic countries and Great Britain, are considering how research can contribute both to an appropriate form of cooperation and to a special effort aiming to strengthen institutions in recipient countries. We find it of great importance that donors with sector programmes integrate research within them. There is a need to draw on donors' research resource bases at home in order to ensure aid's quality and to adapt it to what the respective donor countries do best. Furthermore, there is a special need for involving the research communities in recipient countries in order to ensure aid's relevance and adaptation to local conditions as well as, with time, to strengthen these communities' independent capacity.

## Aid for Learning to Learn

Donors' support for strengthening developing countries' own research capacity can be seen as an attempt to supplement the transfer of resources, technology and knowledge by building a preparedness and capacity for learning in recipient countries. Seen in a longer time perspective, it can be argued that development cooperation has been developed from mostly focusing on financing infrastructure and training local labour to use 'our' technology, to placing more emphasis on formulating economic policy and strengthening institutions to support development efforts. Basically, however, it is still 'our' strategies for developing society – that is, those of the rich Western countries – that characterize development cooperation. This constitutes pressure on recipient countries to make them copy the 'Western development model' – regardless of their own conditions and priorities. In this respect, support for strengthening developing countries' own research capacity can be understood as an effort to improve these countries' capacity for analysing their development problems and working to find solutions independently of donor organizations' ideas and priorities. In a broader sense, this means developing skills and capacity for learning – learning to learn.

This is an aim and a strategy that ought to be given greater emphasis in years to come. If through development cooperation we shall fundamentally contribute to making the world's poor more independent and self-sufficient, it is crucial that we ourselves build a capacity to analyse and learn and find solutions and methods for better utilization of natural and human resources. At the same time, aid organizations ought to place less emphasis on specific recommendations and demands concerning economic policy and the institutional and administrative organization of its implementation. It is interesting that the DAC in its 1997 annual report mentions such considerations in comments about Albert Hirschman, who strongly emphasized that economic activities were best managed decentrally and in accordance with regional and local requirements and priorities (OECD/DAC 1998: 18 f.). This demands that the necessary capacity is available to analyse, decide and implement in both the public and private sectors. DAC's member countries should follow up on such considerations with far stronger support to strengthen developing countries' own research and analytical capacity. This is also one of the main points in the World Bank's *World Development Report 1998/99* (World Bank 1999).

In this connection, it must be emphasized that higher priority for this area should not be given at the expense of the modest support provided by several donor organizations for research in the North on developing countries. The existence of considerable capacity here is a prerequisite for support to research in developing countries. In addition, the independent development research in donor countries is essential for the quality and relevance of development cooperation. It is through this research that actors can gather a great deal of knowledge about and understanding of development problems and conditions that either block or promote realization of development goals.

CHAPTER 12

# The Impact of Aid

> Foreign aid in different times and different places has been highly effective, totally ineffective, and everything in between. Perhaps that is to be expected in a complex endeavour that has spanned half a century, with scores of countries as donors, a hundred countries as recipients, tens of thousands of specific activities, and nearly US$1 trillion in finance. (World Bank: 1998b: 2)

In this chapter, we attempt to find a pattern behind the effectiveness and impact of aid in different societal contexts. Box 12.1 shows that millions of people now benefit from a longer and healthier life, but at the same time there have never been so many absolutely poor people. Does this have anything to do with foreign aid? Yes, if the goals of aid are taken seriously: these goals involve doing something about the problems of poverty and development. Such a perspective can provoke four kinds of reactions.

1. Aid has achieved much, especially with regard to improving the living conditions (longevity, health, education, and so on) for hundreds of millions of poor people, especially in Asia.
2. Aid is a failure, since the media can report that extreme human suffering continues.
3. Aid works effectively in some sectors, countries and contexts, just as ineffectively in other contexts, and neutrally in still other contexts. Differences and variety are the only common characteristics.
4. Aid is of limited significance for both success and failure in development work, which primarily is borne by people, enterprises, organizations and governments in the developing countries themselves.

Most analysts tend towards the third and fourth interpretation (Cassen et al. 1994; Cox et al. 1997; Lipton and Toye 1991; van de Walle and Johnston 1996; World Bank 1998b; Lancaster 1999). There are countless examples of aid saving human life, increasing agricultural production, improving the level of health and education and so forth. But there are also a long series of examples of aid leading to 'white elephants' or landing in the wrong pockets. There is no doubt that actors and resources other than donors and aid are most important for development's direction, successes and crises. But such an assessment of aid is not sufficient in relation to the many resources, policies, strategies and projects that have been invested in aid during the last forty years. Aid's interaction with a series of development factors (private capital flows; political, economic, social and institutional relations, and so on) explains why it is so difficult to draw conclusions about aid's impact in recipient countries. But we must give it a try.

Economists in the World Bank are quite audacious in the *Assessing Aid* report (1998b) and its follow-up, in drawing conclusions about the overall impact of aid on economic growth, poverty reduction, investments and public expenditures and services in developing countries. The World Bank's analysis deserves special attention, partly because it contains interesting figures for aid's total impact on the macro level, and partly because its conclusions can have widespread consequences for aid's future. The World Bank's analysis is based on strong assumptions about aid fungibility: developing countries' governments and other aid recipients can free resources with the help of foreign aid, so they can use their own money in accordance with their own wishes and priorities. Therefore, it has little meaning to evaluate aid effects only in relation to the goals set by the donor-financed projects and programmes. Aid's effects can be understood only in their societal context, and aid's impact must primarily be analysed on the basis of its qualitative and strategic influence on societal processes, institutions and power structures. It is primarily through its strategic influence on these factors that aid can achieve its long-term goals.

This does not mean that the immediate effects of aid are without interest. When aid improves the living conditions and opportunities for a special target group (pregnant women, school-age girls, refugees, landless workers, the handicapped, and so on), it is of value in itself (like humanitarian assistance). It is also of value in the form of strengthening these groups in relation to other groups without similar problems. And it can be of value in the form of changed development processes and power structures in society that reduce these groups' vulnerability and improve their influence. Similarly, aid for environmental protection can often have direct effects in the form of ensuring a sustainable resource base for local producers, as well as a global effect through protection of biodiversity.

This chapter examines aid impact at different levels of recipient societies. Since the launching of the *Assessing Aid* report, much attention – and controversy – has focused on the macro-economic effects of aid in developing countries, especially because of the radical policy recommendations emerging from the debate: to maximize poverty reduction, aid should be allocated primarily to the 'good performers' among developing countries. After discussing the most radical findings and recommendations on the macro-economic impact of aid, we examine the impact of structural adjustment and other forms of programme aid, based on an evaluation of Swedish programme aid and a World Bank study of *Aid and Reform in Africa*.

Project assistance remains the most widely used aid form, and we discuss

### **Box 12.1** Development Achievements, Failures and Challenges

Over the past decade, the international community has formulated a set of quantitative goals for global development and for international development cooperation. In 1996, OECD compiled these into specific goals to be reached between 1990 and 2015. The goals received global support at the UN Millennium Summit in September 2000. Each year, UNDP and the World Bank assess progress in achieving these goals in their respective *Human Development Report* and *World Development Indicators*. The progress for eight goals has been as follows:

1. To halve the proportion of the people in the world living in extreme poverty, that is, at less than US$1 per day. Between 1990 and 1998, the proportion was reduced from 29 to 24 per cent, but the absolute number fell only from 1,276 million to 1,175 million. If the highly uncertain, but generally positive trends for China are excluded, the number of extremely poor increased from 916 to 961 million. With a 'business-as-usual' growth pattern, seventy developing countries lag far behind on the necessary path to reach the goal for extreme income poverty by 2015. Even if the goal were achieved, there would still be 900 million people living in extreme poverty in developing countries. The figures for people living on US$2 or less per day are equally depressing: they have increased from 2.7 billion in 1990 to 2.8 billion in 1998, and are not likely to be decisively reduced before 2015.
2. To halve the proportion of the world's people suffering from hunger. The developing world still has some 826 million undernourished people, which is 'only' some 40 million fewer than in the early 1990s.
3. To halve the proportion of the world's people without access to safe drinking water, and to provide water, sanitation and hygiene to all by 2025. To achieve the water target by 2015 will require providing an additional 1.5 billion people with access to an improved water supply, that is, an additional 280,000 people every single day for the next fifteen years.
4. To enrol all children in primary school; achieve universal completion of primary schooling; and achieve gender equality in access to education. During the 1990s, enrolment increased in all regions of the world. More than seventy developing countries have reached primary net enrolment ratios of more than 80 per cent and the female enrolment ratio has reached almost 90 per cent of male enrolment. Still, 113 million children (of whom 60 per cent are girls) are today not attending school.
5. To reduce maternal mortality ratios by three-quarters, and to provide access for all who want reproductive health services. At an average of

440 per 100,000 live births, maternal deaths in developing countries are twenty times higher than in high-income countries. While contraceptive prevalence has reached nearly 50 per cent in developing countries, around 20 million couples who want to use contraception do not have access to it. The differences in access to reproductive health services are high, both between countries and within countries. In Bangladesh, a woman in the wealthiest fifth of the population is sixteen times more likely to have trained assistance in childbirth as a woman in the poorest fifth.

6. To reduce infant and under-five mortality rates by two-thirds. During the 1990s, both mortality rates were reduced by more than 10 per cent. Still, sub-Saharan Africa has an infant mortality rate of more than 100 per 1,000 live births and an under-five mortality rate of more than 170. Mortality rates have actually increased in eleven countries. There are more than 150 million underweight children in developing countries.
7. To halt and begin to reverse the spread of HIV/AIDS, malaria and other major diseases. The number of new HIV infections decreased in 2000, while the number living with HIV/AIDS is still increasing.
8. To implement national strategies for sustainable development to reverse the loss of environmental resources. The number of countries adopting sustainable development strategies doubled to more than fifty in 1997, but implementation remains minimal.

the impact of project aid in relation to poverty reduction. Most studies of the outcome of aid, however, focus on effectiveness and performance, rather than on impact. We examine what impact lessons can be learned from three evaluations of institutional performance covering the World Bank, Danida and Danish NGOs. Finally, we pull the information together in a summary of what is known about aid impact at different levels of society and through different types and instruments of aid.

## Aid Impact Assessment: A Neglected and Difficult Research Field

Lancaster (1999: 5–10) has identified two main approaches to analysing the impact of aid on development: a 'contextual' approach, which suggests that aid impact is primarily a function of the broader economic and political context in which it is provided; and an 'instrumental' approach, which evaluates aid impact in terms of the success or failure of the programmes and projects it finances. Contextual approaches examine relations of power between donor and recipient; forms of aid and development dependency; ideological implications of the idea of development and of the operations of the aid business; and the role of aid in generating equity (income redistribution and/or empowerment) and in addressing state or market failures through state-building, structural adjustment etc. The instrumental approaches are either anecdotal and polemic in their often journalistic criticism of the aid business, or empirical and management-oriented in their focus on the project and programme cycles of development cooperation or on the capacities of aid agencies and their partners.

There are few well-researched studies of the *impact* of development assistance (this section is based on Folke et al. 2001), especially impact at the local level (see Kruse et al. 1997). The study entitled *Does Aid Work?* (Cassen 1994) dealt with a number of important development cooperation issues, but primarily at a high level of generalization. As we see below, the World Bank has published a summary study of sixty-four projects entitled *Implementing Projects for the Poor – What Has been Learned?* (Carvalho and White 1996). This study ostensibly deals with impact, but in fact focuses on performance, particularly implementation progress and the extent to which project objectives are being achieved.

Impact is usually defined as the long-term, sustainable changes brought about by a given intervention. It is, however, more fruitful to see impact as something that happens from the first day a particular intervention is conceived and unfolds over time. It will obviously depend on the intervention as well as the context how impact is best conceptualized and studied. Projects that have material benefits (production or service delivery) as their primary goal will need an approach different from that needed by projects with capacity-building and empowerment as their main objectives. Sector programmes, which combine a complement of interventions with policy dialogue and capacity-building at sector level, will need yet another approach. Often, impact assessments deal exclusively with project (or programme) objectives (immediate, intermediate and development objectives), that is, with intended impact, but it is equally important to deal with the unintended (and unexpected) consequences of development interventions. This is captured in the simple definition of impact assessment provided by an Oxfam/Novib research project on NGO aid impact: 'Impact assessment is the systematic analysis of the lasting or significant changes – positive or negative, intended or not – in people's lives brought about by a given action or series of actions' (Roche 1999: 21).

It is essential to look at impact in terms of the ways in which the interventions impinge on societal processes. According to Norman Long, the concept intervention should itself be perceived as 'an ongoing, socially constructed and negotiated process', rather than 'the execution of an already specified plan of action with expected outcomes' (Long and Long 1992: 35). Donor-funded interventions are not implemented in a void. They interact with other interventions in a particular area (government- or NGO-supported and the private sector), and they stimulate or reinforce certain types of development and counteract others. The project itself may in many cases foster co-operation and teamwork among people who recognize the advantages of collaborating, but it may also create tension among beneficiaries and non-beneficiaries or exacerbate conflicts between different groups or factions. Thus, the introduction of a project in a particular locality often entails that certain people, individuals and groups, stand to gain, whereas others are left out or even stand to lose. At the same time, the considerable amount of resources (social, political, economic and symbolic) canalized by the project into a particular community might induce people to form strategic groups or alliances in order to capture a share of the expected benefits. Such groups and alliances will in turn reflect the social relations and power structure in the area.

The problems involved in studying aid impact are compounded when the focus shifts from projects to complex programmes. A shift in development cooperation from project aid to sector programmes may in practice involve only a change in scale, where the sector programme components are little more than large-scale projects held together by being within the same sector. Donors, however, emphasize that sector programme support goes into the planning and implementation of overall national and local sector development. Policy dialogue and policy implementation are important aspects. This means that impact studies need to be concerned even more with the political level and its impacts on the complex context of social, economic and political forces, the interaction of which influences the design and implementation of the more specific interventions. The major question then is whether and how the derived benefits emanating from new policies and improved capacities at the sector level, through all these societal processes reach the ultimate beneficiaries (for example, groups of poor men and women).

## Aid and Other Development Factors

Cassen's authoritative study of the effects of aid (1994: 224) concluded that aid has contributed positively to a long series of results and processes: raising food production in South Asia; experimental rural education programmes in Africa; infrastructure investment (power, roads and railways, ports, communications); rural development self-help schemes; strengthening developing country institutions; family planning, and so forth. All actors in development assistance can give similar examples of aid's positive and effective contributions within sectors, regions, institutions, themes.

The question is whether Cassen is also correct in the analysis's basic conclusion about development assistance, that 'the majority of aid is successful in terms of its own objectives' (Cassen 1994: 225). His next sentence is interesting: 'Over a wide range of countries and sectors, aid has made positive and valuable contributions.' When we return to considerations about aid's *contributions*, it is partly because of the methodological problems discussed above, and partly because aid *is* a limited contribution.

In both low-income and middle-income countries (LICs and MICs), total aid amounted to only US$9 per capita in 1999. For LICs, this was a fall from US$13 in 1994, while per capita aid to MICs stagnated. It is evident that very little 'development' can be generated for US$9 per capita per year, considering that aid aims to cover all levels of society, and that a significant part of aid returns to donor countries.

The fact that the poorest people in LICs and those who on average are better off in MICs receive the same level of aid (US$9 per capita per year) shows that poverty reduction is still not the dominant objective of aid in practice. This is seen clearly in Figure 12.1. The poor in sub-Saharan Africa have been exposed to a significant decline in aid per capita, from US$34 to $20. In 1999, the people of Eastern Europe and Central Asia received more aid per capita than Africans: US$23 as opposed to $20. Most of the absolutely poor people in this world live in South and East Asia, but they are the target of only US$3 and $8 in aid per capita per annum. It is very difficult to identify any aid impact in India and China due to the small size of aid (some US$2 per capita) and the large size of their national economies. In 1999, only eight countries received more than US$100 in net aid per capita: Albania, Bosnia-Herzegovina, Honduras, Israel, Macedonia, Namibia, Nicaragua and the West Bank and Gaza, that is, five European and Middle East countries,

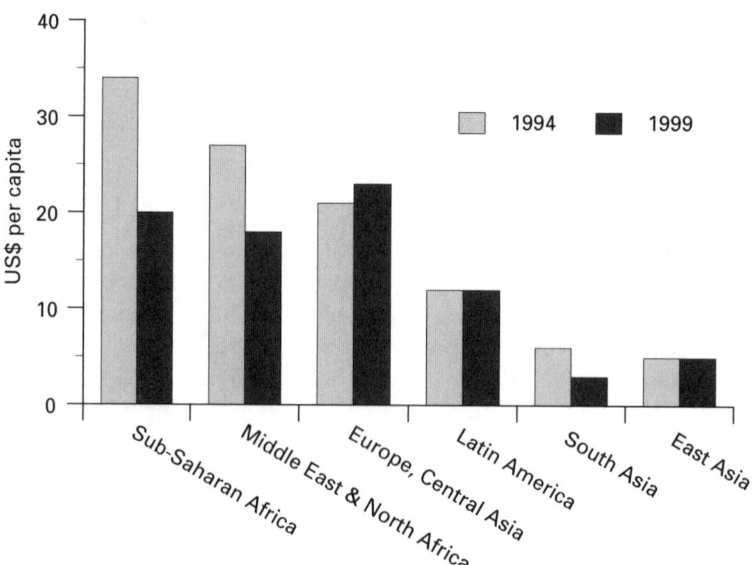


**Figure 12.1** Net official development assistance to regions of developing countries, 1994 and 1999 (*source*: World Bank 2001c, Table 6.10)

two Central American countries, and only one African country (Namibia at US$104 per capita). Development cooperation is politically biased and heavily under-financed.

Figure 12.2 shows that net aid provides a very limited share of gross national income (GNI) even in low-income countries (2 per cent, though 5–7 per cent if China and India are excluded) and even in sub-Saharan Africa (only 4 per cent). In 1999, aid constituted more than 25 per cent of GNI in only four countries: Guinea-Bissau (26 per cent); Malawi (25 per cent); Mongolia (25 per cent); and Nicaragua (33 per cent). Collier (2000: 313) suggests that a country starts to 'drown' in aid only when the share of net aid inflows to GDP exceeds some 12 per cent. In 1999, this applied to sixteen countries.

The low figures for the African average in Figure 12.2 are partly due to the very limited aid to Nigeria (with a population of 124 million), where aid constituted 0.5 per cent of GNI and 1.8 per cent of investments in 1999. In many other African countries, aid has provided more than half of the gross capital formation, yielding strong donor influence on national investments and economic development. Lensink and White (1999) suggest that there is nothing 'bad' in such aid dependence, if countries are on the path towards achieving specific development objectives and gaining access to other sources of capital.

Unavoidably, foreign aid frees national resources for other purposes. In other words, aid is fungible. In the most extreme case, the recipient government can use all local taxes and other sources of income for military

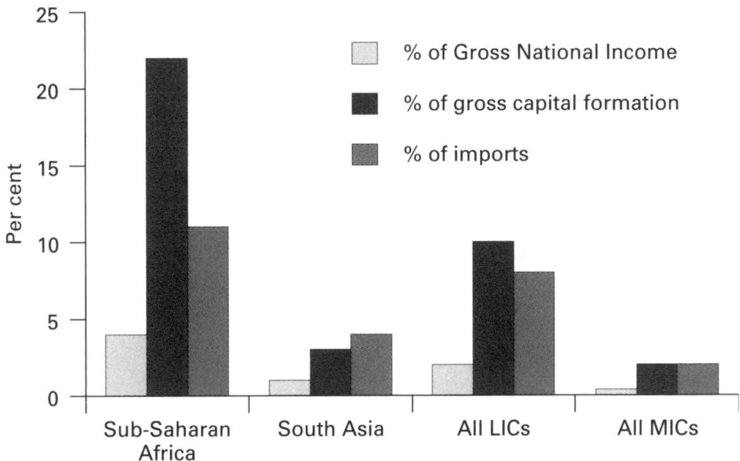


**Figure 12.2** Aid dependency ratios for selected groups of developing countries, 1999 (*source*: World Bank 2001c, Table 6.10)

armaments, extended oppression and luxury consumption (import of Mercedes automobiles and bank accounts in Switzerland are often named as the main examples), if they can just be sure that aid for health and other social sectors, sometimes supplemented by food aid, is sufficient to keep the masses under control. A consequence of this could be that it is increasingly irrelevant whether the individual aid-financed project or programme achieves its narrow goals and has any immediate effects.

We discuss aid's fungibility later in this chapter, but first, with Figure 12.3, show the amounts involved. The most important factor in this context is the amount of aid in relation to the government's total expenditures (for both public investments and operations). Figure 12.3 shows the size of development assistance for 1994 and 1999 in relation to total expenditures by the central government. The clearest results are the considerable variations between countries, and aid's decreasing significance in all countries except Vietnam. The variations are primarily due to the size of aid in relation to the developing country's economy. Another reason for the variations, however, is the differences between countries in relation to the distribution of expenditures between the central and local governments. Finally, aid is also channelled through both NGOs and the private sector, which explains that aid in countries like Burundi amounted to more than 100 per cent of the central government's total expenditures.

In any case, Figure 12.3 shows that aid fungibility is a reality in many developing countries: the amount of aid is large enough for the government to cover much of actual expenditures, but there are usually still considerable resources available for the government to use as it wishes. Mosley and Hudson

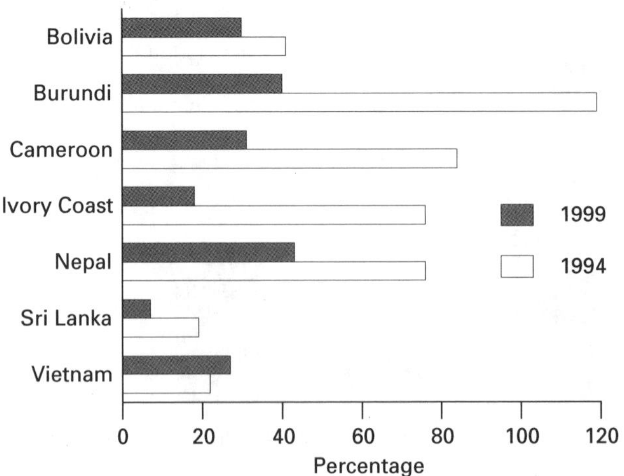


**Figure 12.3** Aid as a percentage of central government expenditures in selected developing countries, 1994 and 1999 (*source*: World Bank 2001c, Table 6.10)

(1997: 19) argue that the fungibility effect has disappeared completely in Africa and other low-income countries, because aid finances far more than the government's *development* expenditures (that is, the investment budget). We find, however, that fungibility is still a reality because the difference between development and recurrent budgets (for operations and maintenance) has become unclear in the poorest countries. They are forced to plan and finance services, maintenance, reconstruction and development activities at one and the same time.

## Macro-effects of Aid

Aid has had/can have many different effects on the society or macro level. On the basis of several country studies of aid's effects, Lele and Nabi (1991: 7) point to four rationales for aid:

1. Aid improves economic policies and the distribution of resources in recipient countries.
2. Aid strengthens technical, management, institutional and administrative capacity and thereby increases the effectiveness of capital.
3. Aid provides income transfers in situations where market forces fail.
4. Aid ensures fulfilment of poor people's basic needs.

To these aid potentials must be added aid's political effects in the form of society-building and democratization. At the same time, the country analyses in Lele and Nabi (1991) point to three negative consequences that aid has had/can have on the society and macro level.

1. Aid increases consumption and reduces savings and investments in the recipient country.
2. Aid promotes growth in the public sector beyond what the national economy can carry.
3. Aid promotes ineffective use of resources, for example, in the form of increased use of capital at the expense of labour.

On the basis of Serageldin (1995), we can go a bit further in summarizing the negative consequences of aid pointed out by the critics.

1. Aid has not worked. It has not promoted economic growth and development in recipient countries. Aid has replaced or reduced domestic savings and investments instead of supplementing and promoting them.
2. Aid causes dependence and inhibits or postpones the necessary economic changes and political reforms in recipient countries. It gives the elite the opportunity to continue policies that are detrimental to development. Aid has also promoted unnecessary state intervention in societal development.
3. Aid is misused. It falls into the hands of the relatively rich and powerful, not the poor and needy. Aid increases the resources of those in power

and thereby their grip on society. This criticism comes from both the left and right sides of the political spectrum.

4. Aid is not nearly as good as trade and direct private investments in getting a development process started. There is therefore no alternative to liberalization, which can integrate developing countries in the world economy far better than aid.

Right-wing opponents of aid emphasize the first two groups of criticism: aid has not promoted economic growth, which is primarily due to the fact that it allows and leads to a *laissez-faire* policy in developing countries, so that the necessary reforms are not made and the correct policies are not carried out. The argument is that there is no direct connection between the size of aid (large or small) given to the individual developing country, and economic growth (high or low) and the size of savings and investments in the same country. This, together with the fact that evaluations of individual projects for most donors have given positive results in up to 60–70 per cent of cases, led Mosley (1986) to point to a micro–macro paradox. Economists generally see a strong correlation between high savings and economic growth. The main problem for economists is therefore to find explanations for why the sum of aid, in the form of resources of considerable size, did not lead to economic growth in developing countries.

Economists gave three explanations. First, aid is not exclusively distributed according to need and effectiveness criteria, which would give most aid to the poorest countries that implement growth-generating economic policies and have the capacity to make use of aid. Historic, strategic, political, commercial and other motives influence donors' aid distribution (as described in Chapter 2). Figures 12.1 and 12.2 show that to a large extent aid has gone to middle-income countries rather than to the low-income countries with the largest number of poor people. Below, we consider the attempts of some World Bank economists to calculate the effects of the ineffective distribution of aid.

The economists' second explanation for the micro–macro paradox was that aid (like commercial loans) is used here and now for consumption or poor investments. Therefore, aid is not well enough integrated into the necessary use of domestic and foreign savings for long-term investments to improve production and capacity and thereby create a basis for future economic growth. Furthermore, aid makes it possible for recipient governments to postpone necessary solutions to the country's problems, especially in relation to imbalances in the economy (foreign trade and debt, inflation and state deficits).

The third explanation is the so-called 'Dutch disease'. All resource transfers from one country to another cause the exchange rate in the recipient country to be revalued, which reduces its export opportunities and ability to compete. This is a problem that the oil-exporting countries have run into, and which has resulted in a high living standard but low growth. In order to avoid this situation, which is seldom sustainable in the long run, recipient countries must use resource transfers for investments rather than consumption. This can be difficult in a developing country that is often in the midst of several crisis situations that demand transfers of income for consumption.

The main argument of these economists was that (a) there are always policies that are out of balance and must be adjusted; (b) adjustments often cost political popularity; (c) foreign aid allows countries not to adjust; (d) thus, small imbalances can grow large; and (e) aid thereby causes macro damage in addition to whatever else it does. On the basis of this logic, the structural adjustment programmes (SAPs), which the World Bank and IMF have supported and insisted upon since the beginning of the 1980s, were ideal for removing the micro–macro paradox and increasing the impact of aid on economic growth. Through SAPs, donors made conditions requiring strong adjustments of economic and other macro policies. The results, however, have been quite ambiguous.

On the one hand, the many studies made in the 1990s (starting with Mosley, Harrigan and Toye 1991; Collier 1997, 2000; Killick 1998; Kanbur 2000) have shown that donor conditionality does not work: many developing countries have approved politico-economic and institutional reforms without implementing them; and donors have accepted this, as they have continued to approve loans and transfer aid. One reason for this is that donor organizations' own success criteria have been to transfer as much money as possible to recipient countries. This applies both to the organizations' responsibility towards the political level in donor countries and the individual staff member in the donor organizations whose career depends on well-functioning aid projects and programmes.

On the other hand, research has found that aid's impact on economic growth and investments *increased* during the period when aid moved up to the macro level with the help of policy dialogue and structural adjustment programmes (Hansen and Tarp 2000). Mosley and Hudson (1997) conclude that aid's effectiveness in promoting growth and investments in developing countries improved from the period 1974–83 to the period 1984–92. The two authors have shown that there were signs of a positive effect of aid on economic growth in two studies in nineteen and twenty-nine developing countries, respectively (Mosley and Hudson 1995, 1996, and summarized in 1997). Mosley and Hudson studied aid's effect on savings, investments, human capital and economic policy in developing countries, and through this, developing countries' economic growth rate. They concluded that for sixty-four developing countries, aid effectiveness improved from the period before to the period after 1983. For seventy-four developing countries, where other data were found, aid effectiveness was positive for the whole period 1974–92. This was due to improved effectiveness after 1984. This is the case, even though the authors confirm other analyses showing that aid increases consumption and reduces savings in developing countries.

Lele and Nabi concluded (in 1991: 460) that aid's consumption-increasing effects must also be judged to be positive: aid helped several Asian countries to maintain poor people's consumption possibilities and limit inflation and pressure on wages, and thereby gave governments in developing countries breathing space to tackle crises. Positive evaluation of a 'breathing space' represents a perspective that is in opposition to the 'doing-nothing' explanation. Once again, we see how difficult it is to draw clear conclusions about the effects of aid. It depends to a great extent on the eyes that see and on the factors and contexts they wish to look at.

## *Assessing Aid* – Overview of the Debate

The World Bank's *Assessing Aid: What Works, What Doesn't, and Why* (1998b), written by David Dollar and Lant Pritchett, was presented as a 'policy research report'. Its 'judgments do not necessarily reflect the views of the World Bank's Board of Directors or the governments they represent' (World Bank 1998b: xi). Still, it 'prompted a vigorous debate embracing the impact of aid on growth, conditionality and selectivity, and the implications for poor performers. Its importance – for donors, for recipients, for poor people – cannot be overstated' (Beynon 2001). In an excellent assessment, Beynon continues:

> The debate has been healthy, but at times hotly contested. Two opposing viewpoints have emerged. According to one, aid only really works when government policies are good, and a more selective allocation of aid to 'good policy/high poverty' countries will lead to larger reductions in poverty. According to the other, aid effectiveness is not conditional on policy and the implications of the former for more selective aid allocations are treated with concern. (Beynon 2001: 1)

The debate is heated because the 'good policy and selectivity' viewpoint is highly ideological in its advocacy of particular good/sound/right policies; it reduces the scope for alternative, independent policy-making by developing countries; and it will have significant costs for the poor living in poorly performing countries with weak/incorrect policy environments. The logic of the *Assessing Aid* viewpoint may be summarized in six points (see Box 12.2).

1. Aid does not always lead to increased economic growth.
2. Economic growth is essential for poverty reduction.
3. Economic growth depends on the quality of economic policies, in particular: inflation control, balanced budget management and trade liberalization.
4. Economic growth and poverty reduction also depend on the quality of the legal-institutional environment (rule of law, accountability, absence of corruption).
5. Development aid should be allocated selectively, viz. to countries with good economic policies and institutional capacities.

6. Countries with poor policies and capacities should be given knowledge and policy ideas (and only promises of money) as incentives to reform.

This position, which has affected the aid allocation criteria of the World Bank, the regional development banks and some large bilateral donors, has been criticized on each of the six points.

1. Overall, aid has promoted economic growth, regardless of national policies. The fact that recipients of much aid have often had low economic growth is due rather to the poverty-orientation of aid, which has gone to countries with weak opportunities in the world economy.
2. Poverty reduction is about much more than the reduction of income poverty that may result from economic growth. It is also about increasing human security, income redistribution and empowerment. The extent and forms of inequality are key starting points and targets for poverty reduction.
3. There is no automatic link between economic policies and macro-economic development on the one hand and the livelihoods of the poor and the scope for poverty reduction on the other.
4. Institutional capacity has been influenced by aid, both negatively (through 'projectitis', 'reformitis', donor competition, and so on) and positively (through capacity-building and policy dialogue). The budget, including its implementation, is a key to enhanced development and aid effectiveness. Improved institutional capacity must be an objective of aid, not a precondition. The countries with the weakest institutional capacities are the countries with the greatest need for aid.
5. Aid should primarily be given to the poorest countries and to countries hit by external shocks, where it is possible to improve economic policies and institutional capacities. The desire for change and the direction of change is more important than past performance.
6. Limiting aid to 'poor performers' to the provision of 'ideas' is wrong for two reasons. First, it makes the poor in poorly performing countries suffer twice (as a result of poor policies and as a result of reduced aid). Second, it is neo-imperialist and donor-centric in its assumption that donors have a monopoly on knowledge about what the right policies are. The ever-changing fads in development thinking and donor beliefs prove that such a position is untenable.

The debate is ongoing, but some elements of agreement are emerging.

First, aid has contributed significantly to a reduction of poverty in recipient countries, through economic growth, income redistribution, improved health and education, that is, a combination of resource transfer, societal change, capacity-building and human resource development. Quantitative, econometric models of aid effects on growth, savings, investments, imports and suchlike cannot capture the whole poverty-reducing impact of aid.

### **Box 12.2** Key Points of the *Assessing Aid* Report

- *Financial aid works in a good policy environment.* Financial assistance leads to faster growth, poverty reduction and gains in social indicators in developing countries with sound economic management. In a weak environment, however, money has much less impact.
- *Improvements in economic institutions and policies in the developing world are the key to a quantum leap in poverty reduction.* When societies desire reform, foreign aid can provide critical support – in ideas, training and finance. Efforts to 'buy' policy improvements in countries where there is no movement for reform have typically failed.
- *Effective aid complements private investment.* In countries with sound economic management, aid acts as a magnet and 'crowds in' private investment by a ratio of almost $2 to every $1 of aid. In highly distorted environments, aid 'crowds out' private investment.
- *The value of development projects is to strengthen institutions and policies so that services can be effectively delivered.* Aid brings a package of knowledge and finance. Aid finance is typically fungible. Thus, choosing such laudable sectors as primary health or education cannot ensure that money is well used. Aid is financing the entire public sector, and the overall quality of policies and institutions is the key to securing a large return from this financing. The knowledge creation supported by aid leads to improvements in particular sectors, whereas the finance part of aid expands public services in general.
- *An active civil society improves public services.* The best aid projects support initiatives that change the way the public sector does business. The top-down, technocratic approach to project design and service delivery has not worked in areas critical for development – rural water supply, primary education, natural resource management and many more.
- *Aid can nurture reform in even the most distorted environments – but it requires patience and a focus on ideas, not money.* In some of the poorest countries of the world, governments are not providing effective policies or services, which is why government-to-government transfers have yielded poor results. Still, there are often champions of local or sectoral reform, and aid at times has been effective in supporting these initiatives. This work is staff-intensive and results in little disbursement of funds.

Making aid more effective in reducing poverty requires five policy reforms:

- Financial assistance must be targeted more effectively to low-income countries with sound economic management. Too much aid is going to middle-income countries that do not need it and countries with poor policies where it is ineffective.

- Policy-based aid should be provided to nurture policy reforms in credible reformers. Conditionality has rarely worked unless there is strong domestic support for reform. In countries with poor policies and no credible reform movement, ideas matter more than money, with assistance better focused on dissemination of ideas and international experience, training future policy-makers and leaders, and stimulating capacity for informed policy debate within civil society.
- The mix of aid activities should be tailored to country and sector conditions. Aid is highly fungible, so donors need to examine a country's overall budget allocation and efficacy of public spending: The better they are, the stronger the case for budget support. In countries with sound policies but weak capacity for delivering services, project aid is better.
- Projects need to focus on creating and transmitting knowledge and capacity. The key role of development projects should be to support institutional and policy changes that improve public service delivery. Even if money does not 'stick' (fungibility), the local knowledge and institutional capacity created by projects can.
- Aid agencies need to find alternative approaches to helping highly distorted countries, since traditional methods have failed in these cases. Ideas matter more than money. Donors need to get away from an 'approval and disbursement' culture that does not value small-scale, staff-intensive activities.

*Source:* World Bank 1998: *Assessing Aid: What Works, What Doesn't, and Why.* Overview: 1–27.

Second, aid is, of course, most effective in developing countries with macro-economic stability, coherent policies and good institutional capacities. It is essential that improved policy-making and capacity-building are aid objectives in all developing countries, particularly in the weakest and least developed countries.

Third, the greatest global effect in terms of income poverty reduction will be achieved through (re)allocating aid to the low-income countries with the largest number of poor people. This is more effective than a reallocation of aid on the basis of only the 'quality' of policies and institutions.

Fourth, economic models can suggest ways to allocate aid so that the largest number of absolutely poor people move out of income poverty. This is critical at a time when the number of poor people is not being reduced significantly because of population growth, HIV/AIDS and so on. These models, however, are primarily relevant to policy-oriented programme aid (budget or balance of payments support, adjustment and some sector programmes) to stable societies.

Fifth, humanitarian assistance, technical cooperation and development projects and programmes should be allocated on the basis of poverty, social and political needs, and institutional opportunities. With very few exceptions where only humanitarian assistance is possible (Afghanistan, People's Republic of Congo, Somalia, Liberia, Sierra Leone), all these aid forms are needed in all low-income countries.

We use this emerging agreement as a foundation for our discussion in Chapter 14 of the future rationale, prospects and design of development aid. First, however, we present the critique in greater depth and the World Bank's response, which leads to a discussion of the logic and implications of selectivity in aid allocations.

## *Assessing Aid* – Implications for Selectivity in Aid Allocations

The *Assessing Aid* report has been criticized on three grounds.

1. Incorrect econometric analyses of the empirical evidence, which cannot support its radical policy recommendations.
2. Inadequate analyses of the political economy and the social context of development cooperation.
3. Unacceptable policy recommendations from an ethical and humanitarian point of view.

*Econometric weaknesses* Hansen and Tarp (2000) show that the World Bank economists' models underlying *Assessing Aid* are not robust. Respecification of the model gives different results. Based on a survey of existing cross-country analyses, they find that the weight of the empirical evidence indicates that there is a robust relationship between aid and aggregate growth, regardless of the policies of recipient countries. While they concur that the marginal benefit of aid in recipient countries is higher when the policy environment is favourable, they are adamant in their criticism of the scientific foundation of the Bank's policy recommendations on selectivity in aid allocations. Similarly, Lensink and White (1999) talk about 'the abuse of cross-country regressions'. They suggest that the impact of aid on economic growth is determined by the stability of aid flows, not by the level of aid.

*Context and political economy* Lensink and White (1999) criticize the policy index being used by the World Bank to determine good and sound policies, economic management and institutional capacity. The Bank considered low inflation, budget surplus, trade openness and institutional quality (security of property rights and efficiency of government bureaucracy), none of which can be said to be clear and beyond dispute on the path towards development.

Some inflation and budget deficits are sometimes needed to promote growth; some trade protection is needed to give indigenous enterprises a chance to invest and develop; and effective state intervention depends on a wide range of factors.

The model's assumptions of linear relationships between policies and growth do not fit with the reality of changing and often contradictory relationships and processes. Countries experiencing external shocks (trade, financial flows, natural disasters, conflicts, population movements, and so on) may perform badly on policies but be in high need of development assistance and often capable of using it effectively. The idea that 'policies matter' to such an extent that they should be the criteria for aid allocations is not supported by more detailed studies of the gaps between policies and implementation. The policies emerging from the dialogue between donors and recipient governments often matter much less to the livelihood of the poor than the resources that actually reach schools and clinics in the communities. Infant and child mortality can be reduced just as well by mother and child health programmes, such as immunization, as by aid-promoted growth.

Furthermore, the assessment of institutional quality is based on surveys among owners of private enterprises, assessing issues such as decision-making predictability, rule of law and its enforcement, political stability, property rights and the extent of corruption. It is not surprising that there is close correspondence between the views of private entrepreneurs on these issues and the economic performance of the developing country. When there is low growth, few investments, private enterprises are not likely to be very happy about the government's handling of the economy; hence, they are likely to give the government a low score on policies regardless of its actual policy performance. Such circular arguments should not serve as a foundation for cross-country regression analyses with far-reaching policy implications.

*The rights of the poor* Performance-based aid allocation and selectivity makes a fundamental break with the rights of the poor everywhere to international solidarity no matter where they live. Needs and rights are being replaced by effectiveness and performance as guiding principles in international development cooperation. An ethical perspective could well be taken to the other extreme: the poor living in countries with corrupt and oppressive regimes deserve more international attention than those living under peaceful conditions with good development prospects. The proposal in the *Assessing Aid* report that poor performers should be given 'ideas, not money' is arrogant, both in terms of its belief in donor supremacy regarding the correct development paths and policies, and in terms of its disregard for the plight of poor and marginalized people.

The difference between a needs-and-rights approach and an effectiveness-and-performance approach lies, of course, in how good and bad performers are defined (how many developing countries and poor people are in each category) and how selective aid allocation will be effectuated (at one extreme: badly performing countries are only given humanitarian assistance and ideas in the form of policy advice and technical assistance). This question is not easily answered. The political sensitivity underlying donor decisions about the political, economic and institutional performance of their partners among independent states in the Third World has reduced the donors' desire to be transparent regarding the extent of selectivity. It took the US Congress several years to approve legislation on a selective approach to economic partnerships with African countries. The Nordic countries have largely stuck to their long-term partnerships with least-developed countries as regards bilateral aid. The EU has taken many steps over the years favouring a more selective approach towards ACP countries, but has continued to have aid programmes in countries with below-average policies. This is partly because the political costs of cutting collaboration with too many ACP countries are considered too high.

The World Bank has also applied performance-based selectivity to the interest-free IDA credits. The allocation among developing countries is based on twenty criteria, and the 'good performers' are allocated approximately twice the average per capita aid – and three to four times as much as the 'poor performers'. The difference in per capita lending between the highest and the lowest quintiles of country performance increased from 1.5 times in 1993–95 to 3.5 times in 1998–2000. Since many countries in the top quintile are relatively small, the bulk of IDA lending goes to the three quintiles with middle-rated performers (World Bank, OED 2001: 57). The twenty components in the Bank's Country Policy and Institutional Assessment can be grouped into four categories (Collier and Dollar 2001: 5; World Bank 2001b: 3).

- *Macro-economic policies:* whether fiscal, monetary and exchange rate policies provide a stable environment for economic activity;
- *Structural policies:* the extent to which trade, tax and sectoral policies create good incentives for production by households and firms;
- *Public sector management:* the extent to which public sector institutions effectively provide services that complement private initiative, such as the rule of law (functioning of the judiciary, police), infrastructure and social services;
- *Social inclusion:* the extent to which policy ensures the full participation of the society through social services that reach the poor and disadvantaged, including women and ethnic minorities.

This index is far-reaching, covering many important development aspects discussed throughout this book. But it is also highly selective and hence ideological and political. Combining a range of unweighted, ideology-flavoured policy assessments by World Bank staff with strong vested interests into a seemingly objective decision-making instrument for aid allocation is pure power politics and has little to do with poverty reduction needs and development partnerships. Collier and Dollar correctly refer to it as 'the Bank's subjective CPIA score' (2001: 4). There is, again, a real risk of circular argument: Bank staff assigns scores on country *policies*, but their scores are unavoidably affected by the state of the national economy, that is, policy *outcomes*. Still, the index is used indiscriminately by World Bank economists in their regression analyses of links between policies and growth (that is, outcomes) and the impact of aid.

World Bank management takes a number of other issues into consideration in its actual decision-making on aid allocation among countries. These include reduction of the performance rating by one-third for countries found (by the Bank) to have serious governance problems – the 'governance discount'.

Does a selectivity ratio of three or four to one (IDA credits per capita) in favour of good performers constitute a fully performance-based aid allocation system? The thrust of the findings and recommendations of the *Independent Evaluation of IDA's Partnership for Poverty Reduction 1994–2000* (World Bank, OED 2001) is that the Bank has not gone far enough in strategic, performance-based, aid allocation, including the use of greater country selectivity. In particular, the evaluation argues that the system has not yet 'captured' all borrowing countries with 'serious governance problems'. The World Bank management's response to this proposition is significant: 'IDA's allocation system has consistently functioned effectively, achieving an allocation that is significantly more performance-based than concessional assistance as a whole ... In particular, management believes that the governance discount has served a very useful function. Lending has been reduced sharply in countries with very weak governance' (World Bank, OED 2001: 57).

In this context the argument seems concerned about punishing 'countries with governance problems' – that is, governments with low scores on the policy index or other political-economic charcateristics not favoured by the Bank – than about reaching the poor and marginalized people in all low-income countries. Some of the evaluation's suggestions for improvements to the performance-based allocation system point to the dilemmas inherent in this approach to increasing aid impact:

> Remove criteria not shown by research to be important for growth and fund research to identify policies that lead to poverty reduction (beyond that achievable by growth alone) ... Assign appropriate weights to the criteria ... Ensure that each criterion rates policy performance rather than level of development, rewarding equally all borrowers doing everything feasible in their situation. Ensure that each criterion can be objectively assessed and that IDA has the capability to assess it. Redefine the governance indicators in light of ongoing consultations and research. (World Bank, OED 2001: 59)

The aim is laudable: maximum poverty reduction in countries with friendly and committed governments. However, the approach is technocratic: knowledge- and management-intensive. The idea of detailed, objective criteria for aid allocation and investment across all developing countries defies all talk of partnership, local ownership and priorities, and respect for national and local political processes, including conflicting interests and disagreements. Paradoxically, at the same time, the technocratic approach to isolating and circumventing 'bad performers' exaggerates the role of policies for poverty reduction and the livelihoods of the poor. We return to this paradox in Chapter 14.

The strength of the Bank economists' research and advocacy of performance-based selectivity and reallocation of aid lies in their call for more aid to the countries with the largest number of poor people. Bank management, Bank researchers, and their external opponents agree that more aid should go to countries in South Asia and sub-Saharan Africa with deep poverty and relatively little aid. From the Bank perspective, this is possible because some 75 per cent of the world's poor live in countries with high poverty *and* good policies. Collier and Dollar have gone far (summarized in 2001) in calculating how global aid ought to be allocated to pull most people out of poverty, based on their models of the impact of aid on growth and poverty reduction. They place 115 developing countries in a figure with four quadrants: (1) poor policy and high poverty; (2) good policy and high poverty; (3) good policy and low poverty; and (4) poor policy and low poverty. The main argument is that aid should increasingly be allocated to the high poverty and good policy countries.

Collier and Dollar (2001: 10) compare actual with 'poverty-efficient' aid allocations (see Figure 12.4). The main reallocation is not from poor to good policy countries, but from middle-income countries (with low poverty) to low-income countries (with high poverty). Collier and Dollar conclude that in MICs, 'aid is not likely to have much impact on poverty' since 'aid is likely to be highly fungible because it is a smaller fraction of the national budget' (2001: 10). The reallocation suggested by the Collier and Dollar model would mean that nineteen of the top twenty recipients of aid (in terms of the aid share of GDP) would be countries in sub-Saharan Africa, with Bangladesh in place fifteen as the only exception.

| POOR POLICY / HIGH POVERTY<br>29% of actual ODA in 1998<br>28% of poverty-efficient ODA | GOOD POLICY / HIGH POVERTY<br>38% of actual ODA in 1998<br>68% of poverty-efficient ODA |
|---|---|
| POOR POLICY / LOW POVERTY<br>6% of actual ODA in 1998<br>0% of poverty-efficient ODA | GOOD POLICY / LOW POVERTY<br>27% of actual ODA in 1998<br>4% of poverty-efficient ODA |

**Figure 12.4** Actual and poverty-efficient aid allocations (*source*: Collier and Dollar 2001: 10)

India and China are particular problems in such calculations – and in real-life decisions on aid allocation. Both countries represent good policy and high poverty situations, though there is some difference: almost 90 per cent of the people in India live for less than US$2 per day, whereas this applies to 'only' half of the Chinese. China has therefore been excluded from the Collier and Dollar calculations, whereas special limits are put on the share of aid that 'ought' to go to India. Without such limits in their models, India should receive about *two-thirds* of global aid (as compared to less than 5 per cent today) because of its high poverty, low per capita income, and reasonably good policies (Beynon 2001: 11). When Collier and Dollar put an artificial limit of 20 per cent on India's share of global aid, the top six recipients of aid in a poverty-efficient allocation would be: India 20 per cent; Bangladesh 19 per cent; Vietnam 8 per cent; Nigeria 8 per cent; Pakistan 7 per cent; and Ethiopia 6 per cent. With present aid allocations, Collier and Dollar estimate that the global aid budget of US$40 billion would lift 16 million people out of poverty. With the policy and poverty-efficient aid allocation, they estimate that an additional 9 million people could be lifted out of poverty. Adding $10 billion to the aid budget would lift 2 and 7 million people out of poverty under the existing and poverty-efficient aid allocations, respectively.

Having critically reviewed the aid effectiveness and selectivity debate, Beynon concludes as follows on aid allocation:

> There needs to be a significant shift in aid from middle income towards low income countries ... Some greater focus on 'good policy' countries is warranted, but in assessing performance donors need to make allowance for the impact of external shocks, while there remains a powerful case for continued engagement in poorly performing countries. Overall, these points will mean shifting aid away from Eastern Europe and Central Asia, Latin America, and the Middle East and North Africa, towards South Asia (especially India) and (to a lesser degree) Sub-Saharan Africa. (Beynon 2001: 3).

## The Impact of Policy-oriented Programme Aid

The debate on the macro effects of aid on growth and poverty discussed above grew out of concern about the impact of structural adjustment programmes on policies, economic development and poverty. As these programmes developed into balance of payments and budget support, there was a need for macro-level impact assessments to supplement the project reviews and evaluations that had dominated the aid business so far. Many analyses of structural adjustment programmes correctly looked at these from a political economy point of view – as external policy interventions by IMF and the World Bank rather than as aid programmes. While there was a tendency during the late 1980s and early 1990s to exaggerate the policy interference by IMF and the World Bank, later analyses concluded that adjustment and policy conditionality had less impact on growth and policy-making in developing countries than claimed by IMF and the Bank. They also had fewer effects in terms of cuts in social services and lay-offs in the public sector than argued by NGOs and opposition groups in developing countries (Engberg-Pedersen et al. 1996; White and Leavy 1999).

In this section, we summarize two impact assessments of programme aid: White's evaluation of Swedish programme aid, entitled *Dollars, Dialogue and Development* (White 1999c); and World Bank researchers' analysis, *Aid and Reform in Africa: Lessons from Ten Case Studies* (World Bank 2001b). This allows a discussion of the impact of aid on policies and policy reforms, which is also a key issue in Collier and Dollar's analysis of development effectiveness (2001). The impact of the new fashion in development cooperation, sector programme support, however, should rather be discussed in a project context.

Programme aid, which is all aid not intended to finance a specific project, and which amounted to 12 per cent of total Swedish aid during the 1990s, is typically policy-based and linked to economic reform. Like most bilateral donors, Sweden, in most cases, has linked its programme aid to policy-based lending and conditionalities set by the World Bank and IMF. While Swedish programme aid declined during the 1990s (from 20 per cent to 5 per cent of Swedish aid), it recorded a significant shift from import support to debt relief and budget support. Import support was criticized for being prone to corruption and inefficiency and for being excessively bureaucratic. In general, programme aid is more vulnerable than other types to general cuts in donor budgets. Although the Ministry of Finance is directly involved in programme aid and is more likely to follow IMF and World Bank policy prescriptions, programme aid has actually been more focused on the poorest countries than Sweden's other development assistance. Swedish programme aid has always had a growth and economic reform objective, but it has occasionally been suspended with reference to violations of good governance. Social sector reform or poverty reduction, however, were very seldom given as the explicit objective.

Based on case studies of Swedish programme aid to eight developing countries and a survey of the literature on structural adjustment and policy-based lending, White concludes as follows on the impact of adjustment and the capacity of donor agencies to promote reform and influence policy change in recipient countries. Since 1980, there has been a dramatic change in the economic policy stance of virtually all developing countries. Domestic political considerations are the prime factor in determining economic and political reform, including the timing and pace of reform. Donors overstate their own importance at the expense of understanding political dynamics in the partner countries. Countries that have reformed have performed better in most economic fields, with the exception of agricultural growth, since the agricultural supply response has been mixed. More intensive reform does not yield additional benefits over those with a lesser extent of liberalization.

Comparing, for example, Uganda and Zambia, reform seems to have been necessary but not sufficient for restoring growth. With a few exceptions, the adjustment programmes did not seem to have been successful in reducing poverty; liberalization seems to have increased inequality also within countries.

According to White, policy dialogue must be seen as a set of processes, where conditionality is only the formal, directive end; other channels and parts of the policy dialogue have often been more effective. Formal conditionality has a mixed record, with outright failures and some success in influencing policies. While bilateral agencies have moved the agenda of political conditionality forward and supported the implementation of economic reforms, they have had little influence on the content of IMF/World Bank programmes. There does not appear to be a 'Swedish position'. Sweden's role in policy dialogue at the country level does not reflect what might have been expected from a 'progressive donor'. There is no evidence of Sweden trying to place poverty more strongly on the conditionality agenda at the country level. Despite talk in the donor community of pro-poor growth, policies proposed by donors focus on influencing growth rather than the pattern of growth.

As regards the impact of Swedish and other programme aid, White notes that aid has supported both imports and debt payments; without aid, imports would have been 20–50 per cent less in the countries studied. Aid has been anti-inflationary, because it has not resulted in an equivalent increase in expenditures, and because aid has provided goods and given credibility to the exchange rate. There has in general been a weak private investment response to aid in the form of funds and policy advice. The impact on the structure of government expenditure has been mixed, meaning that it is not clear that aid has promoted spending on social services. Aid, however, has improved welfare through its support for imports and public expenditures, whereas its impact on growth seems neither particularly strong nor sustainable.

The study edited by the World Bank, *Aid and Reform in Africa*, provides lessons from ten case studies, organized in four groups. These are: (1) successful reformers: Ghana and Uganda; (2) post-socialist reformers: Ethiopia, Mali and Tanzania; (3) mixed reformers: Ivory Coast, Kenya and Zambia; and (4) non-reformers: Democratic Republic of Congo (DRC) and Nigeria. Suggesting with these categories that the success or failure of development depends on the extent of reform undertaken by African governments themselves is a highly political message. This is underlined by the Bank's President Wolfensohn already in the foreword: 'When aid supports a country-owned development strategy, it can lead to sustained growth and poverty alleviation ... When reform is imposed from abroad, even as a *quid pro quo* for aid, it is not sustainable' (World Bank 2001b: xi). But, as we have seen above, the 'country-owned development strategy' has to comprise all the good/right/sound policies advocated by the Bank. If not, a country is characterized as a 'mixed reformer' or even a 'poor performer'.

The study uses the Bank's Country Policy and Institutional Assessment

(CPIA) index as indicators of good policies: absence of high inflation; functioning foreign exchange and financial market; openness to foreign trade; effective rule of law; and delivery of key services such as education. The authors recognize that learning about development policy is an ongoing process. Still, their findings are surprisingly sharp, based on their own case studies and other research.

- The amount of aid that countries have received has had no direct effect on the quality of their macro-economic policies. Reform outcomes can be predicted by underlying political-economic variables, such as the length of tenure of the government and whether the leader was democratically elected. Variables under donors' control have no influence on the success or failure of reform (see also Killick 1998; Mosley, Harrigan and Toye 1995).
- Policy formulation depends primarily on domestic political-economic factors (Rodrik 1999; van de Walle and Johnston 1996). There is no consistent relationship between aid and reform. Still, aid goes to a large extent to countries in need of policy reform with the explicit objective to promote reform. Countries that have devastating economic and political crises (Ghana, Uganda, Nigeria and Congo) tend to move to the extremes, either developing coherent reform movements or declining rapidly. Of these crisis countries, it is those rich in natural resources that tend to descend into civil war (Nigeria, Congo).
- Successful reformers have consultative processes that build consensus for change. However, there is no relationship between formal democratic institutions and good economic policy.
- Large amounts of aid to countries with bad policy sustain those poor policies. Funding allows the delay of reform. Attaching conditions to aid in these cases does not lead to successful policy change.
- Aid plays a significant and positive role in the case of two sustained reformers (Ghana, Uganda). Finance grew as policy improved and increased the benefits of reform, helping to sustain political support.
- Donors do not discriminate effectively among different countries and different phases of the reform process. Donors tend to provide the same package of assistance everywhere and at all times. The lessons from the Ghana and Uganda cases are that donors should concentrate on technical assistance and other soft support without large-scale budget or balance-of-payments support in the phase before governments are serious about reform. If a reform movement develops, finance can be increased as policies actually improve. In the early stage of serious reform, political leaders and technocrats actually welcome conditionality in order to bind themselves to policy change. Once the reform movement is well entrenched, conditionality becomes less useful because it limits participation and disguises ownership.

The statement about a lack of consistent relationship between aid and reform has to be recognized as an 'average' assessment. The World Bank economists argue that this depends on four factors: (1) the country context, including the availability of other sources of income such as export of natural resources; (2) the existence of national reform movements; (3) the phase of reform; and (4) the type of aid ('money or ideas'). This leads to suggestions about effective donor management (or manipulation) of aid types and sequencing, which, in our view, represent socio-political engineering by external forces with little concern for the plight of the poor. Participation and ownership are significant, but (aid) resources are needed for economic investments (such as infrastructure) and public services (such as health and education) during all phases of reform. Based on the ten-country study of Africa, the Bank concludes that 'it is difficult to find a case where reform occurred without a crisis' (World Bank 2001b: 7). This and the view that financial aid may postpone necessary reform produce the proposition that countries in a non-reform or pre-reform situation should be given only ideas (technical assistance and policy advice) and not money in the form of programme aid. The suggestion that 'it takes a crisis' to produce reform can only be characterized as cynical. The limited understanding of needs and politics is seen in the subsequent statement: 'It takes disinterested economic analysis to gauge whether on balance the economy will benefit from the reforms' (World Bank 2001b: 10).

The positive aspect of these analyses is that they start taking politics seriously; the negative aspect is that they often do it poorly, yet with sufficient self-confidence to propose radical reallocation and management of aid in accordance with their analyses. When cross-country regression analyses are applied to the success of governments in adopting and implementing reform programmes, they restrict the scope for proper analysis. For example, Dollar and Svensson (2000) suggest that the outcome of reform programmes can be *predicted* on the basis of the nature of the government: a new, democratically elected government has a 95 per cent probability of success, compared to 67 per cent for an authoritarian government that has been in power for twelve years. Collier and Dollar (2001: 15) find that 'this result makes intuitive sense'. We can only hope that such analyses and predictions are not being used to determine any donor's approach to a partnership with a recipient government, since it would preclude a solid understanding of national politics and of the potential role of the donor.

When Collier and Dollar assess the finding by Knack (2001) that during the period 1982–95 aid was associated with an increase in corruption and a deterioration in bureaucratic quality and the rule of law, they recognize that many projects are now explicitly designed to reduce corruption. Still, they find that aid is a weak instrument for reducing corruption and for strengthening participation and reform. Financial aid cannot 'induce' reform; it can at best sustain national reform efforts. They reserve the role of reform inducement to technical assistance and projects with demonstration effects.

These projects should be knowledge-intensive and are demanding on donor staff, but 'they are unlikely to be significant in the allocation of financing between countries' (2001: 21). We return to this proposition in Chapter 14, but first explore aid impact at the *project* level, with focus on impact in the form of poverty reduction.

## Aid and Poverty Reduction

During the 1990s, poverty reduction again stood at the top of the donors' agenda. In 1990 and 2000, the World Bank published *World Development Reports* that focused on poverty. The poverty reduction strategy of the early 1990s had three main elements.

1. Labour-intensive economic growth with some income redistribution.
2. Investment in human capital through health and education services.
3. Under certain conditions, social security nets for vulnerable population groups, such as victims of structural adjustment (laid-off workers in the public sector and people unable to pay user fees for health services, and so on).

The *World Development Report 2000/2001* recognized the non-income aspects of poverty (related to lack of education, poor nutrition and health, and even powerlessness, voicelessness and vulnerability) and expanded the poverty reduction strategy to include a concern about the opportunity, empowerment and security of the poor, to be achieved through economic growth as well as institutional and social change. The three key concepts cover:

- *Opportunity:* Expanding economic opportunity for poor people by stimulating economic growth, making markets work better for poor people, and working for their inclusion, particularly by building up their assets, such as land and education.
- *Empowerment:* Strengthening the ability of poor people to shape decisions that affect their lives and removing discrimination based on gender, race, ethnicity and social status.
- *Security:* Reducing poor people's vulnerability to sickness, economic shocks, crop failure, unemployment, natural disasters and violence, and helping them cope when such misfortunes occur.

At the UN Summit in Copenhagen in 1995 and at the Millennium Summit in New York in 2000, the world's heads of state and government obligated themselves to eradicate poverty and set goals for the reduction of extreme poverty. Cox and Healey (1997, 2000) have examined the most important donors' relation to poverty reduction, and thus divide them into three groups.

- For the UNDP, the World Bank, Belgium, Canada, Denmark, the EU, Finland, Holland, Norway, Sweden and the United Kingdom, poverty reduction is the main strategic goal.

- For Australia, Italy, Japan, Switzerland, Germany, the USA and Austria, poverty reduction is one among several priorities.
- For France and Spain, poverty reduction has no special priority.

In the 1990s, most donors supported two or three of the elements proposed by the World Bank as the most important strategy, focusing especially on the income aspects of poverty. Cox and Healey noted that the UNDP, Canada, Denmark, Holland, Great Britain and Germany emphasize poverty's many dimensions and the need for participation in poverty reduction. Donors agree on the importance of national ownership and focus on poor people's basic needs within primary education and primary health services, and the gender dimension of poverty reduction. There is more disagreement about the importance and possibilities of a social security net, progressive tax system and land reforms. While the social security nets during the 1990s were being replaced by social funds for development with broader socio-economic development objectives, the contentious issues around income and asset redistribution, land reforms, and so on are still not being addressed by all donors. The World Bank's new triangle of concepts (opportunity, empowerment, security) are politically correct, but do not address the politics of development in terms of conflicting interests, power and oppression (see pp. 3, 4, Chapter 1).

Cox and Healey criticize the donors' poor knowledge about the character and causes of poverty (2000: 58–61). The World Bank's country-specific poverty analyses and analyses of public expenditures have tried to create an analytic point of departure for formulating country strategies. Among others, Toye and Jackson (1996) and Hammer (1996) have criticized the quality of the World Bank's analyses, which in the 1990s, however, were broadened with participatory analyses of poor people's own evaluations of their needs. In 2000, the World Bank published *Voices of the Poor*, which is a major attempt to record the views of 60,000 of the world's poor on their own problems and priorities. Similarly, the poverty reduction strategy papers (PRSPs), discussed in earlier chapters, are meant to upgrade the poverty analyses on behalf of all development partners: government, civil society, private sector, bilateral and multilateral donors, and international NGOs operating in individual developing countries.

The effect of aid on poverty reduction is still something of an enigma. Knowledge about how great a share of aid is aimed directly towards the poor is lacking. Baulch found that it was at most 15–20 per cent of the aid to low-income countries (1996: 8). Cox and Healey (1997, 2000), on the basis of a large comparative study of European aid to poverty reduction, judge that the actual goal-oriented aid is far less than donor rhetoric would imply, that is, than donors' policies and strategies indicate. They note that 'systematic and comprehensive information on the role of the agencies in *specific poverty-focused* interventions is generally not published' (2000: 53). Data available for the mid-1990s point towards a 10–20 per cent share of poverty-focused interventions in bilateral aid portfolios. The World Bank has evaluated that in the mid-1990s, one-third of its total loans were directed towards poverty reduction, and even about one-half of its IDA credits (World Bank 1996b: xi). According to Cox and Healey (1997: 11), these figures are not comparable, however, with other donors' calculations, since few of the World Bank's 'poverty loans' actually contain mechanisms that target aid towards the poor.

The World Bank's analysis of the effects of aid on poverty reduction goes, as we saw in the discussion of the *Assessing Aid* report, via the assumed link between economic growth and decrease in poverty. In 1996, the Bank concluded that growth generally led to poverty reduction, but that there are great variations between countries with regard to the size of poverty reduction. This depends, for example, on distribution of income. The Bank concluded that an improved distribution of income over time reduces poverty. Other analyses (see, for example, IDS 1996) emphasize even more the significance of the existing income distribution and inequality in determining whether growth leads to reduced poverty. The World Bank acknowledged in this connection (World Bank 1998c: 6) that while there is broad agreement about which policies contribute to reduced poverty, there is much more uncertainty about which policies improve income distribution.

## Aid Projects and Poverty Reduction

Aid is mostly carried out through individual projects and programmes. Unfortunately, it is difficult to say anything general about aid projects' impact on poverty reduction for all the reasons already discussed in this chapter. The World Bank's evaluation department, which has a reputation for being the most professional and effective in this business, has published a paper with a devastating assessment of the Bank's interest in impact assessment: 'In tracking the development impact of projects, the Bank has been weak almost across the board ... The Bank has rarely used its lending portfolio to systematically collect evidence on what works in reducing poverty, what does not, and why' (Hanny 2000: 7). The World Bank publishes collections of evaluation results annually. These present examples of output, physical results and measurable improvements (for example, admission of children to primary education) resulting from the projects, and examine implementation difficulties, which the Bank and its partners can do something about, with the hope of increasing long-term effects.

We discuss here two attempts to collect information about aid projects' effects on poverty reduction: a study of several World Bank projects (Carvalho and White 1996), and a comparative study, *European Development Co-operation and the Poor* (Cox et al. 2000).

Carvalho and White (1996) have looked at *Implementing Projects for the Poor: What Has been Learned?* for the World Bank. Their method was to examine what had happened in 1995 with sixty-seven poverty-oriented projects that IDA approved in 1988–90. Carvalho and White used five methods in their approach.

*Examples of results* The authors gave several examples from the Bank's monitoring of the projects. Six million schoolbooks were distributed in Africa; 200,000 more girls attended school in Pakistan; medicine supply was improved; malnutrition was reduced by half among children in 6,000 villages in India; use of birth control was three times as high in Lesotho; nine million books, brochures and pictures were published about health care and hygiene in China; sanitation improved for 200,000 people in slum areas in Uganda; 3,961 km of barriers against soil erosion were constructed in Burundi; 7,000 person-years of employment were created with the help of labour-intensive maintenance of infrastructure in Senegal, and so on. It can be seen that the results are a mixture of physical output that can be traced back to the project, and improved living conditions that cannot be directly connected with the projects, since many other factors also play a role. Nevertheless, it is of course through such improvements that aid has its most comprehensive and tangible results.

*Likely benefits from targeting* Reports show that the World Bank has used eight strategies to improve the chances that projects reach and actually benefit the target groups: (1) focus on basic services, especially primary education and primary health care; (2) focus on backward geographic areas within the individual developing country; (3) goals targeted at women among the poor; (4) ensuring participation by the target group and local NGOs in all phases of the project cycle; (5) ensuring that user fees do not prevent poor people's access to services; (6) simultaneous delivery of services for health, education and water supply in order to exploit complementarity; (7) creation of demand for services through information and education; and (8) development of capacity to meet quickly needs created by disasters and suchlike. We agree that such targeted strategies are necessary, and that they probably have a positive effect on poverty reduction. The size of the effects, however, cannot easily be documented.

*Enhancing contextual impact* On the basis of individual projects, it is possible to influence broader societal processes. Carvalho and White point out four methods: (1) influencing sector policies; (2) initiating user fees and dividing costs to ensure sustainability; (3) using pilot projects in order to experiment before launching large projects; (4) using experiences from earlier projects. These methods are reasonable, but the decisive factor is whether or not they are actually used and ensure broader effects.

*Summary of project performance* Those responsible for projects in the World

Bank must continually evaluate whether the projects can be expected to achieve their development goals and their immediate goals. They use a scale from one to four, where one is best. Carvalho and White collected averages for the sixty-seven poverty-oriented projects and observed that 89 per cent of the projects that had received the character of one or two had a slightly higher average than the average for IDA projects generally. At the same time, they describe (1996: 33) that there are systematic signs of over-optimism and subjectivity in assignment of such grades by those responsible for the projects.

*Managing implementation problems* The authors studied several typical implementation problems that reduced the probable impact: (1) lack of capacity within the project units; (2) problems with project payments and purchases; (3) lack of initiatives by the recipient government, in spite of agreements and promises; (4) disagreements between the project and a structural adjustment programme; (5) destructive external factors. We agree that these are problems and also that improvement can lead to improved impact, but the question is: how and how much?

Cox and Healey go further in suggesting findings on whether the poor benefit from European aid. In seven developing countries, the researchers assessed ninety projects supported by Denmark, Finland, Germany, Netherlands, Sweden, the UK and the EU. The projects were selected by the donors as examples of poverty-oriented interventions, thus their poverty-reducing effects are presumably above average. The overall conclusions of the study on 'perceived impact' are (2000: 92):

- Over 70 per cent of the projects had a positive impact on the poor, and one-third of these had a high impact.
- The interventions were more successful in addressing some dimensions of poverty than others. Donors were most effective at improving the access of the poor to *resources* and *knowledge*, with 80–90 per cent of the sample having a positive impact. They were less able to improve the *livelihoods* and *rights* of the poor very significantly.
- Only one-fifth of the ninety interventions were highly targeted at poor groups. Indeed, 38 per cent made negligible use of targeting mechanisms.
- Though two-thirds were participatory, only 17 per cent of projects were highly participatory.
- Two-thirds of the projects revealed moderate or high levels of gender sensitivity, with an increasing trend in recent years.
- Only one-fifth of projects were judged to be highly likely to be sustainable after donors withdraw.
- Overall, interventions targeted at the poor and involving their participation are systematically associated with greater impact on the poor.

Lancaster (1999) takes a different approach. She provides the following 'across-the-board' summary of assessments by donors of the performance of their projects in Africa, where they typically consider there to be the weakest performance in the developing world. She suggests particular weaknesses in the following sectors and fields: agriculture and rural development, development finance organizations, industrial development, and institutional capacity-building. Fixed capital formation (road construction, and so on) and expansion in social services have been more effective, while economic reform programmes have had mixed outcomes. Lancaster suggests three reasons for below-average performance of particular projects: (1) frequent lack of proven technology for achieving project goals (related for example to family planning, productivity of small farmers and accountability of newly elected governments); (2) too little donor knowledge about developing societies and institutions; and (3) domestic and bureaucratic politics within aid agencies themselves (1999: 48f., 492f.). While this may be a correct assessment, it says more about aid performance and implementation difficulties than about aid effectiveness and impact.

## Evaluation of Institutional Performance in Poverty Reduction

In 1995–96, Danida financed a comprehensive evaluation, *Poverty Reduction in Danish Development Assistance* (Danida 1996a). It was carried out by several groups of consultants based on project studies in Nepal, Uganda and Zimbabwe, and analyses of Danida's policy and strategy documents and procedures (Danida 1996a). The evaluation chose a broad definition of poverty, as deprivation and lack of basic human and social needs and rights. The success criteria were therefore (as in Cox and Healey 1997, Cox et al. 2000) whether aid contributes to strengthening poor people's ability to gain access to and utilize resources, develop secure livelihoods, increase their knowledge and practise their rights.

The general conclusion of the evaluation is positive in relation to Danish bilateral development assistance's contribution to improving poor people's access to resources, services, employment and other development opportunities, as well as their knowledge and ability to improve their livelihoods. It points out that aid has not been sufficiently goal-oriented in relation to poverty reduction. The evaluation contains several important conclusions. These can illustrate how far such a very broad evaluation can come in judging aid's results on the basis of project and document studies, but not real impact studies. Important results are:

- It is not sufficiently clear in Danida's country strategies whether and how the chosen priority sectors contribute in each recipient country to poverty reduction.
- There are examples of contradictory effects of Danida's goal for poverty reduction and other political goals, such as the involvement of the Danish resource base in aid.

- Danida's three-dimensional strategies for poverty reduction (broad-based growth, human resource development and enhanced participation) are a reasonable point of departure. Further work must be based on: economic growth as the necessary but not sufficient condition for poverty reduction; the distribution of growth, income and resources as often more important for the poor than overall growth; and investment in human capital and empowerment of poor women as a necessary part of poverty reduction.
- The evaluated Danida-supported projects contributed to a great extent to improving poor people's resources; to improving significantly their livelihood and knowledge; and to a limited extent to improving their rights.
- The general tendency is that the following types of interventions have a positive effect on poverty reduction: aid directed towards specific poor or vulnerable groups; aid to basic social services; aid to the productive sector; aid that integrates the cross-cutting considerations in other interventions; and aid to public administration reform.

In this enumeration of effective interventions for poverty reduction, we feel that the report goes beyond the findings of its own analyses. It is impossible to say generally, for example, that aid to the productive sector and administration reforms are poverty-reducing. It depends on both the content and the context of the specific interventions.

The World Bank's Operations Evaluation Department has undertaken a major evaluation, *IDA's Partnership for Poverty Reduction 1994–2000*, focusing on whether or not the Bank has implemented the demands raised by its donors during the IDA replenishment negotiations in the 1990s (World Bank OED, 2001). The donors had instructed the Bank/IDA to 'sharpen the poverty focus of its support for country development; direct its assistance ... to expanding access to basic social services, fostering broad-based growth, promoting good governance, and integrating gender and environmental considerations into development efforts; increase its development effectiveness through more selective, more participatory, and better-coordinated country assistance programs' (Box 1: ix). The evaluation concludes:

> Overall, OED finds IDA's performance in relation to its commitments to be satisfactory, but with qualifications. IDA has done much to sharpen the poverty focus of its analytical work, policy dialogue, and lending. The quality of lending and non-lending services has improved. Recently, it has brought governance to the fore. Yet it has made limited progress in integrating private sector development, gender, and environmental sustainability into its country programs. *Taking account of a host of factors not under IDA's control, the development outcomes of IDA programs are rated partially satisfactory.* Much remains to be done by IDA and its partners to meet the multifaceted challenge of supporting sustained, pro-poor, broad-based growth. (Box 2: x)

The OED conclusion on partially satisfactory development outcomes is not drawn from field-based impact studies. It is founded on assessments of weak linkages between IDA priorities and country programmes; operational weaknesses; under-investment in analytical work, institutional capacity-building and governance activities; inadequate selectivity (within and between countries); and insufficient monitoring and evaluation at country and project levels. On most of these findings, one must ask: relative to what?

The bulk of this institutional evaluation of the World Bank has a programmatic approach with analyses looking forward towards a more consistent and effective IDA organization and lending portfolio. The assessment and recommendations are mainstream, or consensus-oriented, in their call for stronger focus on poverty reduction; attention to gender, participation, sustainability and other cross-cutting concerns; greater selectivity at project and country levels, to be achieved through coherent country strategies tied to the PRSPs; and wider and deeper professional capacity in-house. The more substantive findings and recommendations concern needs to do more in agriculture, rural and private sector development, which lack both coherent strategies and resources, and more on governance, in particular rule of law and public financial accountability. Finally, the evaluation calls for a greater 'focus on implementation', with which we can only agree.

Some of the methodological shortcomings of the OED evaluation were avoided by the more focused, yet field-based *Danish NGO Impact Study: A Review of Danish NGO Activities in Developing Countries* (Oakley 1999), which we discussed in Chapter 8. This impact study is based on case studies in Bangladesh, Nicaragua and Tanzania, involving both beneficiary and stakeholder impact assessments and independent analyses. Its conclusions are more in-depth than the evaluations of poverty reduction by Danida and IDA. The NGO Impact Study concludes *inter alia* (pp. 74–96):

- Danish development NGOs and their partners lack an 'impact culture', especially regarding long-term and contextual impact. They are concerned about outputs and immediate impact and can well demonstrate such achievements in the productive and social sectors.
- Understanding impact is particularly weak in complex and integrated projects, which tend to produce an excessive wealth of activity and output data that are seldom used in attempts to discuss impact. This applies even more to the many projects that are aimed at strengthening civil society in partner countries.
- There is little awareness of the 'unintended impact' of project activities. This includes often highly differential impact, where for example the intermediate beneficiaries (for example, direct project participants) tend to benefit more than ultimate beneficiaries. The Danish NGOs seldom analysed their projects as two-way streets and platforms for communities to make use of foreign aid. There is much reference to 'empowerment', but little awareness and evidence of what it means.
- The overall strengths of Danish development NGOs lie in: poverty focus,

especially alleviation of poverty; partnerships with Southern civil society organizations as the backbone of NGO activities; sound appraisal and control of projects to avoid failures; a good record of basic services provision; and broad support to civil society.

- The overall weaknesses of Danish development NGOs lie in: lack of systematic contextual analysis; extensive reporting requirements, but not cost-effective and high-quality monitoring and evaluation; weak human resource base in technical fields, compared with too many generalist and programme staff in Danish NGOs; too many cases of micro-projects by small specialized NGOs, with no wider perspective or advocacy at national level. Despite a 'people-centred' approach to development, a participatory project practice is not widespread, that is, projects are delivered to, not negotiated with, local partners.

These critical findings concern NGOs from a front-runner among donor countries (Denmark). We are convinced that similar impact studies of international NGOs and bilateral and multilateral agencies would yield even more critical findings. There is both need and scope for more effective development cooperation with greater impact on poverty and marginalization.

## Conclusions

Aid impact is uncertain and controversial. At one end, there is an aid industry with vested interests in assuming and claiming impact, often documented through instrumental project cycle analyses (success in delivering outputs and achieving immediate targets) and anecdotal success stories. The typical risk here lies in exaggeration of the influence of aid in general and donors in particular. At the other end, there is the reality of relatively small aid activities that flow into social, economic, political and institutional contexts characterized by deep complexity, weak capacity and consistent turmoil. The World Bank suggested that aid is 'highly effective, totally ineffective, and everything in between'. We may add that aid is sometimes the deciding push factor, sometimes a near waste of resources, and sometimes of little or no significance. The evidence allows the following conclusions:

- Aid has contributed significantly to improvements in people's livelihoods and capabilities through its impact on growth, resource transfers, public services, capacity-building, conflict management and influence on societal change. The remaining challenge and tasks for development cooperation are, however, as large as ever. Contrary to popular belief, the 'aid dependency' of developing countries has decreased on most counts: aid as a percentage of GDP, government budgets, and so on. Annual aid receipts per capita are so low (from US$2 in South Asia to US$20 in sub-Saharan Africa) that the huge objectives of aid cannot be met. From an impact point of view, development cooperation is heavily under-financed.

- Overall, aid has limited influence on national policy-making and reform that depends on domestic political-economic factors. Aid is increasingly integrated into local institutions and processes. Aid impact assessment requires a contextual approach at both local and national levels. Aid impact is increasingly becoming a question of development impact. Consequently, aid impact increasingly suffers from the general gaps between policy-making and implementation in developing countries.
- Aid is – at least partly – fungible with other resources. The success of aid depends on how it impacts on national and local politics, institutions and socio-economic processes, including conflicts and power relations over access to resources. In most low-income countries, aid finances the bulk of the government's development expenditures, meaning that the impact and quality of public policy implementation is partly dependent on donor performance. Government budgets (from resource mobilization, through priority-setting and planning, to implementation and follow-up) are critical to development and aid impact.
- The contribution of aid to reduced poverty could be enhanced significantly, if aid were allocated among countries on the basis of the number of poor people, the extent of poverty, and the form and frequency of external shocks. This requires that poverty reduction becomes the basic policy objective, overriding foreign policy, commercial and other goals. Political biases in aid allocation have been excessive.
- There is insufficient evidence to conclude that some aid forms (technical assistance, development projects, sector programmes, budget support, and so forth) have higher impact on poverty than others, particularly if all the non-income-related dimensions of poverty are included. Guestimates of the actual poverty focus in bilateral and multilateral agency programmes in low-income countries range from 10 to 50 per cent, meaning that it is not known with any precision, but that it is much lower than the donor rhetoric seems to indicate.
- There are few, if any, entirely positive studies of the impact of technical assistance, partly because of the multiple objectives imposed on technical assistance staff, partly because of its high costs. Projects may lack sustainability and broader impact (partly because of the fungibility factor), but they sometimes empower particular target groups through the provision of resources, services, knowledge, access and hence power. The impact of the various forms of programme assistance depends on so many interests, forces and processes between the donor and the ultimate beneficiary that generalizations make little sense. Budget support may be effective in terms of broad development promotion, but its direct contributions to poverty reduction depend on the dialogue between donors and the recipient government on the structure of resource mobilization and allocation and the efficiency of budget implementation.
- Poverty-focused projects are more successful in addressing some dimen-

sions of poverty than others. Projects are most effective at improving the access of the poor to resources and knowledge, whereas projects have less impact on the livelihoods and rights of poor people. With respect to sectors, the limited evidence shows that investments in human capital formation through primary education and health have the greatest impact, whereas agriculture and rural development programmes aiming at broad-based, pro-poor growth face greater implementation difficulties (partly because of conflicting interests) and therefore tend to have less impact. Poverty reduction, however, cannot be achieved without such broad economic development programmes addressing access, distribution and inequality.

- The evidence across types of donors (bilateral and multilateral donors and international NGOs) does not permit clear conclusions on differences in aid impact. Given the emerging consensus on development cooperation during the 1990s, as witnessed in the adoption of global goals and targets and the relative ease with which, for example, the World Bank and international NGOs collaborate, the differences in donor approach and performance are being reduced. For example, NGOs are not systematically better at achieving impact in the form of empowerment of the poor, though they probably have a competitive edge in capacity-building in civil society.

The evaluation of aid's impact is made difficult by the large and complex goals that all donors have formulated for aid cooperation. It is not surprising that there is quite a distance between the rhetoric and the implementation of aid. Nor is it surprising that the 'softer' and more process-oriented the goals become, the more difficult it is to document immediate and long-term effects of aid. It is illogical, however, when some critics conclude that if goal fulfilment cannot be documented, there is something wrong with the goals, and that aid must be concentrated on goals that allow measurement of their fulfilment.

Our defence of ambitious, multi-faceted goals must not be used as an excuse for insufficient implementation in practice of poverty goals and strategies. Distribution of most aid among countries and within sectors can and must reflect poverty reduction to a greater extent than in the past. Targeted aid can be effective and give results when it is combined with utilization of aid's strategic potential to influence local power structures, capacities and processes in developing countries.

CHAPTER 13

# Problems and Challenges of Development Cooperation with States in the South

§ DEVELOPMENT cooperation with poor countries and poor people makes great demands on donors, but also on partners in recipient countries. In preceding chapters, we have described and discussed many of the problems and challenges confronting the involved parties during the different phases of the whole process (see Chapter 1). In this chapter and the next, we focus on selected problems and challenges. The main emphasis is on cooperation with states in the South. Special problem areas in NGO cooperation were discussed in Chapter 8, but several of the problems discussed below are also relevant for NGOs' involvement.

The chapter contains a discussion of the following problems and challenges:

- How are priorities in development cooperation affected by the changed global conditions for development in the Third World, especially with regard to distribution of aid among countries?
- What can donors do about the many weak states and how paternalistic can they allow themselves to be in relation to such states?
- What is the effect of corruption on development cooperation, and what can be done to avoid negative effects?
- What does aid to promote democratization processes involve and what special problems are connected with this?
- What roles in the development process do prominent donor actors such as the World Bank assign more generally to the state?

Discussion of these questions should give an idea of where special needs exist at present, and help find new solutions and more appropriate balances in the relationship between states in the South and official aid agencies.

## Changed Global Conditions for Development

The debate of recent years about globalization's consequences has mostly concentrated around two central questions. The first is whether national economies have become so strongly integrated in transnational and global processes that they have lost their independent significance. The second is whether nation-states in this context have thereby lost their capacity to regulate the economy in accordance with national interests and priorities (Hirst and Thompson 1996). The first theme is discussed in this section; the second in the next.

There is no doubt that the global processes of change during the last decade create new conditions for growth and societal development in developing countries. There are strong disagreements, however, about what these new conditions mean for poor countries' development opportunities and beyond this for foreign aid. These disagreements can be summarized as two opposing conceptions.

One view sees globalization as implying in itself markedly improved opportunities for economic growth, in principle for all countries. The important thing for poor countries is to 'catch the train' – to open their economies and carry out policies that make them attractive for foreign enterprises and investors. The role of aid is to contribute to this, but otherwise the private sector should now take over the leading role in the development process from the states in both North and South. Development cooperation should be privatized.

According to the opposite view, the global processes of change involve markedly deteriorating external conditions for development in poor countries (Degnbol-Martinussen and Lauridsen 2001). They meet even harder competition than earlier in international markets, and they are held back by lack of highly educated workers, entrepreneurs and access to advanced technology. In addition, the poor countries are uninteresting for foreign enterprises and investors. Therefore, these countries need more aid, not primarily in order to integrate them into the world economy, but in order to create fundamental and long-term improvements so that over many years they can develop to a level where they can perhaps benefit from market-led development dynamics. In the short or medium term, they have no chance to achieve this. Instead, for many years yet, they must rely on continued and more massive official aid (see Riddel 1996: 39 ff.).

There are many variations between these two opposing positions, but too few expressly and systematically operate by differentiating between the countries in the Third World on the basis of their widely differing possibilities. In general, long-term loans and direct foreign investments can give badly needed contributions to financing development efforts. Private capital transfers, however, are not determined by needs in the recipient countries; they are determined by the presence of opportunities to earn an attractive profit by access to expanding markets under predictable and stable conditions. Most poor countries cannot live up to these demands and therefore do not receive large amounts of private capital, especially not in the form of direct investments. These countries have small markets with poor and stagnating demand. Their private sectors are small and weak. The political system is often unstable.

Social unrest and even civil war characterize many countries. The economic policy that is being implemented is unclear and incoherent. Their economic infrastructure is undeveloped, and there is often a lack of qualified labour. Their financial systems are underdeveloped. Therefore, these developing countries are not attractive for foreign investors, and the tendency is that when these investors do go into these countries, it is with short-term investments. Then, if problems arise, they can quickly pull their investments out again.

When examining economic globalization more closely, it becomes evident that economic transactions and financial flows are very unevenly distributed among the countries in the world (see Chapter 5; Oman 1994; World Bank 1998a). Among developing countries, only a dozen or so countries have seriously experienced globalization as increased foreign trade, growth in foreign investments and increased injection of foreign capital. For the vast majority of the world's poor countries, globalization has rather manifested itself in the form of marginalization and exclusion from the international growth processes. Transnational economic and financial transactions have in general increased during the last decade, but growth has been concentrated in certain countries and regions, with the USA, Japan and the EU as the three dominating centres of strength. Therefore, it would be more precise to describe the global processes of change as a combination of globalization, regionalization and marginalization – and add to this that aid needs in the marginalized countries have not decreased but, on the contrary, increased.

## Weak States Under External Paternalism

Not only the external conditions for creating material improvements in poor, marginalized countries have deteriorated. Something similar applies to their opportunities to set national priorities and carry out development policies on the basis of their own conditions, because they are exposed to increasing pressure from the dominating actors in the new economic world order. These actors are private transnational corporations and finance institutions, each with an annual turnover higher than the GNP of even medium-sized developing countries. Actors also include official international organizations such as the World Trade Organization (WTO), the IMF and the World Bank, in addition to confederations of states such as the OECD and the EU. These organizations set most of the rules for transnational economic and financial transactions. Moreover, they set the agenda for what individual states, also domestically, can do – for example, with respect to their economic policy towards foreign enterprises and investors.

Several times in this book, we have discussed the conditionalities for soft loans and aid and pointed out that during the last fifteen to twenty years these conditionalities have become more widespread and far-reaching. Whereas earlier they were limited to demands for a specific economic policy, they now include demands for good governance, political-administrative reforms, and more generally the whole division of labour between state and private sector. The aim of such a package of conditionalities is to influence the whole policy process from structuring decision-making processes, to policy formulation, to implementation (see Stokke 1995; Doornbos 1995; Raffer and Singer 1996: Chapter 11).

Many sensible considerations lie behind these demands. Donors justify them by referring to a combination of universal human values – especially human rights – and experiences harvested in industrial countries regarding the most appropriate economic and foreign policies and organization of society. The question is, however, whether the official donors have not gone too far in their efforts to decide how recipient countries should structure their societies, and especially in their attempts to decide the state's form and mode of functioning. In other words, the question is whether cooperation has become external paternalism. We find two fundamental problems here:

- Are experiences from industrial countries and a few successful developing countries really so clear that firm conclusions can be drawn about what development policy and organization of society are best?
- Are developing countries so identical with regard to their potential and the development problems they face that they can all be recommended to follow an almost identical development policy and to organize their societies in the same way?

We cannot answer these questions affirmatively; nor would many representatives of official aid agencies do so. Nevertheless, the prevailing tendency is for donors to seek to press very different countries, which also differ greatly from those countries where experiences have been harvested, to adopt the same development model (see pp. 5, 6, Chapter 1).

In this context, it is interesting that the World Bank's former chief economist, Joseph Stiglitz, has disavowed the so-called Washington consensus as a universal solution for developing countries (Stiglitz 1998). He points out that this consensus concerning the correct macro-economic policy, which the IMF, the World Bank and the US government in particular have arrived at, is based far too much on special experiences in Latin America in the 1980s. With its focus on inflation, budget deficit, deregulation and privatization, this economic policy is inadequate to ensure stability and long-term economic development. Stiglitz emphasizes especially the need also to create robust financial systems that require state regulation. He also emphasizes that privatization in itself does not promote development, but can produce good results only under certain conditions. These include relatively free competition, and this again often demands state regulation. It is not so much Stiglitz's specific criticism and recommendations that are interesting in this context, as his more general appeal for humility and open-mindedness on the part of the World Bank and other global actors in their considerations about correct economic policy.

A further paradox in relation to paternalism towards poor countries' weak states is that while donors demand specific policies to be carried out, they also demand that recipient countries should follow democratic procedures and involve their citizens more in decision-making processes. For weak states in poor and extremely aid-dependent countries, however, it would be difficult to give priority to citizens' expressed preferences if these were in conflict with donors' priorities (Moore 1998). They would then risk losing aid. Thus, the 'dialogue' with donors is actually a limitation of authorities' – and, in its furthest consequence, citizens' – freedom of action.

It is understandable that both bilateral and multilateral organizations wish to formulate global development goals and strategies for their work. It is also understandable that these reflect the predominant norms and ideas in donor countries. It should be obvious, however, that there are limits to how far they can go if they wish to achieve real cooperation and partnership in development efforts. It also ought to be obvious that standardization must be kept at a minimum to make room for far more differentiation in strategies based on the different conditions and national priorities in recipient countries. This also applies in connection with new aid forms such as sector programme assistance, which causes special problems regarding external paternalism and national ownership.

## Aid Forms and Ownership

With the introduction of sector programme aid, several large donor agencies, including Danida, are trying to place greater emphasis on recipient country ownership. The idea entails designing aid so that it supports existing efforts by recipient countries within selected sectors. If recipient countries have not already formulated a cohesive policy, donors see it as their task to provide advice regarding such policy. And if authorities in recipient countries do not have the necessary administrative capacity to implement the sector policies decided upon, donors also see it as part of their responsibility to contribute to building such capacity. If – or when – the necessary prerequisites exist, donors can concentrate on providing budget assistance as well as assistance to interconnected projects and activities within the concerned sectors.

The great and difficult challenge in this context is to unite, on the one hand, donor priorities, and on the other, genuine respect for recipient country ownership and for the priorities of the relevant authorities. Paradoxically enough, uniting these two general considerations can prove to be more difficult to achieve in connection with sector assistance than with traditional aid forms such as project aid. Problems with project aid have already been pointed out, and one of them is, in fact, that within this aid form, authorities in developing countries and those in the power elite have gained too much influence and been able to 'capture' projects and use them in their own patronage systems. To put it bluntly, the problem here is that recipients have gained too much control – too much ownership – not as part of a cohesive national policy, of course, but as part of a national political culture and de facto management of public funds.

With the transition to sector programme assistance, opportunities to capture aid in this way are reduced, because donors also demand that the authorities approve and implement certain policies. Demands of this kind have become significantly more widespread in development cooperation in recent years. One of the common demands is poverty orientation. Donors demand that recipient countries carry out policies that clearly aim to reduce poverty. Other demands relate to consideration for the environment and stronger participation by women in development processes. The point is that these otherwise completely legitimate demands may conflict with national and local priorities in recipient countries. Insistence on meeting these demands can therefore lead to undermining ownership, which is the second aim of this new aid form.

This risk is not necessarily so great in countries with strong political authorities that are dependent on foreign aid only to a modest extent, such as India. But the risk is considerable in countries with weak states and also extreme dependency on aid from outside, as in the case of most countries in sub-Saharan Africa (see Chapter 5).

Among crucial questions to be answered in this context are the following:

1. How far can donors go with regard to formulating specific demands to recipient countries' authorities about their policies and how to organize implementation without at the same time undermining these authorities' independence and maybe even threatening their political survival?
2. How well equipped are donor agencies to make such demands when they take into consideration how complex and varying conditions are in recipient countries?
3. If, in the light of such problems, donor agencies choose to give sector assistance to weak states that pursue policies that conflict with donor priorities, how much responsibility can they give to these authorities for managing aid without coming into conflict with political authorities and taxpayers in donor countries?

The last question also involves a more general problem related to monitoring and evaluating sector programme assistance, regardless of what policies recipient countries decide upon. The problem is that this aid form by definition reduces the individual donor's visibility, since there are several donors within the same sector, and since the assistance is given to activities that are mostly implemented by the recipient countries' authorities themselves. Under such circumstances, it is difficult to isolate the contribution from the individual donor and evaluate whether or not it has been useful. Impact evaluation of all aid is difficult, also impact evaluation of project aid; but with sector programme assistance, donors relinquish in advance control of aid's specific utilization. This can be appropriate seen from the perspective of recipient countries – and it should benefit development – but this does not alter the fact that, seen from a donor perspective, it reduces possibilities for taxpayers and their elected representatives to ensure at home that aid is used correctly and well.

In any case, no simple and indisputable answers can be given to the above questions. A deeper debate on principle is necessary, as well as concrete weighing of opposing goals about aid's use in accordance with donor priorities, on the one hand, and respect for recipient-country ownership on the other. We return to this question in the next chapter.

## Corruption and Political Culture

In many recipient countries, development cooperation is influenced by extensive corruption. It is not possible to obtain a precise picture of how extensive corruption is, but there is no doubt that significant amounts of aid are used for more or less direct forms of bribery. Nor is there any doubt that, as a result of political and personal pressure, large amounts are used for other purposes than those officially agreed upon.

One of the few international organizations that has the fight against corruption as its main goal, Transparency International, argues that corruption in the Third World has increased significantly during the last ten to fifteen years. We find this difficult to judge on the basis of the rather sporadic documentation available. We agree, however, that its scope is so great that corruption not only makes development cooperation considerably more expensive, but it also weakens and distorts many development initiatives and thereby economic and social development in a large number of countries. In addition, corruption contributes to creating local 'aid elites' whose livelihoods depend mostly on aid and who thereby become an interest group that will fight for continued aid, not primarily to support development and poverty reduction in their society, but to ensure themselves continued privileges and income.

There is nothing new in emphasizing corruption's great significance. Many development researchers have done this previously (see for example Myrdal 1968: especially Chapter 20; Maddison 1971; Theobald 1990). However, it is new that more and more official donor organizations have expressly taken this problem up and placed it on the agenda in the debate about development cooperation. Even the World Bank and the IMF, since the mid-1990s, have involved themselves in analyses of corruption's significance for economic development and pointed to possible strategies to combat corruption (World Bank 1996e, 1997a; IMF 1998). We will return to this, but first it could be useful to examine more closely the different forms corruption can take. Instead of attempting to use analytical catagorization (which under all circumstances is difficult), we present several illustrative examples of corruption that, like many others, we have encountered in practice.

One of the most costly forms of corruption appears in connection with large contracts such as those involving aid to development of physical infrastructure. There are many examples of top political leaders and highly placed officials who have demanded considerable sums – up to 15 per cent of the contracted amount – to enter into agreements with private entrepreneurs. Payment of such forms of bribery have most often led to corresponding deductions in the amount that is actually used for infrastructure development.

A less costly but very widespread practice consists in bribing officials and local politicians lower in the hierarchy. In many developing countries, it is necessary to pay desk officers in the administration a 'fee' to persuade them to expedite such matters as building permits in connection with a project, approval of customs-free imports, recruiting employees, or other types of administrative decisions. Bribes are not always paid in the form of money, although this is probably most common in many poor countries where civil servants receive salaries too meagre to support their families. Bribes can also involve indirect payment, as when a donor hires an official's family members and friends in order to expedite matters, or when project leaders allow the use of project vehicles or other equipment for private use by local partners.

A special variety of small-scale corruption among employees directly involved in aid activities is when they take extra fees for extending the services to the target group that have been agreed upon. For example, doctors or other health care personnel can demand payment for consultations and medicine that in principle are already paid for by the donor organization. Again, this can happen directly or in more subtle ways. An example of the latter: a donor has delivered free medicine to a health care project expecting it to be given to patients according to need; in reality, the medicine is transferred to the local pharmacies, which are owned by doctors. The patients are then sent to buy medicine at these pharmacies.

Corruption can also take other forms of fraud and embezzlement, as when aid project employees regularly steal money by delivering false receipts, or receive double reimbursement from several donors. Or they make purchases for the projects and then sell a portion of them to third parties in order to make a profit.

Extensive corruption has often been exposed in connection with foreign aid. This has sometimes led to closing the affected project or programme. In other cases, the donors have preferred to change the procedures in order to make it more difficult to continue corrupt behaviour. This has often meant that aid resources, instead of being channelled through national and local authorities in recipient countries, are placed under the direct control of donors throughout the whole process. This has reduced the possibilities of misuse, but at the same time this form of donor-led aid has also limited the possibilities for integrating development cooperation into the total development efforts in recipient countries.

With the general shift of aid strategies in recent years towards greater transfer of responsibility to developing countries' own authorities, such a procedure is no longer on the agenda. Instead, donors must focus on strengthening a non-corrupt administrative culture and encourage recipient countries to introduce procedures that prevent corrupt behaviour. This usually demands assistance from donors for strengthening the administrative organs responsible for payments, accounting and auditing, and presents great challenges for aid. Transfer of greater responsibility to developing countries' authorities, also those responsible for economic management, involves an expansion of the areas for misuse of aid resources in the many countries where corruption is a central aspect of the administrative culture. At the same time, however, it is possible, in the long run, to change the situation only if the initiative comes from powerful groups and institutions in recipient countries themselves. Experience has clearly shown that donor organizations alone have not been able to lessen corrupt behaviour significantly.

Fighting corruption is of great significance for development cooperation, because it incurs extra costs and because aid resources thus dwindle away and are used for other purposes and for the benefit of other people than those belonging to the target group. Fighting corruption is also important, because its existence can distort the whole profile of development cooperation. 'Big corruption', in connection with contract agreements for construction work and large projects in general, puts development cooperation under particularly acute pressure. It is here that big money can be made. Therefore, it is also here that many leading politicians and officials in recipient countries prefer aid to be concentrated. If donors do not insist on another priority, this can lead to neglect of social areas such as education and health.

Another serious reason for giving high priority to fighting corruption is the importance it apparently has for economic growth and social development. Some authors have argued that the use of bribery and other deviations from formal administrative regulations should be seen merely as a parallel system of decision-making and allocation of resources and money. Analyses commissioned and published by the World Bank indicate, however, that at least certain forms of corruption lead to a notably lower economic growth rate (World Bank 1997a: Chapter 6). Since it is not possible to acquire systematic hard data on corruption's scope and character, these analyses use a survey technique instead. A large number of representatives of private firms are asked about their opinions. Analyses from Transparency International, using a similar approach, rank the countries in the world on the basis – in this case – of a broader survey.

These procedures are debatable, especially since they are followed by regression analyses that aim to show causal relationships between corruption's scope and character on the one hand and economic growth rates on the other. Correlations on a few points are so remarkable, however, that it is worth examining them a more closely.

The analyses indicate that the more widespread corruption is, the lower the economic growth rate over a number of years. More interesting, however, are the results connected with the distinction between (a) opaque and unsystematic corruption and (b) transparent and well-organized corruption. The former has far more serious consequences for investment rates and economic growth than corruption that is systematic. This is not so surprising, since opaque corruption naturally entails a drastic reduction of predictability. In this case, bribers cannot be certain of achieving their goal, since it is unclear who makes the final decision. As a result, bribers will often need to pay a whole series of corrupt officials and politicians.

In spite of the fact that it is clear that extensive and especially opaque corrupt administrative cultures inhibit economic growth and – we can add – socially balanced development, it is not easy to change things. Official donor agencies and NGOs disposed to give priority to combating corruption are confronted with an enormous challenge. Corruption in many developing countries has extremely good conditions for both thriving and increasing.

Among the most important conditions are, first, that public authorities have monopoly-like control over many of the necessary requirements for private production and delivery of aid. This was formerly the case, when many states in the Third World closely regulated investments and activities of individual firms, but although in most places such operational control measures have been dismantled, public authorities' personnel continue to have ample opportunities to demand bribes in connection with issuing various forms of permits. A new growth area for corrupt behaviour is issuing permits for environmentally harmful production and emissions.

Second, corruption thrives due to the wide discretionary powers of individual officials in many countries. Unclear or non-existent deadlines provide further opportunities for demanding payment for expediting a matter.

Third, monitoring and supervision within the state administration and by external organs and the public are generally very weak in most developing countries. Well-functioning organs for parliamentary control are extremely rare. The same is true of well-functioning government auditors or other supervisory authorities. In addition, public access to information about administrative functions, such as that particularly familiar in Scandinavian countries, is almost totally absent in most developing countries. Even if independent media and organizations that wished to expose corrupt behaviour in state administrations were to exist, they would have little chance of functioning properly. Often the only real possibility would be to accuse named persons for corruption in the courts. This is in itself an extreme and demanding step and one that, except in India and a few other developing countries, would rarely lead to a conviction.

A fourth element in this picture is that state employees in many countries receive a salary insufficient to support their families. Thus, these people have actually only two possibilities, and both violate the law: they can take time off from work and have one or more jobs on the side; or they can demand and receive bribes to supplement their incomes.

In many countries, the whole situation is aggravated by considerable political instability. This means that the political system's many institutions are weak and function without clearly defined guidelines and areas of responsibility.

Finally, it should be emphasized that much of the behaviour we consider corrupt is considered by the participating parties in many countries as a natural part of the political and social culture. It is very common in all societies that people divide into groups that share a feeling of solidarity and special mutual obligations. Such groups can be a family or extended family, caste, tribe, clan, religion or ethnic community. The essential thing is that there is a difference in behaviour towards members of one's own group, often called the in-group, in comparison with behaviour towards others, the out-groups, which are often ranked in concentric circles in increasing distances from the in-group. One feels solidarity and an obligation to help and support those who are nearest, and one expects special treatment from them in return. Fellow citizens who are further removed and foreigners, however, are expected to pay for any services.

In principle, all this is no different in poor developing countries from the situation obtaining in rich industrial countries. The consequences, however, are considerably more far-reaching in many developing countries, where there are no fixed procedures for observing formal rules in state administration, or where the element of individual discretion in making each decision is considerable (Theobald 1990: Chapters 3–4). Under such circumstances, it would seem natural for the individual official to benefit members of the in-group when making a decision. This is normally considered nepotism when involving family members and favouritism when involving other forms of social network. On the other hand, others cannot expect preferential treatment as a matter of course unless they perform an extra service, typically in the form of a bribe or other form of gratuity. It is here that actual corruption comes in; seen from the point of view of the officials and others involved, however, it is often experienced as just part of the tradition-based mechanisms for the exchange of goods and services. As such, this is not limited to public administration but also affects the private sector.

Official donor agencies, international NGOs and foreign investors have often condemned corruption in moral terms, but participated in it nevertheless – with reference to the fact that since everyone else does it, they must also.

Here, we have sketched a picture of corruption as a problem for aid and development cooperation, but also as a phenomenon with deep roots in societies where the administrative culture is influenced by personal and social relationships (see Martinussen 1997: Chapter 17). A reduction of the problem's scope and importance therefore demands a very broad and long-term effort focusing partly on formulating precise rules and strengthening capacity in the public sector, and partly on increasing transparency in administration and its public control.

The World Bank has presented a series of proposals for how arbitrary state administration and corruption can be limited (World Bank 1997a: Chapters 6–7, 1997g). Transparency International has also worked out a proposal for fighting corruption (see Pope 1997).

The main emphasis of the World Bank's proposal is placed on formulating rules and procedures that limit officials' opportunities to make decisions based on their own discretion. Furthermore, the Bank recommends that checks and balances be built into the whole public system so that legislative, executive and judicial authorities are given the possibility mutually to control and balance each other. It is also proposed that the administration's accountability to citizens be increased by giving citizens better possibilities for gaining insight into and the right to protest against administrative decisions. Basically, the proposals aim to create changed norms and incentives for officials and politicians that will motivate them to act in accordance with general regulations and without deference to personal relationships or their own interests. Aid can contribute to this through advice on the making of rules and procedures, and donor organizations can contribute directly by refusing to participate in any cooperation that entails corrupt behaviour.

That such an important donor actor as the World Bank focuses on corruption as a problem in development cooperation is in itself indicative of great progress, but we find that the recommendations are based on too much faith in what can be achieved through formal rules and procedures. Corruption is too deeply rooted in many countries for this to be possible. It is embedded in an informal system of mutual obligations and personal relationships in both the public and private sectors. Consequently, much more is required to stamp out corruption, presumably a reorganization of much development cooperation. One of the strategies that has proved fruitful (for example, in Nepal and Uganda) is to give more and better information to local people about existing development projects and the funds given to them. When ordinary citizens are informed (for example, through posters), it is easier for them to find out when aid resources are being used for unauthorized purposes. They are not always able to prevent misuse, but experience shows that the mere fact that many people know about misuse has a preventive effect on corrupt behaviour.

Democratization of the political system can contribute to limiting corruption, but free elections in themselves are far from enough. This has been shown by experiences from India, which has had a democratic form of government since independence. In fact, experiences from other countries that have recently adopted a democratic form of government (for example,

Nepal) show that corruption increases rather than decreases. Politicians in the government in power seem determined to get as much as possible out of their temporary positions, since the opposition could take over at any time. Thus, it is not so much the democratic election system that is decisive in this context. It is to a greater extent other aspects of the democratization process, such as establishment of parliamentary control organs, strengthening the judicial system, free press and public access to information about administrative decisions. The next section considers more broadly the democratization process and the role of aid in this connection.

## Democratization, Human Rights and Aid

Since the end of the Cold War, more and more bilateral donors have placed increasing emphasis on recipient countries' democratization and respect for human rights, both as conditionalities and as development goals (see Chapters 3–4). Multilateral organizations such as the World Bank and the UNDP cannot – within their mandates – explicitly demand or recommend specific political forms of government, but they have moved in the same direction by placing emphasis on people's participation and good governance.

These newer tendencies entail increased interference in recipient countries' political affairs, which raises several problems. There is undoubtedly broad support, in most recipient countries too, for the basic idea of promoting democratization and respect for basic human rights, but there are many contradictory ideas about how these goals can best be realized. There is also great disagreement about at what pace and under whose leadership this whole process should be implemented.

It is not the intention here to deal with the whole complex of questions involved in human rights and democratization in relation to development cooperation (see Tomasevski 1997). We would like, however, to emphasize three problems and challenges in connection with official aid agencies' handling of democracy assistance as an aid form and democratization as conditionality.

The first problem is that few donors have seriously considered what a thorough democratization process implies. There is a tendency for donors to consider democratization as a series of formal rules and procedures such as holding elections with participation of more than one party and establishment of a government on the basis of elected bodies. These are central characteristics of a democratic form of government, but in themselves they are completely insufficient to ensure the more basic elements of a democracy: (a) extensive competition among individuals and organized groups for political positions of leadership; (b) significant genuine participation by citizens in elections of political leaders so that no group of adult citizens is excluded from exerting influence; and (c) extensive observance of civil rights, including freedom of expression, freedom of the press and freedom of association, so that competition and participation become meaningful and genuine (Dahl 1971).

If a form of government is to live up to these demands, it is furthermore necessary for democratic decision-making to be the predominant norm, not only in connection with parliamentary elections and establishing a government, but also within political parties and organizations in general. This also includes respecting and ensuring minority participation and influence. Scandinavian aid agencies have come relatively far in their considerations about democratization as entailing such radical changes in recipient societies (see for example, Danida 1999). Most bilateral donors, however, focus only on the existence of a multiparty system and elections, and the formation of a government on this basis. The problem in this connection is not that donors make these demands, but that in their support of democratization, they focus too narrowly on formal institutions and procedures and too little on the broader political and social requirements that will enable institutions and procedures to function according to intentions. A special paradox is that donors make demands for well-functioning multiparty systems; but at the same time, they refuse to give any form of assistance to strengthening political parties. We have no final proposal for how democracy assistance should be tackled, but we find it necessary that donors engage themselves far more in considerations about how to do this.

The second problem is that both demands and assistance concerning democratization are much too narrowly rooted in Western ideas and norms. The predominant tendency is to transfer models for institution-building and sets of rules known from donor countries themselves. Too little is done to consider how recipient countries' own institutions and traditions for political leadership and people's participation can be developed further. Political parties that follow a Western model are new and foreign elements in the political systems in many developing countries, whereas other types of organizations that have traditionally ensured the involvement of citizen groups in political decision-making processes do exist in many places. It lies outside the scope of this book to examine these aspects more closely, but again we must recommend that donors try to design their aid more on the basis of existing conditions in recipient countries rather than focusing so strongly on simple imitations and transfers of Western models.

The third problem concerns using democratization as conditionality. We find it problematic that aid is sometimes withheld in order to penalize rebellious political leaders who will not comply with donors' demands for specific political reforms. This often doubles the penalty for the people of the country concerned: they must continue to live with an autocratic regime, and at the same time they lose their share of international aid. As our first critical point above indicates, democratization is a long and sweeping process that can hardly be promoted through dictating to those in power, but much more through a long-term process of cooperation, both with those in power and actors in civil society. Clearly, a regime can function so unacceptably that cooperation becomes impossible, but most often there will be room for a more long-term effort in support of the democratization process. In countries with autocratic forms of government, donors can typically win an advantage by moving support from the public sector to civil society's organizations and in this way strengthen their possibilities to exert pressure on authorities.

This is a strategy that many NGOs attempt to follow (see Clark 1991). Nothing, however, prevents official aid agencies from also exerting much more effort to support such institutions as free trade unions, human rights organizations, associations of advocates, free mass media and other civil society organizations that in the long run can contribute to opening the way for democratization. There are some tendencies in this direction, especially in Scandinavian aid agencies' work and in some of the work carried out by USAID. When considered as a whole, however, official aid continues to be mostly tied to and directed towards state institutions in recipient countries. This can be a problem, not only in connection with democracy assistance, but also in a broader sense. Our proposal is not to attempt a general cutting of ties to states in the South but to consider in more differentiated terms how cooperation with these states can be arranged and supplemented with other forms of aid.

## The State as a Development Problem

Most development assistance is given as official aid, that is, from states in the North to states in the South, or from multilateral organizations to states in the South. Many consider this to be a fundamental problem. Representatives of the private sector in both North and South consider the continued confidence in the state as an engine of development to be mistaken and inhibiting for economic development based on market forces and free enterprise (p. 4). They are especially supported in the theoretical development debate by neo-classical economists. Also, representatives of civil society organizations often consider the state to be repressive and to inhibit development for the benefit of resource-weak groups.

We can largely agree that the state can be seen as not only an actor that promotes development but also as part of the development problem itself. We cannot, however, accept the ideologically based rejection of the state. It is not the state as such that is the problem, but rather many concrete states, which in their form and function do not have the capacity to further, or are not good at supporting, the development goals of international development cooperation. Therefore, already at its starting point, the discussion is about how different the states in the South actually are. The aim must be to make a differentiated analysis that reveals the characteristics of the different states and their relations to their surrounding societies that promote development and those that block development. It lies outside the scope of this book to make such an analysis. We would like to contribute a kind of introduction, however, by indicating some of the weaknesses and limitations influencing much of the debate on the role of the state in the development process (see also Martinussen 1997: Chapters 16–18). Because of the World Bank's great influence on this debate, we focus especially on this institution's concept of the state and its significance for development cooperation.

For many years, the World Bank has set the tone for criticism of the state. In the 1980s, the Bank presented many analyses that questioned the state's relevance and effectiveness for the advancement of economic development – which in itself is a bit paradoxical considering that most of the Bank's activities entail loans to and cooperation with state authorities in developing countries. Nevertheless, the main message during this period was that states in recipient countries should reduce their economic role and reduce the size of the public sector through privatization of as many economic activities as possible. With inspiration from prominent neo-classical economists, the World Bank argued for a minimal state that left the management of development to market mechanisms. This has been referred to and criticized in preceding chapters.

It is interesting to note in this connection that the World Bank, since the beginning of the 1990s, has adjusted its viewpoint and today tries to find a more balanced approach between the state-managed model and the market-led model. It acknowledges that state regulation is necessary in order for the market to function properly. State regulation is also necessary in order to ensure consideration for environmental sustainability and to create improvements for the many poor people whose purchasing power is not sufficient to ensure them a share in national economic progress. The World Bank presented its rethinking regarding the concept of the state in the *World Development Report 1997*. Here, ample argumentation is presented for a balanced division of labour between the public and private sectors, and the Bank recommends a two-part strategy for adjustment and institutional development. In the short term, the states in the South should concentrate on matching the role of the state with its capability. For the many weak states, this will mean a considerable reduction of activities. In the longer term, donors should support raising state capability by reinvigorating public institutions so they can perform all the necessary functions that the Bank assigns to the state (World Bank 1997a: especially Chapters 1–4; see also IDS 1998).

In comparison to earlier, the World Bank's report has come a long way towards a more flexible concept of the state based on experience with various forms of division of labour between the public and private sectors rather than a mainly ideological rejection of the state's relevance and capability. There are still some limitations in the Bank's conception of the state that need to be discussed in more detail, however, before donors can accept it as the basis for realistic strategies for institutional development.

First, there is the question of whether the proposed sequence – first focusing activities within existing capability and later building capacity – is correct. For many weak states, this could mean that they must stop activities within areas of great importance for society. Therefore, we find that the recommendations should be made more open. Sometimes, an immediate need will exist to strengthen state capabilities rather than press the state to restrict its activities. Often, a special need will exist to strengthen the state's capacity to mobilize more resources and use them in accordance with national priorities.

Second, the Bank's analysis is weak in relation to state institutions' societal embeddedness. The strong emphasis on state-led development in both very poor and slightly better-off developing countries during most of the post-war period has not been based on economic analyses and their conclusions about what would be best. Preference for the state-led development model by the leading decision-makers was mostly based on political motives. In many poor countries, especially in sub-Saharan Africa, strengthening the role of the state has been a crucial prerequisite for the political elite's domination. In several countries, including those in South Asia, concentration on state-led development has been an essential element of economic nationalism, where domestic control – either public or private – has been more important than maximizing growth. In still other and better-off countries like those in the Far East, the state has received a prominent position in ensuring a cohesive, export-oriented economic development in close cooperation with the private sector. These brief characterizations should not be mistaken for an analysis. They only illustrate the fact that there can be essentially different economic and political reasons why those in power in so many developing countries have concentrated on the state-led development model. Since this aspect is not discussed in the World Bank report, it does not consider the variations in the societal foundation that are crucial in determining what strategies for change are realistic and feasible.

Third, the World Bank's concept of the state is too narrowly focused on growth-related effectiveness. It does refer to the state's role in connection with protection of the vulnerable and the environment, but neither of these is systematically integrated into attempts at outlining strategies for institutional development. In addition, almost all of the state's non-economic functions are omitted, including promotion of national integration (nation-building) and ensuring political stability. This is somewhat surprising considering the report's strong emphasis elsewhere on the importance of orderly and stable political conditions in order to encourage the confidence of private investors.

Fourth, the report's recommendations are influenced by a tendency to overestimate the capacity and capabilities of non-state institutions and organizations. The newest Bank analyses have retained this overestimation from the 1980s and in a certain sense still reflect a basic wish to minimize the state's role. The problem emerges clearly in proposals for sub-contracting several public functions. This can be a relevant and realistic strategy if an effectively functioning private sector exists that can take over such functions and if mechanisms are in place to ensure that the functions are carried out properly and for the benefit of the groups of citizens concerned. These prerequisites do not typically exist in most poor developing countries. Therefore, implementation of the Bank's recommendations will often lead to deterioration rather than the improvements aimed at. A special danger lies in the replacement, through privatization, of state monopolies by private monopolies, which are both ineffective and based on narrow considerations of profit.

Fifth, we find a tendency in the 1997 report to consider effectiveness isolated from social differentiation. Public services for the poor are usually more difficult to perform and more expensive, because these people cannot participate in their financing – or only to a modest extent. Therefore, strategies and priorities cannot be formulated solely on the basis of effectiveness criteria. The World Bank does not do so in other contexts where the focus is more on reducing poverty than in the 1997 report (for example, World Bank 2001a: Chapter 6).

Sixth, it is a cause for concern that the Bank in its definition of the state gives so little emphasis to political processes (like decision-making processes) that define the guidelines and set the priorities for state functions. The analysis is mainly concerned with central and local administration and state-owned enterprises. There is no systematic attempt to understand the political processes as necessary and constructive decision-making processes where citizens and politicians arrive at decisions about what the state should preferably do and when. Politicians and political processes are almost considered as problems and risks that, according to the Bank's view, should not interfere and disrupt the effective state's way of functioning.

Within these six critical points – and especially the first three – there unfortunately lies a general tendency to standardize developing countries (see pp. 5–6, Chapter 1). The World Bank presents many interesting general considerations about how states in the Third World can come to function more effectively and with focus on the most pressing public functions. But in order to be relevant for the preparation of more specific aid strategies, it is necessary to supplement these considerations with much more differentiated analyses that take into consideration how different these countries actually are. As we have indicated, this does not only apply to the state's form and function, but even more to socio-economic conditions, the private sector's development level, and broader relations between the public and private sectors, including civil society and its organizations (see Martinussen 1998b).

The strategies for focusing state functions and strengthening the involved institutions must necessarily be based on differences in all these areas. If these strategies are to be implemented, they must also be based on the existing power relations, so that recommendations do not only aim at the best solutions but the best solutions *possible* under the given conditions. In this lies a great challenge for development cooperation, which with its development goals for the poor must also give preference to priorities and institutional development that especially benefit the resource-weak groups in society.

CHAPTER 14

# Perspectives and Prospects for Development Cooperation in the Twenty-first Century

§ PESSIMISM and despondency, as well as direct criticism, have long pervaded the debate on international development cooperation. Even the most convinced advocates of foreign aid have had to acknowledge that the results have often been disappointing and have not at all lived up to expectations. The critics have sometimes gone so far as to argue that foreign aid has done more harm than good and therefore should be phased out.

We agree that much aid from rich to poor countries has been based on motives that have nothing to do with promoting development and reducing poverty. We also agree that development cooperation has often produced disappointing results, because it has not been properly planned and effective, and is not based on recipient countries' needs and conditions. Furthermore, it must be admitted that considerable resources have ended up in the wrong pockets as a consequence of corruption and misappropriation, and that large sums have actually been used to repay recipient countries' debts to private banks and export firms in industrialized countries.

Many other criticisms could be added on the basis of the analyses in the preceding chapters, and we must also acknowledge that support is decreasing for continuing to transfer aid at the same level as previously. We do not, however, conclude that these are grounds to phase out foreign aid. Rather, we argue that it is time for radical rethinking in order to transform aid and all development cooperation between rich and poor countries. It is time seriously to learn from experience and improve aid, make it more effective and more beneficial from the point of view of recipient countries, and especially from the point of view of the poor. Some optimism is justified in this connection, because considerable improvements have actually been achieved during the last thirty years. As we have seen in Chapter 12, the positive effects of aid have become clearer and more comprehensive in recent years.

On the background of this basic view, we present in this concluding chapter some considerations about future development assistance. Two subjects are in focus: new forms of financing; and achieving both national ownership and effective results through new forms of performance-based aid. We conclude by discussing four aid models that indicate competing tendencies in international development cooperation.

## Aid Through an International Development Fund

We start with considerations about changing the financing of future aid, because decreases or stagnation in aid transfers during recent years makes this question especially urgent. These considerations are directed towards ensuring more stability in mobilization of resources so that the amount of aid becomes separated from having to compete with other public expenditures. This view lies, for example, behind ideas about taxing transnational flows of capital. Other considerations involve a tax on high incomes or payments to poor countries for services of global value. In this and the following section, we discuss some of the proposals presented within these areas. It is not our aim to present the different proposals in detail or to evaluate their feasibility thoroughly. Rather, we present a brief overview of the ideas we find of interest, and which could be worthwhile developing further. We discuss whether or not the ideas are realistic in the sense that they could attract sufficient political support, and also whether or not institutional capacity exists to implement them.

Among the proposals to change the financing and channelling of aid, several deal with taxing rich countries and transferring resources from them to the poorest countries through a joint development fund. As an example of this line of thinking, we refer to a proposal from Keith Griffin and Terry McKinley (1996). They do not think that we can expect any increase in the amount of aid in years to come, which according to them would not make so much difference if only foreign aid were changed in four essential ways.

First, aid should be financed by a tax calculated on the basis of GNP so that the richest countries pay most in relative terms and the countries that are less well off pay somewhat less. Griffin and McKinley propose 0.375 per cent of GNP for the richest countries, decreasing to 0.2 per cent for donor countries with the lowest per capita incomes. They also propose that the group of donor countries be expanded to include several high-income countries outside DAC. Such a procedure would lead to a marked reduction in aid from the Nordic countries and Holland, whereas it would lead to a marked increase in aid from the USA in particular. If some countries should wish to maintain a higher level of aid, this would be no problem. The decisive point for the two authors is that all well-off countries obligate themselves to pay the minimum agreed upon. This would lead to a more just distribution of the burden, and – more important for recipient countries – it would create a much higher degree of predictability than today, when the amount of aid is determined each year by the governments and parliaments in each donor country.

Second, according to this proposal, aid would be channelled through a joint international development fund managed by the UN. Griffin and McKinley find that it is not feasible for so many bilateral and multilateral donors to be involved, each with its special development goals, interests, procedures and working methods. Instead, all resources should be made available to a fund, which – as the third element in the proposal – distributes the resources to the world's poor countries on the basis of a simple assessment of needs. A concrete proposal is that aid should be confined to countries with up to US$2,200 income per capita (measured in terms of purchasing power parity). This would allow almost sixty countries to receive aid from the international development fund, which is much less than the number of countries receiving aid today. Griffin and McKinley also propose that allocation of aid should be based on population, for example, with US$50 per capita to the poorest countries, decreasing to US$30 for countries that are slightly better off. This would lead to a marked increase in aid transfers to, for example, India, which under the present system is one of the countries receiving least aid per capita.

Recipient countries themselves would decide how to use aid. This is the fourth central element of Griffin's and McKinley's proposal. Donor countries should not interfere with the use of aid, nor should they participate in preparation or implementation of development projects and programmes. Only in this way can the large resources, which until now have to a great extent been transferred back to donor countries, be released for use in poor countries.

The threshold values and specific percentages are not the interesting aspects of Griffin's and McKinley's proposal. What is thought-provoking is rather the basic idea of initiating the taxation of high-income countries and transferring the proceeds as a kind of fixed grant to the poorest countries in the world according to guidelines that can in principle be compared with support for regional development within the EU or internally in many industrialized countries. It is doubtful, however, whether such procedures could attract the necessary backing from people in rich countries, including their business communities, which under the present system also have vested interests in aid cooperation. Nor would decision-makers in donor countries who see aid as an instrument of foreign policy find the automatic aspect of the proposal regarding both resource mobilization and country distribution attractive. Moreover, the fact that the proposal operates with the UN as the international authority for channelling aid would meet strong opposition, especially among leading politicians in the US Congress. Their visions for the UN system do not include expanded and new responsibilities, but cutbacks in most areas.

Thus, realistic possibilities to restructure the financing of aid along these lines do not exist, at least in the short term. It could be useful, however, to work further with the basic idea that the amount of aid transfers should be determined by economic capability, and that distribution should be guided by general and transparent criteria rooted in the needs of recipient countries. This does not mean that we can accept the recommendation to disregard who administers aid in recipient countries and how they do it. On this point, Griffin's and McKinley's proposal is obviously naïve in disregarding the role played by powerful elites, also in poor countries. Giving aid to poor countries cannot be a goal in itself. The development goal is to create lasting improvements for poor people in these countries. It would be difficult to find support for the enormous resource transfers involved, if the governing elites do not use aid for this purpose.

Moreover, transfers of resources should not stand alone. It is not only a question of the political will of those in power to use aid for the benefit of poor people. It is also very much a question of whether the necessary institutional and other preconditions exist. This point can be illustrated through a brief comparison with Marshall aid to Western Europe after the Second World War. In the mid-1950s, it became clear that the Marshall Plan had begun to have positive effects on Western Europe's economic growth, and this inspired thoughts about similar strategies for developing countries. American politicians and officials in particular imagined that during the course of five years foreign aid could trigger economic growth in the Far East and South America and after that in the remaining developing countries. What they overlooked, however, were the great differences with regard to the conditions necessary in order to benefit from aid.

What Western Europe needed after the Second World War were investments for rebuilding the destroyed physical infrastructure and production facilities. Human capital, in the form of skilled labour and experienced businessmen and industrialists, was in place as well as the institutional framework for industrial production, trade and financing. These included relevant legislation on property rights and contractual relations, administrative regulations and well-functioning judicial systems.

Exactly such conditions were – and continue to be – rare in developing countries (Degnbol-Martinussen 2001). Therefore, the first large transfers of capital to these countries did not influence economic development anywhere near as favourably as in Western Europe. This led to considerations about whether resource transfers could be combined with the many other forms of aid that we have analysed in this book, including support for building the administrative and institutional capacities of developing countries. We consider it to be of decisive importance that also future resource transfers be combined with such forms of support. Experience has shown, as emphasized especially in Chapter 12, how important it is for the impact of aid that the administrative and broader institutional framework for development efforts are in place.

While keeping this point in mind, we examine further in the next two sections two supplementary forms of resource transfers that Griffin and McKinley argue for, international payments for services and compensation for harmful behaviour. In recent years, other authors and organizations have also examined these possibilities.

## International Payments for Services

Establishment of an international development fund as a global transfer mechanism is for Griffin and McKinley only the first of three desirable types of resource transfer to the world's poor countries. The second type concerns payments for services provided by the poor countries that are not affected by market mechanisms (Griffin and McKinley 1996: Chapter 2) – for example, the environment programmes in developing countries. The effects of these programmes primarily, or mostly, benefit industrial countries, since they deal with sustaining rainforests and biodiversity and often have greater global than local value. Another example is programmes in developing countries aiming to reduce cultivation and export of euphoriants. A third example is health programmes to fight AIDS and other contagious diseases, and a fourth, initiatives to improve women's economic, social and educational position as part of the efforts to reduce birth rates and thereby reduce world population growth. These and other initiatives on the part of developing countries have a value for the world's rich countries that is not determined by the market. Therefore, it would be reasonable for the rich countries to pay for them, not as charity, but as compensation for specific efforts in developing countries that seriously take responsibility for the areas described.

In the 1994 edition of *Human Development Report* (UNDP 1994: 71 ff.), the UNDP presented a proposal for how international payments could be calculated and effectuated. This has been followed up by very comprehensive studies collected in a 1999 publication (Kaul et al. 1999). These new studies explore the question with focus on global public goods, that is, 'goods' with benefits that cannot easily be confined to a single 'buyer' (or set of 'buyers'); yet, once provided, many can enjoy them without payment. A clean environment is one example, global financial stability another. Without a mechanism for collective action, such goods can be and are likely to be under-produced (Kaul et al. 1999: xx). Such goods are also termed 'non-rivalrous' – they can be consumed by many people at the same time – and 'non-excludable' – no one can be barred from consuming them (see Stiglitz 1999).

The thinking that follows from this is that poor countries need considerable transfers in order to be able to afford producing or contributing to the production of global public goods. Developing countries receive transfers in the form of aid, but the authors of the book referred to above find it unreasonable to use aid funds to create global public goods that also benefit rich countries. Instead, there should be financing beside and in addition to development aid. It is estimated that about one-fourth of all aid actually goes to financing global public goods. Thus, as a consequence of this line of thinking, aid should be increased by this one-fourth, and the financing of global public goods should be provided by new funds made available by industrial countries. Since at the same time there is a great under-supply of global public goods that developing countries could contribute to, it follows that far greater funds should be allocated in the future to co-finance them. This applies to the area of environment and other areas referred to above, but also to such areas as crisis prevention and disaster prevention. Here, early initiatives with financing from rich countries could help avoid global public 'bads' and far more costly reactions to crises and emergencies that have broken out (Hamburg and Holl 1999; Mendez 1999). In order to facilitate financing preventive efforts, a special fund is proposed to which rich countries contribute according to their economic capability. Similar funds are proposed to finance creation of other global public goods. An example is a global financial insurance fund, to be used to create international financial stability for the benefit of both rich and poor countries. The IMF has not been able to create such stability for many years (Wyplosz 1999).

The principles behind these proposals should be able to win considerable support, not least because they would facilitate the rewarding of those developing countries that do the most to reduce global problems and create global public goods. These principles, however, can be very difficult to effectuate. One big problem would be to find an organization with the necessary capacity and legitimacy to assess and collect taxes and distribute them as payment to developing countries for globally beneficial activities.

## Compensation for Harmful International Behaviour

Besides payments for services performed by developing countries for the benefit of industrial countries and global development, Griffin and McKinley propose that rich countries pay compensation for the costs they inflict on developing countries.

The most serious area in this respect is probably the trade restrictions maintained by OPEC countries on developing countries' exports of both industrial and agricultural commodities. There can be no doubt that from the point of view of developing countries the negative effects of these restrictions more than equal the total value of official development assistance, perhaps even double that value. This should inspire considerations about compensation or the reduction of trade barriers. Rich countries' high duties on agricultural commodities alone are estimated to inflict an annual loss of welfare on developing countries of US$19.8 billion, equal to about 40 per cent of all foreign aid (World Bank 2001a: 180).

With the establishment of the WTO, one could suppose that this organization would have a mandate broad enough also to require member countries to pay such forms of compensation or to change their policies. The WTO should also be able to use procedures and guidelines similar to those it can now use within areas of international trade already covered by GATT agreements. With the conclusion of the so-called Uruguay round in Marrakech in 1994, the industrial countries made agreements about reducing their trade barriers and trade-distorting policies within several areas, but the effects will hardly benefit the poorest developing countries, especially not the countries in sub-Saharan Africa. Therefore, further liberalization is needed. Until this is accomplished, there is a need to compensate the countries that are shown to suffer losses due to limitations on their export opportunities.

A special and new form of trade barrier that should also be taken into consideration is connected with the increasing demands on enterprises in general to fulfil product and production standards, including standards for environmental sustainability and non-polluting production. Although international adoption of such standards cannot reasonably be characterized as harmful, very few enterprises in developing countries can live up to them. And if they can, it is difficult for them to be certified. At the same time, the existence of these standards weakens enterprises in developing countries considerably in international competition. Here, compensation could be considered, as well as – with a more dynamic aim – special arrangements for upgrading and certifying enterprises in developing countries. UNIDO is working with such arrangements on a modest scale.

Other forms of harmful international behaviour that could justify compensation are industrial countries' strong immigration restrictions on unskilled labour and simultaneous import of highly educated labour. Preventing unskilled labour from seeking work in industrial and other high-income countries inflicts considerable losses on developing countries. It is well known that immigrant workers who actually succeed in receiving work and resident permits, especially in the Middle East, transfer large amounts of money to their home countries. These transfers could be much larger were it not for the fact that so many rich countries, for social and cultural reasons, prevent the free flow of labour. No changes can be expected in this regard, also because liberalization could lead to extreme pressure on wages that would directly harm the already relatively low-salaried workers in high-income countries. But this should not prevent considerations about some form of compensation.

It is even easier to argue for compensation for the brain drain from many poor countries. In this case, rich countries receive direct benefits from highly educated workers whose education has been paid for by developing countries. Many thousands of such people leave their home countries, attracted by the prospects of better salaries and working conditions in high-income countries. This inflicts a direct loss equal to the investments in these people's education. It also inflicts an indirect loss in the form of lower productivity or reduced public and private service. Again, many of the poorest countries are hit hardest, because they already have far too few highly educated people, especially within medical, natural and technical sciences.

A special form of harmful behaviour can be ascribed to the IMF, World

Bank and multilateral financing institutions in general. It can seem slightly polemic to formulate it in this way, but the fact is that these financing institutions normally do not take responsibility for their own mistakes, and the price of these mistakes is often paid by the borrowers. It is generally acknowledged that the Bretton Woods institutions have given bad advice on several occasions, under-financed structural adjustment programmes and extended loans to doubtful projects. The consequences have been losses – direct or indirect – inflicted upon the borrowing developing countries that have not been able to demand compensation (see Raffer and Singer 1996: Chapter 11).

Some of the background for such poor advice has been the Bretton Woods institutions' tendency to propose the same economic and institutional strategies to almost all countries without systematic consideration of special conditions and prerequisites, but interestingly enough also without regard for the effects produced when many countries followed the advice. Raffer and Singer mention as an example the World Bank's recommendation to Ghana to increase cacao production in order to increase export earnings. Ghana took the advice. Other countries such as Ivory Coast, Ecuador and Brazil, however, did the same, also on the Bank's advice, with the result that world market prices fell and completely eliminated Ghana's expected extra earnings (Raffer and Singer 1996: 160). Under such and similar circumstances, it would be reasonable if the countries concerned could be given compensation for bad advice.

Although there are good arguments for compensating developing countries, the idea is not easy to put into practice. Problems would arise similar to those discussed in the previous section, especially those concerned with finding a capable and legitimate institution to mete out the amount of compensation and collect the funds. We find it important, however, to attempt to move towards supplementary forms of financing and resource transfers to the poor countries of the world.

## Financing Through Earmarked Taxes

Harmful behaviour can be extremely difficult to price. It can be difficult to reach international consensus about what harmful behaviour is. Therefore, it may be necessary instead further to develop ideas about earmarking various forms of taxation for development assistance. Proposals of this kind have been presented in various forms since the 1970s, often to ensure the UN in particular a larger and more stable flow of income. This applies, for example, to the so-called Tobin tax, named after the Nobel Prize winner, James Tobin, who in 1978 proposed introducing a tax on international monetary transactions. The main goal was to limit speculation in capital transactions, which often hit the weakest developing countries the hardest. At the same time, Tobin saw an opportunity to ensure the UN large and stable incomes that could finance both development activities and other UN tasks. Since its founding in 1998, the originally French organization, ATTAC, has proposed with increasing intensity taxing financial transactions. With this and other demands for regulating economic globalization, ATTAC has become a rallying place for many NGOs in DAC countries.

It is not specifically the financing of UN activities that interests us here, although the size and character of these activities definitely have great independent significance for the world's poor countries. Tobin's proposal has further perspectives, because a tax on international monetary transactions could be desirable as a central source of financing, not only for UN activities but also for aid activities in general. It would 'only' take a tax amounting to 0.1 per cent of all monetary transactions to collect an annual total of over US$90 billion – double the amount now being given in aid.

Other related proposals involve taxes on international trade, use of fossil fuel ($CO_2$ tax), exploitation of resources from the seabed in international waters, and air transport. In most cases, such proposals aim to bring supplementary financing to the UN, but as referred to above, the aim can be broadened to include additional financing of international development cooperation. The idea is that the proceeds from tax collection – for which each country's authorities would be responsible – would be transferred in smaller or larger amounts to development activities in the world's poorest countries. The taxes could be confined to activities in a small group of better-off countries, but they could also include all such activities regardless of location. The latter model would mean that, for example, businesspeople and those travelling by air in developing countries would also be obligated to contribute to financing aid.

## Aid to Promote Private Capital Transfers

Even with the proposed increases in resource transfers described above, it must be recognized that most developing countries would still have unmet needs for investments and expertise. Therefore, it should be considered how development cooperation can promote private investments and technology transfers – especially to the poorest developing countries. The basic conditions existing in many poor countries do not make them attractive to private investors. Not least the modest size of their markets is a problem for many countries. Aid cannot change this in any decisive way, but other conditions can be changed through support from official donors.

Development banks and other international financial institutions have been trying for a long time to make developing countries adopt macro-economic policies that are more attractive from the point of view of investors. At least as important, however, is support for capacity-building in the many institutions that are decisive preconditions for making the market and the private sector function properly. Especially important in this connection is strengthening developing countries' own financial sector. This is an area that until now has not attracted much attention among official donor organizations; it has been placed on the agenda, however, since the World Bank's and IMF's meeting in Hong Kong in 1997 (see OECD/DAC 1997: 36 ff.).

Joseph Stiglitz has argued convincingly for the importance of strengthening the financial sector in developing countries – including the Asian high-growth countries, where financial crises in 1997–98 could to a great extent be attributed to poorly functioning financial institutions (Stiglitz 1998: 14 ff.). It is not sufficient for developing countries to adopt a 'healthy' macro-economic policy, if at the same time their financial sectors do not function well. In this context, functioning well means that banks and other financial institutions should not allocate savings only on the basis of demand. Rather, they should favour the most productive and commercially viable investments. It is also important that financing institutions continuously monitor the use of their loans and ensure that they are being used in the best possible way, both to promote economic development and to ensure a high repayment rate. All this demands capacity-building within financial sectors and public regulation and control.

Very few developing countries live up to such requirements. The point in the present context, however, is that if they received help to do this, new international forms of financing might open up. For example, the large pension savings in industrial countries could contribute to financing development even in poor developing countries.

## National Ownership, Donor Demands and Sustainability

Having discussed possible future forms of financing in the preceding section, we will now try to broaden the perspective into a discussion of the forms of international cooperation that can be possible against the background of partially conflicting demands and interests in North and South.

In the 1990s, donors made several new political demands on developing countries regarding economic, political, institutional and social aspects of their societies under the headings of human rights, democratization and good governance. At the same time, donors increasingly emphasized that aid is a partnership in which recipients (governments, local institutions and the target groups) should have ownership of aid activities, and these activities should be fully integrated in local institutions and development processes. These two demands and wishes cannot necessarily be fulfilled simultaneously. They will often be conflicting: if donors accept the idea of full ownership, they must also accept national and local priorities that can conflict with donors' conception of and demand for economic liberalization, institutional effectiveness and democratic political leadership.

There are good arguments on both sides of this dilemma. National ownership of aid and its institutional integration are necessary in order to secure aid's relevance and sustainability. Aid must correspond to developing countries' needs and formulated priorities in order to increase the chances that social groups and institutions will benefit from and continue to carry out activities supported by aid.

One of the main conclusions of evaluations of all forms of aid, furthermore, is that aid achieves results with regard to development of institutional capacity in a recipient country only if the aid is integrated in and borne by the developing country's permanent institutions, whether these are within the state or in organized civil society. An organization must have political responsibility for setting priorities, making decisions, implementing activities and monitoring results before it can improve its total capacity. There is no doubt that intensive donor control through project organizations and foreign experts has led to dependency in developing countries' organizations, while also limiting their possibilities to lead and coordinate all development activities.

At the same time, arguments just as good exist for extending the donors' political demands regarding political leadership and societal development in developing countries. Regardless of what one might think of the hard-handed structural adjustment and liberalization policies; demands for equality and the rule of law, transparent forms of leadership, control of corruption etc.; and demands for democratization, decentralization, income distribution and the like; these must be characterized as legitimate donor interests. It is understandable that citizens and politicians in donor countries combine aid funds with political demands.

In this book, we describe how development assistance can contribute to improvement in poor people's living conditions and development opportunities, both through direct, targeted aid and by influencing local development processes and social relations so that poor people can participate in decision-making and gain access to resources. Therefore, it is necessary for aid to make political demands even though this in turn requires great humility and sensitivity in the conscious attempt to influence social relations and political priorities in cooperating countries and partner organizations.

We can illustrate the dilemma that exists between national ownership and donor demands with the widespread wish for aid to be sustainable in a broad sense. This means that aid must be designed so that the intended development activities can be continued, also without donor involvement. It also means that partners in the South must be technically and administratively skilled enough to continue the activities; that they can do this without seriously harming the environment; and perhaps most demanding – that they can finance the activities themselves at some point in time.

It is a correct principle for aid to strive for sustainability in all these respects, but it is a more problematic principle if it is also made unconditional (Riddell 1996: 30 ff.). The consequence of this can be that those who are already best-qualified partners are favoured, whereas aid cannot be given to the poorest groups of people and the weakest authorities who have the greatest need for help. Financial sustainability in particular will usually be impossible to achieve in connection with activities intended to benefit very poor people. Only by taxing society's better-off citizens will it be possible, for example, to offer poor people proper education and other basic social services – and in many poor countries there are simply not enough citizens to tax for such a purpose.

A tendency exists for aid-financed development activities that prove to be sustainable to benefit the economic elite and those with political power. It is they – not the poor – who have the capacity and can mobilize the resources to continue development activities. This tendency has contributed, for example, to making EU change its monitoring and evaluating procedure. Around 1990, EU tried to collect all monitoring of EU-financed projects in a traffic-light system: green evaluation meant that the project seemed to be sustainable; yellow evaluation meant that risks appeared on the horizon that threatened the project's sustainability; and red demanded immediate efforts to save the project's sustainability. Focusing all project success criteria on sustainability could lead, however, to ignoring whether the individual project achieved its goal: for example, to fight poverty and redistribute society's resources.

All in all, the conclusion must be that sustainability should be aimed at as a general principle, but if it conflicts with the donors' basic goals regarding poverty reduction, or if it hinders lasting improvements for poor countries and poor groups of people, then this principle must yield. Instead, the time framework for development cooperation and resource transfers with such countries and groups must be extended if necessary over a longer period of years. Through political dialogue, balance must be created between the demand for goals of national ownership and sustainability on the one hand, and other donor demands for societal change on the other.

Thus, donors and recipients have found themselves in an unavoidable dilemma. National ownership, institutional integration, policy dialogue and fulfilment of political demands for poverty reduction, democratization, equality between genders and generations, respect for human rights and environmental protection all had to be included in donors' development and aid policies.

These many and partially conflicting considerations also manifest themselves concretely in trying to find a balance between continuity and transparency of aid to the individual developing country on the one hand; and on the other, the desire to shift the volume and distribution of aid according to donors' evaluations of developing countries' fulfilment of political demands. Donors acknowledge that rapid shifts would not be beneficial for aid effectiveness, and they therefore react in at least three different ways.

1. With the help of aid conditionality under the leadership of the IMF and the World Bank, donors have tried to force governments in developing countries to fulfil donor demands regarding specific economic and institutional reforms. As discussed in Chapter 12, the World Bank's 1998 report

on aid recognizes that donors cannot force governments to formulate and implement a specific economic policy if there is no political commitment, interest and backing inside the country.

2. Donors attempt to work themselves out of the dilemma through greater selectivity in aid allocation. If the donor gives aid only to developing countries that fulfil the donor's political-economic demands, the described dilemma disappears. When the donor and recipient agree about what 'sound' economic management and political leadership are and how they shall be established in the country (see Chapter 12), the donor has no problem emphasizing national ownership and aid's institutional integration. One can naturally question how real this ownership is, if donors eliminate all developing countries with different conceptions of what comprises sound and correct societal development.
3. Donors attempt to use different forms of aid in different developing countries, so that aid can be adapted to each country's needs, capacity and problems. For example, these forms stretch from budget support to developing countries that donors consider able to utilize aid effectively, because they have sound economic management, political leadership and institutional capacity; over donor-led project aid to civil society in developing countries where governments do not have effective policies and capacity; to humanitarian aid to developing countries in crisis and with wrong policies and poor capacity. Some donors choose between these aid forms, while others – such as the Scandinavian donors – combine aid forms in a long-term, mutually committing cooperation with selected developing countries.

Underlying these various donor responses lies an increasing preoccupation with the role of aid as part of the politics and management of governance in developing countries as well as internationally. We explore the links between aid and governance as a step towards understanding the risks and scope of performance-based aid, which lies at the heart of tensions between politics and management.

## Aid and Governance: Between Politics and Management

The history of international development cooperation spans five decades, each with distinct emphasis and overriding strategies (see Chapters 2–4): modernization and trickle-down through infrastructure programmes in the 1950s and 1960s; basic needs fulfilment through integrated rural development programmes in the 1970s; financial liberalization and policy harmonization through structural adjustment programmes in the 1980s; and human rights and democratization through good governance policy dialogues and programmes in the 1990s. What will be the distinctive features of the first decade of the twenty-first century?

During the 1990s, aid lost its key role in the systemic conflict between East and West. Aid to developing countries declined rapidly and critically in real terms, leading to predictions about the ultimate decline of aid as one of industrial countries' major foreign policy instruments. Aid was relegated from high to low politics, reduced in size, and confined to the work of commercial and especially humanitarian interest groups and agencies. Even the World Bank turned 'human', giving overall priority to poverty reduction and referring to the three billion people living on less than US$2 a day as its primary clients.

Already during the 1990s, reality became much more blurred and complex. The IMF and the World Bank continued to enforce macro-economic adjustment and liberalization, in full accordance with WTO rules and the interests of the dominant economic powers. Aid as a policy instrument received increasing importance (both quantitatively and qualitatively) in political and economic relations with the former enemies in 'transition' countries. In September 2001, however, terrorist attacks on the USA pushed aid back on to the international security agenda. Within a few weeks, the USA settled the much of its debts to the UN. The fact that the US Congress two days after 11 September allocated US$40 billion to relief and reconstruction in Manhattan (almost equivalent to annual global ODA) is a reflection of the fact that *international* development cooperation and humanitarian assistance are heavily under-financed.

In the late 1990s, it seemed as if *performance-based aid allocation* would be the catchword and overriding aid strategy of the coming years. In subsequent sections, we analyse ways to combine three sets of performance criteria: (1) macro-economic stabilization and structural adjustment; (2) good governance, human rights and democratization; and (3) poverty reduction, human development and social diversity. By placing more emphasis on the second and third sets of criteria, we suggest principles for performance-based aid allocation that would retain much of the original needs-fulfilment objectives of aid, and which would be more appropriate to progressive donors such as most Nordic and European countries and UN agencies.

In Chapters 7 and 12, we discussed how the World Bank has moved along this path of softening and widening performance criteria, although much too slowly for our liking. What we referred to as the emerging consensus on poverty-efficient aid allocation recognizes that the greatest impact on global poverty is achieved by reallocating aid from middle-income to low-income countries, thus acknowledging the secondary significance of the much-heralded reallocation of aid from poor to good policy performers. Yet performance-based aid allocation is still being pursued by both multilateral and bilateral donors. Larger aid volumes and less tied aid forms (including budget support) are being provided to what donors consider to be good performers in terms of economic policies and governance practices. Considering that donors also make increasingly explicit strategic choices of institutional partners and sectors within individual recipient countries, it is evident that *selectivity* has become an essential element of international development cooperation and a key feature in donor strategies.

We concluded in Chapter 10 that *selective humanity* has become a threat to fundamental principles in humanitarian assistance. Selectivity in disaster relief is caused by the following trends: there are insufficient resources to meet global relief needs; disaster victims closer to home matter more than victims of recurrent crises and structural poverty; efforts to link relief and development and hence to reduce poor people's vulnerability to future disasters have not been very successful; the international community has reacted to complex emergencies with institutional overload and a shift from humanitarian to security concerns and agencies; and all categories of international agencies (humanitarian, security, development) have increasingly become part of the conflicts that they are trying to relieve or resolve.

*Political and strategic selectivity* is therefore likely to be a characterizing feature of the international aid scene in the first decade of the twenty-first century, but this characteristic expresses a donor perspective only. The underlying development strategy is likely to be influenced by tensions between politics and management in global, national and local governance.

*Politics* refers to explicit aid objectives to empower poor and marginalized people; guarantee equitable access to and distribution of resources; deepen democratic processes; strengthen recipient ownership; and promote equity in the world economy and democracy in international institutions.

*Management* refers to equally explicit aid objectives and strategies to introduce market principles into local service delivery and public sector reform; invest in technocratic priority-setting and resource allocation mechanisms (consultative groups, comprehensive development frameworks, medium-term expenditure frameworks, poverty reduction strategy papers) with heavy donor involvement; base aid allocation between and within countries on assessments by donors of the performance of their partners; and rely on donor-controlled institutions (particularly the IMF and the WTO) to manage integration of developing countries into the world economy.

A number of concepts and strategies are applied in development cooperation as a mixture of politics and management: *policy dialogue*; *partnership*; *capacity-building*; *aid management*; and *institutionalized ownership*. These concepts epitomize the links between politics and management. We see these links as tensions, not as dichotomies, because there is never an either-or situation. The links and the tensions make it appropriate to view aid as a significant element of governance. From a technocratic starting point (for example, project cycle management and technical assistance), aid agencies (bilateral, multilateral and NGOs alike) have moved deeply into governance issues, processes and structures at national, local and international levels.

*Aid and national governance:* with aid management and donor–recipient policy dialogues linked to poverty reduction strategies (involving government and civil society) and public sector reforms (including medium-term expenditure frameworks), it is evident that the current development partnerships constitute significant parts of national governance in aid-dependent countries. The space occupied by aid is probably larger than what is indicated by the relatively low aid dependency figures, because partners have constructed space that comprises both politics and management. Even for NGOs, national partnerships, capacity-building and political advocacy have started to dominate humanitarian assistance and local service delivery.

*Aid and local governance:* decentralization of authority and resources has been a favoured strategy for both donors and recipients for decades. The 'cross-cutting themes' emphasized by most donors point to direct involvement in governance at all levels of society: equality between genders and ethnic and social groups; participation and empowerment; human rights and democratization; and environmental, economic, institutional and social sustainability. Still, partners have only recently begun to view their local interaction in governance terms. We know much more about the operations of local bureaucracies (district administrations, deconcentrated units of central government and local NGOs) than about the intricacies of local politics. But we do know that aid is heavily involved in both conflicts and relatively stable situations, and that aid agencies are trying to understand how they influence local governance, including conflicts and power relations.

*Aid and international governance:* aid has always been part of the governance

**Table 14.1** Changing modes and relationships in development aid

| | Projects and services in the past | Programmes and policies in the present and future |
|---|---|---|
| Controllable and predictable | More | Less |
| Mental model | Simpler, linear | More complex, interlinked |
| Cause–effect attribution | Clearer | Less clear |
| Accountability, transparency | Upwards | 360 degrees, including downwards |
| Power relations | Top-down | Reciprocal |
| Development agencies and staff | More confident | Less confident |
| Language | Technical | Power-related |
| Political sensitivity | Less | More |
| Donor–recipient relationships | Cruder | More nuanced |
| Characteristic procedure | Logical framework | Negotiated principles and process |

*Source:* Chambers et al. 2001: 2.

of international relations, whether as a simple foreign policy tool in the decolonization drive and in the systemic conflict between East and West; or as an expression of international solidarity by international humanitarian movements and governments. During the 1990s, as discussed above, aid to low-income countries was relegated to lower-ranking roles as private forces took over globalization processes through intensified financial flows, trade and investments. Aid was also revived, however, as a powerful governance instrument in the deepening of political and commercial relations with the former Soviet bloc; in the international institutional response to the financial crises in Southeast Asia in 1997–98; in conflict management (containment and resolution) in the former Yugoslavia and other complex emergencies around the world; and in the security-motivated response to international terrorism. In international governance, the decisive question is whether aid will be given a major role in poverty reduction and in the integration of marginalized people, countries and regions into the world economy. We return to this in the final section.

Thus, at all levels, aid is directly engaged in the tensions between politics and management in the design and execution of governance. This has often been presented as dichotomies between aid models and even between development paradigms. In a recent discussion of 'the new dynamics of aid: power, procedures and relationships', Chambers et al. (2001) come dangerously close to presenting a new set of dichotomies (see Table 14.1).

We agree with most of the characteristics indicated by Chambers et al. for 'programmes and policies in the present and future', although we fear that the list contains too much wishful thinking about the approach and performance of donor agencies. While we share such hopes, we see too few signs that aid programmes and agencies have moved out of the self-confident, rationalistic and technocratic approach to aid and development planning and programme design. The tensions between politics and management are found in all types of institutionalized aid relationships and in the mental model and language of development agencies and their staffs. For this reason, we must carefully examine the push for performance-based aid selectivity. It represents the ultimate integration of politics and management.

## Performance-based Aid: Goals and Country Circumstances

For the World Bank and large bilateral donors like USAID, focus is on recipient countries' performance on the macro level: they must implement proper economic policies that limit inflation and ensure balanced national budgets and payments and also create latitude for private investors. They must leave as much as possible to market mechanisms. Furthermore, the authorities must achieve good governance: accountability to citizens, openness in administration, non-discriminatory legislation and respect for human rights. Developing countries that live up to such demands must be favoured in the distribution of aid. This will give better results and create the kind of success that is necessary to maintain support for aid budgets in donor countries. At the same time, such procedures will function as a strong motivation for other developing countries to improve their performance in these areas.

Other donors, such as the Scandinavian countries and UNDP, focus more on performance in social terms, especially reducing poverty and promoting human development. For supporters of performance-based aid, however, the basic idea is the same: the countries and partners that do best should be rewarded. We can follow the arguments for performance-based aid up to a point. It *is* of great importance for aid's effectiveness that authorities in recipient countries adopt policies that promote development and do this effectively with considerable participation by citizens in decision-making processes. It *is* proven that reducing poverty and promoting human development makes great demands on developing countries' policies and capacity. We see three main problems in aid distributed on the basis of performance, however.

We are concerned about the simplistic and occasionally arrogant viewpoints that the IMF in particular and the World Bank have had about the correct macro-economic policies that they have imposed on developing countries in all regions based on the so-called Washington consensus. The World Bank's former chief economist has acknowledged that this model has been too narrowly based on the experience from Latin America (Stiglitz 1998). Likewise, the World Bank's poverty strategy (see Chapter 12) was developed on the basis of experience from East and South Asia, which do not necessarily fit the starker circumstances and the weaker national economies in sub-Saharan Africa, for example. In Chapter 13, we describe the unacceptable consequences of external paternalism for weak states that do not receive support adapted to their needs, capacity and opportunities.

We find it unacceptable to categorize widely different developing countries in only two groups: those that deliver the demanded economic and institutional performance ('performers'); and those that do not ('non-performers'). During the last ten to fifteen years, a long series of reports from the World Bank has been built up around these very crude categories, which both ignore different types of developing countries' widely different circumstances and opportunities and are extremely problematic with regard to methodology (see the discussion of the World Bank's index of good political leadership and institutional capacity).

Finally, the crucial problem of performance-based aid is that poor people living in weak states may be punished twofold. They suffer under corrupt and repressive regimes and ineffective state administrations that do not deliver social services to the public; and they must also witness how poor people in 'well-functioning' neighbouring states receive far more aid – in accordance with the philosophy of performance-based aid.

We do not deny that it is possible to argue in favour of performance-based aid. First, it is almost self-evident that aid's effectiveness increases when the conditions are effective: donors can reach more poor people when governments in developing countries are well functioning, democratic, and so on. Second, it is possible that 'bad' governments in developing countries experience a certain motivating pressure if they can see that neighbouring countries benefit from aid, investments, trade advantages and suchlike. We doubt, however, the strength of this motivation, because corrupt and repressive political leaders themselves are seldom affected when aid is reduced in developing countries that perform badly. Therefore, it is crucial that the criteria for good performance become more extensive and that the categories of developing countries receive more nuances. Recent years' debate about development and aid point to three main groups of political goals for cooperation that can also serve as performance criteria.

- *Macro-economic stabilization and structural adjustment:* the Washington consensus has, as discussed above, been modified towards a mixed economy where state control and market forces are combined, also to ensure sustainable resource utilization, and where state, non-state and private services supplement each other.
- *Good governance, human rights and democratization:* the earlier focus on competition between East and West has been changed to donor demands for multiparty elections and transparent political governance, and gradually to demands for respect of political, civil, social and economic human rights, and democratization.
- *Poverty reduction, human development and social diversity:* after focusing in the 1970s on people's basic needs and in the 1980s on economic growth as the way out of poverty, donors are increasingly working with the political, social and cultural aspects of poverty reduction and inclusion.

As both ends and means to achieve these three main goals, the parties involved in aid focus on building *capacity* in developing countries' institutions and organizations within the state, civil society, the private sector and the target group. We find it important that capacity-building be seen as a necessary part of all three main goals and not be limited to effective economic control and public administration, as has been the tendency in the World Bank's most important publications in the 1990s on aid and the state.

The main problem with performance-based aid is that there is no tendency towards or guarantee for correlation between the three main goals. Correlation would mean that a developing country would 'score' high or low on performance criteria in relation to all three goals simultaneously. It is here, in our judgement, that the World Bank's *Assessing Aid* analysis of future aid (1998b) falls short. The World Bank claims that good macro-economic and structural policies on the one hand, and good governance and effective management on the other, mutually support each other. Although this sounds ideal, evidence is lacking for such a connection. Many examples are found of developing countries with undemocratic political regimes that have carried out 'good' economic policies, and at least as many examples exist of democratic governments that have adopted policies that the national economy could not carry. Emphasizing a connection between good economic management and a capable public sector approaches a tautology (as discussed in Chapter 12) that cannot be used as a criterion for performance-based aid.

Likewise, correlation is not ensured between the two first-mentioned goals (a specific economic policy and a specific form of governance) on the one hand, and achievement of the third goal of poverty reduction and human development on the other. The World Bank's claim that economic growth automatically leads to reduced poverty is doubtful in itself, because income differences and political and social power relations are just as decisive. No systematic connection can be traced between economic growth and political forms of government on the one hand and human welfare and social identity on the other. The third main goal contains many aspects of poverty and livelihoods that are not necessarily connected with developing countries' overall performance in the economic and political fields.

This analysis of lacking correlation leads us to a basic difficulty with performance-based aid that can be formulated in the following question: what main group of development and aid goals should have priority and form the basis of the criteria that donors use to distribute their performance-based aid? Although most donors in the 1990s emphasized poverty reduction as the main goal, there are many differences regarding how they understand poverty reduction and whether they consider a specific economic, institutional and political development as a prerequisite for effective poverty reduction.

Moreover, there is a considerable methodological problem regarding monitoring of performance. The logic behind performance-based aid says on the one hand that the basis for evaluation is the *developing country's* performance, but at the same time that *aid* (and thereby the donor) plays a major role in the performance. The challenge is therefore to ensure that the developing country's own institutions monitor both goal achievement and the various causal factors related to success or failure such as aid's effectiveness, and that the latter is isolated from other causal factors. This is necessary in order to minimize the risk of circular argumentation: aid is reduced, because aid is planned and implemented ineffectively, which leads to poor goal achievement in developing countries. Realistic and fair monitoring and explanation of developing countries' performance in relation to fulfilment of various goals is at least as demanding a task as formulation of simple and reasonable performance goals.

Although there is no guarantee of correlation between the three main groups of development goals, it is of course easier for a developing country with economic resources, stable political conditions and institutional capacity to deliver good performance in relation to poverty reduction and other development goals than a developing country with debt crisis, political conflicts and identity crises, and lack of financial and educated human resources. If aid is concentrated in developing countries of the former type, inequalities in the world will unavoidably increase – at least in the short term. In the medium to long term, developing countries suffering from crises will have poorer possibilities to tackle their various crises, and it is impossible to say anything cogent about what will happen in the long term.

Development assistance must therefore take into account the different point of departure different developing countries have, economically, politically, socially and with regard to resources. Performance-based aid, however, has meaning only if the number of 'developing country types' is limited so that donors can monitor performance in relation to given goals, and so that governments in developing countries have some goals for which to strive. In the following, we discuss only low-income countries, which are and ought to be the main recipients of development assistance and emergency relief. We differentiate between four types of developing countries, or rather between developing countries in four situations.

1. *Performers – developing countries with few crises and good performance:* this group comprises low-income countries with good opportunities to utilize aid effectively and directly for the benefit of the poor target group. These countries have the economic resources, political support and institutional capacity to integrate and utilize aid in accordance with the goals agreed upon with donors.
2. *Reformers – developing countries with significant crises but with clear reform efforts:* this group comprises the large group of low-income countries that – as cause and consequence of the fact that they are low-income countries – struggle with macro-economic imbalance, problems of political legitimacy, ineffective institutions, and/or natural resource problems. At the same time, however, some of these are on the way out of crisis. There is no guarantee that there is any correlation between the three main development goals in these countries. They often have crises in some areas and 'success' in others.
3. *Non-performers – developing countries with significant crises in all dimensions:* this group comprises developing countries where there are simultaneous economic, social and institutional crises, and where there is no politically legitimate state with programmes and capacity to solve these crises. Such developing countries are also found in all regions, but there are many fewer than in the reform category. In addition, there are also social forces and organizations in all these countries that work to find a way out of the crises.
4. *Developing countries in existential crisis:* this group comprises developing countries without a state with a legitimate demand for sovereignty and capacity to manage development in society. These are usually developing countries involved in international or civil wars and state-threatening ethnic

challenges. When one considers the upheavals, crises and disasters that have befallen the Third World during the last fifty years, it is amazing that so few developing countries have found themselves in existential crisis.

Four categories among low-income countries are thus a minimum needed to analyse the different starting points that developing countries have for being able to utilize aid. We have purposely made each category so broad that we thereby do not specify one development goal as the most important. The demarcation between performers and non-performers is thus not only macro-economic balances and institutional capacity. Concentrating aid on developing countries with good economic management and institutional capacity would be a much too narrow form of performance focus. This would be unreasonable in relation to many countries that have focused on other development goals related to poverty reduction, human development, and so forth; countries that have agreed on policies and taken initiatives within all three development goals; or where social interests and organizations fight for these goals, possibly in opposition to those in power.

## Performance-based Aid: Aid Forms and Agencies

The next step in assessing the possibilities for performance-based aid is to examine whether different *aid forms* can be used to fulfil the various needs and opportunities for effective aid in the different developing countries. In Chapter 4, we describe the different aid forms and their use in different aid strategies as they have developed since the 1950s. Today, one can group aid forms in four categories that comprise both aid instruments and strategies.

1. *Development aid to state partners:* this aid form comprises budget and balance-of-payment support, sector programme assistance and similar donor financing of a share of the public expenditures in developing countries. The aim is to 'reward' governments in developing countries with good performance and to support the further development and implementation of what donors consider to be good policies. This aid form solves the dilemma between national ownership and donor demands, because the parties fundamentally agree about major problems and the direction to be taken. It thus uses in a constructive way aid's fungibility in relation to other development resources and activities in the recipient country: as long as the country is moving in the right direction, it is acceptable that aid funds actually contribute to financing all the activities that the government gives priority to and wishes to implement.
2. *Donor-managed development aid:* this aid form is a further development of the well-known project aid, where the donor has considerable control over the formulation, implementation, monitoring and evaluation of activities. It is also found in sector programme support when it is planned with the same phases as in the project cycle. It is clearly found in much development

assistance that aims to develop physical and other forms of infrastructure with the help of donor-controlled contract bids, tied deliveries and investments from the donor country. Also, since the 1990s, this aid form has grown within aid to organizations in civil society, including human rights activities. Its rationale is that with aid as a form of intervention it is possible simultaneously to deliver services to the target group, develop capacity in selected institutions, and influence local power relations and development processes in order to move towards equality and democracy.

3. *Policy advice and technical assistance:* this aid form emphasizes what donors throughout the years have called technology, organization, best practice, advanced knowledge and (in the most recent World Bank reports) 'ideas' (as opposed to money). It comprises the most immaterial aspects of development cooperation: policy dialogue, capacity-building with a minimum of financial support, technical advice, consultancy assistance, scholarships, and so on. Its rationale is that developing countries' greatest problem today is not lack of capital but lack of knowledge about the correct, sound or good development model. From a Nordic perspective, its slightly more modest rationale is that we have experience concerning society's organization (ranging, for example, from the cooperative movement, to welfare society, to decentralization, and institutionalized labour negotiations) that can benefit developing countries.
4. *Humanitarian assistance:* this aid form has as its direct purpose to ensure the survival and development of people in a vulnerable situation. It covers a wide spectrum from emergency relief to guaranteeing the rights of persecuted groups (refugees, ethnic and other minorities, children, excluded groups, and so on). Its rationale is ethical (from relieving suffering to creating opportunities) and involves security policy (minimizing the risk of illegal immigration, terrorism, violent conflicts). A gradual transition may take place from humanitarian assistance to development assistance for poverty reduction, which also focuses on delivering social services within, for example, primary health care and food security. To a great extent, humanitarian assistance cuts across the other three aid forms, since it (1) supports the existing authorities; (2) is usually controlled by donors; and (3) often includes both financial and technical assistance.

The different aid forms have different degrees of relevance and effectiveness for the four types of low-income developing countries that we have identified.

- Aid to developing countries with few crises and good performance (performers) can mainly take the form of untied budget and programme support to the government's regular development activities. Both technical and humanitarian assistance, however, may be necessary, for example, in emergency situations.
- Aid to developing countries with considerable crises but clear reform efforts

(reformers) will typically be more donor-managed and/or aim more to support organizations in civil society. Technical assistance may be required in these countries, since they are involved in developing and implementing greater changes in their national economy and society structure.

- Aid to developing countries with considerable crises in all dimensions (non-performers) will especially take place through technical assistance to promote reforms and social change, and humanitarian assistance targeted to poor and marginalized groups that are exposed to oppressive states and non-functioning state services. Technical assistance can often be combined with donor-managed development assistance implemented in cooperation with NGOs.
- Aid to developing countries in existential crisis will mostly be humanitarian and aim to protect poor and marginalized people, including ethnic and political opposition groups, against assault by often competing state powers. There can also be a role for technical assistance to attempt to build or protect the basic elements of effective and democratic institutions in both the state and civil society.

Thus, good opportunities exist for donors to use different forms of aid that are appropriate for developing countries in different circumstances and with different capacity for good performance. This analysis differs from the recommendations presented in Chapter 12 from the World Bank's *Assessing Aid* report (1998b), especially in three ways. First, humanitarian assistance is integrated into donors' aid instrumentation. Humanitarian assistance does not only involve emergency relief but also targeted poverty reduction and protection of vulnerable and oppositional groups. Thereby, it becomes very useful also in all the developing countries that are not good performers. Second, donor-managed development assistance combined with technical assistance can be extremely useful in developing countries that are in the midst of change (reformers) and therefore cannot yet deliver the demanded performances. One reason for this is that capacity-building can rarely be supported with technical assistance alone; financial assistance is also required in order for developing countries' institutions to learn and develop. Third, using the four categories of developing countries allows a great degree of flexibility for donors as well as a reasonable mutuality in donors' and recipients' obligations.

The basic advantage of this approach to performance-based aid is that both parties' performances must be monitored and evaluated. The *developing country's* performance is evaluated in relation to the conditions and capacity found in the relevant country category. Developing states have a clear interest in improving their performance, since the result is more untied development assistance to the state. Hereby, the incentive that supporters of performance-based aid emphasize is built into aid allocations. The *donor's* performance must be evaluated in relation to the utilization of all aid forms and strategies.

The individual donor and donors as a whole must combine and use all four aid forms in such a way as to maximize developing states' opportunities to gain access to freer aid funding and aid forms. We find it to be of decisive importance that performance demands be directed towards both donor and recipient, since it must be assumed that the developing state is the weak party. It would be unfair if in cooperation and partnership performance demands are laid unequivocally on the weakest part.

We can thus summarize this discussion of aid forms and performance as follows: it is possible to formulate a framework for performance-based aid that takes into account the differences in circumstances and capacity between four types of developing countries; that utilizes differences between aid forms; that gives developing states incentives to improve their performance in utilizing aid; and that at the same time introduces a performance goal for donors' use of the strengths of the various aid forms so that they adapt their aid to the different developing country types.

In Chapter 4, we have grouped donors in the following types according to the main elements in their respective aid goals and strategies: large bilateral donors; small like-minded/progressive donors; the UN system's development programmes; the multilateral development banks; the international NGOs; and the EU. To these we add UN organizations and NGOs that specialize in humanitarian assistance. Interest in performance-based aid is, as we discuss above, greatest among the large bilateral donors and multilateral development banks, with the World Bank in the lead.

The question is therefore whether a division of labour would be possible and effective in connection with a transition towards performance-based aid. The main argument against a division of labour among donors within the framework of a performance-based aid system is that the reward and punishment elements or incentives lose their value and effectiveness if a developing state can receive compensating aid from other donors.

The arguments *for* a division of labour among donors comprise recognition of the differences in their development goals; utilization of their respective strengths; and resistance to extreme donor control that would be an unavoidable result of a joint and coordinated donor policy towards the individual developing country's performance. Finally, there is the pragmatic argument for a division of labour: donors have talked about and worked for donor and aid coordination since the 1960s – to little effect. Aid's effectiveness can therefore be increased if donors could agree to utilize their respective capacities, aid instruments and resources in the best possible way – in reality a coordinated division of labour.

There could be two forms of division of labour. Under the first form, some donors (for example, USAID and multilateral development banks) would tie their aid to developing country performance. Others (for example, small bilateral donors and the UN system) would continue development cooperation characterized by continuity, like that built into the Nordic countries' bilateral cooperation with selected priority partners. An alternative division of labour could be that the different donors tie their aid to different developing country performances in relation to the three main goals for development cooperation: some donors would focus on performance related to macro-economic and structural policy; others on performance related to good governance and democratization; and still others on performance related to poverty reduction and human development.

We consider the arguments for a division of labour among donors to be very strong. It is probable that a certain division of labour of the first type will continue to exist: some donors continue with need-oriented aid (which is most logical within humanitarian assistance), while others move towards performance-based aid. The problem is rather the effectiveness of the second type of division of labour, where donors focus on different developing country performances. This demands investigation of whether different donor types agree about the three main groups of development and aid goals, and whether there are differences in donors' mandates and capacities to contribute to their fulfilment.

The multilateral development banks are still the most important donor actors in relation to the macro-economic and structural development goals. Bilateral donors are still the most important actors in relation to goals concerning developing countries' political leadership and democratization, although most other donors are also trying to enter this area. Almost all donor types give priority to and are active within assistance for poverty reduction and human development.

The next step in combining performance-based aid and the division of labour among donors concerns donors' performances in the use of different aid forms in different categories of developing countries. On the basis of the donors' respective mandates and capacities, one could formulate the following division of labour.

*The large bilateral donors* distribute their aid among all developing country types. The relatively well-functioning (based on donors' political, social and economic criteria) developing states are rewarded with budget support and other programme aid. Developing countries that are in the process of reform efforts are supported by donor-managed development assistance to, among others, organizations in civil society, as are some countries suffering from crisis that perhaps have historic ties to a specific donor. Selected developing countries are given technical assistance, depending on the donor's capacity. All developing countries may be given humanitarian assistance.

The difference between the above donors and the *small like-minded/progressive donors* is that the latter have democratization and poverty reduction as primary development goals and performance criteria. These donors typically focus more on continuity in cooperation with each selected developing country. Therefore, the variation lies in the donor's shifts between the four aid forms, depending on the development situation in the individual cooperating country.

*The UN's development programmes* have fewer possibilities to distribute aid on the basis of performance criteria, because developing states claim the right to receive UN aid. To a certain extent, however, the UNDP, UNICEF and other UN organizations can adapt their aid management to the capacity of the individual developing country to utilize aid effectively.

*International NGOs* work mainly with partner organizations from developing countries' civil society. They can effectively adapt their aid to whether these partner organizations are performers, reformers or non-performers, but there is not always a direct relationship between the developing country's and the NGO partner's capacity.

With respect to country choice and performance criteria, *the EU*'s aid resembles more the bilateral donors than the multilateral organizations. The EU emphasizes continuity in development cooperation and can combine aid forms in accordance with the developing country's capacity and performance. Therefore, the EU is more concerned with performance-based aid forms than with performance-based aid volume.

*The humanitarian organizations* (UN organizations, NGOs, ECHO and others), which mainly deliver humanitarian assistance, distribute their aid primarily according to need. Therefore, performance considerations enter into the picture only when these organizations are drawn towards either development assistance or more political forms of humanitarian interventions. The latter can lead to 'selective humanity', as discussed in Chapter 10.

It is not the aim of this book to recommend the introduction and formulation of a performance-based aid system. We have pointed out several times the great risk that poor groups and even states can suffer doubly under such a system, and that inequities between developing countries are increased. The purpose of the analysis has rather been to find alternatives to the oversimplified ideas concerning performance-based aid that the large bilateral and multilateral donors have worked with since the end of the 1990s.

We have observed that differentiating between four categories of developing countries with different crisis challenges and conditions, and simultaneously differentiating between four different aid forms, can reduce the above-mentioned risk connected with performance-based aid. It can increase the effectiveness of the total amount of aid by also making demands on the different donors' performances in aid delivery.

## Future Aid Models

The analysis in this chapter, and in the book as a whole, allows us to point to some aid models that could influence international development cooperation in the coming years. We define an aid model as a series of connected and internally consistent elements: donor motivation → development and aid goals → choice of cooperation partners in and among developing countries → financing forms → aid forms and strategies. Here, it will suffice to discuss tendencies towards and possible consequences of dividing cooperation into four aid models. We must emphasize that the aid models are described in pure form although it is most likely that they would exist in combination. We also wish to stress that we do not find all models equally attractive. They correspond to tendencies in international development cooperation that are not all positive, seen from a Nordic development policy perspective.

1. *Aid for relief, welfare and conflict containment.* Several factors indicate that taxpayer-financed aid has the greatest chance of surviving as an international pendant to national social welfare provision and conflict resolution. First, people's support for aid has always been greatest in relation to emergency relief, whereas popular confidence in the effectiveness of development assistance has been more limited. Second, competition and wars between political systems during the Cold War have been replaced by social marginalization, differentiation, ethnic conflict, and so on. Such problems relate less to development assistance than to humanitarian assistance combined with security policy initiatives in the form of peace-making and conflict resolution. Third, economic liberalization and globalization involve risks of marginalizing whole countries and societies. Therefore, a division of labour among international organizations could be seen as a good idea: some (for example, the UN and NGOs) take care of the marginalized societies, while others (for example, the IMF and some of the multilateral development banks) support economic integration in the dynamic areas of world society.

Aid in the form of social welfare and conflict resolution would mainly be financed by taxpayers and volunteers in the rich countries. It would be a need-oriented aid form that depended more on the CNN effect (that is, the mass media's description of need and suffering) than on developing countries' performances. Donors' choice of partners in developing countries would be made *ad hoc*, depending on where crises are greatest and where organizations are found that can deliver the necessary services to the suffering populations, local societies and states. Politicization of humanitarian assistance may, however, lead to tougher and more explicit forms of selectivity in humanitarian assistance.

If the connections between social welfare and conflict resolution become very tight, for example, in the form of military support for distributing food and other emergency relief, humanitarian assistance risks losing some of its opportunities to intervene neutrally in conflict situations and to extend its work to targeted poverty reduction and human development. Thus, the linking of emergency relief and development assistance that took place in the beginning and middle of the 1990s would be weakened.

2. *Aid in support of globalization: liberalization and standardization.* Many aid organizations have tried new ways to develop a leading role for the private sector in development processes, especially by promoting private investments from transnational enterprises and local firms. Such an aid model would be

a natural extension of the liberalization and structural adjustment programmes of the 1980s. It quickly became evident, however, that liberalization and privatization alone were not able to promote investments and growth in the private sector. Therefore, as discussed earlier, development research and donors work with a combination of state control and market mechanisms, that is, a form of mixed economy where all actors should be able to find a role in production, distribution, technology development, and so on.

A first reaction is that such a shift back from liberalization to state intervention and mixed economy is an advantage for donor organizations, since development assistance has always been closely connected to state intervention and public services. It is also reasonable, however, to consider it an aid model that supports globalization, because creation of free and stable access to developing countries' markets, labour and natural resources is a basic element that is carried over from structural adjustment programmes. The state intervention that is now referred to lies within the framework of the WTO's regulation of international trade, where the focus is on establishing a level playing field and harmonizing technical and environmental standards.

Another element in globalization support as an aid model is the tendency towards performance-based aid distribution, where the large donors give more aid to developing countries that can document good economic performance: liberalization, trade promotion, transparency, and so on. This aspect of the aid model runs – partly on purpose – into the dilemma that other forms of cooperation between North and South are more effective than traditional forms of development assistance in promoting global economic integration. There will still be plenty of room, however, for technical assistance for economic policy formulation and institutional development in developing countries.

Financing of this aid model could be based on some of the ideas discussed earlier in this chapter. Aid as globalization support should be co-financed by transnational capital that would benefit just as much from aid as developing countries. The attempts made until now by both bilateral and multilateral donors to draw private capital into financing development assistance have received much publicity, but they are very limited in scope. We have still to see a breakthrough of new forms of financing in international development cooperation. Taxpayers in the rich countries still shoulder by far the largest share.

3. *Aid in support of international public goods: transnational problems.* This model, as discussed in the sections on financing earlier in this chapter, will limit aid to global problems that can be solved only through international cooperation. They can mobilize self-interest – and hereby financing – from state and private actors in both industrial and developing countries. To the extent that both activities and benefits are limited to actors in industrial countries, it cannot be considered as aid. The aid element is related to global problems that in order to be solved require international support for activities in

developing countries – problems such as natural resource protection, pollution control, epidemic control, narcotics, fundamentalism, ethnic conflict resolution and other problems of security.

This aid model is attractive to multilateral aid organizations, because they can develop a rationale and a financial foundation that is independent of taxpayers, voluntary contributions and (to a certain extent) politicians in industrial countries. An important problem for the multilateral organizations, however, is also that the solutions to these global problems demand local efforts. Thus, providing global public goods very much resembles traditional development assistance and emergency relief, and its direct effects must be evaluated and defended locally. This limits the multilateral organizations' opportunities for mobilizing independent global financing for these activities.

If bilateral aid organizations should occupy a central position in this aid model, it would demand changing the poverty-reducing components into activities targeted towards global environmental problems, for example. These could include reducing pollution and the plunder of resources in contexts (often in middle-income countries) where the world's environment benefits most from an invested dollar. Such a change would be a radical shift away from need-oriented aid aimed at poverty reduction.

4. *Aid in support of poverty reduction and democratic society-building.* This model corresponds to the bilateral aid that is already being delivered today by most European donor countries and aid organizations. On a more local level, it is the same model used by international NGOs. It is based on solidarity, tax incomes or voluntary contributions, extensive partnerships with developing states and civil society organizations, and aid to all levels and dimensions of social development.

That this aid model is internally consistent, cohesive, and relevant for the low-income countries that house two to three billion of the world's poorest people has been a continuous theme throughout this book. The analysis has shown that publicly supported interventions, even in the most turbulent situations in the marginalized developing countries, have achieved good results through a mixture of innovative experiments, strategy shifts, and continuity in development cooperation.

The aid model does contain a couple of dilemmas, however, that have led to the donor interest in experimenting with performance-based aid. First, donors cannot work for national ownership and institutional integration of aid and at the same time make very precise demands about a specific economic, political, institutional and social model of society in recipient countries. Second, development assistance is a special form of public intervention that in the long term is most effective when the donor minimizes its own role and presence. This produces problems of organizational culture, because aid actors must learn to keep themselves in the background and must be assessed for their contribution to capacity-building and not to direct problem resolution. In concrete terms, this dilemma manifests itself in difficulties in finding the right indicators for aid impact. The result of the individual, donor-financed activity (typically in the form of a project) is naturally of importance for the directly affected groups in the population, but its significance for poverty reduction and other major development goals depends on aid's interaction with the broader societal development processes in developing countries.

In the light of this dilemma it is comforting that the analysis of performance-based aid indicates a direction that can make it possible for individual donors to provide aid in accordance with their respective development and aid goals and within the framework of more effective aid, seen as a whole. Such aid will also take into account the decisive differences between developing countries with regard to their circumstances and capacity to utilize aid. There can be no doubt that the fourth aid model – aid that supports poverty reduction and societal development – is most in accordance with the needs of poor people and developing countries, even though it also involves extensive donor demands for social change in developing countries.

APPENDIX

# Donor Countries and Recipient Countries

Donor countries as understood throughout this book are the members of OECD's Development Assistance Commitee (DAC). They are listed below.

**Table A.1** DAC member countries

| | | |
|---|---|---|
| Australia (1966) | Austria (1965) | Belgium (1961) |
| Canada (1961) | Denmark (1963) | Finland (1975) |
| France (1961) | Germany (1961) | Greece (1999) |
| Ireland (1985) | Italy (1961) | Japan (1961) |
| Luxembourg (1992) | Netherlands (1961) | New Zealand (1973) |
| Norway (1962) | Portugal (1961–74; 1991) | Spain (1991) |
| Sweden (1965) | Switzerland (1968) | United Kingdom (1961) |
| United States (1961) | | |

*Note*: Figures in parentheses indicate the year of joining the DAC. The EU Commission is also member of the Committee.

The DAC list of aid recipients as of January 2000 is reproduced overleaf. Part I countries are recognized as recipients of ODA. Part II countries may receive foreign assistance but this is then counted only as 'official aid' (see Chapter 5).

The DAC List of Aid Recipients as at 1 January 2000

| Part I: Developing countries and territories (official development assistance) | | | | | | Part II: Countries and territories in transition (official aid) | |
|---|---|---|---|---|---|---|---|
| Least developed countries | Other low-income countries (per capita GNP < $760 in 1998) | Lower-middle-income countries and territories (per capita GNP $761–$3,030 in 1998) | | Upper-middle-income countries and territories (per capita GNP $3,031–$9,360 in 1998) | High-income countries and territories (per capita GNP > $9,360 in 1998)[1] | Central and Eastern European countries and new independent states of the former Soviet Union | More advanced developing countries and territories |
| Afghanistan | *Armenia | *Albania | Palestinian Administered Areas | Botswana | Malta[1] | *Belarus | §Aruba |
| Angola | *Azerbaijan | Algeria | Papua New Guinea | Brazil | Slovenia[1] | *Bulgaria | Bahamas |
| Bangladesh | Cameroon | Belize | Paraguay | Chile | | *Czech Republic | §Bermuda |
| Benin | China | Bolivia | Peru | Cook Islands | | *Estonia | Brunei |
| Bhutan | Congo Rep. | Bosnia and Herzegovina | Philippines | Croatia | | *Hungary | §Cayman Islands |
| Burkina Faso | Côte d'Ivoire | Colombia | South Africa | Gabon | | *Latvia | Chinese Taipei |
| Burundi | §East Timor | Costa Rica | Sri Lanka | Grenada | | *Lithuania | Cyprus |
| Cambodia | Ghana | Cuba | St Vincent and Grenadines | Lebanon | | *Poland | §Falkland Islands |
| Cape Verde | Honduras | Dominica | Suriname | Malaysia | | *Romania | §French Polynesia |
| Central African Rep. | India | Dominican Republic | Swaziland | Mauritius | | *Russia | §Gibraltar |
| Chad | Indonesia | Ecuador | Syria | §Mayotte | | *Slovak Republic | §Hong Kong, China |
| Comoros | Kenya | Egypt | Thailand | Mexico | | *Ukraine | Israel |
| Congo Dem. Rep. | Korea Dem. Rep. | El Salvador | §Tokelau | Nauru | | | Korea Rep. |
| Djibouti | *Kyrgyz Rep. | Fiji | Tonga | Palau Islands | | | Kuwait |
| Equatorial Guinea | *Moldova | *Georgia | Tunisia | Panama | | | Libya |
| Eritrea | Mongolia | Guatemala | *Uzbekistan | §St Helena | | | §Macao |
| Gambia | Nicaragua | Guyana | §Wallis and Futuna | St Lucia | | | §Nether- |
| Guinea | Nigeria | Iran | Yugoslavia | Trinidad and Tobago | | | |
| Guinea-Bissau | Pakistan | Iraq | | Turkey | | | |
| | Senegal | Jamaica | | Uruguay | | | |
| | *Tajikistan | Jordan | | Venezuela | | | |
| | *Turkmenistan | | | | | | |

| | | | | | |
|---|---|---|---|---|---|
| Haiti | Viet Nam | *Kazakhstan | Fed. Rep. | | lands |
| Kiribati | Zimbabwe | Macedonia | | Threshold | Antilles |
| Laos | | (former | | for World | §New |
| Lesotho | | Yugoslav Rep.) | | Bank loan | Caledonia |
| Liberia | | Marshall Islands | | eligibility | Northern |
| Madagascar | | Micronesia | | ($5,280 in | Marianas |
| Malawi | | Federated States | | 1998) | Qatar |
| Maldives | | Morocco | | | Singapore |
| Mali | | Namibia | | | United |
| Mauritania | | Niue | | §Anguilla | Arab |
| Mozambique | | | | Antigua and | Emirates |
| Myanmar | | | | Barbuda | §Virgin |
| Nepal | | | | Argentina | Islands |
| Niger | | | | Bahrain | (UK) |
| Rwanda | | | | Barbados | |
| Samoa | | | | §Montserrat | |
| São Tomé | | | | Oman | |
| and Principe | | | | Saudi Arabia | |
| Sierra Leone | | | | Seychelles | |
| Solomon Islands | | | | St Kitts and | |
| Somalia | | | | Nevis | |
| Sudan | | | | §Turks and | |
| Tanzania | | | | Caicos | |
| Togo | | | | Islands | |
| Tuvalu | | | | | |
| Uganda | | | | | |
| Vanuatu | | | | | |
| Yemen | | | | | |
| Zambia | | | | | |

* Central and Eastern European countries and new independent states of the former Soviet Union (CEECs/NIS)
§ Territory
1. These countries and territories will transfer to Part II on 1 January 2003 unless an exception is agreed.

# References


Abbott, K. and D. Snidal (1998) 'Why States Act through Formal International Organisations', *Journal of Conflict Resolution*, Vol. 42, pp. 3–32.

ABD (Aid Book Database) (1999) Statistical annexes on trends in aid flows, prepared by Peter Hjertholm, Development Economics Research Group (DERG), Institute of Economics, University of Copenhagen, available at httm://www.econ.ku.dk/derg/pub.htm

Addison, T. (2000) 'Aid and Conflict', in Tarp (ed.), pp. 392–408.

Adedeji, A. (1995) 'An African Perspective on Bretton Woods', in ul Haq et al.

Adelman, I. (2000) 'The Role of Government in Economic Development', in Tarp (ed.), pp. 48–79.

Akroyd, S. and A. Duncan (1998) 'The Sector Approach and Sustainable Rural Livelihoods', in D. Carney (ed.), *Sustainable Rural Livelihoods: What Contribution Can We Make?*, London: Department for International Development.

Alagapop, M., T. Inoguchi and J.-M. Coicaud (eds) 1998) *The United Nations and the Management of Security Issues*, New York: UN University Press.

Alger, Chadwick F. (ed.) (1998) *The Future of the United Nations System*, New York: UN University Press.

Anderson, M. B. (1996) *Do No Harm: Supporting Local Capacities for Peace through Aid*, Cambridge: Collaborative for Development Action.

Anderson, M. B. and P. J. Woodrow (1989) *Rising from the Ashes*, Boulder, CO and San Francisco, CA: Westview Press and UNESCO.

Annan, Kofi (1997) *Renewing the United Nations: A Programme for Reform. Report of the Secretary-General*, New York: United Nations.

— (1998) *The Causes of Conflict and the Promotion of Durable Peace and Sustainable Development in Africa. Report of the Secretary-General*, New York: United Nations.

Arndt, C. (2000) 'Technical Co-operation', in Tarp (ed.), pp. 154–77.

Ayres, R. L. (1983, *Banking on the Poor: The World Bank and World Poverty*, Cambridge, MA: MIT Press.

Baluch, Bob (1996) 'Poverty, Policy & Aid. Editorial – The New Poverty Agenda: A Disputed Consensus', *IDS Bulletin*, Vol. 27, No. 1.

Barrett, C. B. (1998) 'Food Aid: Is It Development Assistance, Trade Promotion, Both or Neither?', *American Journal of Agricultural Economics*, Vol. 80, No. 3, pp. 566–71.

Bauer, P. T. (1973) *Dissent on Development*, Cambridge, MA: Harvard University Press.

— (1981) *Equality, the Third World, and Economic Delusion*, Cambridge, MA, Harvard University Press.

Baum, Warren C. and Stokes M. Tolbert (1985) *Investing in Development: Lessons of World Bank Experience*, New York: Oxford University Press.

Berg, Elliot J. (1993) *Rethinking Technical Cooperation: Reforms for Capacity Building in Africa*, New York: UNDP and Development Alternatives.

— (1997) 'Dilemmas in Donor Aid Strategies', in Gwin and Nelson.

Bergesen, Helge Ole and Leiv Lunde (1998) *Dinosaurs or Dynamos? The United Nations and the World Bank at the Turn of the Century*, Oslo: Fridtjof Nansen Institute.

Beynon, J. (2001) 'Policy Implications for Aid Allocations of Recent Research on Aid Effectiveness and Selectivity', paper presented at the Joint Development Centre/DAC Experts Seminar on 'Aid Effectiveness, Selectivity and Poor Performers', Paris, OECD, 17 January 2001.

Boone, P. (1994) *The Impact of Foreign Aid on Savings and Growth*, processed, London School of Economics.

— (1996) 'Politics and the Effectiveness of Foreign Aid', *European Economic Review*, Vol. 40, No. 2, pp. 289–329.

Bosch, Margarita (1997) 'NGOs and Development in Brazil: Roles and Responsibilities in a "New World Order"', in Hulme and Edwards, 1997a.

Bossuyt, J., T. Lehtinen, A. Simon, G. Laporte and G. Gorre (2000) 'Assessing Trends in EC Development Cooperation Policy. An Independent Review of the European Commission's External Aid Reform Process', Discussion Paper No. 16, European Centre for Development Policy Management, Maastricht.

Brandt Commission (1980) *North South: A Programme for Survival*, London: Pan Books.

— (1983) *Common Crisis. North South Co-operation for World Recovery*, London: Pan Books.

Branson, W. and C. Jayarajah (1995) *Structural and Sectoral Adjustment: World Bank Experience, 1980–92*, Washington, DC: Operations Evaluation Department, World Bank.

Brundtland, Gro Harlem et al. (1987) *Our Common Future*, Oxford: World Commission on Environment and Development, Oxford University Press.

Buchanan-Smith, M. and S. Maxwell (1994) 'Linking Relief and Development: An Introduction and an Overview', *IDS Bulletin*, Vol. 25, No. 4.

Buira, A. (1996) 'The Governance of the International Monetary Fund', in R. Culpeper and C. Pestieau (eds), *Development and Global Governance*, Ottawa: International Development Research Centre, North–South Institute.

Burnside, Craig and David Dollar (1997) 'Aid, Policies and Growth', Policy Research Working Papers No. 1777, Washington, DC: World Bank.

— (1998) 'Aid, the Incentive Regime, and Poverty Reduction', Policy Research Working Paper No. 1937, Washington, DC: World Bank.

— (2000) 'Aid, Growth, the Incentive Regime and Poverty Reduction', in Gilbert and Vines.

Carlsson, Jerker, Gloria Somolekae and Nicolas van de Walle (eds) (1997) *Foreign Aid in Africa. Learning from Country Experiences*, Uppsala: Nordic Africa Institute.

Carvalho, Soniya and Howard White (1996) *Implementing Projects for the Poor. What Has been learned?*, Washington, DC: World Bank.

Cassen, Robert et al. (1994) *Does Aid Work? Report to an Inter-governmental Task Force*, Oxford: Clarendon Press.

Caufield, Catherine (1997) *Masters of Illusion. The World Bank and the Poverty of Nations*, New York: Henry Holt.

Cernea, Michael (ed.) (1991) *Putting People First: Sociological Variables in Rural Development*, New York: Oxford University Press.

Cerny, Philip G. (1995) 'Globalization and the Changing Logic of Collective Action', *International Organization*, Vol. 49, No. 4.

Chambers, Robert (1997) *Whose Reality Counts? Putting the First Last*, London: Intermediate Technology Publications.

Chambers, Robert et al. (2001) 'The New Dynamics of Aid: Power, Procedures and Relationships', *IDS Policy Briefing*, Issue 15, August 2001.

Chase, R., E. Hill, and P. Kennedy (eds) (1998) *The Pivotal States: A New Framework for US Policy in the Developing World*, New York: W. W. Norton & Co.

Chenery, H. B. and A. M. Strout (1966) 'Foreign Assistance and Economic Development', *American Economic Review*, Vol. 56, No. 4, pp. 679–733.

Chibber, A. (1998) 'Institutions, Policies and Development Outcomes', in R. Picciotto and E. Wiesner (eds), *Evaluation and Development: The Institutional Dimension*, New Brunswick and London: Transaction Publishers (for the World Bank).

Childers, Erskine and Brian Urquhart (1994) *Renewing the United Nations System*, Uppsala: Dag Hammarskjöld Foundation.

Chomsky, N. (1999) *The New Military Humanism: Lessons from Kosovo*, London: Pluto Press.

Cissé, N. D. (1994) 'The Impact of Performance Contracts on Public Enterprise Performance', paper presented at a World Bank conference on 'Changing Role of the State: Strategies for Reforming Public Enterprises', Washington, DC: World Bank.

Clark, John (1991) *Democratizing Development. The Role of Voluntary Organizations*, London: Earthscan Publications.

— (1997) 'The State, Popular Participation and the Voluntary Sector', in Hulme and Edwards, 1997a.

Clarke, W. and J. Herbst (1997) *Learning from Somalia: The Lessons of Armed Humanitarian Intervention*, Boulder, CO: Westview Press.

Clay, E., S. Dhiri and C. Benson (1996) 'Joint Evaluation of European Union Programme Food Aid: Synthesis Report and Summary of Synthesis Report', study commissioned by the Working Group of Heads of Evaluation Service (Development) of the European Union, London, Overseas Development Institute.

Clayton, Andrew (1996) *NGOs, Civil Society and the State: Building Democracy in Transitional Societies*, Oxford: INTRAC.

Colding, B. and P. Pinstrup-Andersen (2000) 'Food Aid as an Aid Instrument: Past, Present and Future', in Tarp (ed.), pp. 195–219.

Collier, Paul (1997a) 'The Failure of Conditionality', in Gwin and Nelson (eds).

— (1997b) 'The Future of MDB Concessional Lending', paper for the Conference on the Future of Multilateral Development Bank Concessional Lending, Overseas Development Council, Washington, DC.

— (2000) 'Conditionality, Dependence and Coordination: Three Current Debates in Aid Policy', in Gilbert and Vines.

Collier, Paul and David Dollar (1999) 'Aid Allocation and Poverty Reduction', Policy Research Working Papers 2041, Washington, DC: World Bank.

— (2001) 'Development Effectiveness: What Have We Learnt?', mimeo, Washington: Development Research Group, World Bank.

Collier, P. and A. Hoeffler (2000) 'Aid, Policy and Peace', first draft, World Bank Research Department.

Collier, Paul et al. (1997) 'Redesigning Conditionality', in *World Development*, Vol. 25, September.

Commission on Global Governance (1995) *Our Global Neighbourhood*, Oxford: Oxford University Press.

Cornia, G. A., R. Jolly and F. Stewart (eds) (1987) *Adjustment with a Human Face. Protecting the Vulnerable and Promoting Growth*, Oxford: Clarendon Press.

COWIconsult (1988a) *Patuakhali and Barguna Area Development Programme, Bangladesh: Identification Report*, Copenhagen: Danida.

— (1988b) *Institutional Aspects of Danish Project Assistance: Issues and Recommendations on Institutional Development*, Copenhagen: Danida.

— (1992) *Institutional Issues in Danida Projects Evaluated During 1990–91*, Copenhagen: Danida.

Cox, A., J. Healey, P. Hoebink and T. Voipio (2000) *European Development Cooperation and the Poor*, Basingstoke: Macmillan.

Cox, Aidan and John Healey (1997) 'Poverty Reduction: A Review of Donor Strategies and Practices', paper for Forum on Key Elements for Poverty Reduction Strategies, OECD Development Centre and Development Assistance Committee, Paris, December 1997.

Cox, Aidan, John Healey and Antonique Koning (1997) *How European Aid Works. A Comparison of Management Systems and Effectiveness*, London and Maastricht: ODI and ECDPM.

Cox, Aidan et al. (1997) *Do the Poor Matter? A Comparative Study of European Aid for Poverty Reduction in India*, Copenhagen: Centre for Development Research (draft).

Cracknell, B. E. (2000) *Evaluating Development Aid: Issues, Problems and Solutions*, New Delhi: Sage Publications.

Cramer, C. and J. Weeks (1998) 'Conditionality and Conflict Reduction', in F. Steward, W. Nafziger and R. Vayrynen (eds), *Economic Causes of Conflict*, Oxford: Oxford University Press.

Culpeper, Roy (ed.) (1997) *The Multilateral Development Banks: Titans or Behemoths?*, Boulder, CO: Lynne Rienner.

Cumming, Gordon (1995) 'French Development Assistance to Africa: Towards a New Agenda?', *African Affairs*, No. 94.

Curry, S. and J. Weiss (1993) *Project Analysis in Developing Countries*, London: Macmillan.

Dahl, Robert A. (1971) *Polyarchy, Participation and Opposition*, New Haven, CT: Yale University Press.

Danida (1988) *Strategisk planlægning. Handlingsplan*, Copenhagen: Udenrigsministeriet/Danida.

— (1991a) *Effectiveness of Multilateral Agencies at Country Level. Case Study of 11 Agencies in Kenya, Nepal, Sudan and Thailand*, Copenhagen: Ministry of Foreign Affairs.

— (1991b) *Effectiveness of Multilateral Agencies at Country Level. European Community in Kenya and Sudan*, Copenhagen: Ministry of Foreign Affairs.

— (1992a) *Evaluation of Danish Assistance to Selected Workers' Education Projects. Synthesis Report*, Copenhagen: Ministry of Foreign Affairs.

— (1992b) *A Future UNIDO. A Study on UNIDO's Comparative Advantages, Areas of Concentration, Organization and Resources*, prepared by COWIconsult and Royal Danish Embassy and UN Mission, Vienna.

— (1994a) *En verden i udvikling. Strategi for dansk udviklingspolitik frem mod år 2000*, Copenhagen: Udenrigsministeriet/Danida.

— (1994b) *Guidelines for Evaluation*, Copenhagen: Ministry of Foreign Affairs/Danida.

— (1996a) *Poverty Reduction in Danish Development Assistance*, Copenhagen: Ministry of Foreign Affairs.

— (1996b) *Plan of Action for Active Multilateralism*, Copenhagen: Ministry of Foreign Affairs.

— (1997) *Assessment of UNIDO. Capacity Development for Sustainable Industrial Development Under Changed Conditions*, Copenhagen: Ministry of Foreign Affairs.

— (1998a) *Guidelines for Sector Programme Support*, Copenhagen: Ministry of Foreign Affairs, May (revised).

— (1998b) *Guidelines for an Output and Outcome Indicator System*, Copenhagen: Ministry of Foreign Affairs.

— (1999) *Evaluation. Danish Support to Promotion of Human Rights and Democratisation* (synthesis report and 8 volumes), Copenhagen: Ministry of Foreign Affairs.

Danish Ministry of Foreign Affairs (2000) *The Multilateral Aid Response to Violent Conflict: More than Linking Relief and Development*, prepared by Centre for Development Research and COWI, Copenhagen.

— (2001) 'Donor Response in Conflict-affected Countries: Implementation Partnerships in Rwanda', issues paper, prepared by Centre for Development Research and COWI, Copenhagen.

Danish Red Cross (1995) *Programming Relief for Development*, workshop proceedings, February 20–22, Danish Red Cross.

De Waal, A. (1997) *Famine Crimes: Politics and the Disaster Relief Industry in Africa*, Oxford: James Currey and Bloomington: Indiana University Press (for Africa Rights and the International Africa Institute).

Degnbol-Martinussen, John (1998) 'Challenges and Opportunities in Danish Development Co-operation', in Bertel Heurlin and Hans Mouritzen, *Danish Foreign Policy Yearbook 1998*, Copenhagen: Danish Institute of International Affairs (DUPI).

— (2001) *Policies, Institutions and Industrial Development: Coping with Liberalisation and International Competition in India*, New Delhi: Sage.

Degnbol-Martinussen, John and Laurids S. Lauridsen (eds) (2001) *Changing Global and Regional Conditions for Development in the Third World*, Roskilde: Roskilde University (Occasional Paper No. 21).

Denning, Stephen (1994) 'Programme Aid beyond Structural Adjustment', Washington, DC: World Bank.

Desai, M. and P. Redfern (eds) (1995), *Global Governance: Ethics and Economics of the World Order*, London and New York: Pinter.

Devarajan, Shantayanan and Vinya Swaroop (2000) 'The Implications of Foreign Aid Fungibility for Development Assistance', in Gilbert and Vines (eds).

DfID (1997) *White Paper. Eliminating World Poverty: A Challenge for the 21st Century*, London.

— (2000) *Departmental Report 2000*, London.

Diehl, Paul Francis (1997) *The Politics of Global Governance: International Organizations in an Interdependent World*, Boulder, CO: Lynne Rienner.

Dollar, David and William Easterly (1998) 'The Search for the Key: Aid, Investment, and Policies in Africa', Washington, DC: Policy Research Working Paper.

Dollar, D. and J. Svensson (2000) 'What Explains the Success or Failure of Structural Adjustment Programs', *Economic Journal*, October.

Doornbos, Martin (1995) 'State Formation Processes under External Supervision: Reflections on "Good Governance"', in Stokke (ed.), 1995.

Duffield, M. (1998) 'Aid Policy and Post-modern ConflIct. A Critical Policy Review', School of Public Policy Discussion Paper, No. 19, University of Birmingham.

— (2001) *Global Governance and the New Wars. The Merging of Development and Security*, London: Zed Books.

ECDPM (European Centre for Development Policy Management) (1996) *Beyond Lomé IV. Exploring Options for Future ACP–EU Cooperation*, Policy Management Report No. 6, Maastricht.

— (2001) *Cotonou Infokit. The New ACP–EU Partnership Agreement.*

ECOSOC (1997) *Operational Activities of the UN for International Development Cooperation: Follow-up to Policy Recommendations of the General Assembly*, E/1997/65, New York, 3 June.

Edkins, J. (1996) 'Legality with a Vengeance: Famines and Humanitarian Relief in "Complex Emergencies"', in *Millennium*, Vol. 25, No. 3, pp. 547–76.

Edwards, Michael and David Hulme (1992) 'Scaling up NGO Impact on Development: Learning from Experience', *Development in Practice*, Vol. 2, No. 2 (June).

Eichengreen, B. and P. Kenen (1994) 'Managing the World Economy under the Bretton Woods System: An Overview', in Kenen (ed.).

Engberg-Pedersen, Poul (1982) *The United Nations and Political Intervention in International Economic Processes. The Case of Technology Transfer*, Centre for Development Research, Research Report No. 1, Copenhagen.

Engberg-Pedersen, Poul and Ted Freeman (1992) *Strategic Choices for UNICEF: Service Delivery, Capacity Building, Empowerment*, Evaluation of UNICEF, Synthesis Report, prepared for the Governments of Australia, Canada, Denmark and Switzerland.

— (1994) *Aid Coordination and Aid Management by Government: A Role for UNDP*, prepared for UNDP Policy Division, New York, August.

Engberg-Pedersen, Poul, John Degnbol-Martinussen and Ted Freeman (1996) *Assessment of UNDP: Developing Capacity for Sustainable Human Development*, prepared for Danida, Centre for Development Research, Copenhagen.

Engberg-Pedersen, Poul et al. (eds) (1996) *Limits of Adjustment in Africa: The Effects of Economic Liberalization, 1986–94*, Centre for Development Research, Oxford: James Currey, London: Heinemann.

European Commission (1996) *Linking Relief and Development*, Bruxelles.

— (1997) *Green Paper on Relations between the European Union and the ACP Countries on the Eve of the 21st Century. Challenges and Options for a New Partnership*, Luxembourg.

Fagen, Patricia Weiss (1995) *After the Conflict. A Review of Selected Sources on Rebuilding War-torn Societies*, Geneva: UNRISD, War-torn Societies Project, Occasional Paper No. 1.

Ferreira, Francisco H. G. and Louise C. Keely (2000) 'The World Bank and Structural Adjustment: Lessons from the 1980s', in Gilbert and Vines (eds).

Folke, S. et al. (2001) *Aid Impact: Development Interventions and Societal Processes*, Research Programme 2001–2004, Copenhagen: Centre for Development Research.

Forss, K., J. Carlsen, E. Froyland, T. Sitari and K. Vilby (1990) *Evaluation of the Effectiveness of Technical Assistance Personnel Financed by Nordic Countries*, Copenhagen: Ministry of Foreign Affairs.

Forster, Jacques and Olav Stokke (eds) (1999) *Policy Coherence in Development Co-operation*, London: Frank Cass in association with EADI.

Fowler, Alan (1997) *Striking a Balance. A Guide to Enhancing the Effectiveness of Non-Governmental Organisations in International Development*, London: Earthscan.

— (ed.) (2000) 'Questioning Partnership: The Reality of Aid and NGO Relations', *IDS Bulletin*, Vol. 31, No. 3.

Fowler, Alan and Kees Biekart (1996) 'Do Private Agencies Really Make a Difference?', in Sogge (ed.).

Fox, J. A. and L. D. Brown (1998) *The Struggle for Accountability: The World Bank, NGOs, and Grassroots Movements*, Cambridge MA: MIT Press.

Franz, W. E. (1996) 'The Scope of Global Environmental Financing: Cases in Context', in R. O. Keohane and M. A. Levy (eds), *Institutions for Environmental Aid: Pitfalls and Promise*, Cambridge, MA: MIT Press.

Frey, B. S. (1997) 'The Public Choice of International Organizations', in D. C. Mueller, *Perspectives on Public Choice. A Handbook*, New York: Cambridge University Press.

Friedmann, John (1992) *Empowerment. The Politics of Alternative Development*, Cambridge, MA: Blackwell.

Fukuda-Parr, S. (1996) 'Beyond Rethinking Technical Co-operation: Priorities for Capacity Building and Capacity Utilisation in Africa', *International Journal of Technical Co-operation*, Vol. 2, No. 2, pp. 145–7.

Ganuza, E. and M. Lundahl (eds) (1995) *Är Sveriges bistånd effektivt?*, Stockholm: SNS Förlag.

George, S. and F. Sabelli (1994) *Faith and Credit: The World Bank's Secular Empire*, London: Penguin.

Gilbert, Christopher L. and David Vines (eds) (2000) *The World Bank. Structure and Policies*, Cambridge: Cambridge University Press.

Gilbert, Christopher L., Andrew Powell and David Vines (2000) 'Positioning the World Bank', in Gilbert and Vines (eds).

Gourevitch, P. (1998) *We Wish to Inform You that Tomorrow We Will be Killed with Our Families: Stories from Rwanda*, New York: Farrar, Straus and Giroux.

Gran, Guy (1983) *Development by People. Citizen Construction of a Just World*, New York: Praeger.

Grant, R. and J. Nijman (eds) (1998) *The Global Crisis in Foreign Aid*, Syracuse: Syracuse University Press.

Green, Reginal Herbold and John Toye (1996) *Multilateral Development Bank Concessional Lending. Forward into the Second Half Century*, Sussex: Institute of Development Studies.

Griesgraber, J. M. and B. Gunter (eds) (1995) *Promoting Development – Effective Global Institutions for the Twenty-first Century*, London: Pluto Press.

— (1996) *The World Bank: Lending on a Global Scale*, London: Pluto Press.

Griffin, Keith (1991) 'Foreign Aid After the Cold War', *Development and Change*, Vol. 22, No. 4.

Griffin, Keith and Terry McKinley (1996) *New Approaches to Development Cooperation*, New York: UNDP, Office of Development Studies.

Grindle, M. S. and M. E. Hilderbrand (1995) 'Building Sustainable Capacity in the Public Sector: What Can be Done?', *Public Administration and Development*, Vol. 15, No. 5, pp. 441–63.

Guba, Egon G. and Yvonna S. Lincoln (1989) *Fourth Generation Evaluation*, Newbury Park: Sage Publications.

Gwin, C. and J. M. Nelson (eds) (1997) *Perspectives on Aid and Development*, OCD Policy Essay 22, Washington, DC: Overseas Development Council.

Hamburg, David A. and Jane E. Holl (1999) 'Preventing Deadly Conflict: From Global Housekeeping to Neighbourhood Watch', in Kaul, Stern and Grunberg (eds).

Hanmer, L., G. Pyatt and H. White (1996) *Poverty in Sub-Saharan Africa: What Can We Learn from the World Bank's Poverty Assessments?*, The Hague: Institute of Social Studies.

Hanna, N. (2000) 'Implementation Challenges and Promising Approaches for the Comprehensive Development Framework', OED Working Paper Series, No. 13, Washington, DC: World Bank, Summer.

Hansen, Henrik and Finn Tarp (2000) 'Aid Effectiveness Disputed', *Journal of International Development*, Vol. 12, pp. 375–98.

Haq, Mahbub ul (1995) *Reflections on Human Development*, New York: Oxford University Press.

Haq, M. ul, R. Jolly, P. Streeton and K. Haq (1995) *The UN and the Bretton Woods Institutions: New Challenges for the Twenty-first Centruy*, London: Macmillan.

Hayek, Friedrich (1976) 'The Mirage of Social Justice', in *Law, Legislation and Liberty*, Vol. II, London: Routledge and Kegan Paul.

Hayter, Teresa (1971) *Aid as Imperialism*, Harmondsworth: Penguin.

Hayter, T. and C. Watson (1985) *Aid: Rhetoric and Reality*, London: Pluto Press.

Healey, John (1996) 'British Programme Aid: Changing Orientations', *IDS Bulletin*, Vol. 27, No. 4.

Heijden, H. van der (1987) 'The Reconciliation of NGO Autonomy, Program Integrity and Operational Effectiveness with Accountability to Donors', *World Development*, 1987.

Hendrickson, D. (1998) 'Humanitarian Action in Protracted Crises: An Overview of the Debates and Dilemmas', in *Disasters*, Vol. 22, No. 4.

Hirst, Paul and Grahame Thompson (1996) *Globalization in Question. The International Economy and the Possibilities of Governance*, Cambridge: Polity Press.

Hjertholm, Peter and Howard White (2000) 'Foreign Aid in Historical Perspective: Background and Trends', in Tarp (ed.).

Hook, S. W. (ed.) (1996) *Foreign Aid. Toward the Millenium*, London: Lynne Rienner Publications.

Hopkins, R. F. (2000) 'Political Economy of Foreign Aid', in Tarp (ed.), pp. 423–49.

Hopkins, Raul, Andrew Powell, Amlan Roy and Christopher L. Gilbert (2000) 'The World Bank, Conditionality and the Comprehensive Development Framework', in Gilbert and Vines (eds).

Howell, Jude (1995) 'Prospects for NGOs in China', *Development in Practice*, Vol. 5, No. 1.

Hulme, David and Michael Edwards (eds) (1997a) *NGOs, States and Donors. Too Close for Comfort?*, Houndmills: Macmillan in association with Save the Children.

— (1997b) 'NGOs, States and Donors. An Overview', in Hulme and Edwards (eds), 1997a.

Huther, J., S. Roberts and A. Shah (1998) *Public Expenditure Reform under Adjustment Lending: Lessons from World Bank Experience*, World Bank Discussion Papers 382, Washington, DC.

IDS (1993) 'The Emergence of the 'Good Government' Agenda: Some Milestones', *IDS Bulletin*, Vol. 24, No. 1.

— (1996) 'Poverty, Policy and Aid', *IDS Bulletin*, Vol. 26, No. 1.

— (1998) 'The Bank, the State and Development', *IDS Bulletin*, Vol. 29, No. 2.

IFRC (2001) *World Disasters Report 2001. Focus on Recovery*, Geneva.

ILO (1973) *Employment, Income and Equality: A Strategy for Increasing Productive Employment in Kenya*, Geneva: International Labour Organization.

— (1977) *The Basic Needs Approach to Development*, Geneva: International Labour Organization.

IMF (1998) *Finance and Developent*, March, Washington, DC.

Inukai, Ichiro (1993) 'Why Aid and Why Not? Japan and Sub-Saharan Africa', in Koppel and Orr (eds).

Iqbal, Z. and R. Kanbur (eds) (1997) *External Finance in Low-Income Countries*, Washington, DC: International Monetary Fund.

Isham, Jonathan and Daniel Kaufmann (2000a) 'How Policies and Institutions Affect Project Performance: Microeconomic Evidence on Aid, Policies and Investment Productivity', in Gilbert and Vines (eds).

— (2000) 'The Forgotten Rationale for Policy Reform: The Impact on Projects', *Quarterly Journal of Economics*.

Islam, Shafiqul (ed.) (1991) *Yen for Development. Japanese Foreign Aid and the Politics of Burden-Sharing*, New York: Council of Foreign Relations Press.

Jackson, R. G. A. (1969) *A Study of the Capacity of the United Nations Development System*, Geneva: United Nations.

Jayarajah, C. and W. Branson (1995) *Structural and Sectoral Adjustment: World Bank Experience, 1980–92*, a World Bank Operations Evaluation Study, Washington, DC: World Bank.

Jayarajah, C., W. Branson and B. Sen (1996) *Social Dimensions of Adjustment: World Bank Experience, 1980–93*, a World Bank Operations Evaluation Study, Washington, DC: World Bank.

Jepma, Catrinus J. (1991) *The Tying of Aid*, Paris: OECD Development Centre.

Jones, S. (1997a) 'Sector Investment Programs in Africa: Issues and Experience', World Bank Technical Paper, 374.

— (1997b) *Sector Investment Programmes in Sub-Saharan Africa: Review of Issues and Experience*, Oxford: Oxford Policy Management.

— (2000) 'Increasing Aid Effectiveness in Africa? The World Bank and Sector Investment Programmes', in Gilbert and Vines (eds).

Kahler, Miles (1995) *International Institutions and the Political Economy of Integration*, Washington, DC: Brookings Institution.

Kaldor, M. (1999) *New and Old Wars: Organised Violence in a Global Era*, Cambridge: Polity Press.

Kanbur, Ravi (1999) 'Prospective and Retrospective Conditionality: Practicalities and Fundamentals', in P. Collier and C. Pattillo (eds), *Investment and Risk in Africa*, Basingstoke: Macmillan.

— (2000) 'Aid, Conditionality and Debt in Africa', in Tarp (ed.), pp. 409–22.

Kanbur, Ravi and David Vines (2000) 'The World Bank and Poverty Reduction: Past, Present and Future', in Gilbert and Vines (eds).

Kapur, D., J. P. Lewis and R. Webb (1997a) *The World Bank: Its First Half Century, 1: History*, Washington, DC: Brookings Institution.

— (1997b) *The World Bank: Its First Half Century, 2: Perspectives*, Washington, DC: Brookings Institution.

Kaul, Inge, Marc Stern and Isabelle Grunberg (1998) *Re-engineering International Development Co-operation and Finance*, New York: Office of Development Studies, UNDP.

— (eds) (1999) *Global Public Goods: International Cooperation in the Twenty First Century*, New York, Oxford University Press.

Kayizzi-Mugerwa, S., A. O. Olukoshi and L. Wohlgemuth (eds) (1998) *Towards a New Partnership with Africa. Challenges and Opportunities*, Uppsala: Nordic Africa Institute.

Kenen, Peter B. (ed.) (1994) *Managing the World Economy. Fifty Years After Bretton Woods*, Washington, DC: Institute for International Economics.

Keohane, R. (1998) 'International Institutions: Can Interdependence Work', *Foreign Policy*, 110 (Spring), pp. 82–96.

Khan, H. A. and E. Hoshino (1992) 'Impact of Foreign Aid on the Fiscal Behaviour of LDC Governments', *World Development*, Vol. 20, No. 10, pp. 1481–8.

Khan, Mushtaq H. (1996) 'A Typology of Corrupt Transactions in Developing Countries', *IDS Bulletin*, Vol. 27, No. 2.

Killick, Tony (1997) 'What Future for Aid?', in *Finance for Sustainable Development: The Road Ahead*, New York: United Nations.

— (1998) *Aid and the Political Economy of Policy Reform*, London and New York: Routledge.

Knack, S. (2001) 'Aid Dependence and the Quality of Governance: Cross-Country Empirical Tests', mimeo, Development Research Group, World Bank.

Koning, A. (1995) *Strengths and Weaknesses in the Management of the European Development Fund*, Maastricht: Working Paper No. 8, ECDPM.

Koppel, Bruce M. and Robert M. Orr (eds) (1993) *Japan's Foreign Aid. Power and Policy in a New Era*, Boulder, CO: Westview Press.

Korten, David C. (1987) 'Third Generation NGO Strategies: A Key to People-centered Development', *World Development*.

— (1990) *Getting to the 21st Century: Voluntary Action and the Global Agenda*, West Hartford, CT: Kumarian Press.

Krueger, A. (1997) *The World Trade Organisation: Its Effectiveness as an Institution*, Chicago, IL: University of Chicago Press.

Kruse, S.-E. et al. (1997) *Searching for Impact and Methods: NGO Evaluation Synthesis Study*, a report prepared for the OECD/DAC Expert Group on Evaluation, Helsinki: Ministry for Foreign Affairs.

Kumar, K. (1998) 'Postconflict Elections and International Assistance', in K. Kumar (ed.), *Postconflict Elections, Democratization and International Assistance*, Boulder, CO and London: Lynne Rienner.

Lancaster, C. (1999) *Foreign Aid and Development in Africa*, Chicago, IL: University of Chicago Press.

Landell-Mills, Pierre and Ismail Serageldin (1991) 'Governance and the Development Process', *Finance and Development*, September.

Lappé, Frances Moore, Rachel Schurman and Kevin Danaher (1987) *Betraying the National Interest*, New York: Grove Press.

Lateef, K. Sarwar (ed.) (1995) *The Evolving Role of the World Bank. Helping Meet the Challenge of Development*, Washington, DC: World Bank.

Lehtinen, Terhi (2000) 'Reforming European Development Cooperation: What Do the Practitioners Think?', ECDPM Discussion Paper No. 23, March.

Lele, Uma and Ijaz Nabi (eds) (1991) *Transitions in Development. The Role of Aid and Commercial Flows*, San Francisco, CA: ICS Press.

Lensink, R. and H. White (1999) 'Assessing Aid: A Manifesto for the 21st Century?', A SIDA Evaluation Report, Stockholm: 99/17:13.

Lipton, Michael and John Toye (1991) *Does Aid Work in India? A Country Study of the Impact of Official Development Assistance*, London: Routledge.

Little, I. M. D. and J. Mirrlees (1974) *Project Appraisal and Planning for Developing Countries*, New York: Basic Books.

Long, Norman and Ann Long (eds) (1992) *Battlefields of Knowledge: The Interlocking of Theory and Practice in Social Research and Development*, London: Routledge.

Macrae, Joanna and Anthony Zwi (eds) (1994) *War and Hunger. Rethinking International Responses to Complex Emergencies*, London: Zed Books, Save the Children (UK).

Maddison, Angus (1971) *Class Structure and Economic Growth. India and Pakistan since the Moghuls*, London: George Allen & Unwin.

Marcussen, Henrik Secher (1996) 'Comparative Advantages of NGOs: Myths and Realities', in Stokke (ed.).

Maren, M. (1997) *The Road to Hell: The Ravaging Effects of Foreign Aid and International Charity*, New York: Free Press.

Marsden, David and Peter Oakley (eds) (1990) *Evaluating Social Development Projects*, Oxford: Oxfam.

Martinussen, John (1996) 'Empowerment of Labour. A Study of ILO-assisted Activities in Support of Third World Trade Unions', in Rudebeck and Törnquist (eds).

— (1997) *Society, State and Market. A Guide to Competing Theories of Development*, London and New Jersey: Zed Books.

— (1998) 'The Limitations of the World Bank's Conception of the State and the Implications for Institutional Development Strategies', *IDS Bulletin*, Vol. 29, No. 2.

Marzouk, Mohsen (1997) 'The Associative Phenomenon in the Arab World: Engine of Democratisation or Witness to the Crisis?', in Hulme and Edwards (eds).

Mason, Edward S. and Robert E. Asher (1973) *The World Bank Since Bretton Woods*, Washington, DC: Brookings Institution.

McGillivray, M. (1999) 'Aid and Public Sector Fiscal Behaviour in Developing Countries', *Review of Development Economics*, Vol. 4, No. 2.

McGillivray, M. and O. Morrissey (2000) 'Aid Fungibility', in 'Assessing Aid: Red Herring or True Concern?', *Journal of International Development*, Vol. 12, No. 3, pp. 413–28.

Meadows, D. H. et al. (1972) *The Limits to Growth*, New York: Basic Books.

Meier, Gerald M. (1989) *Leading Issues in Economic Development*, New York: Oxford University Press.

Mendez, Ruben P. (1999) 'Peace as a Global Public Good', in Kaul, Grunberg and Stern (eds).

Montes, C. and S. Migliorsi (1998) 'Evaluation of European Union Aid (Managed by the Commission) to ACP Countries', Synthesis Report, Brussels.

Moore, Mick (1995) *Institution Building as a Development Assistance Method. A Review of Literature and Ideas*, Stockholm: SIDA.

Moore, Mick (1998) 'Toward a Useful Consensus?', *IDS Bulletin*, Vol. 29, No. 2.

Mosley, Paul (1986) 'Aid Effectiveness: The Micro-Macro Paradox', *IDS Bulletin*, Vol. 17.

— (1997) *Overseas Aid as a Public Good*, Discussion Papers in Economics and Management No. 355, University of Reading.

Mosley, P. and M. J. Eeckhout (2000) 'From Project Aid to Programme Assistance', in Tarp (ed.), pp. 131–53.

Mosley, Paul and John Hudson (1995) *Aid Effectiveness: A Study of the Effectiveness of Overseas Aid in the Main Countries Receiving ODA*, report to the Overseas Development Administration, London.

— (1996) *Effectiveness of Overseas Aid Flows: A Study of 29 ACP Countries*, report to the Commission of the European Communities, Brussels.

— (1997) *Aid Effectiveness: Tests of the Robustness of Macro Relationships*, Discussion Papers in Development Economics, No. 31, University of Reading.

Mosley, Paul, Jane Harrigan and John Toye (1995) *Aid and Power. The World Bank and Policy-based Lending*, Vols 1–2, London and New York: Routledge.

Mustafa, S. et al. (1996) *Beacon of Hope. An Impact Assessment Study of BRAC's Rural Development Programme*, Dhaka: BRAC Research and Evaluation Division.

Myrdal, Gunnar (1968) *Asian Drama. An Inquiry into the Poverty of Nations*, Harmondsworth: Penguin.

Naim, M. (1994) 'From Supplicants to Shareholders: Developing Countries and the World Bank', in United Nations (1994) *International Monetary and Financial Issues for the 1990s*, Vol. IV, New York.

Nelson, P. (1995) *The World Bank and Non-governmental Organisations: The Limits of Apolitical Development*, London: Macmillan.

Nordic UN Project (1991) *The United Nations in Development. Reform Issues in the Economic and Social Field. A Nordic Perspective*, Stockholm: Almqvist & Wiksell.

— (1996) *The United Nations in Development. Strengthening the UN Through Change: Fulfilling Its Economic and Social Mandate*, Oslo.

Nozick, Robert (1974) *Anarchy, State and Utopia*, Oxford: Blackwell.

Oakley, Peter (1999) *The Danish NGO Impact Study. A Review of Danish NGO Activities in Developing Countries. Overview Report*, Copenhagen: Danida.

ODI (1998) *The UK White Paper on International Development – and Beyond*, London.

OECD (1991) *Principles for New Orientations in Technical Co-operation*, Paris.

— (1992) *Development Assistance Manual: DAC Principles for Effective Aid*, Paris.

— (1996) *Shaping the 21st Century: The Contribution of Development Co-operation*, Paris.

— (1999a) *DAC On-line Database*, Paris. Available at http://www.oecd.org/dac

— (1999b) *DAC Scoping Study of Donor Poverty Reduction Policies and Practice: Synthesis Report*, Paris.

— (2001) *Development Cooperation 2000*, Paris.

OECD Development Centre (1996) *Public Support for International Development*, ed. Colm Foy and Henny Helmich, Paris.

OECD/DAC (1996) *Development Co-operation. 1995 Report*, Paris.

— (1997) *Development Co-operation. 1996 Report*, Paris.

— (1998) *Development Co-operation. 1997 Report*, Paris.

— (2000) *Development Co-operation. 1999 Report, The DAC Journal*, Vol. 1, No. 1, Paris.

— (2001) *Development Co-operation. 2000 Report, The DAC Journal*, Vol. 2, No. 1, Paris.

— France (1997) *Development Co-operation Review Series. France*, Paris.

— France (2000) *Development Co-operation Review Series. France*, Paris.

— Japan (1996) *Development Co-operation Review Series. Japan*, Paris.

— Japan (1999) *Development Co-operation Review Series. Japan*, Paris.

— United Kingdom (1994) *Development Co-operation Review Series. United Kingdom*, Paris.

— United Kingdom (1997) *Development Co-operation Review Series. United Kingdom*, Paris.

— USA (1995) *Development Co-operation Review Series. United States*, Paris.

OECF, Japan, and World Bank (1998) *A New Vision of Development Cooperation for the 21st Century*, proceedings of a symposium held in Tokyo, September 1997, Tokyo and Washington, DC.

Olsen, G. R. (2001) 'European Public Opinion and Aid to Africa: Is There a Link?', *Journal of Modern African Studies*, Vol. 39, No. 4.

Oman, Charles (1994) *Globalisation and Regionalisation: The Challenge for Developing Countries*, Paris: OECD.

Paldam, Martin (1997) *Dansk u-landshjælp. Altruismens politiske økonomi*, Aarhus Universitetsforlag.

Parpart, J. L., S. M. Rai and K. A. Staudt (eds) (2000) *Rethinking Empowerment and Development in a Global/Local World: Gendered Perspectives*, London and New York: Routledge.

Parsons, A. (1995) *From Cold War to Hot Peace: UN Interventions 1947–1995*, London: Penguin.

Pearce, Jenny (1997) 'Between Co-option and Irrelevance? Latin American NGOs in the 1990s', in Hulme and Edwards (eds), 1997a.

Pearson, Lester (1969) Commission on International Development, *Partners in Development*, London: Pall Mall Press.

Pope, Jeremy (ed.) (1997) *National Integrity Systems. The TI Source Book*, Berlin: Transparency International (second edn).

Raffer, Kunibert and H. W. Singer (1996) *The Foreign Aid Business. Economic Assistance and Development Co-operation*, Cheltenham: Edward Elgar.

Ramsbotham, O. and T. Woodhouse (1996) *Humanitarian Intervention in Contemporary Conflict*, Cambridge: Polity Press.

Rathgeber, Eva M. (1990) 'WID, WAD, GAD: Trends in Research and Practice', *Journal of Developing Areas*, Vol. 24, No. 4.

Ravallion, Martin and Shaohua Chen (1997) 'What Can New Survey Data Tell Us About Recent Changes in Distribution and Poverty?', in *The World Bank Economic Review*, Vol. 11, No. 2.

Ray, H. N. (1996) *The World Bank. A Third World View*, New Delhi: Indus Publishing.

Reality of Aid Project (1997–98) *The Reality of Aid 1997–98. An Independent Review of Development Cooperation*, London: Earthscan.

— (2000) *The Reality of Aid 2000. An Independent Review of Poverty Reduction and Development Assistance*, London: Earthscan.

Rebien, Claus C. (1996) *Evaluating Development Assistance in Theory and Practice*, Aldershot: Avebury.

Reilly, B. and A. Reynolds (1999) *Electoral Systems and Conflict in Divided Societies*, Washington, DC: National Academy Press.

Reilly, J. E. (ed.) (1999) *American Public Opinion and US Foreign Policy 1999*, Chicago, IL: Chicago Council on Foreign Relations.

Reno, W. (1998) *Warlord Politics and African States*, Boulder, CO: Lynne Rienner.

Richey, Lisa Ann (2000) 'Gender Equality and Foreign Aid', in Tarp (ed.).

Riddell, Roger C. (1987) *Foreign Aid Reconsidered*, London: ODI/James Currey.

— (1995) *Enhancing the Impact of Aid beyond the Confines of Discrete Projects*, Stockholm: Overseas Development Institute, for SIDA.

— (1996) *Aid in the 21st Century*, New York: UNDP, Office of Development Studies.

Riddell, Roger C. et al. (1997) *Searching for Impact and Methods: NGO Evaluation Synthesis Study*, Helsinki: Ministry of Foreign Affairs (a report prepared for the OECD/DAC Expert Group on Evaluation).

Rittberger, Volker (ed.) (1993) *Regime Theory and International Relations*, Oxford: Clarendon Press.

Rix, Alan (1993) *Japan's Foreign Aid Challenge. Policy Reform and Aid Leadership*, London: Routledge.

Roche, Chris (1999) *Impact Assessment for Development Agencies. Learning to Value Change*, Oxford: Oxfam GB with Novib.

Rodrik, D. (1999) *The New Global Economy and Developing Countries: Making Openness Work*, ODC Policy Essay 24, Washington, DC: Overseas Development Council.

Rosenstein-Rodan, Paul (1957) 'Notes on "the Big Push"' in Meier, pp. 281 ff.

Rostow, W. W. (1956) 'The Take-Off into Self-Sustained Growth', *Economic Journal* 66 (March), pp. 25–48.

— (1960) *The Stages of Growth*, Cambridge: Cambridge University Press.

Rowlands, J. (1997) *Questioning Empowerment: Working with Women in Honduras*, Oxford: Oxfam.

Rudebeck, Lars and Olle Törnquist (1996) *Democratisation in the Third World. Concrete Cases in Comparative and Theoretical Perspective*, Uppsala University.

Ruggie, Gerard (ed.) (1993) *Multilateralism Matters*, New York: Columbia.

Ruttan, V. W. (1996) *United States Development Assistance Policy*, Baltimore, MD: Johns Hopkins University Press.

Sahn, D. E. (1994) 'The Impact of Macroeconomic Adjustment on Incomes, Health and Nutrition: Sub-Saharan Africa in the 1980s', in G. A. Cornia and G. K. Helleiner (eds), *From Adjustment to Development in Africa: Conflict, Controversy, Convergence, Consensus?*, New York: St Martin's Press and Basingstoke: Macmillan.

Sandler, Todd (1997) *Global Challenges: An Approach to Environmental, Political, and Economic Problems*, Cambridge: Cambridge University Press.

Schraeder, P. J., S. W. Hook and B. Taylor (1998) 'Clarifying the Foreign Aid Puzzle: A Comparison of American, Japanese, French and Swedish Flows', *World Politics*, Vol. 50, No. 2, pp. 294–323.

Schulpen, L. and P. Gibbon (2001) *Private Sector Development. Policies, Practices and Problems*, CDR Policy Paper, Centre for Development Research, Copenhagen.

Schumpeter, Joseph A. (1934) *The Theory of Economic Development*, Cambridge, MA: Harvard University Press.

Scott, C. V. (1995) *Gender and Development: Rethinking Modernization and Dependency Theory*, Boulder, CO and London: Lynne Rienner.

Seligson, M. A. and J. T. Passe-Smith (eds) (1998) *Development and Underdevelopment: The Political Economy of Global Inequality*, Boulder, CO: Lynne Rienner.

Sen, Amartya (1999) *Development as Freedom*, Oxford: Oxford University Press.

Serageldin, Ismail (1995) *Nurturing Development: Aid and Cooperation in Today's Changing World*, Washington, DC: World Bank.

SIDA (1994) *Evaluation Manual for SIDA* (by Elisabeth Lewin), Stockholm: SIDA.

— (1997) *Development Cooperation in the 21st Century*, Stockholm: SIDA.

Singer, Hans W. and Richard Jolly (eds) (1995) *Fifty Years On: The UN and Economic and Social Development*, *IDS Bulletin*, Vol. 26, No. 4.

Smilie, Ian (1996) 'Mixed Messages: Public Opinion and Development Assistance in the 1990s', in OECD Development Centre.

Sogge, David (ed. with Kees Biekart and John Saxby) (1996) *Compassion and Calculation. The Business of Private Foreign Aid*, London: Pluto Press with Transnational Institute.

Sørbø, Gunnar M. and Peter Vale (eds), *Out of Conflict. From War to Peace in Africa*, Uppsala: Nordic Africa Institute.

South Commission (1990) *The Challenge to the South. The Report of the South Commission*, Oxford: Oxford University Press.

Squire, Lyn (2000) 'Why the World Bank Should be Involved in Development Research', in Gilbert and Vines (eds).

Squire, L. and H. G. van der Tak (1975) *Economic Analysis of Projects*, Baltimore, MD and London: Johns Hopkins and the World Bank.

Stepputat, Finn (1994) *Efter nødhjælpen - fra katastrofe til udvikling?*, CUF Notat, Center for Udviklingsforskning, September.

Stern, Marc (1998) *Development Aid: What the Public Thinks*, Office of Development Studies, Bureau for Development Policy, UNDP, New York, May.

Stewart, Frances (1998) 'Food Aid During Conflict: Can One Reconcile Its Humanitarian, Economic, and Political Economy Effects?', *American Journal of Agricultural Economics*, Vol. 80, No. 3, pp. 560–5.

— (1995) *Adjustment and Poverty: Options and Choices*, New York: Routledge.

Stiglitz, Joseph E. (1998) *More Instruments and Broader Goals: Moving Toward the Post-Washington Consensus*, WIDER Annual Lectures 2, Helsinki, World Institute for Development Economics Research.

— (1999) 'Knowledge as a Global Public Good', in Kaul, Grunberg and Stern (eds), 1999.

— (2000) 'Introduction', in Gilbert and Vines (eds).

Stokke, Olav (ed.) (1989) *Western Middle Powers and Global Poverty. The Determinants of the Aid Policies of Canada, Denmark, the Netherlands, Norway and Sweden*, Uppsala: Scandinavian Institute of African Studies.

— (ed.) (1991) *Evaluating Development Assistance. Policies and Performance*, London, Frank Cass/EADI.

— (ed.) (1995) *Aid and Political Conditionality*, London: Frank Cass/EADI.

— (ed.) (1996) *Foreign Aid Towards the Year 2000: Experiences and Challenges*, London: Frank Cass/EADI.

Subbarao, K. et al. (1997) *Safety Net Programs and Poverty Reduction: Lessons from Cross Country Experience*, Washington, DC: World Bank.

Suhrke, Astri et al. (1997) *Humanitarian Assistance and Conflict*, Bergen: Chr. Michelsen Institute.

Sultana, Parvin and Steen Folke (1999) *Project Impact at the Local Level. A Study of LIFT-Patuakhali*, Copenhagen: Danida (Danish NGO Impact Study, Bangladesh In-depth Study).

Takayanagi, Akio (1997) 'Japan', in Reality of Aid Project, 1997–98.

Tarp, Finn (ed.) (2000) *Foreign Aid and Development: Lessons Learnt and Directions for the Future*, London: Routledge.

Taylor, L. (ed.) (1993) *The Rocky Road to Reform: Adjustment, Income Distribution, and Growth in the Developing World*, Cambridge, MA: MIT Press.

Theobald, Robin (1990) *Corruption, Development and Underdevelopment*, London: Macmillan.

Therkildsen, O., P. Engberg-Pedersen, J. Boesen (1999) 'Sector Support: From Policy Making to Implementation Processes', *Aid Policy and Practice. An Issue Paper from the CDR*, Copenhagen: Centre for Development Research.

Thorbecke, E. (2000) 'The Evolution of the Development Doctrine and the Role of Foreign Aid, 1950–2000', in Tarp (ed.), pp. 17–47.

Tomasevski, Katarina (1997) *Between Sanctions and Elections. Aid Donors and Their Human Rights Performance*, London: Pinter.

Toye, John and C. Jackson (1996) *Public Expenditure and Poverty Reduction: Has the World Bank Got It Right?*, Brighton: Institute of Development Studies.

Udsholt, Lars (1996) *Danish Aid Policies for Poverty Reduction*, Copenhagen: Centre for Development Research.

UN (1995) *The Copenhagen Declaration and Programme of Action*, New York: United Nations.

UNDP (1994) *Human Development Report 1994*, New York: Oxford University Press.

— (1995) *Human Development Report 1995*, New York: Oxford University Press.

— (1996) *Human Development Report 1996*, New York: Oxford University Press.

— (1997a) *Capacity Development*, Technical Advisory Paper 2, Management Development and Governance Division, New York.

— (1997b) *General Guidelines for Capacity Assessment and Development*, Management Development and Governance Division, New York.

— (1997c) *Human Development Report 1997*, New York: Oxford University Press.

UN General Assembly (1995) *Triennial Policy Review of Operational Activities for Development of the United Nations System*, Resolution No. 50/120, 20 December.

— (2001) A/55/1000: 'Report of the High-level Panel on Financing for Development', New York, 26 June.

USAID (2000) *Agency Performance Report 1999*, Washington, DC: Center for Development Information and Evaluation.

Uvin, P. (1998) *Aiding Violence: The Development Enterprise in Rwanda*, West Hartford, CT: Kumarian Press.

Waal, Nicholas van de and Timothy Johnston (1996) *Improving Aid to Africa*, Policy Essay No. 21, Overseas Development Council, Washington, DC.

Wallensteen, P. and M. Sollenberg (1997) 'The End of International War? Armed Conflict 1989–1996', *Journal of Peace Research*, Vol. 34, No. 3, pp. 339–58.

Watkins, Kevin (1994) 'Aid Under Threat', *Review of African Political Economy*, No. 66.

Weiss, T. (1999) *Military–Civilian Interactions: Intervening in Humanitarian Crises*, Lanham, MD: Rowman and Littlefield.

Weiss, T. and C. Collins (1996) *Humanitarian Challenges and Intervention: World Politics and the Dilemmas of Help*, Boulder, CO: Westview Press.

Weiss, T. G. and L. Gordenker (eds) (1996) *NGOs, the UN, and Global Governance*, Boulder, CO and London: Lynne Reinner.

Wheat, Sue (2000) 'What are NGOs Doing Here?', *Courier*, Issue 181 (June/July).

White, Howard (1999a) *Swedish Programme Aid: An Evaluation*, Stockholm: Swedish International Development Co-operation Agency.

— (1999b) 'Aid and Economic Reform', in S. Kayizzi-Mugerwa (ed.), *The African Economy*, London and New York: Routledge.

— (1999c) *Dollars, Dialogue and Development. An Evaluation of Swedish Programme Aid*, Stockholm: Swedish International Development Co-operation Agency

White, H. and J. Leavy (1999) *The Impact of Adjustment Policies. Programme Aid and Reforms*, Stockholm: SIDA Evaluation 99/17:11.

White, Howard and Lois Woestman (1994) 'The Quality of Aid: Measuring Trends in Donor Performance', *Development and Change*, Vol. 25, No. 3.

White, O. C. and A. Bhatia (1998) *Privatization in Africa*, Washington, DC: World Bank.

Williamson, J. (ed.) (1994) *The Political Economy of Policy Reform*, Washington, DC: Institute for International Economics.

Wintrobe, R. (1998) *The Political Economy of Dictatorship*, Cambridge: Cambridge University Press.

Wolf, Susanna and Dominik Spoden (2000) 'Allocation of EU Aid Towards ACP Countries', ZEF Discussion Papers on Development Policy, Bonn, March.

Wolfensohn, James D. (1997a) 'The Strategic Compact: Renewing the Bank's Effectiveness to Fight Poverty', memo from the President, World Bank, 13 February.

— (1997b) 'The Challenge of Inclusion', address by the President of the World Bank to the Annual Meeting of the World Bank and the IMF, Hong Kong, 23 September.

— (1999) 'A Proposal for a Comprehensive Development Framework – a Discussion Draft', available at http://www.worldbank.org/cdf/cdf-text.htm

Woods, Ngaire (2000) 'The Challenges of Multilateralism and Governance', in Gilbert and Vines (eds).

World Bank (1981) *Accelerated Development in Sub-Saharan Africa: An Agenda for Action*, Washington, DC: World Bank.

— (1990) *World Development Report 1990*, New York: Oxford University Press.

— (1991) *The African Capacity Building Initiative. Toward Improved Policy Analysis and Development Management in Sub-Saharan Africa*, Washington, DC: World Bank.

— (1992) *Effective Implementation: Key to Development Impact*, Report of the World Bank Management Task Force (the Wappenhans report), Washington, DC: World Bank

— (1993a) *The East Asian Miracle*, Washington, DC: World Bank.

— (1993b) *Expanding OED's Program of Impact Evaluations: Proposed Principles and Procedures.* Report of Interim Working Group, Washington, DC: World Bank.

— (1994) *Adjustment in Africa: Reforms, Results, and the Road Ahead*, Oxford: Oxford University Press (for the World Bank).

— (1995) *Bureaucrats in Business: The Economics and Politics of Government Ownership*, New York: Oxford University Press (for the World Bank).

— (1996a) *Taking Action to Reduce Poverty in Sub-Saharan Africa. An Overview*, Washington, DC: World Bank.

— (1996b) *Poverty Reduction and the World Bank. Progress and Challenges in the 1990s*, Washington, DC: World Bank.

— (1996c) 'Supporting Peace: The World Bank's Role in Post-conflict Reconstruction', www.worldbank.org

— (1996d) *World Development Report 1996*, New York: Oxford University Press.

— (1996e) *Sustainable Banking with the Poor. A Worldwide Inventory of Microfinance Institutions*, Washington, DC: World Bank.

— (1997a) *World Development Report 1997*, New York: Oxford University Press.

— (1997b) *Global Economic Prospects and the Developing Countries 1997*, Washington, DC: World Bank.

— (1997c) *World Development Indicators 1998*, Washington, DC: (on CD-rom, Discovery).

— (1997d) *Poverty Reduction and the World Bank: Progress in Fiscal 1996 and 1997*, Washington, DC: World Bank.

— (1997e) *IDA in Action 1993–1996. The Pursuit of Sustained Poverty Reduction*, Washington, DC.

— (1997f) *Helping Countries to Combat Corruption. The Role of the World Bank*, Washington, DC: World Bank.

— (1997g) *A Framework for World Bank Involvement in Post-Conflict Reconstruction*, Oxford, Oxford University Press (for the World Bank).

— (1997h) *Global Development Finance 1997*, Washington, DC: World Bank.

— (1998a) *Global Development Finance 1998*, Washington, DC: World Bank.

— (1998b) *Assessing Aid. What Works, What Doesn't, and Why*, New York: Oxford University Press.

— (1998c) *World Development Indicators 1998*, Washington, DC: World Bank.

— (1998d) 'News Release No. 99/1884/S', 15 July.

— (1998e) *Guidelines for the World Bank's Role in Post-conflict Reconstruction*, Washington, DC: World Bank.

— (1998f) *Independent Evaluation of the SPA as a Mechanism to Promote Adjustment and Development in Sub-Saharan Africa*, Washington, DC: World Bank.

— (1998g) *Partnerships for Development: Proposed Actions for the World Bank*, Washington, DC: World Bank.

— (1998h) *Public Expenditure Management Handbook*, Washington, DC: World Bank.

— (1998i) *The Impact of Public Expenditure Reviews: An Evaluation*, Operations Evaluation Study, Washington, DC: World Bank.

— (1999) *World Development Report 1998/99. Knowledge for Development*, New York: Oxford University Press.

— (2001a) *World Development Report. Attacking Poverty*, New York: Oxford University Press.

— (2001b) *Aid and Reform in Africa: Lessons from Ten Case Studies*, (ed.) S. Devarajan and D. Dollar, Washington, DC: World Bank and Sweden: T. Holmgren, Ministry of Foreign Affairs.

— (2001c) *World Development Indicators, 2001*, Washington, DC: World Bank.

— (2002) World Development Report 2002: Building Institutions for Markets, New York: Oxford.

— OED (Operations Evaluation Department) (1997) *Annual Review of Development Effectiveness*, Report No. 17196, Washington, DC: World Bank.

— OED (Operations Evaluation Department) (1998) *The Special Program of Assistance for Africa: An Independent Evaluation*, Washington, DC: World Bank.

— OED (Operations Evaluation Department) (2001) *IDA's Partnership for Poverty Reduction (FY94–FY00). An Independent Evaluation*, Report No. 22158, Washington, DC: World Bank.

*World Development* (1987) special issue on 'Development Alternatives: The Challenge for NGOs', Vol. 15, Autumn.

Wyplosz, Charles (1999) 'International Financial Instability', in Kaul, Grunberg and Stern (eds), 1999.

Yanagihara, Toru and Anne Emig (1991) 'An Overview of Japans' Foreign Aid', in Islam (ed.).

Young, Kate (1993) *Planning Development with Women. Making a World of Difference*, London: Macmillan.

Zimmerman, Robert F. (1993) *Dollars, Diplomacy and Dependency. Dilemmas of U.S. Economic Aid*, Boulder, CO: Lynne Rienner.

# Index